WHO'S THE SAVAGE?

THE EXECUTION OF 38 SIOUX INDIANS BY THE U. S. AUTHORITIES, AT MANKATO, MINNESOTA, FRIDAY, DECEMBER 26.—From a Sketch by W. H. Childs.—See Page 279.

WHO'S THE SAVAGE?

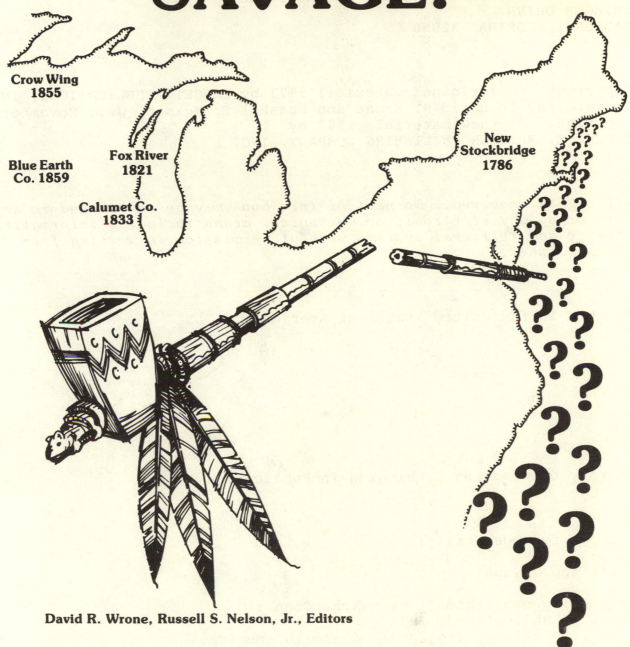

Crow Wing
1855

Blue Earth
Co. 1859

Fox River
1821

Calumet Co.
1833

New
Stockbridge
1786

David R. Wrone, Russell S. Nelson, Jr., Editors

Robert E. Krieger Publishing Company
Malabar, Florida
1982

Original Edition 1982
(Based upon 1973 Edition, Revised & Enlarged)

Printed and Published by
ROBERT E. KRIEGER PUBLISHING COMPANY, INC.
KRIEGER DRIVE
MALABAR, FLORIDA 32950

Library of Congress Cataloging in Publication Data

Main entry under title:

Who's the Savage?

Originally published: Greenwich, Conn :
Fawcett Publications, 1973
      1. Indians, Treatment of--North America.
2. Indians of North America--Government relations.
I. Wrone, David R.   II. Nelson, Russell S.,
1927-
E93.W63 1981   970.004'97   81-17167
ISBN 0-89874-452-0   AACR2

For ELIZABETH M. and DAVID A. WRONE

To the Memory of my parents HELEN and RUSSELL NELSON

Contents

PREFACE

Who's the Savage?, published in October 1973, has been out-of-print for several years. Inquiries from Indian people, teachers, and the general public indicate a continuing interest. Students, always fascinated by the book, search for it only to find the few available copies on restricted reserve. This collection of documents that describes the mistreatment of the Native North American from the days of the Vikings to the present is now available in a new edition.

With great care the editors have revised *Who's the Savage?*. All introductions and headnotes have been re-examined. Many sentences and paragraphs have been re-written. Documents that were repetitious of points made elsewhere were deleted. One document has been added: the map that shows the placement of the national guard during the takeover of the novitiate near Gresham, Wisconsin.

A major change in this new edition is the inclusion of illustrations: maps, photoprints, pictographs, songs, and hymns. Maps help the reader locate some of the most reknown battle sites and forced migration routes. Photoprints portray scenes of cruel treatment, humiliation, and regimentation. Through drawings by Indian people and songs and hymns in several Indian languages, the influence of the dominant population is demonstrated.

The editors have added a bibliography of books found useful in the study of North American Indian history. An index which is also new to this volume enables the reader to utilize the book with some ease.

The editors are fully responsible for the contents. The staff of the Learning Resources Center at the University of Wisconsin at Stevens Point must be thanked for their assistance.

A Note on Illustrations

The hymns are in the Oneida language and are from: A. W. Sickles, *A Collection of Hymns in the Oneida Language* (Toronto: Wesleyan Missionary Society, 1855). The page from the Choctaw Bible is taken from *The New Testament of Our Lord and Saviour Jesus Christ... Pin Chitokaka Pi Okchalinchi Chisvs Klaist In Testament Himona Chahta Anumpa Atoshowa Hoke* (New York: American Bible Society, 1871). The question on arithmetic in Cherokee and English is excerpted from John B. Jones, *Elementary Arithmetic, in Cherokee and English, Designed for Beginners* (Tahlequah: Cherokee National Press, 1870). Jonathan Edwards in *Observations on the Language of the Muhhekaneew Indians* (New Haven: Josiah Meigs, 1788) provided the Pater Noster in the Muhhekaneew language, the tongue spoken by the Stockbridge. All four volumes are in the Rare Book Room, State Historical Society of Wisconsin.

The stylized eagle or thunderbird is adapted from the symbol used by the Society of the American Indians, 1911-1919?, based on an artifact predating the European invasion claimed to have been discovered in an archeological dig near Peoria, Illinois. The calumet was drawn by James F. Frechette, Jr., Menominee. Frances Densmore, "Menominee Music," *Bureau of American Ethnology Bulletin No. 102* (Washington: Government Printing Office, 1932) contains the Menominee war songs. The stick ball is found in W. J. Hoffman's "The Menomini Indians," *Fourteenth Annual Report of the Bureau of American Ethnology* (Washington: Smithsonian Institution, 1896) pp. 3-328. The pictographs are found in Garrick Mallary's treatise on "Picture-writing of the American Indian," *Tenth Annual Report* (1893).

The pictographs representing diseases are from Dakota Sioux Winter Count records. The diseases introduced by Europeans periodically swept the continent inflicting severe losses on tribes. The great Sioux leader Crazy Horse died on September 5, 1877. While in the guard house at Fort Robinson, Nebraska, a soldier ran a bayonet into him. The symbol depicting this is taken from his compatriot American Horse's Winter Count, 1877-1878.

The characters depicting a summons to the religious ceremony of the Great Medicine Lodge or Mide were taken by Mallary from the Chippewa historian of the nineteenth century, George Copway. The pictograph recording a treaty is also Chippewa. The figure on the left holding a flag represents a Chippewa chief; the one on the right, an Assinaboin chief holding a pipe in one hand and a drum in the other. Smoke issues from their mouths. The Chippewa considered the flag an emblem of peace. The Passamaquoddy wikhegan illustrates in pictorial form how the tribe defined relations between themselves and the President of the United States or the Governor of Maine. The white leader is at the top of the pole and any Indian wishing to speak to him must work hard at climbing the pole; the white man with power ought to pity the Indian who goes to such a length to see him.

Photographic reproductions of wood-block prints, lithographs, photographs, land sale announcement, and postcard are through the courtesy of the Iconography Collections of the State Historical Society of Wisconsin except for: "The Hanging of the thirty-eight Sioux" and "Fur trade scene in the northern forest" are through the courtesy of the Minnesota Historical Society; "Struck by the Ree" is by permission of the South Dakota Historical Society; "Chippewa Indians, Lac du Flambeau Reservation," is from the John Anderson collection Stevens Point. John Patrick Hunter gave special permission to use the "Two Stockbridge being Sworn into the Union Army," held by the State Historical Society of Wisconsin.

The data upon which the reservation map is based comes from the Bureau of Indian Affairs regional offices at Ashland and on the reservation.

The Great Wampum Belt is reproduced in the *Second Annual Report of the Bureau of American Ethnology* (1883) while the copper plates appear in the *Fifth Annual Report* (1887). "The Indian Ghost Dance and War" can be located in James Mooney's "The Ghost Dance Religion," *Fourteenth Annual Report*, Part 2.

"Lovewell's Fight" is printed in George Cary Eggleston, *American War Ballads and Lyrics* (New York: G. P. Putnam's Sons, 1889). The figures of Indians fleeing attackers can be located as a detail in the map accompanying Captain John Underhill, *Newes From America...* (London: printed by F. D. for Peter Cole, 1638).

The Captain John Smith incidents are border embellishments of the map found in the modern scholarly edition of his works edited by Edward Arber, *Travels and Works of Captain John Smith...* (Edinburgh: John Grant, 1910).

WHO'S THE SAVAGE?

Introduction

Monday, 30th.—At the request of Maj. Platt, sent out a small party to look for some of the dead Indians— returning without finding them. Toward noon they found them and skinned two of them from their hips down for boot legs; one pair for the Major the other for myself. On the other side of this mountain was a town said to be of the best buildings we had passed. It was destroyed by Gen'l Poor the evening of the engagement.[1]

This entry in the journal of Lieutenant William Barton, dated August 30, 1779, characterizes the atrocious treatment of the Indian people. Descriptions of such treatment of native Americans do not encumber the conventional historical account of America's growth from an uncharted forest and desert to a thriving industrial nation. Any intrusion of the subject into the narrative is incidental and reveals no clear outline of this repugnant subject.

The documents presented here provide a basic insight into the crude and brutal treatment from the age of white exploration of the Indian homeland to the nuclear era. They trace the continuity of the savage act manifested in changing forms throughout the violent course of America's history. This volume devoted solely to the subject can help the reader understand the relationship of these acts to modern civilization. The sad story they tell reveals an extremely rough facet of the American character unknown to the general public. The rich documentary record provides a wide variety of examples given in a convenient chronological arrangement.

The first chapter covers the age of exploration, discovery, and early settlement. The diverse instances from Spanish, French, Swedish, Dutch, and English sources demonstrate that mistreatment derived more from the nature of the emerging European culture than from the eccentricities of a particular nation. Chapter two encompasses the colonial era, roughly from the first great clashes with the Indian people in the late seventeenth century to the crumbling of the European empires in the late eighteenth. French, Russian, English, and Spanish sources represent this phase of white savagery, but the emphasis is upon the English, who dominated the continent then. Chapter three discusses the early years of the United States, focusing mainly on American abuses and atrocities.

Chapter four, 1812-1860, is the period of the early industrial transformation of the nation, a chaotic age. The major emphasis is on removal of the Indians to the West. Chapter five, 1861-1865, covers the Civil War, stressing the war's impact on the Indian. Chapter six,

1866-1899, follows the atrocities associated with the wars against the Plains Indians and the forced movement of the western Indian population to reservations. Part of the chapter considers the era of allotment, when many reservations were broken up and the tribal members were given portions of the holdings. Included also is the dismemberment of the Five Civilized Tribes of Oklahoma. Chapter seven, 1899-1971, stresses a neglected period in white mistreatment of the Indian, which is characterized by the persistent failure of institutions. Russell S. Nelson, Jr. is primarily responsible for the first three chapters. David R. Wrone is primarily responsible for the final four chapters.

The form of white atrocities varied, but the principle of destruction inflicted by an alien civilization upon an entire race did not. In the early years of American expansion brutal military force reduced Indians to docility and harshly directed their lives into a white, Christian pattern. By 1900 federal and local authorities frequently utilized the courts to practice fraud and deceit upon the dissolved tribal nations. Their efficient devastation of the innocent surpassed the previous era. In the instance of Oklahoma, where so many Indians lived, the entrenchment of graft and fraud, accompanied by violence and disdain for Indian dignity and institutions, was comparable to the occupation of a country by a criminal syndicate. Today the inhumanity is ensconced in rigid bureaucratic forms where misguided and mediocre federal and local agencies afflict the Indians with malnutrition, starvation, disease, and poverty—an impact more brutal in terms of lost and twisted lives than any previously mentioned.

The indignant citizen has no devil to pommel. All segments of the population participated in the mistreatment. The documents reveal men of diverse cultural background: frontiersmen, Presidents, city dwellers, militiamen, regular army, immigrants, illiterates, and educated men. The color of skin also varies: whites predominated, but blacks as well as Mexican-Americans and Indians joined in the tragedy. The assiduously nurtured myth that only irregularly disciplined and raw militiamen participated in such acts is found so frequently in standard histories. The documents indicate veteran soldiers and West Point graduates murdered, raped, scalped, and mutilated bodies, and then bribed, lied, and bragged about their deeds of infamy as easily as the equally culpable citizens. George Washington and Andrew Jackson participated in atrocities. Theodore Roosevelt and U. S. Grant condoned them publicly. Abraham Lincoln gave orders to commit them. Obviously all persons did not act in a savage way; nor did all men who performed one act repeat it with every Indian encountered. But it was impossible to predict when and where the brutal conduct would emerge.

Indian people perpetrated atrocities upon whites, blacks, Mexican-Americans, and Indians. The heinous acts of the Indians have so frequently infused popular narratives and film presentations of westward expansion that their existence is known to the average man. Indians practiced slavery. The eastern woodland Menominees held slaves, including prisoners captured while serving as American mercenaries in the 1832 slaughter of the Sauk. Some groups practiced cannibalism. It was not always the symbolic kind of cannibalism, such as eating the heart of the foe to acquire his courage, but instead, devouring the cooked human body for food. Indians murdered innocent civilians, wantonly killed captives, and inflicted tortures upon whites, blacks, Mexicans, and fellow Indians.

An example of Iroquois atrocities against missionaries in the late sixteenth century is found in a Jesuit's relation of the experiences of a fellow Jesuit in the interior of America.

There was no strife as to who should burn him—each one took his turn; thus they gave themselves leisure to meditate some new devise to make him feel the fire more keenly. They hardly burned him anywhere except in the legs, but these, to be sure, they reduced to a wretched state, the flesh being all in shreds. Some applied burning brands to them and did not withdraw them until he uttered loud cries; and, as soon as he stopped shrieking, they again began to burn him, repeating it seven or eight times—often reviving the fire, which they held close against the flesh, by blowing upon it. Others bound cords around him and then set them on fire, thus burning him slowly and causing him the keenest agony. There were some who made him put his feet on red-hot hatchets, and then pressed down on them. You could have heard the flesh hiss, and seen the smoke which issued therefrom rise even to the roof of the cabin. They struck him with clubs upon the head, and passed small sticks through his ears; they broke the rest of his fingers; they stirred up the fire all around . . . fearing that he would die otherwise than by the knife, one cut off a foot, another a hand, and almost at the same time a third severed the head from the shoulders, throwing it into the crowd, where someone caught it to carry it to the Captain Ondessone, for whom it had been reserved, in order to make a feast therewith. As for the trunk, it remained at Arontaen, where a feast was made of it the same day. . . . On the way [home] we encountered a Savage who was carrying upon a skewer one of his half-roasted hands.[2]

After an Algonquian massacre, Timothy Horsfield, militia leader and local politician in Northampton County, Pennsylvania, reports to the governor the attack on the Moravian community of Gnaddenhutten.

In the evening (November 26, 1755), came Joseph Sturges, G. Partch & his Wife the Persons who had excaped out of ye Flames from ye fury of ye Indians, from whom I received the following Accot. of that most Inhuman & Shocking Affair: vizt.

That on Monday ye 24th Instant, an hour before Sun Set Geo: Custard with 2 others of the Neighbours, came to ye Mahoni the Place the Murther was committed at & inform'd Them that in the Evening they might expect a Number of Arm'd Men to be with them all Night; That about 6 o'Clock while they were sitting at Supper 14 in Number they heard the Dog bark very much, & concluding it was the People Custard had inform'd them of, Sturges & 3 more got up to receive them but on opening ye Door 4 Guns were Immediately discharg'd in upon them, which Kill'd one of them immediately, & one of the Balls graz'd on Sturges Chin & set his Hair on Fire, then 4 or 5 More & a third Time when ye Indians immediately rush'd in upon them & kill'd some of them on the Spot, the rest run into an adjoining Room from whence Partch escap'd thro' a Window, & meeting Senseman who was coming down from another House to see what was ye Matter, took Him along with Him but Sturges with 3 Men 3 Women & Child, got up Stairs, at the Head of which was a Trap Door, which they shut down & secured it, in the best Manner they could. The Indians often attempting to force it Open & finding they could not fired in upon them thro ye Cieling, & Roof of the House but without effect upon which they set Fire to ye House, Sturges Watching his opportunity as he thought, while they were Scalping those below, jump'd out the Gable End Window & Partch's Wife following him, they both made their Escape. . . . Partch's Wife being newly come to ye Place & not knowing the Woods crept at a small Distance & hid herself behind a Stump & saw Fabricius who jump'd out of ye Window after her Shot & Scalp'd; and otherwise inhumanly abus'd the rest Perish'd in ye Flames. . . .[3]

There is no attempt to gloss over Indian atrocities. Some of them such as the notorious ones performed by the Apache were recent in origin, and groups practicing them were often undergoing severe stress and dislocation from war, disease, or calamity of nature. Indians were "primitive" in the sense of not being a part of Western civilization; they were not considered civilized people. White men had no such excuse for their actions. Our concern is with the white men's mistreatment.

Genocide was not widely practiced with success. Whites threatened extermination many times and attempted it. During the French occupation of the Great Lakes region, they ordered extermination of the Fox Indians of Wisconsin and persistently tried to accomplish it. The French also attempted this with the Natchez. The Spanish exterminated some California groups and many of the tribal bands in Puerto Rico. Following the forced removal of the Spanish from the Southwest, Americans endeavored to exterminate tribes. At least two tribes perished to the last man, woman, and child; surviving tribes were hunted in the mountains. Although we have erected monuments to the extinct passenger pigeon and the decimated buffalo, no monument exists for these vanished people.

American generals sometimes gave orders to exterminate Indians. In instances such as the Yamasee War and Black Hawk's War, they issued such commands. Failure rested more upon military incompetency than weakness of will. The documentary record reveals that not only the military participated in attempted genocide but also citizens of all economic and social classes. In colonial New England the Puritan fathers fought the proud and doughty Pequot Indians as a tribe by using all possible means—starvation, war, and enslavement—until a mere remnant survived (today in Wisconsin). Genocidal efforts are also documented in the eighteenth-century frontier butchery of pacifist Christian Indians. And finally such attempts are found among many state and local governments, who employed professional exterminators. Exterminators were paid by the scalp, one white man alone collected for several hundred.

Forced population control involving cruel and violent actions consistently marked white policy. Typical of this policy are documents describing the mid-nineteenth-century removal of the tribes living east of the Mississippi River. Military force removed Creek, Seminole, and Cherokee from the South and supervised removal of the lesser tribes to the north. Its presence awed the Chickasaw and Seneca into submission. The death toll among the Indians from disease, climate change, battle deaths, adjustment to the new conditions, and other causes surpassed the number of American prisoners of war who perished on the infamous Bataan Death March of World War II. To the Indians, if not to the white men, removal was a ghastly epoch forever seared into their memories. Indian removal is the single most destructive peace-time act in American history, and its principal director (though not its initiator), Andrew Jackson, is an American folk hero. Another infamous episode in population control was the concentration of the Navajo at Bosque Redondo during the Civil War, a situation similar to the treatment of the Japanese-Americans during World War II. Removal doctrine smacks of totalitarianism, denies principles cherished as innate to representative democracy, and is similar to the apartheid now practiced in the Union of South Africa. The removal concept is not dead. It is still suggested by federal and local government officials from time to time as an alternative to reservation life.

American execution of prisoners of war continually appears in the sources describing the minor Indian wars. To provide examples of each known instance is not necessary to establish this gruesome act as a basic type of atrocity. Two executions are presented in brief form, and one is given wider coverage. The major incident is the mass public hanging of thirty-eight Sioux Indians following their defeat in the revolt of 1862. After hurried courts martial in an emotional atmosphere, Abraham Lincoln ordered their execution. The total number of Indians killed was greater by twenty-six than the number of Nazis executed after the Nuremberg War Crimes Trials in 1945-1946.

Frequently during the Indian wars an Indian warrior, upon surrender or capture, was shot or "strung up" to the nearest tree; no official report was made. At other times public show trials, appealing to the carnival quality of early American public life, tried the warriors and then killed them, providing excellent publicity for the military and their political cronies. Citizens of all walks of life decried these acts but largely to little avail; only rarely was a citizen, governmental official, or military officer ever executed for an atrocity perpetrated against the Indians.[4]

The rape of female Indian prisoners of war and the sexual abuse of Indian women through luxuries, prestige, and better treatment are so common in American military history that the point hardly needs to be made. Brigadier General James Clinton of the Continental Army cautioned the soldiers he sent off to destroy the Iroquois nation in 1779.

> Bad as the savages are, they never violate the chastity of any women, their prisoners. Although I have very little apprehension that any of the soldiers will so far forget their character as to attempt such a crime on the Indian women who may fall into their hands, yet it will be well to take measures to prevent such a stain upon our army.[5]

The mistreatment of dead Indian bodies is the most revolting of the cruel acts which the documents relate. Using swords, saws, knives, and axes, Americans took Indian heads. They piked, staked, mounted, and boiled or tanned them for trophies. Skulls were decorated and used, as by the Vikings of old, as quaffing vessels. Scalping, so common, does not seem to merit a separate treatment. At times the British government purchased Indian, and white scalps, by the bale; state governments paid for the sack full. Citizens and soldiers skinned Indians and used the skin for razor straps, tobacco pouches, leggings, bridles for horses, and hat bands. Parts of the body—jaw bones, ears, private parts of men and women, teeth, fingers, shin bones—served decorative and utilitarian ends, such as bait for animal traps. The disemboweling of Indian women with bowie knives and swords and the mutilation of unborn children also occurred. All of these acts have been included within the body of general documents; only a few have been given special treatment.

Whites frequently assassinated Indian leaders. The list is long, and the methods vary with the era and the need. American officers employed deceit, such as the pretence of negotiations, for the purpose of execution. Hidden assassins sometimes killed leaders on their way to peace councils. Indians were murdered by American officers as they sat unarmed during peace councils. Oglala Chief Crazy Horse perished as a result of a conspiracy to arrest him and ship him to a Florida jail. He fought the arrest sprung upon him during a peace talk and died from an American bayonet thrust into his back. The list of assassinated Indian leaders is very long, and the representative documents presented here merely suggest the base undercurrents moving at the highest level of government.

The attempt by the dominant white group to control the Indians with violent, crude methods is similar to the Spaniards' cruel treatment of the Moors in the seventeenth century and the fascist Croatian pogroms against the Serbians in the twentieth century. In most of the overseas empires carved by Europe, inhuman treatment frequently occurred, and atrocities were often perpetrated, e.g., Boers against Zulus, English against Maoris, French against Berbers. White men and their black, Mexican, and Indian mercenaries' harsh domination of the aboriginal Americans involved fewer victims than the previous Europeans'

atrocities against indigenous populations on other continents.

Notes

1. *Journals of the Military Expedition of Major General John Sullivan Against the Six Nations of Indians in 1779* . . . (Frederick Cook, Comp., Auburn, N.Y.: Knapp, Peck and Thomson, 1887), p. 8.

2. Reuben Gold Thwaites, ed., *The Jesuit Relations and Allied Documents* (73 vols.; Cleveland: Burrows Brothers Co., 1896-1901), XIII, pp. 67, 79.

3. Timothy Horsfield to Robert Hunter Morris, Bethlehem, November 27, 1755, Timothy Horsfield Letter Book 1754-55, The Historical Society of Pennsylvania, Philadelphia.

4. For an example of punishment see George Chalou, "Massacre on Fall Creek," *Prologue,* Vol. IV, No. 2 (Summer, 1972), pp. 109-114.

5. Quoted in William L. Stone, *Life of Joseph Brant* . . . (2 vols., New York: A. V. Blake, 1838), I, p. 404.

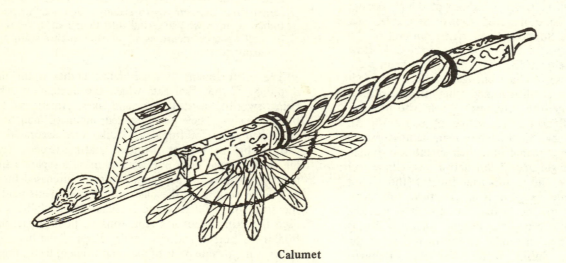

Calumet

The native Americans did not greet the Europeans with bows and arrows and war whoops. On the contrary, they were friendly. The strangers who came from the sunrise in large canoes with sails were their guests. On San Salvador they gathered to watch Christopher Columbus perform the ceremony that claimed the island and much more for King Ferdinand and Queen Isabella. When Columbus gave them gifts, the Indians quickly provided gifts in return. More than forty years later and hundreds of miles to the north, the native Americans crowded around Jacques Cartier as he explored the bays and islands near the mouth of the St. Lawrence River. They smiled and waved, but their large numbers frightened the Frenchmen, who fired their guns into the air to scare them off. Later, when the numbers were less uneven, Cartier exchanged gifts, and in their eagerness to be friendly the Indians gave away even the skins that they wore and departed naked. Almost a century later on Cape Cod two Indians, Samoset and Squanto (who had formerly worked on English fishing ships), greeted the Pilgrims in the English language. Their friendliness with the Pilgrims is known to all.

While the Europeans enjoyed the hospitality of the native Americans, they certainly did not accept them as equals. The Indians were naked "heathens" with little to offer except land, labor, and information. Columbus wanted a western passage to the Orient, not parrots. Cartier wanted a northwest passage to the same fabled place, not animal skins. The Pilgrims merely wanted a home, and their leader, William Bradford, wrote that Squanto "was a special instrument sent of God for their good beyond their expectation."[1]

The pale, hairy, over-dressed strangers used the naked "heathens" to their advantage. Columbus did not find a passage to the Orient. However, the Spaniards who followed up his explorations found wealth beyond their greediest dreams. Cartier also failed in his quest, and only in the next century did the French realize the great value of animal skins. The Pilgrims found a home, and within a decade of their arrival they were joined by hun-

dreds of religious dissenters who quickly occupied the best lands along the New England coast.

The native Americans did not share in these European successes. The Indians of the Southwest were kept busy building and maintaining Christian missions. In the upper St. Lawrence Valley the Indians warred among themselves in their eagerness to supply beaver pelts for guns, knives, and woolen cloth. In New England the Indian tribes, to ease the land shortage, joined the English religious dissenters in the destruction of their mutual neighbor, the Pequot.

The documents in this chapter show how the earliest European explorers and colonizers mistreated the Indian people in order to gain their ends.

1006-1012   Killing Skrellings   Vinland

Five hundred years before the momentous voyage of Christopher Columbus, the Vikings explored the northeastern coastline of North America. In A.D. 986, Bjarni Herjolfson was the first European to see the well-timbered land. On his way from Iceland to join his father in Eric the Red's Greenland colony, Bjarni missed his destination. When he finally arrived in Greenland, he reported his adventures. The Vikings needed timber, and in 1001, Eric's second son Lief, led an expedition that landed at several places, did some exploring, and built houses in Vinland (the Viking name for North America). From this base exploring parties set out, collected a cargo of grapes and timber, and returned to Greenland. Leif's voyage excited the colonists there. Particularly interested in further exploration was his brother Thorvald, who, with a party of Vikings, spent two years in Vinland. The second summer of their stay, they became the first Europeans to see and to kill native Americans (document 1). The *skrellings*, as the Vikings called the native Americans, retaliated, fatally wounding Thorvald. Other Vikings subsequently explored the timbered land. One party under Thorfinn Karlsevni traded with the *skrellings* on their initial meeting with them. This ended violently when Karlsevni's bellowing bull frightened off the *skrellings*, who returned in force and attacked. The heroism of Freydis, Eric's illegitimate daughter, saved the Vikings. Karlsevni then decided that the natural wealth of the country was not worth the risk of lives, and the Vikings departed for Greenland. While they were sailing north along the coast, they

1. William Bradford, *Of Plymouth Plantation, 1620-1647,* ed. by Samuel Eliot Morison (New York: Alfred A. Knopf, Inc., 1953), p. 81.

stopped long enough to kill some *skrellings* who were asleep on the shore (document 2). The following passages are taken from the Vinland Sagas.

Further reading: Samuel Eliot Morison, *The European Discovery of America: The Northern Voyages A. D. 500-1600* (New York: Oxford University Press, 1971).

Document 1
1006   Killing Skrellings   Vinland

From **Voyages to Vinland: The First American Saga**, by Einar Haugen. Copyright 1942 and renewed 1970 by Einar Haugen. Reprinted by permission of Alfred A. Knopf, Inc.

Then they sailed along the coast to the east, into some nearby fjord mouths, and headed for a jutting cape that rose high out of the sea and was all covered with woods. Here they anchored the ship and laid down a gangplank to the shore. Thorvald went ashore with all his company. Then he said, "This is beautiful, and here I should like to build me a home."

After a time they went back to the ship. Then they caught sight of three little mounds on the sand farther in on the cape. When they got closer to them, they saw three skin-covered boats, with three men under each. They split up their force and seized all the men but one, who escaped in his boat. They killed all eight of them, and then returned to the cape. Here they saw a number of mounds in the fjord and guessed that these must be human dwelling places.

After that such a drowsiness fell upon them that they simply could not stay awake, and they all fell asleep. Then a voice cried out to them, so that they all awoke, and this is what the voice said, "Wake up, Thorvald, and all your crew, if you value your lives! Get aboard the ship with your men and hurry away from this country with all speed!" A host of boats was then heading towards them from the inner end of the fjord. Thorvald then said, "We shall set up our breastworks on both sides of the ship and defend ourselves as best we can, but do as little killing as possible." So they did, and after the savages had shot at them for a while, they hurried away as fast as they could.

Thorvald asked if any of his men were wounded. They said they were not.

"I have got a wound under my arm," he said; "an arrow flew between the gunwale and my shield and struck me under the arm, and here is the arrow. This will be the last of me. Now I advise you to make ready for your return as quickly as possible. But me you shall take back to that cape which I found so inviting. It looks as if I spoke the truth without knowing it when I said that I might live there some day! Bury me there with a cross at my head and another at my feet, and ever after you shall call it Crossness."

Document 2
1012   Killing Skrellings   Vinland

From **Voyages to Vinland: The First American Saga**, by Einar Haugen. Copyright 1942 and renewed 1970 by Einar Haugen. Reprinted by permission of Alfred A. Knopf, Inc.

In the Greenland Saga it is told that the Norsemen sold the savages milk. Karlsevni asked the women to carry out vessels of milk and other dairy products. At once the savages wanted to buy this and nothing else. So the trading turned out in this way, that the savages carried their purchases away in their stomachs, while Karlsevni and his men had possession of their furs.

Then it happened that a bull beloning to Karlsevni and his people ran out of the woods and bellowed furiously. The savages were so terrified that they ran to their boats, and rowed along the shore to the south. For three weeks there was no trace of them. But at the end of this time, a vast fleet of Skrelling boats hove into sight, rushing from the south like an angry torrent. This time the savages were waving their sticks at a counter-sunwise direction, and were yelling at the tops of their voices. This time Karlsevni and his men took their red shields and held them aloft. The savages leaped from their boats; the two parties met and started fighting. It was a furious battle, for the savages had warslings to help them. Karlsevni and Snorri watched them lift up a pole with a huge knob on the end, black in color, and about the size of a sheep's

Ball Stick

belly, which flew up on land over the heads of the men, and made a frightening noise when it fell. At this a great fear seized Karlsevni and his followers, so that they thought only of flight, and retreated up the stream. It seemed to them that they were being attacked by savages on every side, and this did not let up before they got back to some cliffs, where they fought a hard battle.

Freydis came out and saw them retreating. She shouted to them, "Why are you running away from these puny fellows, fine men as you are! It looks to me as if you should be able to cut them down like cattle. If I had weapons, I think I could fight better than any of you!"

They paid no attention to what she was saying. She tried to folllow, but had trouble keeping up with them, for she was with child. She went after them into the woods, and the savages started towards her. In front of her lay a dead man, Thorbrand, Snorri's son, whose head had been crushed by a flat rock. Beside him lay his sword, and she picked it up to defend herself. When the savages approached, she pulled out her breasts from under her dress and slapped them with the naked sword. At this the savages were so appalled that they ran down to their boats and rowed away.

Karlsevni and his men now came up to her and praised her good fortune. Two men had fallen of his party, and a great many of the savages, although the latter were far superior in number. They now returned to their camp, dressed their wounds, and talked over who the host might be that had attacked them on land. It had seemed to them as if there were two attacking parties, but now they say that one of these must have been a delusion.

The savages found one of the dead with an axe beside him. One of them picked up the axe and hewed at a tree with it; one after the other tried it, and it seemed to them a great treasure because it cut so well. Then one of them took and struck a rock with it, so that the axe broke. They decided then that it was useless, since it could not withstand stone, and tossed it away.

Karlsevni and his men were now convinced that even though the country was richly endowed by nature, they would always live in dread and turmoil because of the enmity of those who lived there before. So they made ready to break up and return to their own country.

They sailed along the coast to the north. On the shore they found five savages asleep, dressed in leather jackets, and beside them vessels containing animal marrow mixed with blood. Karlsevni judged that these men must have been sent out as spies from this country, and killed them.

| 1492 | Good Servants | San Salvador |
| 1494 | Slaves for Seville | Hispaniola |

The native Americans did not frighten off Christopher Columbus and his men as the *skrellings* had Karlsevni and his party of Vikings. Indeed, on October 12, 1492, his first day in the Indies, Columbus characterized the people on San Salvador as docile and believed that they would make good servants (document 3). The next two days the Spanish explored the island and detained six Indians as guides to help locate Japan. While the quest was unsuccessful, the Spanish monarchs accepted Columbus' reports that he had reached the outlying parts of the Indies, and they supported a second voyage. During this longer stay in America the Admiral had no more success finding the wealth of the Orient than he had had on his first voyage. There were many islands with many inhabitants, but there was little wealth; only birds, cotton, and a few gold trinkets. In 1494, Columbus reviewed the future prospects of the Spanish in the islands in a lengthy memorandum to King Ferdinand and Queen Isabella. One subject that he broached was the enslavement of the islanders. He believed that sending the Indians to the slave market in Seville would be profitable. The Queen strongly objected. Meanwhile, Columbus put his suggestion into effect and shipped several hundred native Americans to Spain (document 4). The brief reference to this shipment of Indian slaves in Andreas Bernaldez's *History of the Catholic Sovereigns* is excerpted here. Bernaldez, curate of Los Palacios near Seville, knew both Columbus and Fonseca, to whom the slaves were delivered. The curate also said that he got further information from "certain papers" that Columbus had deposited with him.

Further reading: Samuel Eliot Morison, *Admiral of the Ocean Sea* (2 vols., Boston: Little, Brown and Company, 1942).

Document 3
| 1492 | Good Servants | San Salvador |

Source: John Boyd Thacher, **Christopher Columbus His Life, His Work, His Remains as revealed by original printed and manuscript records** (3 vols., New York and London: G. P. Putman's Sons, 1903-1904), vol. 1, pp. 530-534.

Thursday, October 11.

After sunset he sailed on his first course to the west. They went 12 miles each hour and up to two hours after midnight they went about 90 miles which are 22½ leagues. And because the caravel *Pinta* was the best sailor and was going ahead of the Admiral, land was discovered by her people and the signs which the Admiral had ordered were made. A sailor called Rodrigo de Traina saw this land first, although the Admiral at 10 o'clock at night being in the stern forecastle saw a light, but it was so concealed that he would not declare it to be land: but he called Pero Gutierrez Groom of the Chamber of the King, and said to him that it appeared to be a light, and asked him to look at it: and he did so and saw it. He also told Rodrigo

Sanchez de Segovia, whom the King and Queen sent with the fleet as Inspector, who saw nothing because he was not where he could see it. After the Admiral told it, it was seen once or twice, and it was like a small wax candle which rose and fell, which hardly appeared to be an indication of land. But the Admiral was certain that they were near land. For this reason, when they said the *Salve* which all the sailors are in the habit of saying and singing in their way and they were all assembled together, the Admiral implored and admonished them to guard the stern forecastle well and search diligently for land and said that to whomever should first see land he would then give a silk doublet, besides the other gifts which the Sovereigns had promised them, which was an annuity of 10,000 maravedis to whomever should first see land. At two hours after midnight the land appeared, from which they were about two leagues distant. They lowered all the sails and remained with the cross-jack-sail, which is the great sail without bonnets, and lay to, standing off and on until the day, Friday, when they reached a small island of the Lucayas, which is called in the language of the Indians, *Guanahani*. Then they saw naked people and the Admiral landed in the armed boat with Martin Alonso Pinzón and Vincente Yañez, his brother, who was captain of the *Niña*. The Admiral took the royal banner and the two captains had two banners of the Verde Cruz, which the Admiral carried on all the ships as a sign, with an F. and a Y. The crown of the Sovereigns surmounted each letter and one was one side of the + and the other the other side. Having landed they saw very green trees and much water and many fruits of different kinds. The Admiral called the two captains and the others who landed and Rodrigo Descoredo, Notary of all the Fleet, and Rodrigo Sanchez of Segovia, and told them to bear him witness and testify that he, in the presence of them all, was taking, as in fact he took possession, of the said isle, for the King and for the Queen, his Lords, making the protestations which were required, as contained more at length in the depositions which were made there in writing. Then many of the people of the island gathered there. The following is in the exact words of the Admiral in his book of his first voyage and discovery of these Indies:

"That they might feel great friendship for us [he says] and because I knew they were a people who would better be freed and converted to our Holy Faith by love than by force—I gave them some red caps and some glass beads which they placed around their necks, and many other things of small value with which they were greatly pleased, and were so friendly to us that it was wonderful. They afterwards came swimming to the two ships where we were, and bringing us parrots and cotton thread wound in balls and spears and many other things, and they traded them with us for other things which we gave them, such as small glass beads and hawk's bells. Finally they took everything and willingly gave what things they had. Further, it appeared to me that they were a very poor people, in everything. They all go naked as their mothers gave them birth, and the women also, although I only saw one of the latter who was very young, and all those whom I saw were young men, none more than thirty years of age. They were very well built with very handsome bodies, and very good faces. Their hair was almost as coarse as horses' tails and short, and they wear it over the eyebrows, except a small quantity behind, which they wear long and never cut. Some paint themselves blackish, and they are of the colour of the inhabitants of the Canaries, neither black nor white, and some paint themselves white, some red, some whatever colour they find: and some paint their faces, some all the body, some only the eyes, and some only the nose. They do not carry arms nor know what they are, because I showed them swords and they took them by the edge and ignorantly cut themselves. They have no iron: their spears are sticks without iron, and some of them have a fish's tooth at the end and others have other things. They are all generally of good height, of pleasing appearance and well built: I saw some who had indications of wounds on their bodies, and I asked them by signs if it was that, and they showed me that other people came there from other islands near by and wished to capture them and they defended themselves: and I believed and believe, that they come here from the continental land to take them captive. They must be good servants and intelligent, as I see that they very quickly say all that is said to them, and I believe that they would easily become Christians, as it appeared to me that they had no sect. If it please our Lord, at the time of my departure, I will take six of them from here to your Highnesses that they may learn to speak. I saw no beast of any kind except parrots on this island." All are the words of the Admiral.

Document 4
1494   Slaves for Seville   Hispaniola

Source: Andreas Bernaldez, "Extracts from the History of the Catholic Sovereigns, Ferdinand and Isabella," **Collections** (Boston: Massachusetts Historical Society, 1843), 3 ser., vol. VIII, pp. 36-37.

In this same year, 1494, in which the vessels arrived from the Indies, leaving in Hispaniola the Admiral and his men, commencing the building of their town, Don Juan de Fonseca sent another squadron with supplies for this colony, of bread, wine, and other provisions, which came in good time; and were of great use to them. The vessels arrived from the Indies in March, 1494, and the squadron with the provisions was dispatched a few days afterwards.

The Admiral had not forgotten the death of the thirty-nine men who had been slain; but made investigation, and ascertained from the Indians themselves, who it was that had killed them: He made incursions into the interior, and

Ferdinand DeSoto's cruelties to Florida Indians.

captured vast numbers of the natives; and the second time that he sent home, he sent five hundred Indian men and women, all in the flower of their age, between twelve years and thirty-five, or thereabouts, all of whom were delivered at Seville to Don Juan de Fonseca. They came, as they went about in their country, naked as they were born; from which they experienced no more embarrassment than the brutes. They were sold, but proved of very little service, for the greater part of them died, from the climate."

1536   Kidnapping Donnaconna   Quebec

In 1534, Jacques Cartier sailed west in search of a passage to the Orient. By late spring he was in the straits of Belle Isle, and unimpressed by Labrador he continued south into the Gulf of St. Lawrence. On the shore of the Gaspé Peninsula he met a group of Indians, traded with them, and before his return to France he kidnapped two sons of Donnaconna, the chief of this tribe of Iroquois Indians. His reports convinced the French government to commission him to lead a second expedition. Late in the summer of 1535, Cartier was back in the Gulf of St. Lawrence. With the help of Donnaconna's sons he proceeded up the St. Lawrence to the village of Stadacona (near the present site of Quebec), where the chief lived. Donnaconna welcomed his sons and the French, who distributed gifts. The French captain wanted guides to take him further upriver to the village of Hochelaga (Montreal), where he hoped to learn more about the "kingdom of Saguenay." The Indians at Stadacona tried to discourage the French from proceeding upriver. Cartier persisted and set out with thirty men. On arrival in Hochelaga he got more detailed information on "Saguenay." By mid-October he was back at his base near Stadacona. Meanwhile, Donnaconna's people and the French had become suspicious of each other. The French spent the winter within a moated fort, armed with cannon. In the spring the captain prepared for the return to France. To insure that the entrance to Hochelaga would remain open to the French, he kidnapped Donnaconna and several Indians with the promise to bring them back to Stadacona within the year (document 5). Five years later Cartier returned to Canada without the Indians. When Donnaconna's people asked about the welfare of the ten kidnapped Iroquois, the captain replied that Donnaconna was an old man and had died, but that the others were rich and well. Actually, only one of them—a child—was still alive in France. The following passage is from the journal of Cartier's second voyage.

Further reading: W. J. Eccles, *The Canadian Frontier 1534-1760* (New York: Holt, Rinehart and Winston, 1969).

Document 5
1536   Kidnapping Donnaconna   Quebec

Source: H. P. Biggar, editor and translator, **The Voyages of Jacques Cartier, Publications** (Ottawa: The Public Archives of Canada, 1924), no. 11, pp. 225-230.

How on Holy Cross Day, the Captain had a Cross set up inside our Fort; and how Chief Donnaconna, Taignoagny, Dom Agaya and their party came, and of the capture of this Chief.

On [Wednesday] May 3, which was the festival of the Holy Cross, the Captain, in celebration of this solemn feast, had a beautiful cross erected some thirty-five feet high, under the cross-bar of which was attached an escutcheon, embossed with the arms of France, whereon was printed in Roman characters: LONG LIVE FRANCIS I. BY GOD'S GRACE KING OF FRANCE. And that day about noon several persons arrived from Stadacona, both men, women and children, who told us that Chief Donnacona with Taignoagny, Dom Agaya and the rest of their party were on their way, which pleased us, as we were in hopes of being able to capture them. They arrived about two o'clock in the afternoon; and as soon as they came opposite to our ships, the Captain went and greeted Chief Donnacona, who likewise was friendly enough but kept his eye constantly fixed on the wood and was wonderfully uneasy. Soon after Taignoagny came up and told Chief Donnacona that on no account should he go inside the fort. Thereupon one of their men brought out some embers and lit a fire for their Chief outside the fort. Our Captain begged him to come on board the ships to eat and to drink as usual, and also invited Taignoagny, who replied that they would go presently. This they did and came inside the fort. Before this however our Captain had been warned by Dom Agaya, that Taignoagny had spoken adversely and had told Chief Donnacona by no

means to go on board the ships. And our Captain knowing this went outside the fort where he had been keeping and saw that at Taignoagny's warning the squaws were hurrying away, and that none but men were left, who were present in considerable numbers. At this the Captain issued his orders for the seizure of Chief Donnacona, Taignoagny, Dom Agaya and two other headmen, whom he pointed out, and he commanded that the others should be driven away. Soon after the chief [Donnacona] entered the fort in company with the Captain, whereupon Taignoagny immediately rushed in to make him go out again. Seeing there was no other chance, our Captain proceeded to call to his men to seize them. At this they rushed forth and laid hands upon the chief and the others whose capture had been decided upon. The Canadians, beholding this, began to flee and to scamper off like sheep before wolves, some across the river, others into the wood, each seeking his own safety. When the above-mentioned had been captured and the rest had all disappeared, the chief and his companions were placed in safe custody.

How at nightfall the Canadians came opposite to our ships to look for their men, and howled and cried all night like wolves; and of the parley and agreement made next day and the presents they offered to our Captain.

At nightfall a large number of Donnacona's people came opposite to our ships, the river [St. Charles] between us, howling and crying like wolves all night long, calling out incessantly, *Agouhanna, Agouhanna*, in the hope of being able to speak to him [Donnacona]. This the Captain would not then allow, nor during the whole of the following morning until about noon, on which account they made signs to us that we had killed or hanged them. And about noon they returned in as great numbers as we had seen during the voyage, prepared for a move of some sort, and remained hidden in the wood, except a few who called out and shouted aloud to Donnacona. At this the Captain gave orders for Donnacona to be brought on deck to address them. And the Captain told him [Donnacona] to be of good cheer, for that after he had had an interview with the king of France, his master, and had related what he had seen at the Saguenay, he would be able, within ten or twelve moons, to come back, and that the king would make him a fine present. At this Donnacona was much pleased and in his speech mentioned it to the others, who gave three great shouts in sign of joy. Then these people and Donnacona made several harangues and went through various ceremonies which, as we did not understand them, it is impossible to describe. Our Captain told Donnacona that his people might cross the river [St. Charles] in all security in order to converse with greater comfort, and that he might reassure them. On learning this from Donnacona, several of the headmen came alongside our vessels in a canoe and began once more their harangues, praising our Captain and making him a present of twenty-four strings of wampum, which is the most valuable article they possess in this world; for they attach more value to it than to gold or silver. When they had chatted and discussed matters together to their heart's content, and had seen that there was no chance for their chief to escape, and that he would be obliged to go to France, the latter commanded them to fetch provisions to eat at sea, and to bring them to him on the following day. Our Captain presented Donnacona with two brass kettles, eight hatchets and some smaller objects such as knives and beads, at which to all appearance he was much pleased, and sent them to his wives and children. The Captain likewise gave some small presents to the Indians who had come to speak with Donnacona, who thanked him extremely for the same. After that they left and went back to their wigwams.

1540   New Mexico
Robbing and Killing among the Pueblo

During the half-century after Columbus's first voyage the Spanish learned that the islands explored by the Admiral were the outlying parts of a new world. The conquistadors who followed up Columbus's voyages explored vast new territories, conquered and enslaved thousands of native Americans, and discovered wealthy empires in Mexico and Peru. These latter conquests whetted Spanish appetites for more gold and silver. They investigated every bit of information about other fabulous places, such as El Dorado, the Mountain of Silver, the Seven Cities of Cibola, and Quivira. Francisco Vasquez de Coronado received a commission from the Viceroy of Mexico to conquer the Seven Cities of Cibola. Information about these places came from a Spanish expedition to Florida that had not been seen for nine years. Then they were chanced upon in northern Mexico and still later seen by Fray Marcos, who followed up the earlier reports of Cibola. The friar saw one of the cities. His findings encouraged the Viceroy of Mexico to organize the Coronado trip to New Mexico. Early in July, 1540, Coronado came to Hawikuh, the first of the seven "golden cities of Cibola." It was a little village, not a golden city. Exploration soon revealed that there was no Land of Cibola. A disappointed but undaunted Coronado ordered the main body of the army to camp in the Rio Grande valley for the winter. The Spanish set up headquarters in the land of the Tigeux. It was here that trouble broke out between the conquistadors and the Indians (document 6). Meanwhile, exploring parties who had set out in several directions brought back reports of visiting many Indian villages, the Grand Canyon, and the rich country of Quivira. An Indian named the Turk, who returned from the Northeast with the exploring party

under Hernando de Alvardo, described a land whose riches made the former dreams of Cibola seem dim. The Turk's tale revived hopes of finding wealth that would rival that of the Aztecs. In the spring Coronado led an expedition to Quivira. The trip was long and difficult. The Indians whom the Spanish met along the way knew nothing of Quivira. Ysopete, an Indian who had accompanied the expedition, early expressed doubts about the truth of the Turk's story. Coronado became suspicious and put the Turk in chains. He was strangled after he confessed that his story was a plot to get the Spanish onto the plains, where they would die or at least be greatly weakened. The following passages are from a *Narrative of the Expedition ... by* Pedro Castenada de Nájera, who accompanied Coronado.

Further reading: John Francis Bannon, *The Spanish Borderlands Frontier 1513-1821* (New York: Holt, Rinehart and Winston, 1970).

Document 6
1540   New Mexico
Robbing and Killing among the Pueblo

Source: George P. Hammond and Agapito Rey, editors and translators, **Narratives of the Coronado Expedition, 1540-1542**, Coronado Cuarto Centennial **Publications, 1540-1940** (Albuquerque: The University of New Mexico Press, 1940), vol. II, pp. 223-227.

Why Tigeux revolted, and the punishment inflicted upon its people without any one of them being to blame.

We have already told how the general arrived at Tigeux, where he found Don García López de Cárdenas and Hernando de Alvarado; how he sent the latter back to Cicuye, and how Alvarado brought Captain Bigotes and the governor of the pueblo as prisoners. The latter was an old man. The people at Tigeux did not feel well about these arrests. This ill feeling was aggravated by the general's desire to gather some clothing to distribute among the soldiers. For this purpose he sent for an Indian chief of Tigeux with whom we were already acquainted and with whom we were on good terms. Our men named him Juan Alemán because they said he had some resemblance to a certain Juan Alemán living in Mexico. The general spoke with him, asking him to furnish three hundred or more pieces of clothing which he needed to distribute to his men. He replied that it was not in his power to do this, but in that of the governors'; that they had to discuss the matter among the pueblos; and that the Spaniards had to ask this individually from each pueblo. The general ordered it thus and provided that certain chosen men who were with him should go to ask for it. As there were twelve pueblos, some were to go on one side of the river and some on the other. As all this was unexpected, the natives were not given time to discuss or consult about the matter. As soon as a Spaniard came to the pueblo, he demanded the supplies at once, and they had to give them, because he had to go on to the next one. With all this there was nothing the natives could do except take off their own cloaks and hand them over until the number that the Spaniards asked for was reached. Some of the soliders who went along with these collectors, when the latter gave them some blankets or skins that they did not consider good enough, if they saw an Indian with a better one, they exchanged it with him without any consideration or respect, and without inquiring about the importance of the person they despoiled. The Indians resented this very much.

In addition to what has been narrated, an outstanding person, whose name I shall omit to spare his honor, left the pueblo where the camp was and went to another one a league distant, and on seeing a beautiful woman in the pueblo, he called her husband down below and asked him to hold his horse by the bridle while he went up; and, as the pueblo was entered from the top, the Indian thought that he was going to some other place. While the native was detained there, some commotion took place, the man came back, took his horse, and rode away. When the Indian climbed to the upper part, he learned that he had ravished or had attempted to ravish his wife. Accompanied by other prominent persons in the pueblo, he came to complain, saying a man had outraged his wife, and told them how it had taken place. The general ordered all the soldiers and persons in his company to appear before him, but the Indian could not identify the man, either because he had changed clothes or for some other reason. But he said he would recognize the horse because he had held it by the rein. He was led through the stalls, and when he saw a blossom-colored horse covered with a blanket, he said that the owner of that horse was the man. The owner denied it, saying that the Indian had not recognized him, and perhaps he was mistaken also in the horse. In the end he went away without getting any redress for what he had demanded.

On another day an Indian from the army who was guarding the horses came bleeding and wounded, saying that the Indians of the land had killed one companion and were driving the horses before them to their pueblos. The soldiers went to round up the horses, many of which were found missing, including seven mules belonging to the general.

One day Don García López de Cárdenas went to visit the pueblos and to get an interpreter from them. He found the pueblos inclosed by a palisade and heard a great shouting inside, with horses running around as in a bull ring and the Indians shooting arrows at them. The natives were all up in arms. Cárdenas could do nothing because they refused to come out into the field, and as the pueblos are strong they could not be harmed. The general ordered Don García López de Cárdenas to go at once with the rest of the force and surround a pueblo. This was the pueblo where the greatest damage had been done and where the incident of the Indian woman had taken place.

The general went ahead, accompanied by many captains, such as Juan de Zaldívar, Barrionuevo, Diego López, and Melgosa. They caught the Indians so unawares that they soon took possession of the high terraces, but at great risk because the defenders wounded many of our men with arrows which they shot from the inside of their houses. In much danger our men remained on the top during the day, the night, and part of the following day, taking good shots with crossbows and harquebuses. Down on the ground the mounted men, together with many Indian allies from New Spain, built some heavy smudge fires in the basements, into which they had broken holes, so that the Indians were forced to sue for peace. Pablo de Melgosa and Diego López, the alderman from Seville, happened to be in that place and they answered their signs

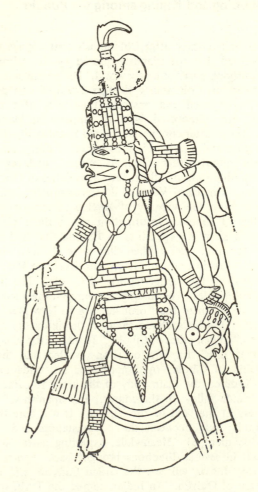

Pre-Columbian copper plate from Georgia

for peace by similar ones, which consisted of making a cross. The natives soon laid down their arms and surrendered at their mercy. They were taken to the tent of Don García, who, as was affirmed, did not know of the peace and thought that they were surrendering of their own accord, as defeated men.

As the general had ordered them not to take any one alive, in order to impose a punishment that would intimidate the others, Don García at once ordered that two hundred stakes be driven into the ground to burn them alive. There was no one who could tell him of the peace which has been agreed upon, as the soldiers did not know about it either, and those who had arranged the terms of peace kept silent, believing it was none of their business. Thus when the enemies saw that their comrades were being tied and that the Spaniards had started to burn them, about one hundred who were in the tent began to offer resistance and defend themselves with what they found about them and with stakes which they rushed out to seize. Our footmen rushed the tent on all sides with sword thrusts that forced the natives to abandon it, and then the mounted men fell upon them; as the ground was level, none escaped alive except a few who had remained concealed in the pueblo and who fled that night. These spread the news throughout the land, telling how the peace that was granted them had not been kept. This resulted in great harm later. After this incident, and as it snowed on them, the Spaniards abandoned the pueblo and returned to their quarters at the time when the army arrived from Cíbola.

1605   Filling the Ship's Complement   Maine

By the beginning of the seventeenth century the English had a detailed knowledge of the east coast of North America. English fishermen, pirates, and colony promoters, such as Sir Humphrey Gilbert and Sir Walter Raleigh, provided the necessary information. Success in overseas commercial adventures in Russia, Turkey, Africa, and later in India encouraged the wealthy of London and Plymouth to consider seriously the colonization of America. The purpose of Captain George Waymouth's voyage to northern Virginia (a name applied to the East Coast from Florida to Canada) was to explore and map an area whose economic potential had already been demonstrated by previous English voyages. Waymouth and his crew explored the Maine coast, traded with the Indians, and established cordial relations. Soon, English suspicions of native Americans outweighed the beneficial effects of this cordiality. Waymouth believed that the Indians planned to ambush the English. Thus, he decided to head back to England. James Rosier, who accompanied Waymouth and had been to America before, described the capture of five Indians to fill the ships' crew prior to sailing home (document 7). On arrival in Plymouth promoters of

the colonization of northern Virginia used the prisoners to help publicize the richness of America. Two of the prisoners Skicowaros and Tahanedo, eventually got back to Maine with exploring and colonizing expeditions.

Further reading: Charles M. Andrews, *The Colonial Period of American History* (4 vols., New Haven: Yale University Press, 1934-1938), Vol. I.

Document 7
1605   Filling the Ship's Complement   Maine

Source: James Rosier, **A True Relation of the most prosperous voyage made this present yeere 1605, by Captaine George Waymouth, in the Discovery of the land of Virginia**; . . . (London: printer, Geor. Bishop, 1605), no pagination. Courtesy of The Newberry Library, Chicago.

About eight a clocke this day we went on shore with our boats, to fetch aboord water and wood, our Captaine leauing word with the Gunner in the shippe, by discharging a musket, to giue notice if they espied any Canoa comming: which they did about ten a clocke. We therefore being carefull they should be kindly entreated, requested me to go aboord, intending with dispatch to make what haste after he possibly could. When I came to the ship, there were two Canoas, and in either of them three Saluages; of whom two were below at the fire, the other staied in their Canoas about the ship; and because we could not entice them abord, we gaue them a Canne of pease and bread, which they carried to the shore to eat. But one of them brought backe our Canne presently and staid abord with the other two; for he being yoong, of a ready capacity, and one we most desired to bring with us into England, had receiued exceeding kinde usage at our hands, and was therefore much delighted in our company. When our Captaine was come, we consulted how to catch the other three at shore, which we performed thus.

"We manned the light horseman with 7 or 8 men, one standing before carried our box of Marchandise, as we were woont when I went to traffique with them, and a platter of pease, which meat they loved: but before we were landed, one of them (being so suspitiously fearefull of his owne good) withdrew himselfe into the Wood. The other two met us on the shore side, to receiue the pease, with whom we went by the Cliffe to their fire and sate downe with them, and whiles we were discussing how to catch the third man who was gone, I opened the box, and shewed them trifles to exchange, thinking thereby to have banisht feare from the other, and drawen him to returne: but when we could not, we vied little delay, but suddenly laid hands upon them. And it was as much as fiue or sixe of us could doe to get them into the light horseman. For they were strong and so naked as our best hold was by their long haire on their heads: and we would haue beene very loath to haue done them any hurt, which of necessity we had beene constrained to haue done if we had attempted them in a multitude, which we must and would, rather than haue wanted them, being a matter of great importance for the full accomplement of our voyage.

"Thus we shipped fiue Saluages, two Canoas, with all their bowes and arrowes.

. . .

The names of the fiue Saluages which we brought home into England, which are all yet aliue, are these.

1. Tahánedo, a Sagamo or Commander.
2. Amoret
3. Skicowaros } Gentlemen
4. Maneddo
5. Sassacomoit, a servant."

1623   Poisoned Wine   Virginia

On Good Friday, March 22, the Indians simultaneously attacked the Virginians who lived on both sides of the James River. By day's end more than three hundred and fifty colonists had been killed. The organizer of this "Massacre of 1622" was Opechancanough, successor to Powhattan. Since the English had arrived in 1607, Powhattan had been responsible for a tenuous peace with the white men. The peace was maintained first by his relations with John Smith, then by the English kidnapping his daughter Pocahontas, and then by her subsequent marriage to John Rolfe. The famous chief supplied the colonists with food and prevented the many small tribes from waging war on the English. While there were many instances of violence and threats of violence, there was no general attack by one party against the other. When Powhattan died in 1618, Opechancanough became head of the Indian confederacy that his predecessor had organized for protection against the Indian people to the west. As recently as a year before the "massacre" Opechancanough had given the Virginians a pledge of perpetual peace, and the colonists were unaware of the chief's well-laid plans to destroy them.

Those colonists who survived the Good Friday attacks abandoned their farms and fled to the more heavily populated parts of the colony. The capital, Jamestown, was saved by a forewarning, and plans were made there to strike back at the enemy. The Virginians sent to England for more military supplies and dispatched military expeditions to attack the Indian villages. One Virginian, Edward Waterhouse, called the "massacre" a blessing and said that now there was no reason to tolerate the Indians anymore.

By the spring of 1623, Opechancanough was ready for peace. Many of his people were dead, and the remainder were hungry. The colonial officials agreed, and military

representatives met with the Indians to return English prisoners to their homes. At one of these meetings on May 22, 1623, Captain William Tucker concluded the treaty of peace with a toast of poisoned wine (document 8). Many Indians died that day, but Opechancanough, who had received a special invitation, did not attend the meeting. In 1644 he tried again to destroy the Virginians. During this latter war the colonists captured the old chief and took him to Jamestown, where a soldier, out of vengeance, shot him in the back.

Further reading: Richard L. Morton, *Colonial Virginia* (2 vols., Chapel Hill: The University of North Carolina Press, 1960), vol. I.

Document 8
1623   Poisoned Wine   Virginia

Source: Robert Bennett to Edward Bennett, from Bennetes Wellcome, June 9, 1623; Susan M. Kingsbury, editor **The Records of the Virginia Company** (4 vols., Washington: Government Printing Office, 1906-1935), vol. IV, pp. 221-222.

Newse I have not anye worthe the wryting but onlye this. The 22 of Maye Captin Tucker was sente with 12 men in to Potomacke Ryver to feche som of our Engleshe which the Indianes detayned, and withall in culler to conclude a pease with the great Kinge Apochanzion; soe the interpreter which was sente by lande with an Indian with hime to bringe the kinge to parle with Captain Tucker broughte them soe. After a manye fayned speches the pease was to be concluded in a helthe or tooe in sacke which was sente of porpose in the butte with Capten Tucker to poysen them. Soe Capten Tucker begane and our interpreter tasted before the kinge woulde tacke yt, but not of the same. Soe thene the kinge with the kinge of Cheskacke, [*their*] sonnes and all the great men weare drun [*torn*] howe manye we canot wryte of but yt is thought some tooe hundred weare poysend and thaye comyinge backe killed som 50 more and brought hom parte of ther heades. At ther departure from Apochinking the worde beinge geven by the interpreter which strode by the kinge one a highe rocke. The interpretour, the worde beinge paste tumbled downe, soe they gave in a volie of shotte and killed the tooe kinges and manye alsoe as ys reporte to the cownsell for serten. Soe this beinge done yt wilbe a great desmayinge to the blodye infidelles. We purpose god willinge after we have wedid our Tobaco and cornne with the helpe of Captn Smythe and otheres to goe upon the Waresquokes and Nansemomes to cute downe ther corne and put them to the sorde. God sende us vyctrie, as we macke noe question god asistinge.

1637 Burning Mystic Fort Connecticut

The carnage at Mystic Fort on May 26, 1637, proved to be the climax of the Pequot War. In less than an hour more than four hundred Pequot died by fire and sword at the hands of the English colonists and their Indian allies. The Pequot, whose name in the Algonquian language means "destroyers," were a fearsome tribe who had moved in among the other Indian tribes a few years before the English began to colonize New England. When the colonists first arrived in numbers in 1620, the coastal tribes were weak, having suffered great losses in a pestilence that swept through their villages in 1616-1617. Indeed, several months passed before the Pilgrims met native Americans face to face. The Puritans, who arrived a decade later and in greater numbers than the Pilgrims, met a similar situation. Unlike the Virginians the New Englanders expanded rapidly inland, not only west from Massachusetts Bay but also south to Narragansett Bay and southwest

Captain John Smith takes the King of Pamunkey prisoner 1608.

into the Connecticut Valley. The interior tribes whom the English met had not been weakened by the pestilence and were inveterate enemies of each other. Among these were the Narragansett, and Mohegan and the Pequot. Both the Narragansett and the Mohegan disliked and feared the Pequot, who had split off from the Mohegan. For a time these three groups of Indians and the English maintained a precarious peace. The killing of ten Englishmen by Indians between 1634 and 1636, however, prompted the Puritans of Massachusetts to send a punitive expedition against the Indians on Block Island and to demand that the Pequot in Connecticut surrender those responsible for the killings. The Puritans drove the Block Islanders from their homes and then went on to Pequot Harbor, where they destroyed and looted the homes of the Indians. The Pequot retaliated with attacks against the English in Connecticut. The New England colonists decided to exterminate the troublesome Pequot. In this effort they were joined by the Narragansett and the Mohegan. The attack on the Pequot Fort on Mystic River under the command of Captain John Mason, described by Captain John Underhill, a participant, crushed the resistance of the Pequot (document 9). In the next few months the allied forces hunted down the enemy, and those not killed were distributed as captives among their Indian neighbors.

Further reading: Alden T. Vaughan, *New England Frontier: Puritans and Indians, 1620-1675* (Boston: Little, Brown and Company, 1965).

Document 9
1637 Burning Mystic Fort Connecticut

Source: John Underhill, Newes From America: or, a New and Experimentall Discoverie of New England; containing A True Relation of their War-like proceeding these two years last past, with a Figure of the Indian Fort, or Palisado (London: printed by F. D. for Peter Cole, 1638), pp. 36-40. Courtesy of The Newberry Library, Chicago.

Having imbarqued our souldiers, wee weighed ankor at *Seabrooke* Fort, and set sayle for the *Narraganset Bay*, deluding the *Pequeats* thereby, for they expected us to fall into *Pequeat* River; but crossing their expectation, bred in them a securitie: wee landed our men in the *Narraganset Bay*, and marched over land above two dayes journey before wee came to *Pequeat*, quartering the last nights march within two miles of the place, wee set forth about one of the clocke in the morning, having sufficient intelligence that they knew nothing of our coming: Drawing neere to the Fort, yeelded up ourselves to God, and intreated his assistance in so waightie an enterprise. We set on our march to surround the Fort, Captain *Iohn Mason*, approching to the West end, where it had an entrance to passe into it, my selfe marching to the Southside, surrounding the Fort, placing the *Indians*, for wee had about three hundred of them without, side of our souldiers in a ring battalia, giving a volley of shotte upon the Fort, so remarkable it appeared to us, as wee could not but admire at the providence of God in it, that souldiers so unexpert in the use of their armes, should give so compleat a volley, as though the finger of God had touched both match and flint: which volley being given at breake of day, and themselves fast asleepe for the most part, bred in them such a terrour, that they brake forth into a most dolefull cry, so as if God had not fitted the hearts of men for the service, it would have bred in them a commiseration towards them: but every man being bereaved of pitty fell upon the worke without compassion, considering the bloud they had shed of our native Countreymen, and how barbously they had dealt with them, and slaine first and last about thirty persons. Having given fire, wee approached neere to the entrance which they had stopped full, with armes of trees, or brakes: my selfe approching to the entrance found the worke too heavie for mee, to draw out all those which were strongly forced in. We gave order to one Master *Hedge*, and some other souldiers to pull out those brakes, having this done, and laid them betweene me and the entrance, and without order themselves, proceeded first on the South end of the Fort: but remarkable it was to many of us; men that runne before they are sent, most commonly have an ill reward. Worthy Reader, let mee intreate you to have a more charitable opinion of me (though unworthy to be better thought of) then is reported in the other Booke: You may remember there is a passage unjustly laid upon mee, that when wee should come to the entrance, I should put forth this question: shall wee enter: others should answer againe; What came we hither for else? It is well knowne to many, it was never my practice in time of my command, when we are in garrison, much to consult with a private souldier, or to aske his advise in point of Warre, much lesse in a matter of so great a moment as that was, which experience had often taught to mee, was not a time to put forth such a question, and therefore pardon him that hath given the wrong information: having our swords in our right hand, our Carbins or Muskets in our left hand, we approched the Fort. Master *Hedge* being shot thorow both armes, and more wounded; though it bee not commendable for a man to make mention of everything that might tend to his owne honour; yet because I would have the providence of God observed, and his Name magnified, as well for myself as others, I dare not omit, but let the world know, that deliverance was given to us that command, as well as to private souldiers. Captaine *Mason* and my selfe entring into the Wigwams, hee was shot, and received many Arrowes against his headpeece, God preserved him from any wounds; my selfe received a shotte in the left hippe, through a sufficient Buffe coate, that if I had not beene supplyed with such a garment the Arrow would have pierced through me; another I received

betweene necke and shouldiers, hanging in the linnen of my Head-peece, others of our souldiers were shot some through the shoulders, some in the face, some in the head, some in the legs: Captaine *Mason* and my selfe losing each of us a man, and had neere twentie wounded most couragiously these *Pequeats* behaved themselves: but seeing the Fort was to hotte for us, wee devised a way how wee might save our selves and prejudice them, Captaine *Mason* entring a Wigwam, brought out a firebrand, after hee had wounded many in the house, then hee set fire on the West-side where he entred, my selfe set fire on the South end with a traine of Powder, the fires of both meeting in the center of the Fort blazed most terribly, and burnt all in the space of halfe an houre; many couragious fellowes were unwilling to come out, and fought most desperately through the Palisadoes, so as they were scorched and burnt with the very flame, and were deprived of their armes, in regard the fire burnt their very bowstrings; and so perished valiantly: mercy they did deserve for their valour, could we have had opportunitie to have bestowed it; many were burnt in the Fort, both men, women, and children, others forced out, and came in troopes to the *Indians*, twentie and thirtie at a time, which our souldiers received and entertained with the point of the sword; downe fell men, women, and children, those that scaped us, fell into the hands of the *Indians*, that were in the reere of us; it is reported by themselves, that there were about foure hundred soules in this Fort, and not above five of them escaped out of our hands. Great and dolefull was the bloudy sight to the view of young souldiers that never had beene in Warre, to see so many soules lie gasping on the ground so thicke in some places, that you could hardly passe along. It may bee demanded, Why should you be so furious (as some have said) should not Christians have more mercy and compassion: But I would referre you to *Davids* warre, when a people is growne to such a height of bloud, and sinne against God and man, and all confederates in the action, there hee hath no respect to persons, but harrowes them, and sawes them, and puts them to the sword, and the most terriblest death that may bee: sometimes the Scripture declareth women and children must perish with their parents; sometime the case alters: but we will not dispute it now. We had sufficient light from the word of God for our proceedings.

1643   Governor Kieft's War   New Netherland

William Kieft, governor of New Netherland from 1638 to 1647, managed to involve the colony in five years of intermittent war with the Indians. The conflict centered in the lower Hudson Valley from Staten Island to Westchester to Long Island, where farming had replaced the fur trade as the major economic activity of both colonists and Indians. Kieft acted quickly to demand satisfaction from Indians who were involved in transgressions against white men. In 1640 he dispatched a military force against the Raritan Indians for refusing to pay a tax, for attempting to steal a sloop, and for killing some pigs. On arriving at the Raritan village the force demanded payment according to their instructions, proceeded to kill several Indians, and captured and tortured the chief's brother. In February, 1643, the governor granted the petition of three councillors to attack several bands of Indians who had fled from their northern neighbors to New Amsterdam, begging protection. These Indians, like many others in the vicinity had been harassed by the colonists and had harassed the colonists. Squabbles developed over livestock eating the Indians' unfenced planted fields, the Indians' ferocious dogs feeding on the colonists' livestock and poultry, and the presence of the "Indian-givers" on land that they had sold to the Dutch. David Peterson de Vries chronicled the Dutch attacks on the Indians at Pavonia across from Manhattan and on the Indians at Corlaer's Hook in Manhattan. De Vries farmed on Staten Island. He had previously lost tenants and property in Indian attacks, but he believed that Kieft's aggressiveness only aggravated the tense situation (document 10). Soon after the attacks the Indians made a peace. In late summer of 1643, however, the Indians launched attacks from Staten Island to Poughkeepsie to Long Island. The only safe place was New Amsterdam. For example, de Vries was burned out, and he returned to Holland. Intermittent fighting continued for two years. On August 31, 1645, the Dutch and at least ten bands of Indians formally established peace. The following day New Amsterdam celebrated a Thanksgiving. Perhaps a thousand Indians had lost their lives since 1640, and the population of New Netherland had declined, but principally from emigration rather than from wartime casualties.

Further reading: Allen W. Trelease, *Indian Affairs in Colonial New York: The Seventeenth Century* (Ithaca: Cornell University Press, 1960).

Document 10
1643	Kieft's War	New Netherland

Source: Henry C. Murphy, editor and translator, David Peterson de Vries, **Voyages from Holland to America, A.D. 1632 to 1644, Collections** (New York: New York Historical Society, 1857), 2 ser., vol. III, part I, pp. 114-116.

The 24th of February, sitting at a table with the governor, he began to state his intentions, that he had a mind to *wipe the mouths* of the Indians; that he had been dining at the house of Jan Claesz.Damen, where Maryn Adriaensz, and Jan Claesz.Damen, together with Jacob Planck, had presented a petition to him to begin this work. I answered him that there was no sufficient reason to under-

take it; that such work could not be done without the approbation of the *twelve men*; that it could not take place without my assent, who was one of the twelve men; that moreover I was the first patroon, and no one else hitherto had risked there so many thousands, and besides being patroon, I was the first to come from Holland or Zeeland to plant a colony; and that he should consider what profit he could derive from this business, as he well knew that on account of trifling with the Indians we had lost our colony in the South river at Swanendael, in the Hoere-kil, with thirty-two men, who were murdered in the year 1630; and that in the year 1640, the cause of my people being murdered on Staten Island was a difficulty which he had with the Raritaense Indians, where his soldiers had for some trifling thing killed some Indians, and brought the brother of the chief a prisoner to the *Mannates*, who was ransomed there, as I have before more particularly related. But it appeared that my speaking was of no avail. He had, with his co-murderers, determined to commit the murder, deeming it a Roman deed, and to do it without warning the inhabitants in the open lands, that each one might take care of himself against the retaliation of the Indians, for he could not kill all the Indians. When I had expressed all these things in full, sitting at the table, and the meal was over, he told me he wished me to go to the large hall, which he had been lately adding to his house. Coming to it, there stood all his soldiers ready to cross the river to Pavonia to commit the murder. Then spoke I again to Governor William Kieft: "Stop this work; you wish to break the mouths of the Indians, but you will also murder our own nation, for there are none of the farmers who are aware of it. My own dwelling, my people, cattle, corn, and tobacco will be lost." He answered me, assuring me that there would be no danger; that some soldiers should go to my house to protect it. But that was not done. So was this business begun between the 25th and 26th of February in the year 1643. I remained that night at the governor's, sitting up. I went and sat in the kitchen, when, about midnight, I heard a great shrieking, and I ran to the ramparts of the fort, and looked over to Pavonia. Saw nothing but firing, and heard the shrieks of the Indians murdered in their sleep. I returned again to the house by the fire. Having sat there awhile, there came an Indian with his squaw, whom I knew well, and who lived about an hour's walk from my house, and told me that they two had fled in a small skiff; that they had betaken themselves to Pavonia; that the Indians from Fort Orange had surprised them; and that they had come to conceal themselves in the fort. I told them that they must go away immediately; that there was no occasion for them to come to the fort to conceal themselves; that they who had killed their people at Pavonia were not Indians, but the Swannekens, as they call the Dutch, had done it. They then asked me how they should get out of the fort. I took them to the door, and there was no sentry there, and so they betook themselves to the woods. When it was day the soldiers returned to the fort, having massacred or murdered eighty Indians, and considering they had done a deed of Roman valour, in murdering so many in their sleep; where infants were torn from their mother's breasts, and hacked to pieces in the presence of the parents, and the pieces thrown into the fire and in the water, and other sucklings were bound to small boards, and then cut, stuck and pierced, and miserably massacred in a manner to move the heart of stone. Some were thrown into the river, and when the fathers and mothers endeavoured to save them, the soldiers would not let them come on land, but made both parents and children drown,—children from five to six years of age, and also some old and decrepit persons. Many fled from this scene, and concealed themselves in the neighbouring sedge, and when it was morning, came out to beg a piece of bread, and to be permitted to warm themselves; but they were murdered in cold blood and tossed into the water. Some came by our lands in the country with their hands, some with their legs cut off, and some holding their entrails in their arms and others had such horrible cuts, gashes, that worse than they were could never happen. And these poor simple creatures, as also many of our own people, did not know any better than that they had been attacked by a party of other Indians,—the Maquas. After this exploit, the soldiers were rewarded for their services, and Director Kieft thanked them by taking them by the hand and congratulating them.

1644   New Sweden
Send Soldiers to Destroy the Indians

During the brief history of the colony of New Sweden, 1638-1655, the Swedes competed for possession of the lower Delaware Valley with the Dutch, the English, and the Indians. Johan Printz, governor of New Sweden from 1643 to 1653, promoted plans for the expansion of settlement, built fortifications, and protested Dutch and English presence there. He also deplored the boldness of the Indians in the neighborhood, whose audacity increased when they noticed that the colony was not growing. In a report to the company dated June 11, 1644, the governor requested soldiers to clear out the Indians in the immediate vicinity (document 11). He believed that they were of no economic value and that they would only become more troublesome. With the Indians who lived nearby destroyed, Printz reasoned that the colonists could open

a vigorous fur trade with the more distant tribes and at the same time retain possession of the valley against the incursions of the Dutch and the English. The soldiers were not sent. The Indians were not destroyed, but like the Dutch and the English in America, the Swedes had no use for Indians who interfered with their plans.

Further reading: Charles M. Andrews, *The Colonial Period of American History* (4 vols., New Haven: Yale University Press, 1934-1938), vol. II.

Document 11
1644   New Sweden
Send Soldiers to Destroy the Indians

Source: Amandus Johnson, editor and translator, **The Instructions of Johan Printz, Governor of New Sweden** (Philadelphia: The Swedish Colonial Society, 1930), pp. 117-118.

Nothing would be better than to send over here a couple of hundred soldiers, and [keep here] until we broke the necks of all of them in this River, especially since we have no beaver trade whatsoever with them but only the maize trade. They are a lot of poor rogues. Then each one could be secure here at his work, and feed and nourish himself unmolested without their maize, and also we could take possession of the places (which are the most fruitful) that the savages now possess; and when we have thus not only bought this river, but also win it with the sword, then no one, whether he be Hollander or Englishman, could pretend in any manner to this place either now or in coming times, but we should then have the beaver trade with the Black and White Minquas alone, four times as good as we have had it, now or at any past time. And if there is some delay in this matter it must nevertheless in the end come to this and it cannot be avoided; the sooner the better, before they do us more harm. They are not to be trusted, as both example and our own experience show, but if I should receive a couple of hundred good soldiers and in addition necessary means and good officers, then, with the help of God, not a single savage would be allowed to live in this River. Then one would have the passage free from here unto Manathans, three small days' journey across the country from this River at Zachikans.

II
The White Man Stays
1675-1774

By the mid-seventeenth century thousands of native Americans were well-acquainted with Europeans. Those who lived along the Atlantic Coast from Nova Scotia to Florida, those who lived from the lower St. Lawrence River to the Great Lakes, and those who lived in the upper Rio Grande Valley, had seen and had begun to trade with Europeans. Many hundreds more native Americans learned of the white men from their neighbors through trade and used European goods long before they saw any white men.

During these ever-increasing contacts few native Americans were really safe from the white men, who invariably demanded the cooperation of the native peoples in economic, political, and social affairs. The white men expected the Indians to give up their land and trade their furs on white men's terms. They also expected the Indian people to support them in their wars with each other and against their Indian brothers. The Spanish in particular expected the "heathen" to become Christian.

The English aggressively moved west from the Chesapeake Bay and coastal New England. In the mid-1670s the Virginians and the New Englanders crushed the Doeg, Susquehannock, Wampanoag, and other tribes who resisted their advance. The Spanish mercilessly punished the religious leaders of the Pueblo who resisted the soul-saving work of Christian missionaries. In 1680, the Pueblo, unlike Indians along the Atlantic Coast, drove the Spanish from their country. The French relentlessly pursued the beaver in the Great Lakes region, where they fought the Iroquois Confederacy of New York for control of the fur trade.

In the eighteenth century the English, French, and Spanish continued their expansionist activities into the interior of North America, frequently clashing with each other, and involving the native Americans in European rivalry for control. The encroachments of the English in Carolina forced many tribes to look to the Spanish in Florida for protection, and some, such as the Yamassee, fled south for their lives. Others, such as the Tuscarora, moved north under the protection of the Iroquois Confederacy. In northern New England the Abnaki, as in the past, depended on the French for protection from the English. For two groups, the Fox in Wisconsin and the Natchez in Louisiana, there were no French rivals nearby to protect them. French power crushed the Fox and destroyed the culture of the Natchez.

In these wars against each other and against the native Americans, the Europeans frequently had Indian allies. The French, for example, had the support of the Illinois and other tribes in their wars against the Fox. The English had Indian allies in their wars against the Tuscarora and the Yamassee. When the French and English clashed in the Ohio Valley in the mid-eighteenth century, the French, who claimed sovereignty over the region, sent an Indian war party led by a mixed blood, Charles de Langlade, to chastise the Miami, who had been trading with the English. One of the traders got away, reported what took place, and brought with him a message from the Miami. The message illustrates the effects of English-French rivalry on the tribe.

> Brother Onas [The Iroquois-language name for the governor of Pennsylvania].
> We your Brethren the Twightwees [Miami], have sent You by our Brother Thomas Burney, a Scalp, and Five Strings of Wampum, in Token of our late unhappy Affair at the Twightwees Town, and whereas our Brother has always been kind to us, hope he will now put us in a method how to act against the French, being more discouraged for the Loss of our Brother the Englishman who was killed, and the five who were taken Prisoners, than for the Loss of ourselves [Burney reported that fourteen Indians were killed and the town destroyed], and notwithstanding the two Belts of Wampum, which were sent from the Governor of Canada, as a Commission to destroy us, we shall hold our Integrity with our Brothers, and are willing to die for them, and will never give up this Treatment, although we saw our great Piankashaw [a tribe of the Miami] King (which commonly was called Old Britain by us) taken, killed and eaten within a hundred Yards of the Fort before our Faces—We look upon ourselves as lost People, fearing that our Brothers will leave us, but before we will be subject to the French, or call them Our Fathers, we will perish here.[1]

While the English and French were disrupting the lives of the Indian people between the Appalachian Mountains and the Mississippi River, the Spanish, long since returned to the upper valley of the Rio Grande, kept the Pueblo of New Mexico busy at work.[2]   About this same time some native Americans had their first contact with Europeans.   In 1745 the Aleut met the Russians, who came to Attu and Agattu in search of furs.

Trade, Christianity, and war all had an immeasurable impact on the native American.   The Indian people accepted the white men's material goods, but their complaints about the abuses of the traders were unending. White traders cheated, beat, and enslaved the Indians, often after getting them drunk on rum.   The Indians participated in white men's wars, but during wartime, colonial officials offered bounties to encourage killing Indians. White bounty hunters seldom bothered to check whether their victim belonged to a tribe that had "taken up the hatchet."   In the mid-eighteenth century the native Americans could assume that their white neighbors hated them and that their lives were not safe in the face of the white men's fury.

Notes

1. Martha L. Simonetti, assistant project director, George Dailey and George R. Beyer, editors, *Records of the Provincial Council 1682-1776*, National Historical Publications Commission Microfilm Publication Program (26 rolls, Harrisburg: Pennsylvania Historical and Museum Commission, 1966), roll #A4, vol. M, p. 175.

2. For an example of complaints against the cruelty of Spanish officials read the report of Fray Carlos José Degado in 1750 in *The Spanish Tradition in America* (Charles Gibson, ed., New York: Harper & Row, Publishers, 1968).

1675   Killing the Wrong Indians   Virginia

The outbreak of war in Virginia in 1675 ended thirty years of peace between the native Americans and the English.   In 1646, Necotowance, successor to the murdered Opechancanough, acknowledged that the Powhattan and allied tribes held their land from the King of England and agreed to pay an annual tribute of twenty beaver skins to the governor.   In effect, Necotowance had agreed that his people would live on land reserved for their exclusive use.   Additional regulations attempted to keep the two groups separated from each other. Mutual fear and distrust, however, made relations between the native people and the English difficult.   The aggressive expansion of the Virginians disturbed the tribes, and violent clashes occurred from time to time.   News of these clashes turned into rumors of a general Indian war among the English, who still remembered Opechancanough's attempts to destroy them in 1622 and 1644.

In 1675 violent clashes between the two peoples led to war.   Thomas Mathew, a landowner on the Potomac River frontier, was neighbor to the Doeg and to the Susquehannock who lived north of the river in Maryland.   The Susquehannock, who recently had moved south from the Susquehanna Valley, were at peace with the English but suffered a food shortage.   With the Doeg as guides the Susquehannock sought food in Virginia.   On one of their forays some hogs were taken from Mathew's plantation. The English pursued these raiders, got back the hogs, and punished the Indians.   In retaliation the Doeg attacked Mathew's plantation.   A small force of Virginians under Colonel George Mason and Major George Brent dashed into Maryland, accused the first Indians they saw, and started to shoot.   Thomas Mathew describes the outbreak of war in a history that he wrote in 1705 (document 12). Of course, the Susquehannock sought revenge by raiding the homes of the English.   The result was a general war, known in the history of colonial Virginia as Bacon's Rebellion.   Almost two years later, in May, 1677, the native Americans and the Virginians assembled to sign a peace treaty.   Again the Indian people acknowledged that they held their land from the King of England.   The Virginians conceded that the aggressive English expansion had contributed to the outbreak of war and agreed that in the future English law would protect the Indian subjects of the King from aggressive Virginians.

Further reading: Wilcomb E. Washburn, *The Governor and the Rebel: A History of Bacon's Rebellion in Virginia* (Chapel Hill: The University of North Carolina Press, 1957).

Document 12
1675   Killing the Wrong Indians   Virginia

Source: T. M. [Thomas Mathew], "The Beginning, Progress, and Conclusion of Bacon's Rebellion, 1675-1676," Charles M. Andrews, editor, **Narratives of the Insurrections 1675-1690** (New York: Barnes & Noble, Inc., 1952, reprint), pp. 16-17.   By permission of Harper & Row, Publishers.

My Dwelling was in Northumberland, the lowest County on Potomack River, Stafford being the upmost; where having also a Plantation, Servant's, Cattle, etc., My Overseer there had agreed with one Robt. Hen to come thither, and be my Herdsman, who then Lived Ten Miles above it; But on a Sabbath day Morning in the summer Anno 1675, People in their Way to Church, Saw this Hen lying th'wart his Threshold, and an Indian without the Door, both Chopt on their Heads, Arms and other Parts, as if done with Indian Hatchetts.   Th' Indian was dead, but Hen when ask'd who did that? Answered "Doegs Doegs," and soon Died, then a Boy came out from under a Bed, where he had hid himself, and told them, Indians had come at break of day and done those Murders.

From this Englishman's bloud did (by Degrees) arise Bacons Rebellion with the following Mischiefs which

Overspread all Virginia and twice endangered Maryland, as by the ensuing Account is Evident.

Of this horrid Action Coll: Mason who commanded the Militia Regiment of Foot and Capt. Brent the Troop of Horse in that County, (both dwelling Six or Eight Miles Downwards) having speedy notice raised 30 or more men, and pursu'd those Indians 20 Miles up and 4 Miles over that River into Maryland, where landing at Dawn of Day, they found two small Paths. Each Leader with his Party took a Separate Path and in less than a furlong, either found a Cabin, which they Silently Surrounded. Capt. Brent went to the Doegs Cabin (as it proved to be) Who Speaking the Indian Tongue Called to have a *Matchacomicha Weewhip i.e.* a Councill, called presently Such being the usuall manner with Indians. The King came Trembling forth, and wou'd have fled, when Capt. Brent, Catching hold of his twisted Lock (which was all the Hair he wore) told him he was come for the Murderer of Robt. Hen, the King pleaded Ignorance and Slipt loos, whom Brent shot Dead with his Pistoll. Th' Indians Shot Two or Three Guns out of the Cabin, th' English shot into it, th' Indians throng'd out at the Door and fled, The English Shot as many as they cou'd, so that they Kill'd Ten, as Capt. Brent told me, and brought away the Kings Son of about 8 Years old, Concerning whom is an Observable Passage, at the End of this Expedition; the Noise of this Shooting awaken'd th' Indians in the Cabin which Coll: Mason had Encompassed, who likewise Rush'd out and fled, of whom his Company (supposing from that Noise of Shooting Brent's party to be Engaged) shott (as the Coll: Inform'd me) Fourteen before an Indian Came, who with both hands Shook him (friendly) by one Arm Saying *Susquehanougs Netoughs i.e.* Susquehanaugh friends, and fled, Whereupon he ran amongst his Men, Crying out "For the Lords sake Shoot no more, these are our friends the Susquehanoughs."

1676   Massachusetts and Rhode Island

The Capture of Philip's Wife and Son

Thirty Shillings for King Philip's Head

King Philip's War was an attempt by the Indian people to drive the English from southeastern New England. Philip was the son of Massasoit, the great friend of the Plymouth colonists. After the deaths of Philip's father (in 1661) and his elder brother (in 1662), he became the sachem of the Wampanoags who lived at Mount Hope. He was a proud young man who looked on the continuous English expansion as the death blow to the Indian way of life. Hunting, particularly for beaver, was poor. Farming, especially with the colonists and their livestock trespassing, was difficult. Tensions between the Indians and the English increased with each trespass, theft, and assault. The young sachem tried to rally the Wampanoags to

organize and defend themselves. The older chiefs favored continued accommodation: Philip favored pressured negotiation.

The colonists, especially those in Plymouth, believed Philip was not only a trouble maker but also a conspirator. The Wampanoag's attack on Swansea in June, 1675, confirmed their suspicions. Quickly the English set out after Philip. He escaped. Indian attacks on English settlements increased, and by the beginning of the new year Indian tribes from Maine to Connecticut joined the war against the colonists. The English, hoping to end the war by capturing Philip, pursued their illusive enemy, who escaped

again and again. The colonists took some satisfaction in capturing and killing the sachems of Philip's allies. They gloated over the capture and sale of his wife and son. A description by a contemporary, Increase Mather, (document 13) is given. Finally in August, 1676, the New Englanders rejoiced over the killing of their great enemy. With Philip's death the Indian attacks decreased, and within the next year all Indian tribes, both friend and foe, suffered from strict confinement to territory specified by the colonists. The pursuit and death of Philip was related by a participant, Captain Benjamin Church, to his son Thomas (document 14).

Further reading: Douglas Edward Leach, *Flintlock and Tomahawk: New England in King Philip's War* (New York: The Macmillan Company, 1958).

Document 13
1676   Massachusetts and Rhode Island
The Capture of Philip's Wife and Son

Source: Increase Mather, A Brief History of the War with the Indians in New-England From June 24, 1675. (When the first Englishman was Murdered by the Indians) to August 12, 1676. When Philip . . . , the principal Author and Beginner of the War, was slain, . . . (London: printed by Richard Chiswell, 1676), pp. 44-45. Courtesy of The Newberry Library, Chicago.

August 1. Captain *Church* with thirty English-men and twenty Indians following *Philip* and those with him, by their track took twenty and three Indians. The next morning they came upon *Philip's* head Quarters, killed and took about an hundred and thirty Indians, with the loss of but one Englishman. In probability many of the English Souldiers had been cut off at this time, but that an Indian called *Matthias,* who fought for the English, when they were come very near the Enemy, called to them in their own Language with much vehemency, telling them they were all dead men if they did but fire a Gun, which did so amuse and amaze the Indians, that they lost a great advantage against the English. *Philip* hardly escaped with his·life this day also. He fled and left his *Peag* behind him, also his *Squaw* and his Son were taken Captives, and are now Prisoners in *Plymouth*. Thus hath God brought that grand Enemy into great misery before he quite destroy him. It must needs be bitter as death to him, to lose his Wife and only Son (for the Indians are marvelous fond and affectionate towards their Children) besides other Relations, and almost all his Subjects and Country too.

Document 14
1676   Massachusetts and Rhode Island
Thirty Shillings for King Philip's Head

Source: T. C. [Thomas Church], **Entertaining Passages Relating to Philip's War which began in the Month of June, 1675, as also of Expeditions More lately made Against the Common Enemy, and Indian Rebels, in the Eastern Parts of New-England: with Some Account of the Divine Providence towards Benj. Church Esqr.** (Boston: printed by B. Green, 1716), pp. 42-45. Courtesy of The Newberry Library, Chicago.

Capt. *Church* being now at *Plymouth* again weary and worn, would have gone home to his Wife and Family, but the Government being Solicitous to ingage him in the Service until *Philip* was slain, and promising him satisfaction and redress for some mistreatment that he had met with: He fixes for another Expedition; he had soon Volunteers enough to make up the Company he desired and Marched thro' the Woods, until he came to Pocasset. And not seeing nor hearing of any of the Enemy, they went over the Ferry to *Rhode-Island*, to refresh themselves. The Captain with about half a dozen in his company took Horse & rid about eight miles down the *Island* to Mr. Sanfords where he had left his Wife; who no sooner saw him but fainted with the surprize; and by that time she was a little revived, they spy'd two Horse men coming a great pace. Capt. *Church* told his company that those men (by their riding) came with Tydings. When they came up they proved to be Maj. *Sanford* and Capt. *Golding*: who immediately ask'd Capt. *Church, What he would give to hear some News of Philip?* He reply'd, *That was what he wanted?* They told him. *They had rid hard with some hopes of overtaking of him, and were now come on purpose to inform him, That there was just now Tydings from* Mount-hope; *An* Indian *came down from thence (where* Philips *Camp now was) on to* Sand Point *over against* Trips, *and hollow'd, and made signs to be fetch'd over; and being fetch'd over, he reported, That he was fled from* Philip, *who* (said he) *has kil'd my Brother just before I came away, for giving some advice that displeased him.*

And said, *he was fled for fear of meeting with the same his Brother had met with.* Told them also, *That* Philip *was now in* Mount-hope *Neck.* Capt. *Church* thank'd them for their good News, and said, he hop'd by to Morrow Morning to have the Rogues Head. The Horses that he and his company came on standing at the door, (for they had not been unsaddled) his Wife must content her self with a short visit, when such game was a-head; they immediately Mounted, set Spurs to their Horses, and away. The two Gentlemen that bro't him the Tydings, told him, *They would gladly wait upon him to see the event of this Expedition.* He thank'd them, and told them, he should be as fond of their company as any Mens; and (in short) they went with him. And they were soon at *Trips* Ferry (with Capt. *Churches* company) where the deserter was; who was a fellow of good sense, and told his story handsomely: he offered Capt. *Church* to Pilot him to *Philip*, and to help to kill him, that he might revenge his Brothers death. Told him, That *Philip* was now upon a little spot of Upland that was in the South end of the miery Swamp just at the foot of the Mount, which was a spot of ground that Capt. *Church* was well acquainted with. By that time they were got over the Ferry, and came near the ground half the Night was spent, the Capt. commands a halt, and bringing the company together he asked Maj. *Sanford* & Capt. *Goldings* advice, what method was best to take in making the on-set, but they declining giving any advice; telling him, *That his great Experience & Success forbid their taking upon them to give advice.* Then Capt. *Church* offered Capt. *Golding*, that he should have the honour (if he would please to accept of it) to beat up *Philips* headquarters. He accepted the offer and had his alotted number drawn out to him, and the Pilot. Capt. *Churches* instructions to him were to be very careful in his approach to the Enemy, and be sure not to shew himself until by day light they might see and discern their own men from the Enemy. Told him also, That his custom in the like cases was to creep with his company on their bellies, until they came as near as they could; and that as soon as the Enemy discovered them they would cry out; and that was the word for his men to fire and fall on. Directed him when the Enemy should start and take into the Swamp, they should pursue with speed, every man shouting and making what noise they could; for he would give orders to his Ambuscade to fire on any that should come silently. Capt. *Church* knowing it was *Philips* custom to be fore-most in the flight, went down to the Swamp and gave Capt. *Williams* of *Situate* the command of the right wing of the Ambush, and placed an *English-man* and an *Indian* together behind such shelters of trees, &c. that he could find, and took care to place them at such distance as none night pass undiscovered between them, charg'd 'em to be careful of themselves, and of hurting their friends; And to fire at any that should come silently thro' the Swamp: But it being some-what further thro' the Swamp than he was aware of, he wanted men to make up him Ambuscade: having placed what men he had, he took Maj. Sanford by the hand, said, *Sir, I have so placed them that 'tis scarce possible* Philip *should escape them.* The same moment a Shot whistled over their heads and then the noise of a Gun towards *Philips* Camp. Capt. *Church* at first tho't it might be some Gun fired by accident: but before he could speak, a whole Volley followed, which was earlier than he expected. One of *Philips* gang going forth to ease himself, when he had done, look'd round him, & Capt. *Golding* thought the *Indian* looked right at him (tho' probably 'twas but his conceit) so fired at him, and upon his firing, the whole company that were with him fired upon the enemies shelter before the *Indians* had time to rise from their sleep, and so over shot them. But their shelter was open on that side next the Swamp, built so on purpose for the convenience of flight on occasion. They were soon in the Swamp and *Philip* the foremost, who starting at the first Gun threw his Petunk and Powder horn over his head, catch'd up his Gun and ran as fast as he could scamper, without any more clothes than his small breeches and stockings, and ran directly upon two of Capt. *Churches* Ambush; they let him come fair within shot, and the English mans Gun missing fire, he bid the *Indian* fire away, and he did so to purpose, sent one Musket Bullet thro' his heart, and another not above two inches from it; he fell upon his face in the Mud & Water with his Gun under him. By this time the Enemy perceived they were way laid on the east side of the *Swamp*, tack'd short about. One of the Enemy who seem'd to be a great surly old fellow, hollow'd with a loud voice, & often called out, *iootash, iootash*, Capt. *Church* called to his *Indian Peter* and ask'd him, *Who that was that called so?* He answered, It was old *Annowon Philips* great Captain, calling on his Souldiers to stand to it and fight stoutly. Now the Enemy finding that place of the *Swamp* which was not Ambush'd, many of them made their escape in the *English* Tracks. The Man that had shot down *Philip*, ran with all speed to Capt. *Church*, and informed him of his exploit, who commanded him to be Silent about it, & let no man more know it, until they had drove the *Swamp* clean, but when they had drove the *Swamp* thro & found the Enemy had escaped, or at least the most of them; and the Sun now up, and so the dew gone, that they could not so easily Track them, the whole Company met together at the place where the Enemies Night shelter was; and then Capt. *Church* gave them the news of *Philips* death; upon which the whole Army gave Three loud *Huzza's*. Capt. *Church* ordered his body to be pull'd out of the mire on to the Upland, so some of Capt. *Churches Indians* took hold of him by his Stockings, and some by his small Breeches, (being otherwise naked) and drew him thro' the Mud unto the Upland, and a doleful great, naked, dirty beast, he look'd like. Capt. *Church* then said, *That forasmuch as he had caused many an* English mans body *to lye unburied and rot above ground, that not one of his bones should be buried.* And calling

his old *Indian* Executioner, bid him behead and quarter him. Accordingly, he came with his Hatchet and stood over him, but before he struck he made a small Speech directing it to Phillip; and said, *He had been a very great Man, and had made many a man afraid of him, but so big as he was he would now chop his Ass for him;* and so went to work, and did as he was ordered. *Philip* having one very remarkable hand being much scarr'd; occasioned by the splitting of a Pistol in it formerly. Capt. *Church* gave the head and that hand to *Alderman*, the *Indian* who shot him, to show to such Gentlemen as would bestow gratuities upon him; and accordingly he got many a Peny by it. This being on the last day of the Week, the Captain with his Company returned to the Island, tarryed there until Tuesday; and then went off and ranged thro' all the Woods to *Plymouth*, and received their *Praemium*, which was *Thirty Shillings per* head for the Enemies which they had killed or taken, instead of all Wages; and *Philips* head went at the same price. Methinks it's scanty reward and poor incouragement; tho' it was better than what had been some time before. For this March they received *Four Shillings* and *Six Pence* a Man, which was all the Reward they had, except the honour of killing *Philip*. This was in the latter end of August, 1676.

c. 1640-1680 Hanging Conspirators New Mexico

In August, 1680, the people of Pueblo country drove the Spanish from the upper valley of the Rio Grande. The Spanish had begun to establish themselves in the valley in the early seventeenth century. In 1599, Juan de Oñate set out for New Mexico to win fame and fortune. His expedition brought him neither, but it renewed Spanish interest in the territory, especially among Christian missionaries. The latter got the support of the royal government, and in 1609, Don Pedro de Peralta was sent north from Mexico as governor. He founded Santa Fe that same year. Royal commands and Franciscan missionaries, not material successes, kept the Spanish in New Mexico. Their presence strongly tested the patience of the Pueblo, who resented supplying goods and labor for the survival of their foreign overlords. The Pueblo especially resented the sternly imposed life of the mission. Spanish officials, lay and clerical, insisted that traditional Indian beliefs and religious practices be stamped out. Thus, they struck out harshly at the Indian religious leaders, who were suspected of conspiring against the Franciscans. Sergeant Major Diego López Sambrano testified to this point in the royal investigation of the Pueblo Revolt of 1680 (document 15). One of the Indian religious leaders mentioned by López was Popé of Taos. Released by the Spanish authorities after one of their roundups of native religious leaders, Popé returned to Taos, where he put a plan into effect to destroy the Spanish. The Pueblo were so successful that fifteen years passed before the Spanish reconquered the upper Rio Grande valley.

Further reading: John Francis Bannon, *The Spanish Borderlands Frontier 1513-1821* (New York: Holt, Rinehart and Winston, 1970).

Document 15
c. 1640-1680   Hanging Conspirators   New Mexico

Source: "[Declaration] of Diego Lopez [Sambrano, . . . December 22, 1681]." C. W. Hackett, editor, **Revolt of the Pueblo Indians of New Mexico and Otermin's Attempted Reconquest 1680-1682**, Coronado Cuarto Centennial Publications, 1540-1940 (Albuquerque: The University of New Mexico Press, 1942), vol. IX, part II, pp. 298-301.

To the eighth question of the interrogatory, he said that what he believes before God and his conscience, as a Christian, is that they are very well content with the idolatrous life they are living, practising sorcery and making idolatrous offerings, because it is what they have always desired, it not having been possible to wean them away from it either by the labors of the many apostolic religious who have been here, or by the punishment inflicted by the various governors and ministers over a period of more than forty years in these parts. This declarant knows of and has witnessed these punishments since the time of the government of Don Fernando de Arguello, who hanged, and lashed, and imprisoned more than forty Indians. And in the year '50, during the government of General Concha, he discovered another plot to rebel which the sorcerers and chief men of the pueblos had arranged with the enemy Apaches, and for that purpose the Christians, under the pretext that the enemy was doing it, turned over to them in the pastures the droves of mares and horses belonging to the Spaniards, which are the principal nerve of warfare. They had already agreed with the said apostates to attack in all the districts on the night of Holy Thursday, because the Spaniards would then be assembled. The said rebellion was discovered because of Captain Alonso Vaca and other soldiers having followed a drove of mares which the Indians were driving off, and the aggressors being overtaken, they declared that the Christians of the pueblo of Alameda and Sandia had turned them over to them, and that they were all plotting and conspiring with all the said Apaches to rebel and destroy the whole kingdom, and to be left in freedom as in ancient times, living like their ancestors. The Spaniards returned with this news and with a knife belonging to a Christian Indian of the pueblo of Alameda, to the presence of the alcalde mayor of the said district, who was Captain Juan Garciá Olgado. He notified the said governor, and on investigating the case the treason was uncovered, and many Indians were arrested from most of the pueblos of this kingdom. As a result

nine leaders were hanged and many others were sold as slaves for ten years. Later another chastisement was visited upon the Piros here for the same crime, during the government of General Don Fernando de Villanueva, when six Indians were hanged and others were sold and imprisoned, for in addition to their crimes and conspiracies they were found in an ambuscade with the enemy Apaches in the Sierra de la Madalena, where they killed five Spaniards, among them the alcalde mayor, who was killed by one of the six Christian Indians, called in his language El Tanbulita, who was hanged. Despite all these punishments, another Indian governor of all the pueblos of Las Salinas, named Don Esteban Clemente, whom the whole kingdom secretly obeyed, formed another conspiracy which was general throughout the kingdom, giving orders to the Christian Indians that all the horse droves of all the jurisdictions should be driven to the sierras, in order to leave the Spaniards afoot; and that on the night of Holy Thursday, just as they had plotted during the government of General Concha, they must destroy the whole body of Christians, not leaving a single religious or Spaniard. This treason being discovered, they hanged the said Indian, Don Esteban, and quieted the rest, and when the property of the said Indian was sequestered there was found in his house a large number of idols and entire kettles full of idolatrous powdered herbs, feathers, and other trifles. Despite all that he has stated, which is a matter of public knowledge throughout this army—and in case of necessity he offers to prove it—during the government of General Don Juan Francisco Treviño the Indians, continuing their abuses and superstitions, had bewitched the father preacher, Fray Andrés Durán, guardian of the pueblo of San Ildefonso, a brother of his, the wife of the said brother, and an Indian interpreter named Francisco Guiter, who denounced the said sorcerers. Forty-seven Indians were arrested, all of the Teguas nation, four of whom, because of having declared that they had committed the witchcraft referred to, were sentenced to be hanged, both for the above crimes and for other deaths which were proved against them, the *autos* of which the secretary, Francisco Xavier, verified, he being commissioned to do so by the said señor general. This declarant assisted him in making the arrests and in gathering up many idols, powders, and other things which he took from the houses of the sorcerers and from the countryside. The said señor general having examined the *autos* with his secretary, who was Luis de Quintana, he sentenced the four of them to death, and that they be taken to the place where they had committed the crime for execution. Two were turned over to this declarant to be hanged, one in the pueblo of Nambé and the other in that of San Felipe; another hanged himself while alone; and his lordship ordered Sargento Mayor Andrés Gómez to have the fourth hanged in the pueblo of Los Jemez. All this was done, and of the others who remained, numbering forty-three, some he released with a reprimand, and others he condemned to lashings and imprisonment.

While they were under arrest all the members of their nation attempted to kill the said general, and for this purpose one morning more than seventy Indians armed with macanas and leather shields entered the house where the said general was, filling two rooms with people. They brought with them some eggs, chickens, tobacco, beans, and some small deerskins—this declarant, who was present, being unable to detain them—and on being asked what they wanted, they said resolutely to the said general that they had come so that they might give up to them the sorcerers who were imprisoned; that he should pardon them; and that they would make amends. Among the prisoners was one named Popé who has been the cause of the present rebellion. The said general pacified the Indians, saying to them, "Wait a while, children; I will give them to you and pardon them on condition that you forsake idolatory and iniquity." This declarant interceded for them, and also Captain Francisco García, who was present and was protector of the natives. The said general not wishing to accept any of the things they brought him, one of the Indians who was in the second room called out, "Leave it there if he does not want it." Whereupon he [the governor] ordered this declarant to receive it and to give them some woolen blankets, and he released and gave up the prisoners and allowed them to go. After some days this declarant said to some of those who had come to ask for the said Indians: "Come and tell me why so many of you people came armed to see the governor." They told him, "We came determined to kill him if he did not give up the said prisoners, and, on killing him, to kill the people of the villa as well," saying that for this purpose they had left an ambuscade in the hills. This declarant asking them where they would have gone afterward if they had done what they said, and whether the Apaches would not have killed them in the sierras, they let it be understood, with much feeling, that in order to defend the sorcerers whom they asked for they would have gone to the sierras even though the Apaches did kill them. Thus he replies to the question.

c.1730   Illinois, Wisconsin and Louisiana Destroy the Renard and the Natchez

In the early eighteenth century the Fox (Renard) in Wisconsin and the Natchez in Louisiana impeded French activities in the Mississippi Valley. French exploitation of North America centered on the fur trade. Within a century of Samuel de Champlain's arrival in 1608 in the St. Lawrence Valley, the French had extended trade with the Indians from the Atlantic Coast to the western Great Lakes and the upper Mississippi Valley. Trade prospered. The long wars with the Iroquois Confederacy of New York and with the Anglo-Americans had ended. And under a system whereby the trade was leased to the commanders of the western military posts, profits were given

to all concerned. Only the Fox of Wisconsin interfered. Earlier these people had been the cause of trouble at Detroit, where the French and their Indian allies besieged the Fox in their fort, pursued them after they had fled the fort, and thoroughly thrashed them. The survivors returned to their brothers in Wisconsin, where they disrupted French trade first with the Illinois and later on with the Sioux. The French would not tolerate middlemen whose activities reduced profits and caused intratribal warfare. With their Indian allies the French struck hard at the Fox in Wisconsin. In the summer of 1730 they set off to the southeast, apparently to seek the protection of the Iroquois Confederacy. Just south of Lake Michigan the Fox decided to make a stand. Nicholas Coulon, sieur de Villiers, commander of the French fort on the St. Joseph River, reported on the progress of the war against the Fox to the Marquis de Beauharnois, governor-general of New France (document 16). Those Fox who got away fled to the Sauk, who gave them protection. They continued to be troublesome to the French, and in 1733, Beauharnois ordered their extermination (document 17). Complete success did not come to the French, and later the Sauk and Fox resisted, in turn both British and American expansion westward.

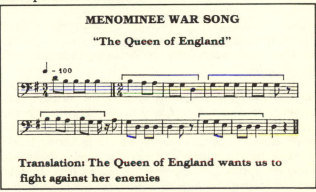

MENOMINEE WAR SONG

"The Queen of England"

Translation: The Queen of England wants us to fight against her enemies

About the same time that the Fox suffered defeat south of Lake Michigan, the Natchez failed in their attempt to halt French expansion in Louisiana. Unlike most native North Americans the Natchez were not migratory hunters and farmers but were a settled agricultural people sufficiently wealthy to support a monarchy. Their leader was the Great Sun, who ruled over several villages, each with a leader of the Sun caste. These little Suns ruled over the people who were called Stinkards. The latter submitted themselves completely to the little Suns, and in turn, both the Stinkards and the little Suns were completely submissive to the Great Sun. Around 1714 the French constructed Fort Rosalie near the village of the Great Sun. When a newly appointed commander of the fort, Chépart, decided he wanted the site of a village (called White Apple) ruled by a man second in rank to the Great Sun, relations between the two peoples became strained. Chépart's demand angered the Natchez, who elaborately planned and swiftly carried out an attack on their French neighbors.

The Natchez destroyed Fort Rosalie on November 28, 1729, and ordered a Stinkard to kill Chépart. Monsieur Périer, the governor of Louisiana, had supported Chépart's demand for the village, and the French, again with Indian allies, attacked the Natchez villages in 1730. The Natchez who survived these attacks crossed to the west bank of the Mississippi River, fortified themselves, and awaited the next French move. Antoine Simor Le Page du Pratz, an engineer who lived in the colony at the time of the war, discussed the surrender of the Natchez in his history of Louisiana (document 18).

Further reading: Louise Phelps Kellogg, "The Fox Indians During the French Regime," *Proceedings, 1907* (Madison: The State Historical Society of Wisconsin, 1908), vol. 55, pp. 142-188 and John R. Swanton, *Indian Tribes of the Lower Mississippi Valley and Adjacent Coast of the Gulf of Mexico*, Bureau of American Ethnology, *Bulletin 43* (Washington: Government Printing Office, 1911).

Document 16
1730   Destroy the Renard   Illinois

Source: Reuben Gold Thwaites, editor, **The French Regime in Wisconsin—II 1727-1748, Collections** (Madison: The State Historical Society of Wisconsin, 1906), vol. 17, pp. 116-117.

Our tribes were very anxious to spare the renards' lives, and proposed an act of treachery to me. Their design was that I should promise Them their lives, that I should make them come out And that they would fall on them. It was in nowise their intention to do so; their only object was to secure captives. I opposed this, seeing it could only result in sparing the lives of those wretches, who would undoubtedly Continue on their way to The jroquois. Every day they found fresh subjects on which to speak to me. They came back twice with their children and with collars, to move me. But although they had been pale, I made them turn as if painted red, by telling them that all their words were in vain And that they were not to come back again. They addressed themselves to Monsieur de St Ange, who listened to them no more than I did. Nevertheless, We fired some shots at them as they reentered their fort. They suffered much from hunger because, for four days previous to Their flight, they lived only on *apichimonts*. [Note on original manuscript: "These are Their coverings made of skins."] Monsieur de Noyelles arrived with the nations of His post, which gave us a reinforcement of a hundred men; these would have been very Useful to us, had the Savages been willing to mount guard night and day, but as soon as the least bad weather set in, they would not come out of their cabins and we were not enough Frenchmen to man the entire contravallation.

The Renards held out for twenty-three days. On the 8th of September, we had the finest weather in the world until an hour from sunset, when a Terrible storm of wind and rain arose which lasted until the night, which was very dark and Foggy, so that, in spite of all I could say to our Savages, I was unable to make them guard all The outlets. The Renards took advantage of this to come out of their fort and flee. We perceived this at first from the crying of the children which we heard, and we learned it from a Sauteux [Chippewa] woman who came into the trench to surrender. I at once prepared to pursue them at day-break. We followed them with Our Savages and routed them, and more than 200 warriors were killed. No other chief Escaped except Licaouais, of whom, however, we have no information. The others were made prisoners and placed in The hands of the Kaôquias [Kiowa], who will assuredly not spare their lives. Those who escaped from us threw away all they had, even to their powder-horns in order that they might escape; but few remain. The prisoners told us that they had fought against The Scioux [Sioux] in the spring and very likely this is true. I Found their village very small, although I do not refer to that in which they were shut up, But to two Of their Camps which I saw in the prairies where they had lived during The summer. Our Quicapoux [Kickapoo] and mascoutins [Mascouten] did wonders on this expedition, and all did equally well, vying with one another. Had it not been for The desertion of 300 Kaôkias who had only just abandoned Monsieur de St. Ange, and for the absence of 100 men from my camp who had gone Hunting to supply us with food, not a single Renard would have escaped. I can assure you, Monsieur, that we made The renards fast, but that we fasted almost as much as They. My son, who has just come out of The action, will give you whatever details I may have omitted. I take the liberty, Monsieur, of begging your protection for Him. I have had no more urgent desire, than to Send Him to you that he may have The honor of bringing you this News.

Document 17
1733   Destroy the Renard   Wisconsin

Source: Reuben Gold Thwaites, editor, **The French Regime in Wisconsin—II, 1727-1748, Collections** (Madison: The State Historical Society of Wisconsin, 1906), vol. 17, pp. 182-183.

Monseigneur—The Renards [Fox] have at last abandoned their fort in which there remained only Fifty of them in all: (Forty Warriors and 10 Boys from twelve to thirteen years of age). They went to la Baye to beg Monsieur de Villiers to ask their Father to have mercy on them. He has brought here four of the principal men among them, Two of them being Former Chiefs. The instigator of all their misdeeds whose name is Kiala is among these. I am sending the Sieur de Villiers at once to return to la Baye with orders to take every proper precaution, by means of the Nations which Are faithful to us, to bring all the Renards to Montreal or to destroy them. If we succeed I shall disperse them among our Villages of settled savages. I think, Monseigneur, that to send them to France with the view of distributing them among the islands would be the most advantageous for the Country because here they could always desert to the English. I am Having the three others taken to Quebec with two women and I send back The hostage with the Sieur de Villiers, as he may be of use to us.

The Sieur de Villiers also has orders, If that Wretched Remnant will not obey, to kill Them without thinking of making a single Prisoner, so as not to leave one of the race alive in the upper Country if possible. If he is obliged to exterminate the Men, the women and Children who remain will be brought here, Especially the Children. I Hope, Monseigneur, that if this step meets with the success that I expect from it, we shall be in a Position next year to make all our Nations of the Lakes attack the Chicachas [Chickasaw]. As I have written to Detroit and to all the Posts in the Neighborhood of the Mississipy to go there, I expect that there will be a number of Bands in the Field. Thirty Men from sault St. Louis and from the Lake of two Mountains have gone there lately.

The Village of the Sakis [Sauk], Monseigneur, has been restored to its former Condition.

I remain with very profound respect, Monseigneur, Your very Humble and very obedient servant,

Beauharnois

Montreal, July 1st, 1733.

Document 18
1731   Destroy the Natchez   Louisiana

Source: [Antoine Simor] Le Page du Pratz, **Histoire de la Louisiane**, ... (3 vols., Paris, 1758), vol. III, pp. 318, 321-327. Selection translated by Thomas S. Soroka. Rare Book Collection, State Historical Society of Wisconsin, Madison.

The Destruction of Natchez by Mr. Périer,
Governor of Louisiana.

Peace was restored to the city. The public thought no more of the war with the Natchez; but Mr. Périer, the Commanding general, ever on active duty, neglected no effort to uncover any place where the Natchez might have taken refuge. After a careful search, he was informed that the Natchez had completely abandoned the eastern bank of the St. Louis River, without a doubt, to avoid exposure to importunate and dangerous visits from the Chatkas [Choctaw]. And to be better hidden from the French, they pulled completely back to west of the river near the Silver Bayou. The distance from their fort to the mouth of the Red River was close to sixty miles.

. . .

The Misters Périer [the governor and his brother, de Salvert, Lieutenant General of the Colony] left with their army; favorable weather seconded their activity. They finally arrived without any obstacles upon the refuge of the Natchez. To reach it, they had to wade up the Red River, from that the Black River and from there the Silver Bayou, which is connected to a small lake stretching to not far from the fort built by the Natchez to sustain themselves against the French.

The Generals sent some soldiers from this side to scout. These were happy enough to come upon and surprise a young boy who was enjoying fishing. At the sudden approach of the French soldiers, his fear was so great that he was unable to cry out, because his sighting of them and his capture by them occurred in the same instant. These soldiers, instructed by the prudence of these generals, mollified his fear and took him away. Misters Périer flattered the boy and promised not only to spare him but also anything else that might be promised in such parallel circumstances. Having regained his strength, this child indicated a path which the army followed. In a while, they traversed a small forest at the edge of which they found themselves before a clearing upon which stood the fortress of the enemy, which was laid seige to as soon as discovered. An officer who has only much valor makes a good Captain of Grenadiers; but when courage, prudence, and vigilance march in step with the Generals, victory accompanies them and makes them succeed.

Having been instructed in these principles from their youth, the Misters Périer always put them into practice.

The enemy fort was scarcely discovered and surrounded, when they began preparations to storm it. Animated by the presence and ardor of their generals, the soldiers take to their task with alacrity.

The Natchez, fear-stricken at the sight of an enemy so vigilant, shut themselves up in their fort, having neither time nor confidence to hold a council. Despair takes the place of the prudence which now abandons them. They have no idea what to do when they see a trench reach the fort. Weapons are passed out; they smear themselves with paint in order to make a final effort in a sortie showing more rage than valor. The soldiers who see them for the first time in this extraordinary attire become at first frightened. But their generals, comporting themselves with ardor in the face of the greatest dangers, reassure their troops who hunt down the enemy and force him, to return with losses to his fort.

The old colonists deride the war tactics of the natives because experience makes all things familiar. But I think that the most resolute Roman Legions would have been terrified at the sight, for the first time, of a troop of men looking not unlike devils pouring out of hell bent on attack. Imagine seeing a troop of men tall, well built, and entirely nude but for a loin cloth, having their whole bodies smeared and painted in distinct areas of black, red, yellow, or grey from head to foot. A few red and black feathers are worn in their hair like a crest; their cinctures dangle with bells of several sizes and gourds quarter filled with small stones. Add to all this the noise the warriors make jumping about, their continual *hou hou* filling the air and neighboring woods. If we put all these things together, we will have a sketch of the portrait I am trying to paint; but I am obliged to confess that nothing compares with the original.

The reception which our troops gave the Natchez taught them to hold themselves close. And although the trench from our side had almost been completed, our generals were impatient that the mortars were not yet in a position to bombard the enclosure. Finally they began a battery and the third round fell in the middle of the fort, where women and children were ordinarily sheltered. We soon heard terrible cries from that very sight. Reacting painfully to the groaning of their women and children, the men made a signal and requested a possibility to capitulate. The Misters Périer had the satisfaction of seeing an obstinate enemy reduced to submission in three days time. Their style of seige, we should relate brought about the surrender of some of the most fortified bases; it was by the very same means that the generals had previously reduced the Fort of Arguin in Africa. As a consequence, one should not be surprised if our August Monarch, always attentive to recompense merit, raised the Misters Périer to the rank of General Officers and our Governor to Lieutenant General.

After having requested a capitulation, the Natchez raised difficulties that occasioned comings and goings till the night which they awaited to profit from. They requested until morning for the conclusion of the articles of capitulation. The night was granted them. But the gate remained guarded and they were not able to make the kind of escape at which they had succeeded in the war of Mr. de Loubois. During this time they attempted to profit from the dark of night and the apparent placidness of the French. They tried then an escape considerably different from the first. No guard heard them; but thanks to the vigilance of Misters Périer, it was discovered soon enough to capture the larger number of them, who were forced to return to the fort. Those few who had succeeded joined up with others who were being hunted down and together retreated to the Tchicachas [Chickasaw]. The remainder listened to discretion: Among these numbered the Grand Sun and his wives, several warriors, many more women, young people and children.

The French army re-embarked and took the Natchez slaves to New Orleans. They were imprisoned there; but since these prisons were too small to contain all these people for a longer time, taking care to keep them away from access to escape, the women and children were sent to the King's plantation and to others. Among these women was one chief's wife, *Bras-pique*, who reminded me how she had once tried to save the French from a disaster with which they had been menaced and to which they succumbed in spite of the efforts this princess had made.

Some time later these slaves were sent to the Isle of S. Domingue. So, all traces of this Nation were wiped out of the Colony. This is in fact what came about. Those few who had escaped had less than one tenth the number of women that would have been needed to revive the Nation. And so was this nation destroyed, once the most brilliant in the Colony and the most useful to the French.

TEYERIHWAHKWATHA
While shepherds watched their flocks by night.

Shi ha di nonh ne kats he nen,
Eh ta geh wah hon tyen,
Ne Kon di ronh ya geh re non,
Wat kon dih swat be te.

Toh sa se wah te ronn ni se,
Se wa ni gon ra geh;
Se wats hen non ni hak tenh non,
Ne jon gwe ta gwe gon.

Da wed I se sa na ta gon,
Eh on gweh wa ha ton;
Ke ris tus Ro ya ner na ah,
Ne wa te nyen denh stonh.

Ka ronh ya gon ne ex ha ah,
Ne n'on gweh en ye gen:
Ron wa nya ta ra gwe non ni,
Kats he nen o ron to.

Wa gen ron ne Se raph nen genh,
Ne wa tyoh swat he ne!
Ka ronh ya geh ro non gon ton,
Ni yoh e ne genh ji.

Ra on we senh tse ra Ni yoh,
Onh went ja geh ka yen:
Ka yan 'renh on gweh a go wenhk,
Yo dah sa we on weh.

Mr. de Salvert left Louisiana with the laurels he had gathered and returned to France to receive the applause of the Court. Mr. Périer, our governor, was also summoned there some time later. He was recompensed as was his due for his services, rendered with firmness and equity, qualities which made him missed by all the honest men of the Colony.

1710-1712   South Carolina
Abusive Indian Traders

Native Americans enjoyed the white men's material goods: woolen blankets, metal pots and hatchets, guns and ammunition, rum and brandy. Indeed, white men's tobacco, pipes, and wampum were preferable to home products. Trade between the two groups began early and rapidly expanded to include more and more Indians and a greater variety of products. For white men's goods, native Americans traded furs and deerskins and, on occasion, slaves. The commerce revolved around an elaborate credit system. Merchants supplied traders, who went to Indian towns to trade or established posts where Indians came in to trade. Indians usually were in debt to the traders, and the traders in turn were in debt to the merchants. The Indian people bitterly and frequently complained of the abusive treatment dealt out to them by traders to whom they were in debt. In response, all European governments attempted to regulate the Indian trade to prevent abuses and to keep the peace between the two peoples. No regulatory system worked with much success. Selections from the minutes kept by the commissioners of the Indian trade in South Carolina illustrate the Indians' complaints and the commissioners' decisions (document 19).

Further reading: Verner W. Crane, *The Southern Frontier 1670-1732* (Ann Arbor: The University of Michigan, 1929, r. 1956).

Document 19
1710-1712   South Carolina
Abusive Indian Traders

Source: W. L. McDowell, editor, **Journals of the Commissioners of the Indian Trade September 20, 1710-August 29, 1718** (Columbia: South Carolina Archives Department, 1955), pp. 3-4, 5, 10-11.

Thursday, September 21, 1710

Present: Ralph Izard, Esq., *President*, Col. James Risbee, Mr. John Raven, Mr. John Guerard, and Col. Wm. Rhett.

Col. Hugh Grainge was chosen and sworn a Comissioner.

The Apalachia Indians appeared and complains by Cockett, the Interpreter, who was sworn.

The Board ordered that Ventusa, an Appalachia Indian, and his Wife are to continew as free People till Phillip Gilliard by a Hearing before the Board can prove the Contrary.

Massony, another Indian of the Appalachias, to be free till Capt. Musgrave can make it other Wayes appeare.

Diego, an Appalachia Indian, to continew free till Richd. Edghill prove otherwise.

Wansella, an Ellcombe Indian, is ordered to be a free Man till Mr. John Pight can prove him a Slave by any Order from the Government.

Coloose, a free Indian Woman given Mr. Pight by their own People, the Commissioners thinck itt unreasonable for her to be a Slave and doe order her to be set free.

The Apalachia Indians desire that their People may be restrained from leaving their own Town and goeing to reside at the Assapallago Town.

They complain against Capt. Musgrove that he went this Spring to their Town and demanded Indians to goe and hoe his Corn and if they did not answer his Demands he would beat them.

Jess Crosley, a Trayder, being jealous of a Whore of his, beat and abused an Apalachia Indian Man in a barbarous Manner and also bete Jno. Cocket till he spitt Blood, for onely desiring him to forbear beating the Indian.

Ordered that Jno. Wright, Esq., Agent, doe forthwith issue out his Warrant to take the said Crosley and have him brought before the Comissioners to answer to such notorious Abuses as he has committed amongst the Indians.

Phillip Gilliard, a Trader, took a young Indian against her Will for his Wife, and cruelly whipped her and her Brother for accepting a few Beades from her, to the great Greife of the Indians there present. One Carpenter justifies [*sic*] that the said Gilliard made a Woeman drunk with Rum and locked her up from her Mother, offering to kill the Mother because she would not leve her Daughter behind her.

. . .

October 28, 1710

. . .

Capt. Musgrove complains that the Creek Indians owe him for Part of 200 Lbs. Powder and 500 Lbs. Bulletts ever since they went to War against the Chactaw Indians. Upon Enquirey and a full Hearing of the Kings being present at this Board, they find that Capt. Musgrove forced the said Powder and Bullets upon the Indians, for which the Indians made him reasonable Sattisfaction for said Powder and Bulletts as has been suffitiently made appear before this Board.

Ordered that the Indians, per the Interpreter, be acquainted therewith which was accordingly done and they dismissed very well sattisfied.

Ordered that upon John Dixon, Charles Peirce, or James Alford, or any of them making Oath that they heard the Tomolla King declare Masoony a Slave, that then the said Indian be Capt. Musgrave's Slave; otherwise he is to have his Freedom.

. . .

July 27, 1711

. . .

And also gave Information of severall Cheif Men of the Yamossees which came down to make Complaints against several Traders. Ordered that the said Indians doe now attend this Board, and also Mr. John Cockett and Mr. Wm. Bray to be Interpreters. The Indians and the two Interpreters accordingly attended and the Interpreters ware sworn and declares as followes:

That an Agent having bin sent up amongst them to redress their Greivances and to acquaint them that their Rum Debts shoold be forgiven them, they were come down to know if they might depend upon that Assurance. Mr. President answered that the said Agent was sent by this Board to redress their Grievances and had ordered with the Assembly that their Rum Debts shoold not be paid. Mr. President also acquainted the said Indians that itt was impossible att this Distance wholy to restrane the Traders from carrying up Rum and advised them to lay what Restraint they could upon their People to prevent their buying Rum from the Traders.

Mr. President acquainted the Indians that the Agent had Orders to inform them that they ware not obliged to pay their Relation [s'] Debts which they had not ingaged for. And also advised the Indians to use their utmost Indevor to pay their just Debts and for the Future to take care not to run in Debt with the Traders. The Indians answered they were preparing to goe to War and a'hunting to pay their Debts. The Indians complained that several white Persons are setled within the Limitts of their Settlement, whereby the said Indians are damnified by the Stock of the white Men. Mr. President answered they shoold be protected in the Possession of their Land and that those Persons who are setled within their Limitts shoold effectualy be prosecuted. The Indians also acquainted this Board that they had further Complaints to make.

July 28, 1711

. . .

Mr. Agent appearing before this Board acquainted them that Capt. John Cochran had sold a free Indian Brother to Anto. Pussimy, then belonging to the Youhau Town, and that the Evidences were the said Agent, Mr. Wm. Magett and Wm. Bray.

Read a Letter from Mr. John Barnwell to the Board.

Ordered that Capt. John Cochran and Capt. Wm. Maggett be sent for. Mr. Cockett, Mr. Bray and the Indians were sent for and attended. And the Indians complained that Tho. Jones, John Whitehead, Joseph Bryan, Robt. Steale, John Palmer and Barnaby Bull are setled in the Limitts of their Land and desired they might be removed. The President answered that effectual Care shoold be taken to remoove them.

The Indians farther complained that Cornelius Macarty took away the Wife and Child of an Indian that was gon to War and that Geo. Wright took away a free Woman that had a Husband in Tomatly Town. Answered Care shoold be taken to right them.

. . .

Mr. Bray and Mr. Stephen Beadon were ordered to attend this Board, who attended accordingly. Mr. Bray was directed according to the Purport of his Bond to send to New York to bring back an Indian Woman and Child who had bin free and was sold thither by him.

1718   Demon Rum   Pennsylvania
1746   New York

One of the most persistent complaints of the native Americans was against the liquor traffic. Rum, brandy, and other spirits were important items in the Indian trade and were equally important for toasts during negotiations for land purchases and peace treaties. Liquor made the native Americans "wild" men, and chiefs regularly asked government officials to forbid the distribution of rum among their people. At a meeting in Philadelphia in June, 1718, a chief of the Conestoga asked the Pennsylvania officials to enforce the prohibition against rum shipments to his town. The governor answered the chief the same day (document 20). Native Americans knew rum made them "wild" men, but few could resist the liquid demon. A member of the religious group, the Unitas Fratrum (Moravian Brethren), who, with a fellow missionary, visited several towns of the Six Nations in New York in 1746, graphically described the effects of rum on the residents of a Seneca town (document 21).

Further reading: Wilbur R. Jacobs, *Wilderness Politics and Indian Gifts: The Northern Colonial Frontier 1748-1763* (Stanford, California: Stanford University Press, 1950).

Document 20
1718   Demon Rum   Pennsylvania

Source: Martha L. Simonetti, assistant project director, George Dailey and George R. Beyer, editors, **Records of the Provincial Council, 1682-1776**, National Historical Publications Commission Microfilm Publication Program (26 rolls, Harrisburg: Pennsylvania Historical and Museum Commission, 1966), roll #A2, vol. E, pp. 48-51.

But they [the Conestoga] must Crave Leave to add one thing further vizt That they have Reason to think the Authority of this Governmt is not Duly Observed for that Notwithstanding all Our former Agreements that Rum should not be brought amongst them it is Still Carried in Great Quantities, They had been doubtfull with themselves whether they should mention this, because if they were Supply'd with none from hence, they would be from Maryland, which would be a means of Carrying their Peltry thither, but there have been such Quantities of that Liquor Carried of Late amongst them by Loose persons who have no fixt Settlements that they are Apprehensive Mischief may arise from it that tho they are perfectly Well Inclined when Sober Yet they cannot answer for their People when Drunk and Least any Inconveniencies may Ensue from thence to this Government whom they so much Respect, as well as to their own people they Desire this may be taken into Consideration in Order to be prevented & redressed by all proper Measures.

Shecokkenecan added that ther Young men about Pextan had been lately so Generally debaucht with Rum Carried Amongst them by Strangers that they now Want all Manner of Clothing & Necessarys to go a hunting, Wherefore they Wish it would be so Ordered that no Rum should be brought amongst them by any except the Traders who furnish them with all Other Necessary's & who have been used to Trust them & Encourage them in their Hunting.

...

The Governour's Sensible they may have too just Cause to Complain of Loose [illegible] fellows bringing Quantities of Rum amongst them to their Great Injury, that this had not for Some time Past been Sufficiently Lookt after but the Governour would Speedily take Care to have it in a Great Measure prevented. That they of their parts must Endeavour to Prevent their Women & Young people from Coming to Philadelphia to Purchase & Carry up Rum from hence Which too many were ready to Deliver them privately for their Skins. And that when they meet with any brought amongst them they should Stave it as they had formerly been Ordered & undertook to Do.

Document 21
1746   Demon Rum   New York

Source: "Diary of the Journey of Br. Cammerhoff and David Zeisberger to the Five Nations from May 3-14 to August 6-17, 1750," Wm. M. Beauchamp, editor, **Moravian Journals relating to Central New York, 1745-1766,** Onondaga Historical Association (Syracuse: The Dehler Press, 1916), pp. 73-79.

Thursday, 21 June-2 July. I passed a sleepless night, partly because of the flies, and partly because I was very tired and suffering with dreadful pains in my head. David was much concerned about me, and said I looked very sick and miserable. I prayed to the Lord to help us in our trials. We prepared for our journey, and named our quarters Tgarihontie's Monument, because he is by name a Senneka [Seneca]. As we continued we saw many tracks of elks; they, as well as buffaloes, abound in this country. It was about 10 miles from our resting place to Zonesschio, where we arrived quite early in the morning. The village consisted of 40 or more large huts, and lies in a beautiful and pleasant region. A fine large plain, several miles in length and breadth, stretches out behind the village. The river Zonesschio, from which the town derives its name, flows through it from S.S.E. to N.N.W., and empties into Lake Ontario. The road from here to Ohio leads W.S.W., 70 or 80 miles from here. The Ohio River flows from N.E. and makes a curve of S.E. and then S., emptying into the Mississippi. It is a very rapid river, with many falls in the upper part, but afterward is said to flow on a fine smooth stream.

When we caught sight of the town we heard a great noise of shouting and quarreling there, from which we could infer that many of the inhabitants were intoxicated, and that we might expect to have an uncomfortable time. On entering the town we saw many drunken Indians, who all looked mad with drink. We inquired for the lodge of the chief Garontianechqui, and were obliged to pass through the whole village in order to reach it. On our way we were everywhere surrounded by drunken savages. The sachem was not at home, but his wife, an aged, good little woman, stood outside of the hut and gave us a kindly welcome, urging us, however, to enter, as a great drunken crowd surrounded the dwelling and wanted to approach us. We went in and sat down, but were immediately followed by the drunken savages, some of whose faces wore an expression more dreadful than anything we had ever seen, showing that they had been in this frightful state of intoxication for some days. Our Gajuka grew anxious and perplexed, and left very hastily, as he no doubt feared some trouble in store for us. In the meantime the sachem's wife sent for her husband. He came, after much delay, but was drunk like the rest. He, however, recognized us and bade us welcome, expressing his pleasure at seeing us. The house was soon filled with savages, who made a terrible noise, yelling frightfully. Our lives being in danger we were led to a small hut near by, which they thought more secure. It was quite a narrow place, with so little space that 6 or 7 men could scarcely stand within. We sat down in a corner and waited to see how matters would proceed. The old chief came to us and wanted to converse. He said that his house was the largest in town, and the meeting place for the Council as well as their fortress, so that he could not keep the drunken Indians out of it. We told him to go away and sleep until he was sober, which he promised to do, for we wanted to talk over our affairs with him to-morrow. His wife brought us some food, which was only half cooked because of the drunken

Indians, but we had no opportunity or quiet time in which to eat it.

Although they gave us Garontianechqui's youngest brother as a protector, a man about 30 years old, yet his presence was of no avail; great crowds came in to see us, men and women, who, with but few exceptions, were intoxicated and kept up a frightful noise. A few of those who were partly sober, tormented us with all sorts of questions. One in particular, who could speak a little broken English, was especially annoying. He told us that he was the only one who understood English, and gave us to understand that we should use him as interpreter in our affairs. David, however, told him to speak to us in Maquai, as we found that language more intelligible than his English, which was very imperfect. We told them that we had come from Onondago, where we had held a council with the Indians, and had merely come here to visit them. There were some Twightwees here, who had been present at the treaty in Lancaster two years ago. They live farther down the Ohio, and are very tall, fine looking Indians, but a very savage and rough people.

After we had spent several hours in this noise, and there seemed to be no means of keeping off or protecting ourselves against the drunken savages, the sachem's wife begged us to go up into their garret. She gave us her brother-in-law as guard to keep them off, (the drunkards). They all appeared to fear that we might be hurt. We climbed up into the loft, which was a veritable prison, only large enough for us to lie side by side. It was under a shingle roof, on which the sun shone, intensely hot. At the gable end there was a hole, barely large enough for David to creep out, and I could effect an exit only with great difficulty. David and I sat there together; I very tired and trying in vain to eat some of our half cooked beans and corn. David at last, after several attempts, succeeded in making me some tea. It was a difficult matter to conceal anything from the drunken savages. We comforted one another with the Daily Word, and felt assured of the Lord's presence with us in this distressing situation.

During the afternoon the second chief, who had been in Philadelphia, named Hagastaes, visited us. He was, however, so drunk that we could have no sensible conversation with him, and we only signified to him that on the morrow we would like to speak with him and Garontianechqui, and therefore wished them to be sober. He then left us. We heard and saw more noise and confusion than we had yet witnessed anywhere. The sachem's wife did her utmost to keep off the drunken savages, and we were no longer much annoyed by them. Notwithstanding our miserable couch, we felt secure, believing that the Lord had led us here, and that we were safe under the shadow of His wings.

Friday, June 22-July 3. We spent a very noisy night; the confusion and noise never ceased, and the drinking was kept up all night long. There were about 200 drunken people in the town. They procure the rum in canoes from

Oswego, as the Zonesschio flows into Lake Ontario, which is about one day's journey from here. High falls in the river make it impossible for them to descend in their canoes, and they must carry them up and down. Rum causes them to lose all self-control, and when they have once begun to drink, they cannot stop till they have consumed all the liquor in the town. David and I deliberated as to what we had best do under these circumstances, for there appeared no prospect of a change. We finally decided to remain to-day and start on our return to Onondago tomorrow.

Soon after both chiefs, Garontianechqui and Hagastaes came to us, as we had told them that we would converse with them to-day. They were, however, both, and one in particular, still as much under the influence of liquor as yesterday. They put several questions, and always came back to the same idea, that we had been sent with a message from the Governor or Conrad Weisser, and were commissioned to invite them to come to Philadelphia. We assured them several times that such was not our errand, and reminded them of our Brethren Tgarhontie and Tgirhitontie, Anuntschi, etc., and of what had been said to them in Philadelphia by Tganiatarechoo or Pyrlaeus. We told them that we had been sent by our Brethren to renew and confirm our covenant with them on various subjects. At the same time we related, as briefly as possible, the chief points of our affairs in Onondago.

David repeated these several times in order to see whether they had fully grasped the idea. The task seemed to be a hopeless one, and so we told them that we would leave here to-morrow and return to Onondago, in order there to await our answer from the Council. Thereupon they tried to persuade us to remain at least two days longer. By that time all the liquor would have been consumed, and they would then call the chiefs together, in order to speak to us. We told them, however, that we could not postpone our leaving any longer than to-day, and that we would start to-morrow at break of day, for we had said that they should cease drinking, in order to be in a condition to speak to us to-day.

They repeatedly urged us to remain and then left. We, however, were decided on carrying out our intention of leaving here on the morrow. We therefore asked the sachem's wife, who had cared for us so faithfully, to prepare some Indian meal for our journey. From the whole state of affairs we plainly saw that on this visit we could accomplish nothing here, but only keep the promise made in Philadelphia, to acquire a more correct knowledge of the land of the Sennekas and their people. In Philadelphia we and our people had formed an incorrect idea of the Sennekas, as they had there given quite a different impression of themselves, and had adopted French manners, whereas, in their own country they were perfectly natural, and showed themselves in their true colors. Although in Philadelphia we took all pains to explain to them our connection with Aquanoschioni, yet we saw

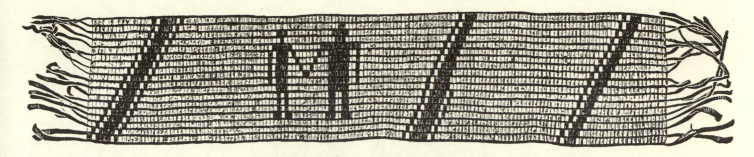

The Great Wampum Belt given to William Penn in 1682 at
Shakamaxon under the Treaty Tree

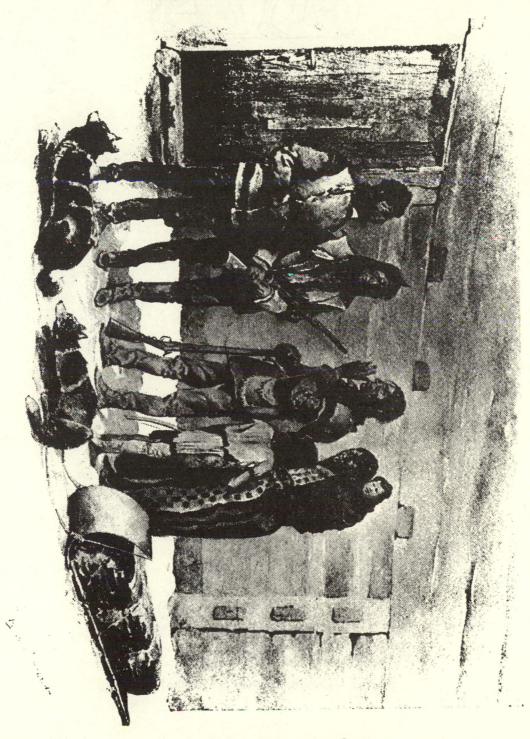

Fur trade scene in the northern forest

Pre-Columbian copper plate from Illinois

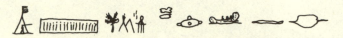

Summons to Mide ceremony

Starvation
(Sioux)

Captain John Smith fights the King of the Pamunkey

clearly that they understood little or nothing, and were still in the dark as regarded our affairs. We did not feel as if they felt as kindly and affectionately toward us as did the Onondagos and Gajukas [Cayuga].

On the whole, the Sennekas are a much rougher and more savage nation than the Gajukas and Onondagos. I do not see how, at the present time, any one of our Brethren can possibly subsist and live among the Sennekas, while, on the contrary, among the Gajukas and Onondagos we felt that the Lord was opening a way for us, and that our mission and what we are trying to do is being made plain to them. From the very beginning of our entrance into the land of the Sennekas, David and I had both experienced a strange, unaccountable feeling of depression, as if Satan and all the heathen powers of darkness were seeking to resist us. We comforted each other with the Daily Word, and entreated the Lord to protect us against the snares of Satan.

I remained in our hut very tired. In the evening, when I left our prison for a short time, I could scarcely walk, as I had eaten very little for several days. During the afternoon my faithful David tried to make some tea for me. It was a great undertaking, for he was obliged to procure the water half a mile to and from, and had to pass all the houses, filled with drunken Indians. On his way back with the kettle of water, several of the drunken savages caught him and drew him into a house, took his kettle, drank the water, and it was only after many efforts that he succeeded in regaining the kettle. He returned to the spring and filled it a second time, but some drunken savages pursued him again. He, however, ran too quickly for them and gained the hut, but by a long circuit through long grass. David then boiled the water, with much trouble and fear, and we refreshed ourselves with some tea, the only nourishment I had taken in two days.

In the afternoon Garontianechqui's third brother, who was still sober, came to see us and conversed much with us. He was a fine looking man and resembled our Gottlieb in Gnadenhutten. We again told him of our intention to start early to-morrow morning, and gave him a piece of tobacco and several pipe-stems, to present to the chiefs when they were sober. We asked him to tell them that we deeply regretted having come such a long distance without being able to talk with them. For his wife we left some thread and needles, and desired her to bake some corn bread this evening for our journey. She was prevented from doing so, however, by the drunken Indians, and we could procure none. Toward evening David went out once more, and on his return a troop of drunken women came rushing madly toward him. Some of them were naked, and others nearly so. In order to drive them away he was obliged to use his fists, and deal out blows to the right and left. He climbed up a ladder, but when he had scarcely reached the top they seized it and tore it from under his feet, but he regained our retreat in safety.

In the meantime the yelling and shrieking continued frightfully in the whole village. It is impossible to describe the confusion to any one who has not witnessed it. Late in the evening Garontianechqui's wife brought us the Indian meal she had prepared for our journey. It was most providential, for without it we could not have started. One of the chiefs, Hagastaes, visited us quite late, but he was still drunk, and we could have no conversation with him. He was not satisfied with our plan of leaving to-morrow. We went to sleep, sure of the Lord's protecting care, praying Him to have mercy on this miserable people and bring them into His fold.

Saturday, 23 June-4 July. During the whole night the orgies continued in the town, and I scarcely slept at all. Early, at first dawn of day, we both arose, packed up and prepared for our journey. At first we did not venture to leave without giving notice, and as we could not go down into the hut from within, David did his utmost to awake our protector by repeated calls. We also rapped vigorously to arouse him, but all to no purpose; and we looked upon it as a special providence of the Lord that the Indian did not awake. He might, perhaps, have made our departure known in the town, and thus we would have incurred the risk of being detained. As we had told them yesterday that we intended to leave early this morning, we resolved to depart quietly, asking the Lord to guide us. David was obliged to jump out of the opening and search for the ladder, which the savages had removed. We then wished to throw out our packs, but David's was so large that he found it necessary to open it, and cast down its contents singly. All this was done amid the great fear of being seen by the drunken savages. The Lord watched over us in such a manner that all the drunken savages were in their huts, not a creature to be seen. Even the dogs, numbering nearly 100 in the whole village, were all quiet, wonderful to relate, and not a sound was heard. A dense fog covered the town, so that we could not see 20 steps before us. A squaw stood at the door of the last hut, but she was sober and returned our greeting quietly. In short we saw clearly that the Lord Himself had removed all obstacles from our path, so that we could depart unhindered. Our feelings on climbing the hill on which the town lies, can be more easily imagined than described. Our hearts were filled with gratitude for this signal deliverance, while at the same time they yearned with pity toward this people, for whom we entreated the Lord to open to them the gates leading to the way of life, now so doubly barred by His enemies and Satan. David and I will certainly never, as long as we live, forget our sojourn in Zonesschio.

1745-1747   Greeting the Aleut   Aleutian Islands

Almost one hundred and fifty years after the native Americans first began to deal with white men around St. Augustine, Jamestown, Quebec, and Santa Fe, their far distant brothers, the Aleut, met white men for the first time. The white men were Russians who explored the far northwestern islands of the New World after crossing the vast expanses of Siberia. In 1639 they founded the port of Okhotsk in eastern Siberia. In the early years of the next century Russian explorers reached the tip of the Kamchatkan Peninsula. Rumors of a large country to the east prompted Peter the Great to send an expedition under Fleet Captain Vitus Bering in search of this country. Bering led two expeditions into the Eastern Ocean (the Northern Pacific), the first in 1725 and the second in 1732. Apparently neither of these official voyages made contact with the Aleut. In the fall of 1745 the people on Attu first learned about white men when a ship sent out by a Siberian merchant, Mikhail Nevotsikoff, arrived at their island. In the next years the fabulous wealth of fur-bearing animals attracted the attention of more merchants, sailors, and hunters. The early relations between the Russian fur-seekers and the people of Attu and Agattu (two of the Near Islands of the Aleutian chain) were summarized by a German scholar, J.L.S., in 1776. His work was translated into English by the Reverend William Coxe and, along with other material on Russian activities in the Eastern Ocean, was published in 1780 (document 22).

Further reading: Hubert Howe Bancroft, *History of Alaska, 1730-1885* (San Francisco: The History Co., 1886) and James R. Masterson and Helen Brower, editors and translators, "Bering's Successors 1745-1780; Contributions of Peter Simon Pallas to the History of Russian Exploration toward Alaska," *Pacific Northwest Quarterly* (Seattle, 1947), vol. 38, pp. 35-83, 109-155.

Document 22
1745-1747   Greeting the Aleut   Aleutian Islands

Source: William Coxe, **Account of the Russian Discoveries between Asia and America, to which are added, The Conquest of Siberia, and The History of the Transactions and Commerce between Russia and China** (2d ed., rev., London: printed by J. Nichols, 1780), pp. 29-36. The first part of Coxe's book is a translation of **Neue Nachrichten von denen neuentdekten Insuln in der See Zwischen Asien und Amerika; aus mitgetheilten Urkunden und Auszugen** verfasset von J.L.S. [identity unknown] (Hamburg und Leipzig: Friedrich Ludwig Gleditsch, 1776). Courtesy of The Newberry Library, Chicago.

Voyages in 1745.—*First discovery of the* Aleutian
Isles *by* Michael Nevodtsikoff.

A Voyage made in the year 1745 by Emilian Bassoff is scarce worth mentioning; as he only reached Beering's Island; and two smaller ones, which lie South of the former, and returned on the 31st of July, 1746.

The first voyage which is in any wise remarkable, was undertaken in the year 1745. The vessel was a Shitik named Eudokia, fitted out at the expence of Aphanassei Tsebaefskoi, Jacob Tsiuproff and others; she sailed from the Kamtchatka river Sept. 19, under the command of Michael Nevodtsikoff a native of Tobolsk. Having discovered three unknown islands, they wintered upon one of them, in order to kill sea-otters of which there was a large quantity. These islands were undoubtedly the nearest Aleütian Islands: the language of the inhabitants was not understood by an interpreter, whom they had brought with them from Kamtchatka. For the purpose therefore of learning this language, they carried back with them one of the Islanders; and presented him to the chancery of Bolcheretsk, with a false account of their proceedings. This islander was examined as soon as he had acquired a slight knowledge of the Russian language; and as it is said, gave the following report. He was called Temnac, and the name of the island of which he was a native was Att [Attu]. At some distance from thence lies a great island called Sabya, of which the inhabitants are denominated Kogii: these inhabitants, as the Russians understood or thought they understood him, made crosses, had books and fire arms, and navigated in baidars or leathern canoes. At no great distance from the island where they wintered, there were two well-inhabited islands: the first lying E.S.E. and S.E. by South, the second East and East by South. The above-mentioned Islander was baptised under the name of Paul, and sent to Ochotsk.

As the misconduct of the ship's crew towards the natives was suspected, partly from the loss of several men, and partly from the report of those Russians, who were not concerned in the disorderly conduct of their companions, a strict enquiry was instituted; in consequence of which the following circumstances relating to the voyage were brought to light.

According to the account of some of the crew, and particularly of the commander, after six days sailing they came in sight of the first island on the 24th of September, at mid-day. They passed it, and towards evening they discovered the second island; where they lay at anchor until the next morning.

The 25th several inhabitants appeared on the coast, and the pilot was making towards shore in the small boat, with an intention of landing; but observing their numbers increase to about an hundred, he was afraid of venturing among them, although they beckoned to him. He contented himself therefore with flinging some needles amongst them: the islanders in return threw into the boat some sea-fowl of the cormorant kind. He endeavoured to hold a conversation with them by means of the interpreters, but no one could understand their language. And now the crew attempted to row the vessel out to sea; but the wind being contrary, they were driven to the other side of the same island, where they cast anchor.

The 26th, Tsiuproff having landed with some of the crew in order to look for water, met several inhabitants: he gave them some tobacco and small Chinese pipes; and received in return a present of a stick, upon which the head of a seal was carved. They endeavoured to wrest his hunting gun from him; but upon his refusing to part with it and retiring to the small boat, the islanders ran after him; and seized the rope by which the boat was made fast to shore. This violent attack obliged Tsiuproff to fire; and having wounded one person in the hand, they all let go their hold; and he rowed off to the ship. The Savages no sooner saw that their companion was hurt, than they threw off their cloaths, carried the wounded person naked into the sea, and washed him. In consequence of this encounter the ship's crew would not venture to winter at this place, but rowed back again to the other island, where they came to an anchor.

The next morning Tsiuproff and one Shaffyrin landed with a more considerable party: they observed several traces of inhabitants; but meeting none they returned to the ship, and coasted along the island. The following day the Cossac Shekurdin went on shore, accompanied by five sailors: two of whom he sent back with a supply of water; and remained himself with the others in order to hunt sea-otters. At night they came to some dwellings inhabited by five families: upon their approach the natives abandoned their huts with precipitation, and hid themselves among the rocks. Shekurdin no sooner returned to the ship, than he was again sent on shore with a larger company, in order to look out for a proper place to lay up the vessel during winter: In their way they observed fifteen islanders upon an height; and threw them some fragments of dried fish in order to entice them to approach nearer. But as this overture did not succeed, Tsiuproff, who was one of the party, ordered some of the crew to mount the height, and to seize one of the inhabitants, for the purpose of learning their language: this order was accordingly executed, notwithstanding the resistance which the islanders made with their bone spears; and the Russians immediately returned with their prisoner to the ship. They were soon afterwards driven to sea by a violent storm, and beat about from the 2d to the 9th of October, during which time they lost their anchor and boat; at length they came back to the same island, where they passed the winter.

Soon after their landing they found in an adjacent hut the dead bodies of two of the inhabitants, who had probably been killed in the last encounter. In their way the Russians were met by an old woman, who had been taken prisoner, and set at liberty. She was accompanied with thirty-four islanders of both sexes, who all came dancing to the sound of a drum; and brought with them a present of coloured earth. Pieces of cloth, thimbles, and needles, were distributed among them in return; and they parted amicably. Before the end of October, the same persons, together with the old woman and several children, returned dancing as before, and brought birds, fish, and other provision. Having passed the night with the Russians, they took their leave. Soon after their departure, Tsiuproff, Shaffyrin, and Nevodtsikoff, accompanied with seven of the crew, went after them, and found them among the rocks. In this interview the natives behaved in the most friendly manner, and exchanged a baidar and some skins for two shirts. They were observed to have hatchets of sharpened stone, and needles made of bone: they lived upon the flesh of sea-otters, seals, and sea-lions, which they killed with clubs and bone lances.

So early as the 24th of October, Tsiuproff had sent ten persons, under the command of Larion Belayeff, upon a reconnoitring party. The latter treated the inhabitants in an hostile manner; upon which they defended themselves as well as they could with their bone lances. This resistance gave him a pretext for firing; and accordingly he shot the whole number, amounting to fifteen men, in order to seize their wives.

Shekurdin, shocked at these cruel proceedings, retired unperceived to the ship, and brought an account of all that had passed. Tsiuproff, instead of punishing these cruelties as they deserved, was secretly pleased with them; for he himself was affronted at the islanders for having refused to give him an iron bolt, which he saw in their possession. He had, in consequence of their refusal, committed several acts of hostilities against them; and had even formed the horrid design of poisoning them with a mixture of corrosive sublimate. In order however to preserve appearances, he dispatched Shekurdin and Nevodtsikoff to reproach Belayeff for his disorderly conduct; but sent him at the same time, by the above-mentioned persons, more powder and ball.

The Russians continued upon this island, where they caught a large quantity of sea otters, until the 14th of September, 1746; when, no longer thinking themselves secure, they put to sea with an intention of looking out for some uninhabited islands. Being however overtaken by a violent storm, they were driven about until the 30th of October, when their vessel struck upon a rocky shore, and was shipwrecked, with the loss of almost all the tackle, and the greatest part of the furs. Worn out at length with cold and fatigue, they ventured, the first of November, to penetrate into the interior part of the country, which they found rocky and uneven. Upon their coming to some huts, they were informed, that they were cast away upon the island of Karaga, the inhabitants of which were tributary to Russia, and of the Koraki tribe. The islanders behaved to them with great kindness, until Belayeff had the imprudence to make proposals to the wife of the chief. The woman gave immediate intelligence to her husband; and the natives were incensed to such a degree, that they threatened the whole crew with immediate death: but means were found to pacify them, and they continued to live with the Russians upon good terms as before.

The 30th of May, 1747, a party of Olotorians made a descent upon the islands in three baidars, and attacked the natives; but, after some loss on both sides, they went away. They returned soon after with a larger force, and were again compelled to retire. But as they threatened to come again in a short time, and to destroy all the inhabitants who paid tribute, the latter advised the Russians to retire from the island, and assisted them in building two baidars. With these they put to sea the 27th of June, and landed the 21st of July at Kamtchatka, with the rest of their cargo, consisting of 320 sea-otters, of which they paid the tenth into the customs. During this expedition twelve men were lost.

1756   Cash for Scalps   Pennsylvania

It was common for European governments, especially the governments in the English colonies, to offer bounties to rid the community of pests. Bounty laws offered premiums for killing crows, squirrels, and wolves. In order to receive payment the bounty hunter brought in the ear or scalp or head of the bird or animal. This evidence of having killed a pest was marked at the time of payment of the premium. During a time of trouble with the Indians, colonials paid out cash for scalps and, on occasion, for heads of the Indian enemy. During the 1720s war between the French and English along the disputed New Brunswick-Maine border, the Massachusetts Bay government passed "An Act to encourage the prosecution of the Indian enemy and rebels." Captain John Lovewell and his men, who reputedly took the scalps of ten sleeping Indians and marched through Boston with the victory souvenirs on hoops, collected £1000. For this and subsequent exploits Lovewell and his men were celebrated in poetry and song.

In Pennsylvania the government hesitated in its organization of defense against the French and Indians in the winter of 1755-1756. Thus, residents of Philadelphia raised money by private subscription to encourage the killing of two Delaware war chiefs (document 23). The following spring, when the colony began to organize for its defense, the governor included premiums for scalps and prisoners in his declaration of war (document 24).

Further reading: Francis Parkman, *A Half-Century of Conflict,* 2 vols., (Boston, 1892) and by the same author, *Montcalm and Wolfe,* 2 vols., (Boston, 1884).

Document 23
1756   Cash for Heads   Pennsylvania

Source: **The Pennsylvania Gazette**, Philadelphia, January 1, 1756.

Seven Hundred Dollars Reward.
Notice is hereby given, That the sum of SEVEN HUNDRED PIECES OF EIGHT is raised by Subscription among the Inhabitants of the City of *Philadelphia*, and now offered, with the Approbation of his Honour the GOVERNOR, as a Reward for any Person or Persons who shall bring into this City the Heads of SHINGAS, and Captain JACOBS, Chiefs of the *Delaware Indian* Nation; or Three Hundred and Fifty Pieces of Eight for each, provided that due Proof is made of being the real Heads of Said *Shingas* or Captain *Jacobs*, they having received many Favours from this Government and now treacherously deserted our Interest, and become the principal Instruments in alienating the Affections of the *Indians* from his Majesty and the People of this Province.

N.B. *It is expected that this Subscription will soon be considerably increased.*

Document 24
1756   Cash for Scalps   Pennsylvania

Source: **Minutes of the Provincial Council of Pennsylvania, from the Organization to the Termination of the Proprietary Government** [Colonial Records], (16 vols., Harrisburg, 1838-1853), vol. VII, pp. 88-90.

By the Honourable ROBERT HUNTER MORRIS, *Esquire, Lieutenant Governor and Commander-in-Chief of the Province of Pennsylvania, and Counties of New Castle, Kent, and Sussex, upon Delaware:*

A PROCLAMATION.

Whereas, the Delaware tribe of Indians, and others in Confederacy with them, have for some Time past, without the least Provocation, and contrary to their most Solemn Treaties, fallen upon this Province and in a most cruel, savage, and perfidious Manner, killed and butchered great Numbers of the Inhabitants, and carried others into barbarous Captivity; burning and destroying their Habitations, and laying waste the Country. *And Whereas,* notwithstanding the friendly Remonstrances made to them by this Government, and the Interposition and positive Orders of our faithful Friends and allies the Six Nations, to whom they owe Obedience and Subjection, requiring and commanding them to desist from any further Acts of Hostility against us, and to return to their Allegiance, the said Indians do still continue their cruel Murders and Ravages, sparing neither age nor Sex; I have, therefore, by and with the Advice and consent of the Council, thought fit to issue this Proclamation; and do hereby declare the said Delaware Indians, and all others who, in Conjunction with them, have committed Hostilities against His Majesty's Subjects within this Province, to be Enemies, Rebels, and Traitors to His Most Sacred Majesty; And I do hereby require all his Majesty's Subjects of this Province, and earnestly invite those of the neighbouring Provinces to embrace all Opportunities of pursuing, taking, killing, and destroying the said Delaware Indians and all others confederated with them in committing Hostilities, Incursions, Murders, or Ravages upon this Province. *And Whereas*, sundry of our good Friends and Allies the Six Nations, and other friendly Indians, are seated upon and do inhabit the Country to the Northward of the Mouth of a River falling into the Sasquehannah, called Cayuga Branch, and those of the Six Nations now in Town have desired that our Hostilities against the said Enemy Indians might not, therefore, be carried on more Northerly than a Line extending from the Mouth of the said Cayuga Branch, at an Indian Town called Diahoga, or Tohiccon, to the Station Point between the Provinces of New York and Jersey, at the Indian Town called Cashetunk, upon Delaware; the said Indians promising us their hearty and best Assistance. I do, therefore, hereby declare that the Indians living and being to the Northward of a Line drawn from the Mouth of the said Cayuga Branch to the said Station Point are not included in this Declaration of War.

And Whereas, many Delaware and other Indians abhorring the ungrateful, cruel, and perfidious Behaviour of that Part of the Delaware Tribe and others that have been concerned in the late inhuman Ravages, have removed into the settled and inhabited Parts of the Country, put themselves under the Protection of this and the neighbouring Governments, and live in a peaceable Manner with the King's Subjects; *I do therefore declare*, that the said friendly Indians that have so separated themselves from our said Enemies, and all others who shall join or act with us in the Prosecution of this just and necessary War, are expressly excepted out of this Declaration, and it is recommended to all Officers and others to afford them Protection and Assistance. *And Whereas*, the Commissioners appointed with me to dispose of the Sixty Thousand Pounds lately granted by Act of General Assembly for His Majesty's Use, have, by their Letter to me of the Tenth Instant, agreed to pay out of the same the several Rewards for Prisoners and Scalps herein after specified; and, therefore, as a further Inducement and Encouragement to all his Majesty's Liege People, and to all the several Tribes of Indians who continue in Friendship and Alliance with us, to exert and use their utmost Endeavour to pursue, attack, take, and destroy our said Enemy Indians, and to release, redeem, and recover such of his Majesty's Subjects as have been taken and made Prisoners by the same Enemies; *I do* hereby declare and promise, that there shall be paid out of the said Sixty Thousand Pounds to all and every Person and Persons, as well Indians as Christians not in the Pay of the Province, the several and respective Premiums and Bounties following, that is to say: For every Male Indian Enemy above Twelve Years Old who shall be taken Prisoner and deliver'd at any Forts garrisoned by the Troops in the Pay of this Province, or at any of the County Towns to the Keepers of the common Jails there, the Sum of One Hundred and Fifty

Spanish Dollars or Pieces of Eight; For the Scalp of every Male Indian Enemy above the age of Twelve Years, produced as Evidence of their being killed, the Sum of One Hundred and Thirty Pieces of Eight; For every Female Indian taken Prisoner and brought in as aforesaid, and for every Male Indian Prisoner under the Age of Twelve Years taken and brought in as aforesaid, One Hundred and Thirty Pieces of Eight; For the Scalp of every Indian Woman, produced as Evidence of their being killed, the Sum of Fifty Pieces of Eight; And for every English Subject that has been taken and carried from this Province into Captivity that shall be recovered and brought in and delivered at the City of Philadelphia to the Governor of this Province, the Sum of one Hundred and Fifty Pieces of Eight, but nothing for their Scalps; And that there shall be paid to every Officer or Soldier as are or shall be in the Pay of this Province who shall redeem and deliver any English Subject carried into Captivity as aforesaid, or shall take, bring in, and produce any Enemy Prisoner, or Scalp as aforesaid, one-half of the said several and respective Premiums and Bounties.

Given under my Hand and the Great Seal of the Province, at Philadelphia, the Fourteenth Day of April, in the Twenty-Ninth Year of His Majesty's Reign, and in the Year of our Lord One Thousand Seven Hundred and Fifty-Six.

ROBT. H. MORRIS.

By His Honour's Command,
Richard Peters, Secretary.
"GOD SAVE THE KING."

1763	Massacres!	Pennsylvania
1768		Pennsylvania
1774		Upper Ohio Valley

By the mid-eighteenth century it became increasingly unsafe for Indians to live near white men. With feelings of fear and hatred the English colonists, in particular, struck out at their Indian neighbors. Indian attacks terrified white men. A paragraph of a letter from Carlisle, printed in *The Pennsylvania Gazette*, July 31, 1755, conveyed the colonists' distress.

We are now in the utmost Confusion, not knowing what Hand to turn to, being more afraid of the Indians (whom we doubt not were the late Murderers on the new Road) than the French. Our Back Settlers are in general fled, and are likely to be ruined for the Loss of their Crops and Summer's Labour; several of them on Juniata having left some Part of their Household Furniture in Flight, and since, going back to fetch or hide it, have found every Thing broken and destroyed by the Indians, and their Horses in the Corn-fields.

For the next three years settlers in central Pennsylvania were subjected to such "confusion." In 1758 the raids ended. Four years of peace followed, deserted farms were reoccupied, and Pennsylvanians poured west to take up new lands along the road to Fort Pitt. In the summer and fall of 1763 this tranquil scene was closed by Indian raids associated with Pontiac's War. One group of white men, the Paxton Boys, decided that their life-long neighbors, the Conestoga, aided and abetted the enemy (document 25). On December 14, 1763, the Paxtons destroyed the village of the Conestoga. Two weeks later they broke into the workhouse in Lancaster and killed the Indians who had been secured there under the protection of the local authorities. County Clerk Edward Shippen and Sheriff John Hay reported the murders to Governor John Penn (document 26). Later the assassins marched toward Philadelphia to murder the Indians who were on Province Island under the protection of the Pennsylvania government. The governor issued the Riot Act, declaring the Paxtons outlaws, subject to arrest by anyone. No arrests were ever made.

Even when the murderer of his friendly Indian neighbors was arrested, he was not tried and punished. Frederick Stump killed six Indians who came to his house, and the next morning traveled fourteen miles to kill four more Indians just to keep the previous six murders quiet. The news got out anyway. Stump was arrested, jailed in Carlisle, but freed by armed men who broke into the jail in broad daylight (document 27).

Personal revenge was the only way for native Americans to punish white neighbors who were killers. Logan, a chief of the Mingo and a long-time friend to the English, lost his entire family when white men killed their Indian neighbors in the upper Ohio Valley in 1774. Chief Logan sought and achieved his vengeance (document 28).

Further reading: Randolph C. Downes, *Council Fires on the Upper Ohio: A Narrative of Indian Affairs in the Upper Ohio Valley until 1795* (Pittsburgh: The University of Pittsburgh Press, 1940).

Document 25
1763   Massacres!   Pennsylvania

Source: R. C. [Redmond Conyingham], "Smith's Narrative. Paxton Boys," **Lancaster Intelligencer and Journal**, Lancaster, Pennsylvania, May 16, 1843.

I was an early settler in Paxton, a member of the congregation of the Rev. Mr. Elder. I was one of the chief actors in the destruction of Conestogue, and in storming the Workhouse in Lancaster. I have been stigmatized as a murderer. No man, unless he were living at that time in Paxton, could have an idea of the sufferings and anxieties of the people. For years the Indians had been on the most friendly terms, but some of the Traders were bought by the French; these corrupted the Indians. The savages unexpectedly destroyed our dwellings and murdered the unsuspicious.—When we visited the wigwams in the neighborhood, we found the Indians occupied in harmless sports, or domestic work. There appeared no evidence that they were any way instrumental in the bloody acts perpetrated in the frontiers.

Well do I remember the evening when ———— [The blanks are left for names for obvious reasons.] stopt at my door; judge my surprise when I heard his tale: "Tom, followed the Indians to the Big Island; from thence they went to Conestogue; as soon as we heard it five of us ————, ————, ————, ————, ————, rode off for the village. I left my horse under their care, and cautiously crawled where I could get a view: I saw Indians armed; they were strangers; they outnumbered us by dozens. I returned without being discovered: "we meet to-night at ———— ; we shall expect you, with gun, knife and ammunition." We met, and our party, under cover of the night, rode off for Conestogue. Our plan was well laid; the scout who had traced the Indians was with us; the village was stormed and reduced to ashes. The moment we were perceived an Indian fired at us, and rushed forward brandishing his tomahawk. Tom cried "mark him," and he fell by more than one ball; ———— ran up and cried out, "it is the villain who murdered my mother." This speech roused to vengeance, and Conestogue lay harmless before us. Our worst fears had been realized; these Indians who had been housed and fed as the *pets* of the province, were now proved to be our secret foes: necessity compelled us to do as we did.

We mounted our horses and returned. Soon we were informed that a number of Indians were in the Workhouse at Lancaster. ———— was sent to Lancaster to get all the news he could. He reported that one of the Indians concerned in recent murders was there in safety. Also that they talked of re-building Conestogue, and placing these Indians in the new buildings.

A few of us met to deliberate; Stewart proposed to go to Lancaster, storm their *castle*, and carry off the assassin. It was agreed to; the whole plan was arranged. Our clergyman did not approve of our proceedings further. He thought every thing was accomplished by the destruction of Conestogue, and advised us to try what we could do with the Governor and Council. I with the rest was opposed to the *measure* proposed by our good pastor. It was painful to us to act in opposition to his will, but the Indian in Lancaster was known to have murdered the parent of ———— , one of our party.

The plan was made. *Three* were chosen to break in the doors, five to keep the keepers, &c., from meddling; Captain Stewart to remain outside, with about twelve men, to protect those within, prevent surprise, and keep charge of the horses.—The three were to secure the Indian, tie him with strong cords, and deliver him to Stewart. If the three were resisted, a shot was to be fired as a signal. I was one of them who entered; you know the rest; we fired; the Indians were left without life; and we rode hastily from Lancaster. Two of the Indians killed in Lancaster were recognized as murderers.

This gave quiet to the frontiers, for no murder of our defenceless inhabitants has since happened.

The foregoing was communicated by a father to his son, in Carlisle, and by that gentleman to the writer.—R.C.

Document 26
1763   Massacres!   Pennsylvania

Source: Martha L. Simonetti, assistant project director, George Dailey, and George R. Beyer, editors, **Records of the Provincial Council 1682-1776**, National Historical Publications Commission Microfilm Publication Program (26 rolls, Harrisburg: Pennsylvania Historical and Museum Commission, 1966) roll #A6, vol. S, pp. 437, 448, 450-451.

Lancaster, 14th December 1763
Evening

Honoured Sir,

One Robert Edgar a hired Man to Captain Thomas McKee living near the Borough, acquainted me to day that a Company of people from the Frontiers had killed and scalped most of the Indians at the Conestogoe Town early this Morning, he said he had his information from an Indian boy who made his Escape. Mr. Slough has been to the place and held a Coroners Inquest on the Corpses, being Six in number. Bill Sawk and some other Indians were gone towards Smith's Iron Works to sell brooms; but where they are now we cant understand. And the Indian's, John Smith & Peggy his Wife, and their Child, and young Joe Hays were abroad last night too and lodged at one Peter Savars about two miles from hence. These last came here this afternoon, whom we acquainted with what had happened to their Friends, & relations, and advised them to put themselves under our protection which they readily agree'd to; and they are now in Our Work House by themselves, where they are well provided for with every necessary—Warrants are issued for the apprehending of the Murderers, said to be upwards of fifty men well armed and mounted. I beg my kind Compliments to Richard Penn, & I am with all due Regards

Sir, Your Honours Obliged Friend,
and most humble Servant
Edw'd: Shippen

The Hon:ble John Penn Esq:r governor

Lancaster 27:th Decem:r 1763 PM.

Honoured Sir,

I am to acquaint your Honour that between two and three of the Clock this afternoon, upwards of an hundred armed Men from the Westward rode very fast into Town, turned their Horses into Mr. Sloughs (an Innkeeper) Yard and proceeded with the greatest precipitation to the Work House, stove open the door and killed all the Indians and then took to their Horses and rode off, all their business was done and they were returning to their horses before I could get half way down to the Work house. The Sheriff and Coroner, however, & several others got down as soon as the rioters but could not prevail with them to stop their hands. Some people say they heard them declare they would proceed to the Province Island & destroy the Indians there I am with great respects

Sir
Your Honours
Most Obedient humble Servant
Edw:d Shippen

The Hon:ble Jno Penn Esq:r Gov:r

A Letter to the Governor from John Jay, Esq., Shff. of Lancasr. Co'ty.

Lancaster, the 27 Decemr., 1763

Sir:

Agreeable to your Orders to me when at Philadelphia, I here inclose a List of the names of the Indians found killed at the Indian Town in Conestogoe Manor with the names of the Survivors, fourteen in number, whom I found, on my Return, had been collected & placed in the Work house of this County; by my Son, with the assistance of John Miller & Robt Beaty (who by appointment of Messrs. Hockley & Peters, had the Care of the Indians belonging to the Town) where they are properly taken care of, & fed, & wait for your Honours further directions relating to them.

I likewise agreeable to your Order give herewith an account of the Effects and Papers which have been found belonging to the said Indians, which now remain in the possession of the said Miller and Beatty in trust for the Indians, to witt:

Three Horses

A Writing on Parchment purporting an Article of Peace & Amity concluded between the Governor of Maryland & the Chiefs of the Conestogoe & other Indians.

A Writing on Parchment purporting An Article of Agreement between William Penn Proprietary &ca. of Pennsylvania and the King of the Indians inhabiting in or about the River Susquehannah and other Indian Nations dated the three & twentieth day of the second month called April in the Year one thousand seven hundred & one.

A Letter (which seems to be under the Lesser Seal of the Province) signed W. Keith, dated Philadelphia May 26: 1719 directed to Civility & the rest of the Indian Chiefs at Conestogoe.

A Letter (which seems to be under the Lesser Seal of the Province), signed W. Keith, dated Philada., 5th

May, 1719, directed to Civility, or Tagotelessa, & the Indian Chiefs at and near Conestogoe.

A Writing purporting a Letter signed James Logan dated the 22nd 4 mo. 1717 directed to Civility & the other Indian Chiefs at Conestogoe.

A Paper (which seems to be under the Lesser Seal of the Province) signed James Logan purporting An Order of Council held at Philadelphia Septr. 28th: 1708 or a Request to the Indians to apprehend Nichole Godin on suspicion of several treasonable Practices against the Government.

And Two Belts of Wampum.

Decemr. 27th, 1763, P.M.

Honoured Sir:

Since writing the above, the poor Indians whom we imagined were placed in safety are destroyed. A number of Persons to the amount (by their appearance), of fifty or Sixty, armed with Rifles, Tomahawks, &ca. suddenly about Two o'Clock rushed into the Town & immediately repaired to the Work House where the Indians were confined, & notwithstanding all opposition of myself and the Coroner, with many others broke open the Work House, and have killed all the Indians there, being the fourteen mentioned in the List to have survived the former Affair at their Town. After which they in a Body left the Town without offering any insults to the Inhabitants, and without putting it in the power of any one to take or molest any of them without danger of Life to the Person attempting it; of which both myself and the Coroner by our opposition were in great danger.

I have since the above affair taken from Messrs. Miller & Beatty the above mentioned Papers and Belts of Wampum, which I shall keep till I have orders from your Honour, & anything further that I can find belonging to the Indians, shall be properly taken care of.

As it is rumored that the people with a Superior Force intend an Attack on the Province Island, with a view to destroy the Indians there, I think proper to mention it to your Honour, & shall do all in my power not only to apprehend the Offenders but to preserve the Peace of the County.

I beg your Honours directions, which I shall endeavour punctually to observe, being

Your Honours Most Obedt. Humble Servt.,
JOHN HAY

To the Honble. JOHN PENN, Esqr., Governor of the Province of Pennsylvania, & ca.

List of the Indians killed at the Indian Town in Conestogoe Manor:

	Their Indian Names
Sheehays	Sheehays,
George	Wa-a-shen,
Harry	Tee-Kau-ley,
A son of Sheehays	Ess-canesh,
Sally, an Old Woman	Tea-wonsha-i-ong,
A Woman,	Kannenquas,

List of the Indians belonging to the Conestogoe Town in the Work House at Lancaster:

Captain John	Kyunqueagoah,
Betty, his Wife	Koneenasee,
Bill Sock	Tenseedaagua,
Molly, his Wife	Kanianguas,
John Smith	Saquies-hat-tah,
Peggy, his Wife	Chee-na-wan,
little John, Capt. John's Son	Quaachow,
Jacob, a Boy	Shae-e-kah,
Young Sheehays, a Boy	Ex-undas,
Chrisley, a Boy	Tong-quas,
little Peter, a Boy,	Hy-ye-naes,
Molly, a little Girl	Ko-qoa-e-un-quas,
a little Girl	Karen-do-uah,
Peggy, a little Girl	Canu-kie-sung.

The names taken from Peggy, Wife of Jno. Smith, and Betty, wife of Captain John.

pme.
John Hay.

Document 27
1768   Massacres!   Pennsylvania

Source: Martha L. Simonetti, assistant project director, George Dailey and George R. Beyer, editors, **Records of the Provincial Council 1682-1776**, National Historical Publications Commission Microfilm Publication Program (26 rolls, Harrisburg: Pennsylvania Historical and Museum Commission, 1966) role #A7, vol. T, pp. 215-216, 254-255.

At a Council held at Philadelphia on Tuesday 19th January 1768.

. . .

The Assembly's Message of the 13th instant, with a Draft of an Answer thereto, and the Bill for removing the Settlers on the Indian Lands, with a proposed amendment, were laid before the Board, but referred to a future consideration, on Account of a Melancholy piece of intelligence just brought to Town, of the Murder of several Indians on the Susquehanna, which required the immediate attention of the Board.

Mr. William Blyth of Penns Township, in Cumberland County, being just arrived in Town, in Order to give information to his Honour the Governor, of the Murder of Ten Indians, lately committed by Frederick Stump, at Middle Creek, in that County, appeared at the Board, and being examined on Oath, related what is contained in the following Deposition, taken in Council, before the Chief Justice, who was expressly desired to attend for that purpose, viz.t—

The Deposition of William Blyth of Penns Township in the County of Cumberland, Farmer, being sworn on the Holy Evangelists of Almighty God., saith

That hearing of the Murder of some Indians by one Frederick Stump, a German, he went to the House of George Gabriel, where he understood Stump was, to enquire into the Truth of the Matter; that he there met with Stump and several others, on the 12th of the present Month January; and was there informed by the said Stump Himself, that on the Sunday Evening before, being the 10th of the Month, Six Indians, to Wit, the White Mingo, an Indian Man named Cornelius, one other Man named John Campbell, one other man named Jones, and two Women, came to his (Stumps) House, and being in Drink, and Disorderly, he endeavoured to persuade them to leave his House, which they were not inclined to do, and he being apprehensive that they intended to do him some Mischief, killed them all, and afterwards, in order to conceal them, dragged them down to a Creek near his House, made a hole in the Ice, and threw them in. And that the said Frederick Stump further informed this Deponent, that fearing News of his killing the Indians might be carried to the other Indians, he went the next Day to two Cabbins about fourteen Miles from thence, up Middle Creek, where he found One Woman, two Girls and One Child, which he killed in order to prevent their carrying intelligence of the Death of the other Indians, killed as aforesaid, and afterwards put them into the Cabbins and burnt them. That this Deponent afterwards sent four Men up the Creek, to where the Cabbins were, to know the Truth of the Matter, who upon their Return, informed him that they had found the Cabbins burnt, and discovered some remains of the Limbs of some Indians who had been burnt in them, and further saith not—

William Blyth,
Sworn at Philadelphia
    the 19th day of January 1768
    before Me Will:m Allen—.

At a Council held at Philadelphia on Thursday 4 February 1768.

Mr. James Cunningham from Carlisle being sent for by Order of the Governor, appeared at the Board, and was immediately examined with regard to what he knew concerning the Rescue of Frederick Stump and John Ironcutter from the Gaol at Carlisle and his Deposition was taken and is as follows.

The Deposition of James Cunningham of Lancaster County concerning the Rescue of Frederick Stump & John Ironcutter from the Gaol at Carlisle.

James Cunningham of Lancaster County, Farmer, being sworn on the Holy Evangelists of Almighty God, deposeth and saith, that on Friday, the Twenty Ninth day of January last, about Nine or Ten o'Clock in the Forenoon as he was sitting at Breakfast with John Armstrong Esquire in the Town of Carlisle in the County of Cumberland, he was surprised to see a Number of Armed Men surrounding on a sudden the public Gaol in the said Town, that He and the said John Armstrong apprehending that the said Company were come with an Intention to Rescue from the said Gaol a certain Frederick Stump and John Ironcutter, who were confined there for the Murder of a Number of Indians, they both instantly Ran to the said Gaol in order to prevent if possible the execution of so wicked and illegal a Design. That when they got up to the Gaol the said John Armstrong made his way through a Number of Armed Men, who stood before the Door of the said Gaol, which was open, and Guarded by four Men, who stood within the Door with Arms in their Hands: that the said Armstrong, and John Holmes, high Sheriff of the said County, both attempted to go into the Door of the Gaol, but were several times pushed back and prevented: that as the said John Armstrong stood on the Steps under the Door he addressed himself frequently to the Armed Company who were about him, and used many arguments to persuade them to desert from their Lawless undertaking, and told them, among other things, that they were about to do an Act which would subject themselves and their Country to Misery. That while the said Armstrong was speaking, this Deponent saw one of the Armed Men take hold of him, and draw him down the said Steps, upon which the said Armstrong by violence pushed back the Person who had hold of him, and regained his Stand on the said Steps, saying at the same time that they should take his Life before they should rescue the Prisoners. This Deponent further saith, that while the said John Armstrong and Robert Miller and William Lyon Esquire and the Reverend John Steel who had joined the said Armstrong, were endeavouring to disperse the said Company, several other Armed Men appeared within side of the said Gaol, to the very great Surprise of everyone with the two Prisoners above mentioned in their Possession, whom they brought forward, and after pushing the said Armstrong, Miller, Lyon, Steel, Holmes and this Deponent by Violence and crowding from before the said Gaol Door, carried them off with Shouts and Rejoicing, and immediately left the Town. This Deponent further saith that he cannot with certainty declare what Numbers were in the Company which made the said Rescue, but that from the best Judgment he could form they were Seventy or Eighty, all Armed with Guns, and some Tomahawks. —This Deponent further saith on his solemn Oath, that he does not know nor has any personal knowledge of any one of the Persons he saw in the said Armed Company, concerned in the said Rescue, and that after the said Company had left the Town, the Reverend Mr. Steel came to the said John Armstrong and William Lyons and John Holmes and informed them that the said Rescuers desired they would come to and confer with them at the Plantation of John Davis, to come to some Terms with them; That the said three last mentioned Persons immediately mounted their Horses and went towards the said Davis's, but informed this Deponent on their Return, that the said Company had altered their Resolution and had gone on without waiting for them, and further saith not.

                                        James Cunningham
Taken and Sworn before the Governor and Council at Philadelphia, before me   Recorder of the city
                                        February the 4th 1768
                                        Benjamin Chew, Recorder

Document 28
1774   Massacre!   Upper Ohio Valley

Source: **The Pennsylvania Journal; and Weekly Advertiser,** Philadelphia, February 1, 1775. The translator of Logan's speech was his brother-in-law, John Gibson, an Indian trader. He sent his translation to James Madison, who forwarded it to William Bradford, printer of the **Pennsylvania Journal.** Gibson's wife and son were among Logan's relatives who were killed by white neighbors in May, 1774. Logan wrongly accused Michael Cresap of the murders. Cresap killed Indians but not these people. The history of Logan's speech is discussed in Irving Brant, **James Madison** (6 vols., Indianapolis: Bobbs-Merrill Company, Inc., 1941-1961), vol. I, pp. 272-291.

"Extract of a letter from Virginia.

"I make no doubt, but the following specimen of Indian eloquence and mistaken valour, will please you; but you must make allowances for the unskilfulness of the interpreter.

The Speech of *LOGAN*, a Shawanese [Mingo] Chief, to Lord *DUNMORE*

"I appeal to any white man to deny, if ever he entered Logan's cabin hungry, and I gave him not meat; if ever he came cold or naked, and I gave him not cloathing. During the course of the last long and bloody war, Logan remained idle in his tent, an avocate for peace; nay, such was my love for the whites, that those of my own country pointed at me as they passed by, and said, "Logan is the friend of white men." I had even thought to live with you, but for the injuries of one man, Col. Cressop, the last spring, in cold blood and unprovoked cut off all the relations of Logan, not sparing even my women and children. There runs not a drop of my blood in the veins of any human creature. This called on me for revenge. I have sought it,—I have killed many.—I have fully glutted my vengeance. For my country, I rejoice at the beams of peace; but do not harbor the thought, that mine is the joy of fear. Logan never felt fear: He will not turn his heel to save his life. Who is there to mourn for Logan? Not one."

III
A Revolution Gives Birth to a Republic
1776-1810

For the native Americans the War for Independence was a disaster. Hundreds lost their lives. Thousands lost their homes. All along the frontier line of settlement from New York to Georgia, state militiamen and Continental troops clashed with the native peoples. When the war began, both the Americans and the British attempted to neutralize the Indians. The attempts failed. The aggressiveness of frontiersmen in western Pennsylvania, Virginia, and Carolina confirmed for the Indians what they already knew: the Americans wanted the lands west of the Appalachian Mountains. The Cherokee in western Carolina and Tennessee fought to retain their lands with little aid from the British. The Shawnee and other groups between the Ohio River and the Great Lakes fought for their lives and homes with assistance from the British at Detroit. The Six Nations of the Iroquois Confederacy entered the war disunited. The Oneida and Tuscarora were neutral, or at least did not openly aid the British, and on occasion helped the Americans. The Onondaga divided among themselves. Some joined the Oneida, and others joined the British. The Mohawk, Cayuga, and Seneca actively supported the British in the war with the colonists.

Despite American military efforts, when the preliminary articles of peace were signed with the British in November, 1782, the native peoples were still dominant west of the mountains. Only the Cherokee, as a result of military conquest, had ceded land to the Americans. The Shawnee and other tribes remained in control of the land west and north of the Ohio River and had not ceded an inch. The Six Nations, although weakened, still held sway over most of the land they had occupied before the war began. The Indians' strong position, however, had no influence at the peace table. The British ceded the territory to the Americans.

After the war the United States informed the native peoples that they had been conquered, that the United States would dictate the terms of peace with them, and that lands would be allotted to the tribes. The Indians were shocked and angered. The Mohawk leader, Joseph Brant, traveled among the tribes of New York and Ohio imploring them to stand together and not to cede any land. The choice for the Indians was clear: cede land to the American government or go to war. The latter choice was out of the question. There were no war supplies at hand.

Thus, in a series of meetings the Indians ceded territory to the United States.

In effect, the land cessions were unenforceable. The chiefs denounced the treaties, and the American military was too weak to open the territory for survey, sale, and settlement. Meanwhile, the frontiersmen and the Indians continued to clash violently. State militiamen punished their recalcitrant Indian neighbors, as they had during the War for Independence. Such action opened little land to settlement. Only the state of New York, through negotiations, succeeded in acquiring lands from the Six Nations.

The negotiations displeased the Six Nations. They had not been defeated on the battlefield. Some of the Mohawk had already moved to Canada, where representatives from each of the Six Nations would later join them. Those who remained in New York ceded some lands rather than go to war. In these negotiations even those Indians who had remained neutral during the war and those who had openly assisted the Americans lost territory to New York. The Oneida and Tuscarora, lived in poverty and, in order to survive, sold some of their land in 1785. The latter tribe moved in large numbers to Canada. The former tried for a time to exist on their greatly reduced territory.

When the United States government was reorganized under the Constitution, the native Americans were still dominant west and north of the Ohio River. This vast region, now consisting of Ohio, Indiana, Illinois, Michigan, and Wisconsin, was organized by Congress in 1787 into the Northwest Territory. Only a small portion in the southeast was open to settlement. Indeed, Indian resistance to white westward expansion increased rather than diminished. The combined efforts of several tribes defeated the United States Army in 1790 and again in 1791. A third military expedition in 1794 was successful enough to call a meeting between the United States and the chiefs of the Northwest Territory. The resulting Treaty of Greenville opened to settlement some of the territory that the Americans had wanted many years earlier.

Americans poured into the ceded lands, even before survey and sale. Within a few years of the Treaty of Greenville it was obvious that more land must be acquired from the Indians. For a time the United States got land relatively peacefully in negotiations with impoverished chiefs. Then Indian resistance began to build up under the leadership of the Shawnee war chief, Tecumseh. He worked indefatigably to unite his Indian brothers in peaceful resistance against white expansion. He believed that strength through unity would command the respect of the United States government. His aim—Indian unity—clashed directly with the goal of William Henry Harrison, the governor of Indiana Territory, whose task it was to open the land between the Ohio River and the Great Lakes to settlement. These mutually antagonistic aims could not be accomplished peacefully. In the second war with Great Britain, the War of 1812, Tecumseh supported the British in order to save his people's territory from the Americans. He lost.

The American mistreatment of the native peoples during the early decades of United States history far exceeded anything done in those same years by the British in Canada, the Spanish in California, or the Russians in Alaska. The Six Nations roundly denounced the British for ceding their territory to the United States in 1782. The British in return granted land in Ontario to the refugee Iroquois. Several California tribes opposed Spanish expansion northward. The Spanish warred against the Seri, Yuma, Mojave, and other tribes and enslaved Indian captives. In these conflicts the Spanish usually were on the defensive, and mistreatment, while certainly present, did not compare in brutality with American actions toward the eastern Algonquian and Iroquoian tribes. There were many complaints about abuses committed against the Aleut by the Russian fur hunters and traders; these were reflected in the ukases of the emperor and the orders of company managers. But here again, in comparison with the American frontiersmen's treatment of the Delaware and Shawnee, the Aleut were fortunate that the first white men to exploit their islands were not from the United States.[1]

1776   Tennessee
Plundering and Burning the Cherokee Towns 1781

The Cherokee resented the steady westward advance of the Americans. Between the end of the Cherokee War, (1761-1762) and the beginning of the War for Independence, agreements that ceded land to the Georgians, Carolinians, and Virginians had not received the approval of all the chiefs. When the Americans and British went to war, the Cherokee saw an opportunity to drive the settlers away from the Watauga and Holston rivers in eastern

1. The comparison is based on E. Palmer Patterson II, *The Canadian Indian Since 1500* (Don Mills, Ont.: Collier-Macmillan Canada Ltd., 1972); Jack D. Forbes, *Native Americans of California and Nevada* (Healdsburg, California: Naturegraph Publishers, 1969); P. Tikhmenev, *The Historical Review of the Russian-American Company and its activity up to the present time* (2 vols., St. Petersburg: printed by Edward Velmar, 1861-1863). Tikhmenev's volumes were translated by Dimitri Krenov for the Works Progress Administration in 1939-1940.

Tennessee. Joined by some Tories they began attacking the frontier settlements in the summer of 1776. The raids aroused the settlers from southwestern Virginia to northwestern Georgia, as well as those in eastern Tennessee. Militiamen from Virginia, North and South Carolina, and Georgia soon mobilized to strike hard at the out-numbered enemy. William Moore reported on his expedition against the Cherokee towns to his superior, Brigadier-General Griffith Rutherford of the North Carolina state troops (document 29). The out-numbered Cherokee, who had got little of the expected aid from the British, soon were crushed, and their towns plundered and burned. Land cessions to the Americans brought an end to the war a year after it had begun.

Not all the Cherokee agreed with the older chiefs' decision to cede hunting grounds to bring about a peace. The dissenters followed their most important spokesman, Dragging Canoe, who moved down the Tennessee River to Chickamauga Creek. Dragging Canoe and his Chickamauga Cherokee followers sporadically raided the frontier settlements during the next four years. Beginning in 1781 and continuing into 1782 the land-hungry frontiersmen destroyed the Chickamauga towns. Arthur Campbell, an early settler and prominent land holder in eastern Tennessee, described the expeditions against the Chickamauga in a letter to Thomas Jefferson, the governor of Virginia (document 30).

Further reading: Jack M. Sosin, *The Revolutionary Frontier 1763-1783* (New York: Holt, Rinehart and Winston, 1967).

Document 29
1776   Tennessee
Plundering and Burning the Cherokee Towns

Source: **North Carolina University Magazine**, new series, vol. VII, no. 3 (Chapel Hill, February, 1888), pp. 90-93.

Brigadier General Rutherford:

DEAR SIR—After my Compliments to you, This is to Inform you, that Agreeable to your Orders I Enlisted my Company of Light horse men, and Entered them into Service the 19th of Oct. From thence we prepared ourselves and Marched the 29th Same Instant as far as Catheys fort, Where we Joined Capt Harden and Marched Over the Mountain to Swannanoa. The Next day Between Swannanoa & French Broad River we Came upon fresh Signs of five or six Indians, upon which we Marched very Briskly to the ford of hominy Creek, where we expected to join the Tryon Troops. But they not Meeting according to appointment, we were Necessitated to Encamp and Tarry for them. Our men being extremely anxious to pursue the aforesaid Indians, After the Moon arose we sent out a Detachment of 13 men Commanded by Capt Harden

& Lieut Woods. They Continued their pursuit about 8 miles and Could Make no Discovery, Untill Day-light appear'd, then they Discovered upon the frost, that One Indian had gone Along the road; they pursued Very Briskly about five miles further and came up with sd Indian Killed and Scalped him. The Remainder of them, we apprehended, Had gone a Hunting off the Road, upon which they returned Back to Camp, where we waited to Join the Tryons. They Coming up Towards the Middle of the day we Concluded to stay (to Refresh our horses which was fatigued with the Over Nights March) till the Next Morning. But to our Great Disadvantage we lost several of our Horses, which Detained us the Ensuing day. Then we pursued our march as far as Richland Creek, where we Encamped in a Cove for the Safety of our horses; but in Spite of all our Care, the Indians Stole three from us that Night by which we perceived that the Enemy was alarmed of our Coming. We followed their Tracks the next day as far as Scots place, which appeared as if they were Pushing into the Nation Before us Very fast & Numerous. From Scots place we took a Blind path which

led us Down to the Tuckyseige river through a Very Mountainous bad way. We Continued our march Very Briskly in Expectation of Getting to the Town of Too Cowee before Night. But it lying at a Greater Distance than we Expected, we were obliged to tie up our Horses, & Lay by till Next morning, when we found a ford and crossed the river & then a Very large Mountain, where we came upon a Very plain path, Very much used by indians Driving in from the Middle Settlement to the Aforesaid Town. We Continued our march along sd path about two Miles when we Came in Sight of the town, which lay Very Scattered; then we Came to a consultation to see which was the best Method to attack it. But our small army Consisting of but 97 men, we found we were not able to surround it, So we Concluded and rushed into the Centre of the town, in Order to surprise it. But the Enemy Being alarmed of our coming, were all fled Save two, who Trying to make their Escape Sprung into the river, and we pursued to the Bank, & as they were Rising the Bank on the Other Side, we fired upon them and Shot one of them Down & the Other Getting out of reach of our shot, & Making to

LOVEWELL'S FIGHT

Of worthy Captain Lovewell, I purpose now to sing,
How valiantly he served his country and his king;
He and his valiant soldiers did range the woods full wide,
And hardships they endured to quell the Indian's pride.

'T was ten o'clock in the morning when first the fight begun,
And fiercely did continue until the setting sun;
Excepting that the Indians some hours before 't was night
Drew off into the bushes and ceased awhile to fight.

But soon again returned, in fierce and furious mood.
Shouting as in the morning, but yet not half so loud;
For as we are informed, so thick and fast they fell,
Scarce twenty of their number at night did get home well.

And that our valiant English till midnight there did stay,
To see whether the rebels would have another fray;
But they no more returning, they made off towards their home,
And brought away their wounded as far as they could come.

Of all our valiant English there were but thirty-four,
And of the rebel Indians there were about fourscore,
And sixteen of our English did safely home return,
The rest were killed and wounded, for which we all must mourn.

Our worthy Captain Lovewell among them there did die,
They killed Lieutenant Robbins, and wounded good young Frye,
Who was our English chaplain; he many Indians slew,
And some of them he scalped when bullets round him flew.

Young Fullam, too, I'll mention, because he fought so well,
Endeavoring to save a man, a sacrifice he fell:
But yet our valiant Englishmen in fight were ne'er dismayed.
But still they kept their motion, and Wymans captain made,

Who shot the old chief Pagus, which did the foe defeat,
Then set his men in order, and brought off the retreat;
And braving many dangers and hardships in the way,
They safe arrived at Dunstable, the thirteenth day of May.

Popular colonial ballad of Captain John Lovewell's band of Indian hunters' defeat in a fight with Indians in the Maine woods, May 8, 1725

the Mountain. Some of our men Crossed the river on foot, & pursued, & Some went to the ford & Crossed on horse, & headed him, Killed & Scalped him with the other. Then we Returned into the town, and found that they had Moved all their Valuable effects, Save Corn, Pompions, Beans, peas & Other Triffling things of which we found Abundance in every house. The town consisted of 25 houses, Some of them New Erections, and one Curious Town house framed & Ready for Covering. We took what Corn we stood in need of, and what Triffling Plunder was to be got, and then set fire To the Town. Then we concluded to follow the Track of the Indians, which Crossed the river, & led us a Direct North Course. We Continued our march about a Mile, and then we perceived a Great pillar of Smoke rise out of the mountain, which we found arose from the Woods Being Set on fire with a View as we supposed to Blind their Track, that we Could not pursue them; Upon which Capt Mcfadden & Myself took a small party of men in Order to make further Discoverys, and left the main Body Behind upon a piece of advantageous Ground until our Return. We marched over a Large Mountain & Came upon a Very Beautifull River which we had no Knowledge of. We crossed the river & Immediately Came to Indian Camps which they had newly left; we went over a Second mountain into a large Cove upon South fork of sd river where we found a Great deal of sign, Several Camping places & the fires Burning Very Briskly. Night Coming on we were Obliged to Return to our main Body A While Before day. When day appeared we made Ready and marched our men Until the place we had Been the Night Before. Our advance Guard Being forward Perceived two Squaws and a lad, who Came down the Creek as far as we had Been the Night Before, and when they Perceived our Tracks they were Retreating to the Camp from whence they Came, which was within 3 Quarters of a mile. The Signal was Given, then we pursued and took them all three Prisoners. Unfortunately our men shouted in the Chase and fired a Gun which alarm'd them at the Camp & they Made their Escape into the Mountains. The Prisoners led us to the Camp where we found abundance of plunder, of Horses and other Goods, to the amount of Seven Hundred Pounds. We took some horses Belonging to the poor Inhabitants of the frontiers which we Brought in, & Delivered to the owners. Our provisions falling short, we were Obliged to steer homeward. That night we lay upon a prodigious Mountain where we had a Severe Shock of an Earthquake, which surprised our men very much. Then we steered our course about East & So. East two days thro' Prodigious Mountains which were almost Impassable, and struck the road in Richland Creek Mountain. From thence we marched to Pidgeon river, Where we Vandued off all Our Plunder. Then there arose a Dispute Between me & the whole Body, Officers & all, Concerning Selling off the Prisoners for Slaves. I allowed that it was our Duty to Guard Them to prison, or some place of safe Custody till we got the approbation of the

Congress Whether they should be sold Slaves or not, and the Greater part Swore Bloodily that if they were not sold for Slaves upon the spot, they would Kill & Scalp them Immediately. Upon which I was obliged to give way. Then the 3 prisoners was sold for £ 242. The Whole plunder we got including the Prisoners Amounted Above £ 1,100. Our men was Very spirited & Eager for Action, and is Very Desirous that your Honnour would order them upon a second Expedition. But our Number was too Small to do as Much Execution as we would Desire. From Pidgeon river we marched home and Every Man arrived in health and safety to their Respective Habitation. Capt Mcfadden is Going to see your Honor at Congress, and if I have Been Guilty of a Mistake in my Information, it's Possible he may Acquaint you Better. Col. McDowell, Capt Davidson and me have sent for one of the Squaws this Day to Come to my house, in order to Examine her by an Interpreter, & we will Give you as Good an account as we Can Gather from her, Concerning the State of the Indians. Dear Sir I have one thing to remark, which is this, that where there is separate Companys United into one Body, without a head Commander of the whole I shall never Embark in such an Expedition Hereafter; for where Every Officer is a Commander there is no Command. No More at present. But Wishing you sir, with all true friends to Liberty all Happiness, I am sir Yours, &c.

WILLIAM MOORE
On the service of the United Colonies.
November 7th 1776.

Document 30
1781   Tennessee
Plundering and Burning the Cherokee Towns

Source: William F. Palmer et al., editors, **Calendar of Virginia State Papers and Other Manuscripts** (11 vols., Richmond: Superintendent of Public Printing, 1875-1893), vol. I, pp. 434-437.

Arthur Campbell to Govr Jefferson
Sir,
The Militia of this, and the two Western N. Carolina Counties have been fortunate enough to frustrate the designs of the Cherokees. On my reaching the frontiers I found the Indians meant to annoy us by small parties and carry off Horses. To resist them effectually, the apparently best measure was to transfer the War without delay to their own borders. To raise a force sufficient and provide them with provision and other necessaries seem'd to be a work of time, that would be accompanied with uncommon difficulties, especially in the Winter season: our situation was critical, and nothing but an extraordinary effort could save us, and disappoint the views of the enemy: all the miseries of 1776 came fresh in remembrance, and to avoid a like scene, men flew to their arms

and went to the field. The Wattago men, under Lieut: Col. Sevier, first marched to the amount of about 300. The Militia of this, with that of Sullivan County, made 400 more, the place of rendezvous was to be on this side of the French River. Col: Sevier with his men got on the path before the others, and by means of some discoveries made by his scouts he was induced to cross the River in pursuit of a party of Indians that had been coming towards our settlements. On the 16th of December, he fell in with the party, since found to consist of 70 Indians, mostly from the Town of Chote, out of which was killed 13, and he took all their Baggage in which were some of Clinton's Proclamations and other documents expressive of their hostile designs against us.

After this action the Wattago Corps tho't proper to retreat into an Island of the River. The 22d I crossed the French River, and found the Wattago Men in great want of provisions. We gave them a supply from our small stock: and the next day made a forced march towards the Tenasee. The success of the enterprise seemed to rest on our safely reaching the further bank of that River: as we had information the Indians had obstructed the common fording places, and had a force ready there to oppose our crossing. The morning of the 24th I made a feint towards the Island Town, and with the main Body pass'd the River without resistance at Timotlee.

We were now discovered—such of the Indians we saw seemed to be flying in consternation. Here I divided my force, sending a part to attack the towns below, and with the other, I proceeded towards their principal Town Chote. Just as I pass'd a defile above Toque, I observed the Indians in force stretching along the Hills below Chote, with an apparent design to attack our van there without their view; but the main body too soon came in sight, for me to decoy them from off the Hills. So they quietly let us pass on in order, without firing a gun, except a few scattering shot at our Rear, at a great distance from the Clefts. We soon were in possession of their beloved Town, in which we found a welcome supply of provisions.

The 25th Major Martin went with a Detachment, to discover the rout the enemy were flying off by; he surprised a party of Indians, took one scalp, and Seventeen Horses loaded with clothing, skins and House furniture: he discovered that most of the fugitives were making towards Telico and the Hiwasee. The same day Capt Crabtree of the Virginia Reg was detached with 60 men to burn the Town of Chilhowee: he succeeded in setting fire to that part of it, situated on the South side the river, altho' in the time he was attacked by a superior force. He made his retreat good.

The 26th Major Tipton of the Carolina Corps was detached with 150 Mounted Infantry with orders to cross the River, dislodge the enemy on that side, and destroy the Town of Tilassee: at the same time Major Gilbert Christian with 150 foot, were to patrol the Hills on the south side Chilhowee, and burn the remaining part of that

Town. This party did their duty well, kill'd three Indians and took nine prisoners: the officer of the Horse, by an unmilitary behaviour failed in crossing the River. This Trip took two days.

In the time the famous Indian Woman Nancy Ward came to camp, she gave us various intelligence, and made an overture in behalf of some of the Chiefs for peace; to which I then evaded giving an explicit answer, as I wished first to visit the vindictive part of the nation, mostly settled at Hiwasee and Chistowee: and to distress the whole as much as possible, by destroying their habitations and provisions.

The 28th, we set fire to Chote, Scitigo, and little Tuskeego, and moved our whole force to a Town on Telico River called Kai-a-tee, where I intended a Post, for to secure a Retreat, and to lay up provisions in. This evening Major Martin on returning from a patrol, attacked a party of Indians, killed two, and drove several into the River. The same evening in a skirmish, we lost Capt: James Elliott, a gallant young officer, being the first and only man the Enemy had power to hurt, on the Expedition, the Indians lost three men on the occasion. The 29th I set out for Hiwasee, distant about 40 miles, leaving at Kai-a-tee, under Major Christian a Garrison of 150 men. The 30th we arrived at Hiwasee and found the Town of the same name abandoned. In patroling the environs, we took a sensible young warrior, who informed us, that a Body of Indians with McDonald, the British Agent, and some Tories, were at Christowee, twelve miles distant, waiting to receive us. I had reason to believe the enemy had viewed us from the Hills above Hiwasee: for which reason, I ordered our Camp to be laid off, fires kindled, and other shews made, as if we intended to stay all night. At dark, we set out with about 300 men (the Wattago men refusing to go further) crossing the River at an unexpected Ford, and that night got near the Town. Early in the morning of the 31st we found that the enemy had fled in haste the evening before, leaving behind them, as they had done at the other Towns, allmost all their corn and other provisions, together with many of their utensils for agriculture, and all their heavy household furniture: with part of their stocks of Horses, Cattle and Hogs. These Towns, I expected would have been contended for, with obstinacy: as most of the Chickamogga People had removed hence after their visitation in 1779. Our Troops becoming impatient, and no other object of importance being in view, it was resolved to return homeward. Major Martin with a detachment were ordered by Sattoga, and the other Towns on the Telico River. in his route he took four prisoners, from whom he learnt that several of the Chiefs had met a few days before, in order to consult on means to propose a Treaty for peace. As I found the Enemy were humbled, and to gain time, I took the Liberty to send the Chiefs a message, a copy of which I send herewith, as the fulfilment thereof will require your Excellencies further Instructions and in which I expect N. Carolina will assist, or that Congress will take upon themselves the whole. I believe advantageous promises of peace may easily be obtained with a surrender of such an extent of Country, that will defray the Expenses of the war. but such terms will be best insured by placing a Garrison of two hundred Men, under an active officer, on the banks of the Tenasee.

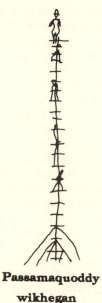

Passamaquoddy

wikhegan

Our whole loss on this Expedition was one man killed by the Indians, and two wounded by accident. It would have been very pleasing to the Troops, to have met the whole force of the nation at once on equal ground: but so great was the panic that seized them, after seeing us in order over the Tenasee, that they never ventured themselves in sight of the Army, but on rocky clefts or other inaccessible ground to our mounted Infantry. By the Returns of the Officers of different detachments, we killed 29 men, and took 17 Prisoners, mostly women and children. the number of wounded is uncertain. besides these, we brought in the family of Nancy Ward, who for their good offices, we considered in another light.

The whole are in Major Martins' care at the Great Island, until the sense of Government is known how they are to be disposed of. The Towns of Chote, Scittigo——Chilhowee Togue, Micliqua, Kai-a-tee, Sattoogo, Telico, Hiwasee, and Chistowee, all principle Towns, besides some small ones, and several scattering settlements, in which were upwards of one thousand Houses, and not less than fifty thousand Bushels of Corn, and large quantities of other kinds of provisions, all of which, after taking sufficient subsistance for the army whilst in the Country, and on its return, were committed to the flames, or otherwise destroyed. No place in the Over H. Country remained unvisited, except the small Town of Telasee, a scattering settlement in the neighborhood of Chickamogga, and the Town of Caloogee, situated on the sources of the Mobile.

We found in Okanastoters Baggage, which he left behind in his fright, various manuscripts, Copies of Treaties, Commissions, Letters, and other Archives of the nation, some of which shows the double game that people have been carrying on during the present War. There seemed to be not a man of honour among the Chiefs, except him of Kai-a-tee, whom I would willingly have discriminated, had it been in my power. Never did a people so happily situated, act more foolishly in loosing their livings, and their Country, at a time an advantageous neutrality was held out to them but such is the consequence of British seduction.

The enemy in my absence did some mischief in Powell's Valley, and on the Kentucky path near Cumberland Gap: besides three children that they scalped on Holstein: one of the perpetrators of which, we knock'd up on our return, and retook a number of Horses. The Botetout and Montgomery Militia were too slow in their movement to do any service. The Virginia Militia that served with me on the Expedition expects to be paid in the same manner with those that served last year in Carolina.

What provisions were needed on our seting out, were purchased on short credit, which I trust will be punctually paid on the first application. Your Excellency will please to excuse the length of this narration. I thought it my duty to give a circumstantial detail of facts, as the undertaking had something singular in it, and may lead to important consequences.

1778   Upper Ohio Valley
The Squaw Campaign

The Shawnee, Delaware, Mingo, and other peoples who lived north of the Ohio River had greater success in retaining their lands during the War for Independence than did the Cherokee. For example, the Shawnee harassed the Kentucky settlements almost without interruption during much of the war. After the frontiersmen murdered one of their chiefs, Cornstalk (a friend to the Americans), the Shawnee began to raid the settlements along the upper Ohio River. By this time (1777) the tribesmen regularly received supplies from the British at Detroit, who hoped that the Indians' raids would divert American troops to the Ohio Valley. These troops then would not be available to resist the British offensive under General John Burgoyne in northern New York. The United States earlier had garrisoned Pittsburgh and sent Brigadier General Edward Hand to recruit Pennsylvania militiamen for an invasion of Indian country. The want of volunteers and supplies delayed Hand's organization of a campaign. He did, however, lead a small force into Ohio to destroy British military stores that, he suspected, would be used by the Indians against the settlers. In a letter to Jasper Yeates, a lawyer in Hand's hometown of Lancaster, Pennsylvania, the general described the expedition (document 31). As an old man, one of the participants also related the details of the fight (document 32). News of Hand's activities, more than British military supplies, convinced most of the Indians of the upper Ohio Valley to support the Shawnee in their raids against the white men.

Further reading: Randolph C. Downes, *Council Fires on the Upper Ohio: A Narrative of Indian Affairs in the Upper Ohio Valley until 1795* (Pittsburgh: University of Pittsburgh Press, 1940).

Document 31
1778   Upper Ohio Valley
The Squaw Campaign

Source: Reuben Gold Thwaites and Louise Phelps Kellogg, editors, **Frontier Defense on the Upper Ohio, 1777-1778**, Draper series, vol. III (Madison: State Historical Society of Wisconsin, 1912), pp. 215-216.

FORT PITT 7th March 1778

DEAR YEATES—I omitted writing to you by the last Opertunity Because I had nothing material then to Communicate, & Expected by this to have Mighty feats to declare, having recd, intelligence that a Quantity of Stores were lodged at Cayahaga, I formed a Project of Seizing them by Surprise, during the Season in which the Savages might Suppose us to be inactive. A party nearly Amounting to 500 Chiefly Westmoreland Militia Offerd themselves for this Service, but unluckily the heavy Rains that fell soon after we set Out, together with the Melting of the snow raised the Waters to such a degree, that after Swiming Some Creek's & going round the heads of others we were obliged to relinquish our Design, about 40 miles up Beaver Creek we discovered Indian Tracts & Sent out reconnoitring Parties some of them returnd & Informd they had found a Camp Containing between 50 and 60 Indians. I conjectured they were Warriors coming into Our Settlements & proceeded to Attack them But to my great Mortification found only one Man with some Women & Children. the Men were so Impetuous that I could not prevent their Killing the Man & one of the Women. another Woman was taken & with difficulty Saved. the remr. escaped.

The prisoner told us that ten Miles higher, Ten Moncy [Munsee] men were Making salt. I detached a party to Secure them, they turn'd out to be 4 Women & a Boy, of these one Woman only was Saved. Notwithstanding this Savage Conduct I verily believe the Party would Behave well if they had men to contend with. You will be Surprised in performing the Above great exploits I had but one man (a Captn.) Wounded, & one Dround'd.

I cant yet give you the Information you desire of your Indian Brother but will inform myself if I can.

The Virginia Commissioners have not Arrived here nor can I learn Any thing of them. I beg my Love to all Your Family. My respects to Mr. Shippens &ca. & am Dear Yeates your Affectionate Kinsman

EDWD: HAND

To Jasper Yeates Esqr. Lancaster

Document 32
1778   Upper Ohio Valley
The Squaw Campaign

Source: Contributor: Samuel Murphy, **Draper Notes**, 33 vols., vol. 3 (1846), Series S, pp. 28-32, Draper Manuscripts, Division of Archives and Manuscripts, The State Historical Society of Wisconsin, Madison.

General Hand's expedition—This was in the winter 1777-78 with a slight fall of fresh snow. About 400 men: Col. Providence Mounts of Mounts Creek, wh empties in Youghogany, was out—Col. Wm Crawford, Maj. Brenton, Capt. John Stephenson, Capt. Scott, &c. Wm Brady, a blacksmith of Pittsburgh, was chosen pilot: Simon Girty* was out, & wanted the appointment.

On the way out, Maj. Brenton lost his horse, & he got Simon Girty to remain with him—they found the horse, & rejoined the army just at the close of the fight or rather firing on the Indian town, in the forks of Neshaneck and Shenango and on the Eastern bank of the latter—Orders had been given as they approached the town to surround it, but Col. Mounts did not fully accomplish his part, & left a gap, & Pipe's wife & children got off—a little fall of snow on the ground. This pipe was the brother of Capt. Pipe. The mother of the Pipes, an old squaw was pursued & shot at repeatedly when Thos Ravenscroft (. . .) ran up to the old squaw & tried to pull her away—but the bullets still flying & had a ball through his legging; when a Major came up & put a stop to firing—when it was ascertained that the only injury she had rec'd was the loss of an end of a little finger. An old squaw was shot by Lt. Hamilton & wounded in the leg—mistaking her for a warrior; & a soldier ran up & tomahawked her, & a second ran up & shot her. Pipe shot and wounded Capt. Scott and disabled his arm, & when nearly ready to shoot again—some one shot Pipe, & Reasin Virgin passing sunk the tomahawk in his head. Then commenced a wild yelling & shooting, without giving the least heed to Hand & to the officers. A few cabins only were there, a little plunder obtained. This was about midday in Feb. or March.

That afternoon a party started off for a small Indian settlement several miles up the Mahoning at a place called the Salt Licks. Simon Girty went as pilot: They did not reach the place till in the night—found the warriors all absent hunting—found a few squaws there, & took prisoner & brought her off—the others were left. A small

---

*This was the notorious Simon Girty, who late in March of 1778 left Pittsburgh to join the Indians against the Americans.

Indian boy out with a gun shooting birds was discovered & killed—and several claimed the *honor*; & it was left to Girty to decide—& his decision was, that one Zach. Connell killed the lad.

At the first town, the mother of Pipe was left in the town. An old Dutchman scalped the squaw that had been killed & put the scalp in his wallet with his provisions—and in swimming a stream on return the Dutchman lost off his wallet—& exclaimed pathetically "O, I loss my prosock & my sculp." This was long a byword with the troops. . . .

1779   New York
Burning of the Towns of the Six Nations

For two years Tories and Indians raided the New York and Pennsylvania frontier. The Mohawk, Cayuga, and Seneca were the most active of the Six Nations in the attacks on the Americans in the Mohawk and Wyoming valleys. In August and September, 1779, the United States Continental Army struck back. Major General John Sullivan commanded a military expedition that assembled at Easton, Pennsylvania, in the early summer. His army marched northward to Wyoming, where they waited for supplies. Then on July 31, the army headed for Tioga and nearby Chemung, destroying Indian towns and crops along the way. After burning Chemung, Sullivan returned to Tioga, where he was joined by Brigadier General James Clinton's force, which had marched southward from the Mohawk Valley, laying waste to Indian villages. The combined army moved north into New York on August 26, burning towns and crops for three weeks. Excerpts from the journals of Sullivan's officers describe the destruction (document 33).

By mid-September the army was again back in Tioga. Forty towns, one hundred and sixty thousand bushels of corn, and untold quantitites of vegetables and fruits had been destroyed. Of the almost five thousand men on the campaign, fewer than forty lost their lives. The Tories and Indians had kept a close watch on the progress of the American force and used guerrilla tactics against the soldiers; only at Newtown was there heavy fighting. The Tories and Indians lacked the manpower and supplies needed to stop the Sullivan-Clinton expedition.

Meanwhile, a small American army under Colonel Daniel Brodhead had marched north from Pittsburgh to destroy the Seneca towns. The colonel reported the destruction and plundering of five hundred acres of corn and vegetables.

The immediate effect of the campaigns was a hungry winter for the Indians. Thousands went to Niagara, where the British tried to feed them. In the spring the British urged the Indians to return to their homes to plant their fields. About the same time that the Indians returned to their homes, they began to organize into war parties. At-

tacks on the settlers resumed in the summer of 1780 and continued through the next two years.

Further reading: Barbara Graymont, *The Iroquois in the American Revolution* (Syracuse: Syracuse University Press, 1972).

Document 33
1779   New York
Burning the Towns of the Six Nations

Source: Frederick Cook, compiler, **Journals of the Military Expedition of Major General John Sullivan against the Six Nations** (Auburn, N.Y.: Knapp, Peck and Thomas, 1887), pp. 229-230, 27, 75, 112, 113.

From the Journal of Major James Norris:

[August] 11, [1779] The Army recd orders to march to Tioga, about two Miles from Sheshekonunck plain the troop forded the river where the Stream was rapid and pretty deep, notwithstanding the men all came safe over, except one who was carried down the Current a considerable distance, and saved by Lieut Col Barber Adjt Genl at the hazzard of his own Life—The Cattle and pack Horses were as fortunate as the Troops—After advancing about one mile through a rich bottom covered with strong and stately Timber which shut out the Sun, & shed a cool agreeable twilight; we unexpectedly were introduced into a Plain as large as that of Sheshekonunck, call'd *Queen Easter's* Plantation—it was on this plain near the bank of the Susquehanna that *Easter* Queen of the Seneca Tribe, dwelt in Retirement and Sullen majesty, detached from all the Subjects of her Nation—The ruins of her Palace are still to be seen; surrounded with fruit Trees of various kinds—At the East end of the plain, the Tioga River forms a junction with the Susquehanna—We now find ourselves happily arrived at Tioga, with our Army & Fleet, our Troops generally in health and spirits, and fewer accidents happening on the march than could be expected in the same distance, thro a Mountainous, wild, uncultivated Country—It appears by the Number of hides lying on the ground that the Indians have lately had an Encampment at this place. By the place of burial seen here, one would be led to think this was once an Indian Town, but there was no Vestiges of Hutts or Wiggoms—Whether through principle of Avarice or Curiosity, our Soldiers dug up several of their graves and found a good many laughable relicts, as a pipe, Tomahawk & Beads &c—

12th The Genl gave orders for a fort and four Block houses to be built at this place for the Security of the Fleet and Stores which are to be left here under a pretty strong Garrison, after the Army moves into the Indian Country—and this movement will take place as soon as Genl Clinton, who is coming down the Susquehanna, joins us with his Brigade—This afternoon Intelligence came by a small scout sent out yesterday, that the Enemy at Chemoung [Chemung], an Indian Town 15 Miles distant up the Cayuga branch, were about moving off upon hearing of our Arrival at Tioga—in consequence of which the main body of our Army marched at 8 oClock this Evening in order to be ready by Day break for surprising Chemoung; our march was attended with difficulty & fatigue, having a thick Swamp and several dangerous defiles to pass,—We arrived however between dawning & Sun rise, but to our no small mortification found the Town abandon'd & two or three Indians only to be seen sculking away—According to the accounts of those who pretend to be acquainted with Indian Citys, this seems to have been a pretty Capital place—It consisted of about 40 Houses built chiefly with split and hewn Timber, covered with bark and some other rough materials, without Chimnies, or floors, there were two larger houses which from some extraordinary rude Decorations, we took to be public Buildings; there was little Furniture left in the Houses, except Bearskins, some painted feathers, & Knicknacks—in what we supposed to be a Chapple was found indeed an Idol, which might well enough be Worshipd without a breach of the 2d Commandt, on account of its likeness to anything either in heaven or Earth—About Sun rise the Genl gave orders for the Town to be illuminated—& accordingly we had a glorious Bonfire of upwards of 30 Buildings at once: a melancholy & desperate Spectacle to the Savages many of whom must have beheld it from a Neighboring hill, near which we found a party of them had encamped last night—And from appearances the inhabitants had left the Town but a few hours before the Troops arrived—Genl Hand with some light Infantry pursued them about a mile, when they gave him a Shot from the Top of a Ridge, & ran according to their Custom, as soon as the fire was return'd; but unfortunately for us, the Savages wounded three Officers, killed Six men and wounded seven more—they were pursued but without effect—Our next Object was their fields of Indian Corn—about 40 Acres of which we cut down and distroyed—In doing this Business, a party of Indians and Tories, fired upon three Regimts across the River, killing one and wounded five—having compleated the Catastrophe of the Town and fields, we arrived at Tioga about Sun set the same day, verry much fatigued having march'd not less than 34 miles in 24 hours, without rest in the Extreamest heat—

American

From the Journal of Lieut. Erkuries Beatty:

MONDAY, [August] 30th, [1779] Raind a little last night and partly all this day by Showers near half the Army out to day cutting up Corn which is in great Abundance here; the party out of our Brigade went over the River where the corn Chiefly grows, went up the River about 2 miles then took up a large branch of the River (which bears near S.W.) one Mile burnt 5 houses and destroyed all the corn in our way. Our Brigade Destroyed about 150 Acres of the best corn that Ever I saw (some of the Stalks grew 16 feet high) besides great Quantities of Beans, Potatoes, Pumpkins, Cucumbers, Squashes & Watermellons, and the Enemy looking at us from the hills but did not fire on us. The Army lay on this ground all day and draw'd 16 Days flower and the Army was put on half allowance of provision which the men submitted to with a great deal of chearfulness.

From the Journal of Lieut.-Col. Henry Dearborn:

[September] 14th, [1779] . . . .

This [Genesee] is much the leargest Town we have met with it consists of more than 100 houses is situate on an excellent piece of land in a learge bow of the river. It appears the savages left this place in a great hurry & confusion as they left learge quantities of corn husk'd & some in heeps not husk'd & many other signs of confusion.

15th At six o'clock the whole Army ware turn'd out to destroy the corn in & about this town which we found in great abundance. we ware from 6 o clock to 2 P M in destroying the corn & houses It is generally thought we have destroy'd 15,000 bushels of corn at this place. The meathod we took to destroy it was to make large fires with parts of houses & other wood & then piling the corn on to the fire ading wood as we piled on the corn which Effectually destroyd the whole of it. . . .

About the same day's work Serg't Major George Grant wrote:

15. The whole of the army this morning with the greatest cheerfulness went about destroying the Corn, Beans, &c, which they effected by 12 o'clock. . . .

From the Journal of Serg't Major George Grant:

[September] 22, [1779]. Marched to Caiuga [Cayuga Castle] 1 mile distant. This town is large and commodius, consisting of 50 houses mostly well built. The party went immediately to destroying corn, &c, with which this place abounds, but the water very bad and scarce. Here was found some salt of the Indians making from the Salt Springs which are in this country. Found several muskets here branded with the brand of the United States, also a few Regimental coats, blue, faced with white.

23. The most part of the day taken up in destroying scattering towns, corn, &c. within two and three miles all around this town. About 4 o'clock marched for another

town distant about 4 miles but could not learn any name for it and here halted for this night.

24. This morning went to destroying corn, beans and Orchards. Destroyed about 1500 Peach Trees, besides Apple Trees and other Fruit Trees. This Town consisted of 13 houses; Then marched for 18 miles, the first 12 the land exceedingly good, the other 6 not extraordinary.

1607-1781   Eastern U.S.
The Indians' History of Indian-White Relations

1782   Upper Ohio Valley
The Gnaddenhutten Massacre

Native American orators regularly related the history of Indian-white relations. These Indian histories can be found in fragments in the minutes of meetings between the native peoples and the Europeans. A more complete history was put together by the Moravian missionary, John Heckewelder, from the orations of Delaware chiefs. The narration begins with the arrival of the English in Jamestown and ends with a Delaware chief's statement in April, 1781, that the white men will kill them all, even the Christian Indians who he was addressing at the time (document 34).

Eleven months later a military expedition under Colonel David Williamson disarmed and bound more than ninety Delaware who had accepted the Christian teachings of the Moravian Brethren. The Christian Indians formerly had lived in three towns, Schoenbrunn, Salem, and Gnaddenhutten in eastern Ohio. During the War for Independence both the frontiersmen and the Indians in the Ohio country suspected that the Christian Indians aided the enemy. The suspicions increased as the attacks by the Shawnee, Delaware, and other tribes on the settlers continued. In 1781 the Delaware forced the Christian Indians to move farther from the Americans to Sandusky. In February, 1782, the believing Indians got permission from the Delaware to return to their former homes to get their personal possessions. While they packed, Colonel David Williamson arrived in Gnaddenhutten. George Henry Loskiel's account of the massacre, as Heckewelder suggested, is excerpted (document 35).

Further reading: Randolph C. Downes, *Council Fires on the Upper Ohio: A Narrative of Indian Affairs in the Upper Ohio Valley until 1795* (Pittsburgh: University of Pittsburgh Press, 1940).

Document 34
1607-1781   Eastern U.S.
The Indians' History of Indian-White Relations

Source: Rev. John Heckewelder of Bethlehem, **An Account of the History, Manners, and Customs of the**

Indian Nations: who once inhabited Pennsylvania and Neighbouring States, Transactions (Philadelphia: Historical Literary Committee of the American Philosophical Society, 1819), vol. I, pp. 59-65. Rare Book Collection. The State Historical Society of Wisconsin, Madison.

INDIAN RELATIONS OF THE CONDUCT
OF THE EUROPEANS TOWARDS THEM.

Long and dismal are the complaints which the Indians make of European ingratitude and injustice. They love to repeat them, and always do it with the eloquence of nature, aided by an energetic and comprehensive language, which our polished idioms cannot imitate. Often I have listened to these descriptions of their hard sufferings, until I felt ashamed of being a *white man*.

They are, in general, very minute in these recitals, and proceed with a great degree of order and regularity. They begin with the Virginians, whom they call the *long knives*, and who were the first European settlers in this part of the American continent. "It was we," say the Lenape [Delaware], Mohicans, and their kindred tribes, "who so kindly received them on their first arrival into our country. We took them by the hand, and bid them welcome to sit down by our side, and live with us as brothers, but how did they requite our kindness? They at first asked only for a little land on which to raise bread for themselves and their families, and pasture for their cattle, which we freely gave them. They soon wanted more, which we also gave them. They saw the game in the woods, which the Great Spirit had given us for our subsistence, and they wanted that too. They penetrated into the woods, in quest of game, they discovered spots of land which pleased them; that land they also wanted, and because we were loth to part with it, as we saw they had already more than they had need of, they took it from us by force and drove us to a great distance from our ancient homes."

"By and by the *Dutchemaan* [Dutch] arrived at *Manahachtánienk*," [Manhattan] (here they relate with all its details what has been said in the preceding chapter.) "The great man wanted only a little, little land, on which to raise greens for his soup, just as much as a bullock's hide would cover. Here we first might have observed their deceitful spirit. The bullock's hide was cut up into little strips, and did not cover, indeed, but encircled a very large piece of land, which we foolishly granted to them. They were to raise *greens* on it, instead of which they planted *great guns*; afterwards they built strong houses, made themselves masters of the Island, then went up the river to our enemies, the Mengwe [Iroquois], made a league with them, persuaded us by their wicked arts to lay down our arms, and at last drove us entirely out of the country." Here, of course, is related at full length, the story which we have told in the first chapter. Then the Delawares proceed.

"When the *Yengeese* [Yankees] arrived at *Machtitschwanne*, [Massachusetts] they looked about every where for good spots of land, and when they found one, they immediately and without ceremony possessed themselves of it; we were astonished, but still we let them go on, not thinking it worth while to contend for a little land. But when at last they came to our favourite spots, those which lay most convenient to our fisheries, then bloody wars ensued: we would have been contented that the white people and we should have lived quietly beside each other; but these white men encroached so fast upon us, that we saw at once we should lose all, if we did not resist them. The wars that we carried on against each other, were long and cruel. We were enraged when we saw the white people put our friends and relatives whom they had taken prisoners on board of their ships, and carry them off to sea, whether to drown or sell them as slaves, in the country from which they came, we knew not, but certain it is that none of them have ever returned or even been heard of. At last they got possession of the whole of the country which the Great Spirit had given us. One of our tribes was forced to wander far beyond Quebec; others dispersed in small bodies, and sought places of refuge where they could; some came to Pennsylvania; others went far to the westward and mingled with other tribes.

To many of those, Pennsylvania was a last, delightful asylum. But here, again, the Europeans disturbed them, and forced them to emigrate, although they had been most kindly and hospitably received. On which ever side of the *Lenapewihittuck*, [Delaware River] the white people landed, they were welcomed as brothers by our ancestors, who gave them lands to live on, and even hunted for them, and furnished them with meat out of the woods. Such was our conduct to the white men [Swedes and Dutch], who inhabited this country, until our elder brother, the great and good MIQUON, [William Penn] came and brought us words of peace and good will. We believed his words, and his memory is still held in veneration among us. But it was not long before our joy was turned into sorrow: our brother Miquon died, and those of his good counsellors who were of his mind, and knew what had passed between him and our ancestors, were no longer listened to; the strangers who had taken their places, no longer spoke to us of sitting down by the side of each other as brothers of one family, they forgot that friendship which their great man had established with us, and was to last to the end of time; they now only strove to get all our land from us by fraud or by force, and when we attempted to remind them of what our good brother had said, they became angry, and sent word to our enemies the Mengwe, to meet them at a great council which they were to hold with us at *Loehauwake* [Easton] where they should take us by the hair of our heads, and shake us well. The Mengwe came, the council was held, and in the presence of the white men, who did not contradict them, they told us that we were women, and that they had made us such; that we had no right to any land, because it was all theirs; that we must be gone; and that as a great favour they permitted us to go and settle further into the country, at the place which they themselves pointed out at Wyoming."

Thus these good Indians, with a kind of melancholy pleasure, recite the long history of their sufferings. After having gone through these painful details, they seldom fail to indulge in bitter, but too just reflections upon the men of Europe. "We and our kindred tribes," say they, "lived in peace and harmony with each other, before the white people came into this country; our council house extended far to the north and far to the south. In the middle of it we would meet from all parts to smoke the pipe of peace together. When the white men arrived in the south, we received them as friends; we did the same when they arrived in the east. It was we, it was our forefathers, who made them welcome, and let them sit down by our side. The land they settled on was ours. We knew not but the Great Spirit had sent them to us for some good purpose, and therefore we thought they must be a good people. We were mistaken; for no sooner had they obtained a footing on our lands, than they began to pull our council house down first at one end and then at the other, and at last meeting each other at the centre, where the council fire was yet burning bright, they put it out, and extinguished it with our own blood! with the blood of those who with us had received them! who had welcomed them in our land! Their blood ran in streams into our fire, and extinguished it so entirely, that not one spark was left us whereby to kindle a new fire; we were compelled to withdraw ourselves beyond the great swamp, and to fly to our good uncle the *Delamattenos*, [Wyandots], who kindly gave us a tract of land to live on. How long we shall be permitted to remain in this asylum, the Great Spirit only knows. The whites will not rest contented until they shall have destroyed the last of us, and made us disappear entirely from the face of the earth."

I have given here only a brief specimen of the charges which they exhibit against the white people. There are men among them, who have by heart the whole history of what took place between the whites and the Indians, since the former first came into their country; and relate the whole with ease and with an eloquence not to be imitated. On the tablets of their memories they preserve this record for posterity. I, at one time, in April 1787 [1781?], was astonished when I heard one of their orators, a great chief of the Delaware nation, go over this ground, recapitulating the most extraordinary events which had before happened, and concluding in these words: "I admit there are good white men, but they bear no proportion to the bad; the bad must be the strongest, for they rule. They do what they please. They enslave those who are not of their colour, although created by the same Great Spirit who created us. They would make slaves of us if they could, but as they cannot do it, they kill us! There is no faith to be placed in their words. They are not like the Indians, who are only enemies, while at war, and are friends in peace. They will say to an Indian, "my friend! my brother!" They will take him by the hand, and at the same moment destroy him. And so you (addressing himself to the Christian Indians) will also be treated by them before long. Remember! that this day I have warned you to beware of such friends as these. I know the *long knives*; they are not to be trusted."

Eleven months after this speech was delivered by this prophetic chief, ninety six of the same Christian Indians, about sixty of them women and children, were murdered at the place where these very words had been spoken, by the same men he had alluded to, and in the same manner that he had described.

Document 35
1782   Upper Ohio Valley
The Gnaddenhutten Massacre

Source: George Henry Loskiel, **History of the Missions of the U.B. among the Indians**, Christian Ignatius Latrobe, translator, (London: The Brethren's Society for the furtherance of the gospel, 1794), pp. 175-182. Rare Book Collection, The State Historical Society of Wisconsin, Madison.

The Governor of Pittsburg thought it but just, to release the believing Indians who with Brother Schebosch were taken prisoners last year by the Americans in Schoenbrunn. The Indians arrived safe in Sandusky, and Brother Schebosch went to Bethlehem, to give a circumstantial account of the present situation of the Indian congregation. The humane behavior of the Governor at Pittsburg greatly incensed those people, who, according to the account given in the former Part of this History, represented the Indians as Canaanites, who without mercy ought to be destroyed from the face of the earth, and considered America as the land of promise given to the Christians. Hearing that different companies of the believing Indians came occasionally from Sandusky to the settlements on the Muskingum to fetch provisions, a party of murderers, about one hundred and sixty in number, assembled in the country near Whiling and Buffaloe, determined first to surprise these Indians, and destroy the settlements, and then to march to Sandusky, where they might easily cut off the whole Indian congregation. As soon as Colonel Gibson, at Pittsburg, heard of this black design, he sent messengers to our Indians on the Muskingum to give them timely notice of their danger: but they came too late. They however received in all the settlements early intelligence of the approach of the murderers, time enough for them to have saved themselves by flight; for a white man, who had narrowly escaped from the hands of some savages, warned them with great earnestness to fly for their lives. These savages, having murdered and impaled a woman and a child, not far from the Ohio, arrived soon after at Gnadenhuetten, where they expressed to our Indians their

fears, that a party of white people, who were pursuing them, would certainly kill every Indian they met on the road. But our Indians, who at other times behaved with great caution and timidity, if only the least appearance of danger existed, showed now no signs of fear, but went to meet real danger with incredible confidence.

This was undoubtedly owing to an idea, that they had nothing to fear from the Americans, but only from the Indians. However on the 5th of March, Samuel, an assitant, was called from Schoenbrunn to Salem, where all the assistants in those parts met, to consult whether they should fly upon the approach of the white people; but both those of Salem and Gnadenhuetten were of opinion, that they should stay. Samuel advised, that everyone should be left to act accord[ing] to his own sentiments, and thus they parted. When Samuel returned to Schoenbrunn, some Brethren accompanied him part of the way, and he declared that such love and harmony prevailed among the believing Indians, as he had never seen before.

Meanwhile the murderers marched first to Gnadenhuetten where they arrived on the 6th of March. About a mile from the settlement they met young Schebosch in the wood, fired at him and wounded him so much that he could not escape. He then, according to the account of the murderers themselves, begged for his life, representing that he was Schebosch the son of a white Christian man. But they paid no attention to his entreaties and cut him in pieces with their hatchets. They then approached the Indians, most of whom were in their plantations, and surrounded them, almost imperceptibly, but feigning a friendly behavior, told them to go home, promising to do them no injury. They even pretended to pity them on account of the mischief done to them by the English and the savages, assuring them of the protection and friendship of the Americans. The poor believing Indians, knowing nothing of the death of young Schebosch, believed every word they said, went home with them and treated them in the most hospitable manner. They likewise spoke freely concerning their sentiments as Christian Indians, who had never taken the least share in the war. A small barrel of wine being found among their goods, they told their persecutors on enquiry, that it was intended for the Lord's Supper, and that they were going to carry it to Sandusky. Upon this they were informed that they should not return thither, but go to Pittsburg, where they would be out of the way of any assault made by the English or the savages. This they heard with resignation, concluding, that God would perhaps choose this method to put an end to their present sufferings. Prepossessed with this idea, they cheerfully delivered their guns, hatchets and other weapons to the murderers, who promised to take good care of them and in Pittsburg to return every article to its rightful owner. Our Indians even showed them all those things, which they had secreted in the woods, assisted in packing them up, and emptied all their bee-hives for these pretended friends.

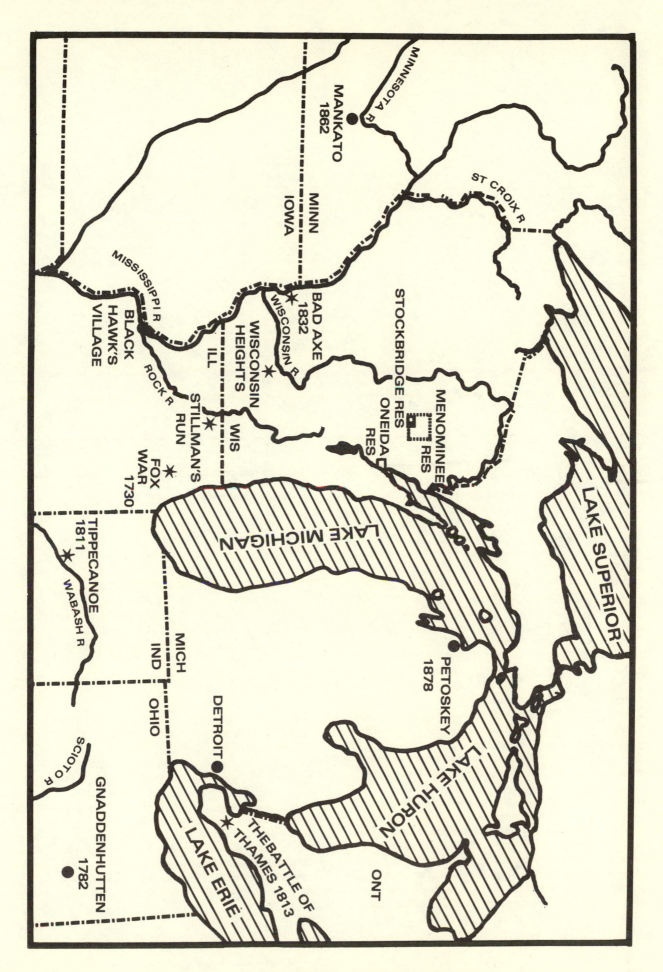

The Great Lakes 18th-19th Centuries

In the mean time the assistant John Martin went to Salem and brought the news of the arrival of the white people, to the believing Indians, assuring them that they need not be afraid to go with them, for they were come to carry them into a place of safety, and to afford them protection and support. The Salem Indians did not hesitate to accept this proposal, believing unanimously that God had sent the Americans, to release them from their disagreeable situation at Sandusky, and imagining them when they had arrived at Pittsburg, they might soon find a safe place to build a settlement and easily procure advice and assistance from Bethlehem. Thus John Martin with two Salem Brethren returned to Gnadenhuetten, to acquaint both their Indian Brethren and the white people with their resolution. The latter expressed a desire to see Salem, and a party of them was conducted thither and received with much friendship. Here they pretended to have the same good will and affection towards the Indians, as at Gnadenhuetten, and easily persuaded them to return with them. By the way they entered into much spiritual conversation, our Indians, some of whom spoke English well, giving these people, who feigned great piety, proper and scriptural answers to many questions concerning religious subjects. The assistants Isaac Glikkiken and Israel were no less sincere and unreserved in their answers to some political questions started by the white people, and thus the murderers obtained a full and satisfactory account of the present situation and sentiments of the Indian congregation. In the mean time the defenseless Indians at Gnadenhuetten were suddenly attacked and driven together by the white people, and without resistance seized and bound. The Salem Indians now met the same fate. Before they entered Gnadenhuetten, they were at once surprised by their conductors, robbed of their guns and even of their pocket knives, and brought bound into the settlement. Soon after this, the murderers held a council, and resolved by a majority of votes, to murder them all the very next day. Those who were of a different opinion, wrung their hands, calling God to witness, that they were innocent of the blood of these harmless Christian Indians. But the majority remained unmoved, and only differed concerning the mode of execution. Some were for burning them alive, others for taking their scalps, and the latter was at last agreed upon; upon which one of the murderers was sent to the prisoners, to tell them, that as they were Christian Indians, they might prepare themselves in a Christian manner, for they must all die tomorrow.

It may be easily conceived, how great this terror was, at hearing a sentence so unexpected. However they soon recollected themselves and patiently suffered the murderers to lead them into two houses, in one of which the Brethren and in the other the Sisters and children were confined like sheep ready for slaughter. They declared to the murders that though they could call God to witness that they were perfectly innocent, yet they were prepared and willing to suffer death. But as they had at their conversion and baptism made a solemn promise to the Lord Jesus Christ, that they would live unto him and endeavor to please him alone in this world, they knew that they had been deficient in many respects, and therefore wished to have some time granted, to pour out their hearts before Him in prayer, and to crave His mercy and pardon. This request being complied with, they spent their last night here below in prayer, and in exhorting each other to remain faithful unto the end. One Brother, called Abraham, who for some time past had been in a lukewarm state of heart, seeing his end approaching, made the following public confession before his brethren: "Dear Brethren! it seems as if we should all soon depart unto our Savior, for our sentence is fixed. You know that I have been an untoward child, and have grieved the Lord and my brethren by my disobedience, not walking as I ought to have done. But yet I will now cleave to my

THE PATER NOSTER
In the Language of the Muhhekaneew Indians

Noghnuh, ne spummuck oieon, taugh mauweh wneh wtukoseauk neanne annuwoieon. Taugh ne aunchuwutammun wawehtuseek maweh noh pummeh. Ne annoihitteech mauweh awauneek noh hkey oieheek, ne aunchuwutammun, ne aunoihitteet neek spummuk oiecheek. Menenaunuh noonooh wuhkamauk tquogh nuh uhhuyutamauk ngummauweh. Ohquutamouwenaunuh auneh mumachoieaukeh, ne anneh ohquutamouwoieauk numpeh neek mumacheh annehoquaukeek. Cheen hquukquaucheh siukeh annehenaunuh. Panneeweh htouwenaunuh neen maumtehkeh. Keah ngwehcheh kwiouwauweh mauweh noh pummeh; ktanwoi; estah awaun wtinnoiyuwun ne aunoieyon; hanweeweh ne ktinnoieen. Amen.

Savior with my last breath, and hold him fast, though I am so great a sinner. I know assuredly, that He will forgive "me all my sins, and not cast me out." The Brethren assured him of their love and forgiveness, and both they and the Sisters spent the latter part of the night in singing praises to God their Savior, in the joyful hope, that they should soon be able to praise him without sin.

When the day of their execution arrived, namely the 8th of March, two houses were fixed upon, one for the Brethren and another for the Sisters and children, to which the wanton murderers gave the name of slaughter houses. Some of them went to the Indian Brethren and showed great impatience, that the execution had not yet begun, to which the Brethren replied, that they were all ready to die, having commended their immortal souls to God, who had given them that divine assurance in their hearts, that they should come unto him, and be with him for ever.

Immediately after this declaration the carnage commenced. The poor innocent people, men, women, and children were led, bound two and two together with ropes, into the above-mentioned slaughter houses and there scalped and murdered.

According to the testimony of the murderers themselves, they behaved with uncommon patience and went to meet death with cheerful resignation. The above-mentioned brother Abraham was the first victim. A Sister, called Christina, who had formerly lived with the Sisters in Bethlehem, and spoke English and German well, fell on her knees before the captain of the gang and begged her life, but was told, that he could not help her.

Thus ninety-six persons magnified the name of the Lord, by patiently meeting a cruel death. Sixty-two were grown persons, among whom were five of the most valuable assistants, and thirty-four children.

Only two youths, each between fifteen and sixteen years old, escaped almost miraculously from the hands of the murderers. One of them, seeing that they were in earnest, was so fortunate as to disengage himself from his bonds, then slipping unobserved from the crowd, crept through a narrow window, into the cellar of that house in which the Sisters were executed. Their blood soon penetrated through the flooring, and according to his account, ran in streams into the cellar, by which it appears probable, that most, if not all of them, were not merely scalped, but killed with hatchets or swords. The lad remained concealed till night, providentially not one coming down to search the cellar, when having with much difficulty climbed up the wall to the window, he crept through and escaped into a neighboring thicket. The other youth's name was Thomas. The murderers struck him only one blow on the head, took his scalp, and left him. But after some time he recovered his senses and saw himself surrounded by bleeding corpses. Among these he observed one Brother, called Abel, moving and endeavoring to raise himself up. But he remained lying as still as though he had been dead, and this caution proved the means of his deliverance: for soon after, one of the murderers coming in, and observing Abel's motions, killed him outright with two or three blows. Thomas lay quiet till dark, though suffering the most exquisite torment. He then ventured to creep toward the door, and observing nobody in the neighborhood, got out and escaped into the wood, where he concealed himself during the night. These two youths met afterwards in the wood, and God preserved them from harm on their journey to Sandusky, though they purposely took a long circuit, and suffered great hardships and danger. But before they left the neighborhood of Gnadenhuetten they observed the murderers from behind the thicket making merry after their successful enterprise, and at last setting fire to the two slaughter houses filled with corpses.

Providentially the believing Indians, who were at that time in Schoenbrunn, escaped. The missionaries had immediately upon receiving orders to repair to Fort Detroit,

sent a messenger to the Muskingum to call our Indians home, with a view to see them once more, and to get horses from them for their journey. This messenger happened to arrive at Schoenbrunn the day before the murderers came to Gnadenhuetten, and having delivered his message, the Indians of Schoenbrunn sent another messenger to Gnadenhuetten to inform their brethren there and at Salem of the message received. But before he reached Gnaddenhuetten, he found young Schebosch lying dead and scalped by the way side, and looking forward, saw many white people in and about Gnadenhuetten. He instantly fled back with great precipitation and told the Indians in Schoenbrunn what he had seen, who all took flight and ran into the woods. They now hesitated a long while, not knowing whether to turn or how to proceed. Thus when the murderers arrived at Schoenbrunn the Indians were still near the premises, observing everything that happened there, and might easily have been discovered. But here the murderers seemed as it were struck with blindness. Finding nobody at home, they destroyed and set fire to the settlement, and having done the same at Gnadenhuetten and Salem, they set off with the scalps of their innocent victims, about fifty horses, a number of blankets and other things, and marched to Pittsburg, with a view to murder the few Indians lately settled on the north side of the Ohio, opposite to the Fort. Some of them fell sacrifice to the rage of this blood-thirsty crew, and a few escaped. Among the latter was Anthony, a member of our congregation, who happened then to be at Pittsburg, and both he and the Indians of Schoenbrunn arrived after many dangers and difficulties safe at Sandusky.

The foregoing account of this dreadful event was collected, partly from what the murderers themselves related to their friends at Pittsburg, partly from the account given by the two youths, who escaped in the manner above described, and also from the report made by the Indian assistant Samuel of Schoenbrunn, and by Anthony from Pittsburg, all of whom agreed exactly as to the principal parts of their respective evidences.

1788   Massachusetts
The Mashpee Lose Their Right to Govern Themselves

The Mashpee, descendants of the Wampanoags and other New England tribes, lived in South Shore, Massachusetts. In 1760 in the petition of Reuben Cognetew, a Mohegan, and other residents of Mashpee, a committee of the King's Privy Council ordered the governor of Massachusetts Bay to investigate Cognetew's complaints. The petitioners protested "that the English Inhabitants of the said Province have of late Years unjustly encroached upon the said Lands and hindered and obstructed the Indians in the just Right they have to fish in the River Mashbee within the said Limits."* The result of the investigation was a law, enacted by the government of Massachusetts Bay in 1763, that incorporated the inhabitants of Mashpee into a district. In effect, the law enabled the residents to govern themselves pretty much in the same manner as the other inhabitants of Massachusetts Bay governed themselves in their towns. The major difference was the requirement that two of the five overseers—the town clerk and the treasurer—must be Englishmen. In 1767 the law was renewed. During the War for Independence some of the Indians in Mashpee volunteered to serve on the side of the Americans. Their services were accepted. At the war's end independence for the Americans deprived the Mashpee of their rights to govern their own district. In 1788 and 1789, Massachusetts enacted legislation that placed the Mashpee under the control of overseers, who resided in neighboring counties. In effect, the inhabitants of Mashpee became wards of the state. The most comprehensive of the three laws is reprinted here (document 36).

Unlike the native Americans who lived along the frontier of settlement in New York, Ohio, and Tennessee, the Mashpee were not burned out of their homes and killed by their white neighbors. Far worse: they lost their political independence in a state where the most outspoken protesters against British oppression lived.

Further reading: Marion Vuilleumier, *Indians on Cape Cod* (Taunton, Mass.: Wm. S. Sullwold Publishing, 1970).

Document 36
1788   Massachusetts
The Mashpee Lose Their Right to Govern Themselves

Source: 1788, Chapter 38. **Acts and Laws of the Commonwealth of Massachusetts** [1788-1789] (reprint, Boston: Wright & Potter Printing Company, State Printer, 1894), pp. 64-67.

AN ACT FOR THE BETTER REGULATING OF THE INDIAN, MULATO AND NEGRO PROPRIETORS AND INHABITANTS OF THE PLANTATION CALLED **MARSHPEE, IN THE COUNTY OF BARNSTABLE.

Whereas the provisions already made by law respecting the Indian, Mulatto, & Negro proprietors and inhabitants of the plantation called Marshpee, *in the County of* Barnstable, *are insufficient to the well ordering & managing their affairs, and protecting them and their property against*

Acts of the Privy Council of England. Colonial Series, edited by W. L. Grant, James Munro and Sir Almeric W. Fitzroy (6 vols., London: His Majesty's Stationery Office, 1908-1912), vol. IV (1746-1766), pp. 460-461.
**Modern spelling is Mashpee.

the arts & designs of those who may from time to time be disposed to take the advantage of their weakness:

Be it therefore Enacted by the Senate and House of Representatives, in General Court assembled, and by the authority of the same, that a Board of Overseers shall be established, consisting of five discreet and disinterested persons, (two of whom to be inhabitants of the County of *Barnstable,* and the other three of the adjoining Counties) and shall be appointed as is herein after directed, which Overseers are hereby vested with full power and authority to regulate the police of the said plantation, to establish rules and regulations for the well ordering and managing the affairs, interest and concerns of the said *Indian* and other proprietors and inhabitants, as well with respect to the improvement and leasing out of their lands and Tennements, regulating their streams, ponds & fisheries, perambulating their lines, and meeting out lots for their particular improvement, as with respect to their bargains, contracts, wages and other dealings, and to take due care of their poor, and that their Children be bound out to suitable persons, of sober life and conversation. And the said Overseers are impowered and directed to hold stated meetings, elect a moderator, Secretary and Treasurer, and may if they judge it necessary, appoint some suitable person or persons to act under their direction, as a Guardian or Guardians to the said *Indian* and other proprietors, and to carry into execution, their said regulations and orders (which Guardian or Guardians shall give bonds to the said Board of Overseers for the faithful discharge of their trust and to render in to the said Overseers, and settle their accounts once every year and oftener if required; and whenever the said Board shall judge the continuance of the said Guardians in their said trust, inexpedient or unnecessary, they may remove them.

And be it enacted, that the said Board of Overseers or the Guardians whom they may appoint, are hereby vested with power and authority to demand and receive any property, dues or wages, which now are or hereafter may be detained, withheld from or justly owing, to said proprietors or any of them, by any person or persons, and to institute and bring forward in their own names and capacities, any action or actions for the recovery thereof; as likewise for any illegal entries or trespasses, which have been or may be made or committed on their lands, tenements, fisheries and other property; or for any fraud or injury done to them or any of them, and the same action or actions to pursue to final judgment and execution; And shall at all times have full power and authority to examine adjust and settle all accounts and controversies between them or any of them, and any white person or persons, for voyages or other services and transactions which remain unsettled, or which may hereafter be done or arise as likewise to adjust and bring to a settlement all accounts and proceedings of any former Guardian, Trustee or Overseer, taking effectual care, that justice be done therein; And may also bind by Indenture, the Children of the poor of the said proprietors to suitable persons, of sober life and conversation, as they the said Overseers or Guardians may judge necessary and convenient.

And be it further Enacted, that no lease, indenture, covenant, bond, bargain or contract in writing, made by any of said proprietors, shall be of any validity, unless it be made by or under the direction of said board, Guardian or Guardians, or with their consent and approbation, nor shall any action be brought against any of the said proprietors upon any account, for goods sold and delivered, services done and performed, or for money had and received, to the use of another, unless such account shall have been first examined by the said Overseers, Guardian or Guardians, and by them approved.

And be it further Enacted, that the said Overseer shall keep a fair and regular account of all their transactions, and of all the rents and profits arising from their the said proprietors lands, tenements and fisheries or otherwise, and of all money, wages or incomes, which they may receive from time to time, belonging to the said proprietors or any of them, and shall destribute to them, their respective rights dues and shares, after deducting the reasonable expence of conducting their said business, payment of their just debts, and (from the common profits,) providing for the sick and indigent and reserving from time to time, such sum or sums as can conveniently be spared, for the support and continuance of religious instruction among them, and the Schooling of their children; And they the said Overseers shall state their accounts annually, and lay the same before the Governor and Council for approbation and allowance: And the Governor with the advice of the Council is hereby authorized and impowered, to appoint such overseers, and to fill up vacancies whenever by death, resignation, removal out of the Commonwealth, or otherwise, they may happen to displace them or any of them for want of ability or integrity, or other reasonable cause, and to audit their accounts.

And be it Enacted, that no liberty or pretended liberty, from the proprietors or any of them, for cutting off any wood, timber or hay, milking pine trees, carrying off any ore or grain, or for planting or improving any of said lands or tenements, without the approbation of said Overseers, Guardian or Guardians, shall be any bar in any of their action or actions, *Provided* nothing herein shall be construed to defeat any lease or indenture heretofore made agreeably to law. And the lands and tenements of said proprietors, shall not be liable to be taken in execution for debt. And if any of said proprietors shall be committed in execution for debt, he she or they shall have the same benefit, from an Act intitled, "An Act for the relief of poor prisoners who are committed by execution for debt," as any white person now hath, who has no estate, their being proprietors notwithstanding, and the oath shall be varied accordingly.

And be it further Enacted, that all laws heretofore made

respecting the said *Marshpee Indians* be, and hereby are repealed.   *January 30, 1789.*

1801   Indiana
"Heavy Complaints of Ill Treatment"

1810   Indiana
Tecumseh Explains How the United States Got Land from the Indians

Even before George Washington became president, prominent political figures recognized that the native Americans never would acknowledge their defeat in the War for Independence. Article 3 of the Northwest Ordinance of 1787 already reflected the abandonment of the idea that the Indians had been defeated in the war. Under the Ordinance dealings with the Indians would always be in good faith, lands and property would not be taken without their consent, and their property, rights, and liberty would never be disturbed except in just and lawful wars authorized by Congress. Two years later Washington's Secretary of War, Henry Knox, filed his report on Indian affairs. Knox believed that there were two ways to end the hostilities between the Indians and white men north of the Ohio. The United States could war against the refractory tribes, or the United States could write treaties of peace, explicitly define rights and limits, rigidly observe the terms, and punish violators. Knox favored treaties of peace. The United States should acknowledge the native peoples' ownership of the land and purchase only some of the land. Then as white settlement increased, the supply of game would decrease, and the Indians would become poor and sell their land for a small consideration.

It was impossible to put Knox's second suggestion into effect. The native Americans fought to keep their land. After five years of war the Indians agreed, in 1795, to a large cession of land at the Treaty of Greenville. In this treaty the United States acquired three-fourths of the present state of Ohio along with a large section of the present state of Indiana around Vincennes. Six years later William Henry Harrison, the first governor of Indiana Territory, sent a report to the Secretary of War on the adverse effects of American settlement on the Indians who lived within or near the ceded territory (document 37).

Harrison's task was to keep peace between the native peoples and the frontiersmen and at the same time acquire land from the Indians. This was next to impossible to accomplish. He was under instructions from President Jefferson "to live in perpetual peace with the Indians, . . ." and "to draw them to agriculture, to spinning and weaving." Jefferson reasoned that "when they withdraw themselves to the culture of a small piece of land, they will perceive how useless to them are their extensive forests, and will be willing to pare them off from time to time in exchange for necessaries for their farms & families." The

President also wrote that "we shall push our trading houses, and be glad to see the good and influential individuals among them run in debt, because we observe that when these debts get beyond what the individuals can pay, they become willing to lop them off by a cession of lands."*

Between 1802 and 1809 the governor got chiefs of the Kickapoo, Wea, Delaware, Kaskaskia, Potawatomi, Sauk and Fox, and other tribes to cede millions of acres to the United States. Tecumseh, the Shawnee war chief, knew only too well what Harrison was about. In 1810 he went to see the governor to protest the Treaty of Fort Wayne, where Harrison got some chiefs to cede three million acres. In his speech Tecumseh reviewed the grievances of the Indian people against the United States (document 38).

Further reading: Reginald Horsman, *Expansion and American Indian Policy, 1783-1812* (Lansing: Michigan State University Press, 1967); Francis Paul Prucha, *American Indian Policy in the Formative Years: The Indian Trade and Intercourse Acts 1790-1834* (Cambridge: Harvard University Press, 1962); Glenn Tucker, *Tecumseh Vision of Glory* (Indianapolis and New York: The Bobbs-Merrill Company, Inc., 1956).

Document 37
1801   Indiana
"Heavy Complaints of Ill Treatment"

Source: Logan Esarey, editor, **Messages and Letters of William Henry Harrison, Collections** (2 vols., Indianapolis: Indiana Historical Commission, 1922), vol. 7 [vol. I, 1800-1811], pp. 25-31.

July 15th, 1801

Sir

For the last ten or twelve weeks I have been constantly engaged in receiving visits from the Chiefs of most of the Indian nations which inhabit this part of the Territory. They all profess and I believe that most of them feel a friendship for the United States—but they make heavy complaints of ill treatment on the part of our Citizens. They say that their people have been killed—their lands settled on—their game wontonly destroyed—& their young men made drunk & cheated of the peltries which formerly procured them necessary articles of Cloathing, arms and ammunition to hunt with. Of the truth of all these charges I am well convinced. The Delaware Chiefs in their address to me mentioned the loss of six persons of their nation, since the treaty of Greenvill having been killed by the White people—& I have found them correct as to number.

*Thomas Jefferson to William Henry Harrison, Washington, February 27, 1803, *Messages and Letters of William Henry Harrison,* edited by Logan Esarey, *Collections* (2 vols., Indianapolis: Indiana Historical Commission, 1922), vol. 7 [vol. I, 1800-1811], pp. 70-71. Courtesy of Indiana Historical Bureau.

In one instance however the White boy who killed the Indian was tried and acquitted as it was proved that it was done in self defence. In another instance the Murderer was tried and acquitted by the Jury, altho it was very evident that it was a cruel and unprovoked murder. About twelve months ago a Delaware was killed in this Town by a Citizen of the Territory against whom a bill has been found by the grand. He was however escaped and it is reported that he has gone to Natchez or New Orleans. But the case which seems to have affected the Indians more than any other is the murder of two men

Whooping-cough

and one woman of this same nation about three years ago. This cruel deed was perpetrated on this side of the Ohio, forty or fifty miles below the falls & is said to have been attended with circumstances of such atrocity as almost to discredit the whole story—were it not but too evident that a great many of the Inhabitants of the Fronteers consider the murdering of Indians in the highest degree meritorious—the story is this. About three years ago two Delaware men and a woman were quietly hunting in the neighbourhood of the Ohio—I believe on the waters of Blue river their Camp was discovered by two men I think of the name of Williams—brothers—and these Williams mutually determined to murder them for the purpose of possessing themselves of about fifty dollars worth of property and the trifling equipage belonging to the hunting Camp of a Savage. They thought it too dangerous to attack them openly as one of the Indians well known to the white people by the name of Jim Galloway or Gilloway—was remarkable for his strength and bravery. They approached the camp as friends & as I am toled they have since confessed asked leave to stay at the Indians Camp and hunt for a few days. Their request was granted & they remained until a favorite opportunity offered to carry their design into effect—& the then Indians were murdered. Altho they were missed by their friends it was a long time before their fate was ascertained. The murderers thinking themselves safe from the length of time which has elapsed, now begin to talk of the affair, and one of them is said to have declared that he was very nearly over-powered by the Indian after he had wounded him—that he had closed in with him and the Indian was on the point of getting the better of him when his brother to whom the murder of the other Indian had been committed came to his assistance. Altho I am convinced that the facts above stated are all true—yet so difficult is it to get testimony in a case of this kind, that I have not as yet been able to get the necessary depositions on which to ground an application to the Executive of Kentucky for the delivery of these people to Justice. Whenever I have ascertained that the Indian boundary line has been encroached on by the white people I have caused the Intruders to withdraw. But as the boundary line seperating the Indian land from that to which the title has been extinguished has not been run—nor the manner in which it is to run precisely ascertained either at this place or in the country on the Mississippi called the Illinois—it is impossible to tell when encroachments are made on the Indians at those two places. As this is an object of considerable importance to the Citizens of the Territory I must beg you Sir to obtain the directions of the President to have it done as soon as possible. The people have been about petitioning Congress on this subject—Untill it was observed that the President was authorized by law to cause all the boundaries between the lands of the U.N. States & the Indian tribes to be ascertained and marked—Untill their boundaries are established it is almost impossible to punish in this quarter the persons who make a practice of Hunting on the lands of the Indians in violation of law and our Treaty with that people. This practice has grown into a monstrous abuse. Thousands of the wild animals from which the Indians derive their subsistance have been distroyed by the white people. They complain in their speeches to me that many parts of their Country which abounded with game when the general peace was

Smallpox

made in 1795 now scarcely contains a sufficiency to give food to the fiew Indians who pass through there. The people of Kentucky living on the Ohio from the mouth of the Kentucky river down the Mississippi make a constant practice of crossing over on the Indian lands opposite to them every fall to kill deer, bear, and buffaloe—the latter from being a great abundance a few years ago is now scarcely to be met with, in that whole extent. One white hunter will distroy more game than five of the common Indians—the latter generally contenting himself with a sufficiency for present subsistance—while the other eager after game hunt for the skin of the animal alone. All these Injuries the Indians have hitherto borne with astonishing patience but altho they discover no disposition to make war upon the United States at present—I am confident that most of the tribes would eagerly seize any favorable opportunity for that purpose—& should the United States be at war with any of the European nations who are known to the Indians there would probably be a combination of nine tenths of the Northern Tribes against us—Unless some means are made use of to conciliate them. The British have been unremitted in their exertions to preserve their

influence over the Indians resident within our Territory ever since the surrender of the Forts upon the Lake—& those exertions are still continued—last year they delivered a greater quantity of goods to their Indians than they have been ever known to do—and I have been lately informed that talks are now circulating amongst them, which are intended to lesten the small influence we have over the Indians—I cannot vouch for the truth of this report—but I think it very probable that the British will redouble their efforts to keep the Indians in their Interest as a mean of assisting them in any designs they may form against Louisiana which it is said will be shortly delivered up to the French.

I have had much difficulty with the small tribes in this immediate Neighbourhood—viz.—the Peankashaws, Weas & Eel river Indians, these three tribes form a body of the greatest Scoundrels in the world—they are dayly in this town in considerable numbers and are frequently intoxicated to the number of thirty or forty at once—they then commit the greatest disorders—drawing their knives and stabing every one they meet with—breaking open the Houses of the Citizens killing their Hogs and cattle and breaking down their fences. But in all their frolicks they generally suffer most severely themselves they kill each other without mercy, some years ago as many as four were found dead in the morning—& altho these murders are actually committed in the streets of the town, yet no attempt to punish them has ever been made. This forbearance has made them astonishingly insolent & on a late occasion (within 8 weeks) when one of these rascals had killed without provocation two of the Citizens in one of the Traders Houses in this place, & it was found impossible to apprehend him alive, he was put to death. This peice of Justice so exasperated those of his tribe in the neighbourhood that they actually assembled in the borders of the town with a design to seize some favourable opportunity of doing mischief—the Militia were ordered out and their resentment has subsided.

Should you think proper to garrison Fort Knox with a small body of troops it will be the means of keeping the Indians under much better controle when they come here to trade—& would enable the civil Magistrates to punish those who violate the laws. Inded I do not think that a military force is so necessary on any part of the fronteers as at this place—the inhabitants tho fully able to repulse them when aware of their designs are constantly in danger from their treachery. Five Hundred Warriers might introduce themselves into the settlement undiscovered by the White people—& after doing all the mischief in their power might make—their escape with as much facility. I do not indeed apprehend in the least that the neighbouring tribes have any inclination to make open war upon us—I fear only the effect of some sudden resentment arising from their constant intercourse with the people of this town. In this intercourse causes of irritation are constantly produced twice within a few weeks an appeal was made to arms by both parties—one occasioned by some drunken Indians attempting to force a House in which one was killed and an other wounded. The other at the time when the two white men were killed as above mentioned. Luckily however no other mischief was done in either instance.

The Indian Chiefs complain heavily of the mischiefs produced by the enormous quantity of Whiskey which the Traders introduce into their Country. I do not believe there are more than Six Hundred Warriers upon this River

Measles

(the Wabash) and yet the quantity of whiskey brought here annually for their use is said to amount to at least six thousand Gallons. This poisonous liquor not only incapacitates them from obtaining a living by Hunting but it leads to the most attrocious crimes—killing each other has become so customary amongst them that it is no longer a crime to murder those whom they have been most accustomed to estem and regard. Their Chiefs and their nearest relations fall under the strokes of their Tomhawks & Knives. This has been so much the case with the three Tribes nearest us—the Peankashaws, Weas, & Eel River Miamis that there is scarcely a Chief to be found amongst them.

The little Beaver a Wea Chief of note well known to me was not long since murdered by his own son. The Little Fox another Chief who was always a friend to the white people was murdered at mid day in the Streets of this by one of his own nation. All these Horrors are produced to these Unhappy people by their too frequent intercourse with the White people. This is so cirtain that I can at once tell by looking at an Indian whom I chance to meet whether he belong to a Neighbouring or a more distant Tribe. The latter is generally well Clothed healthy and vigorous the former half naked, filthy and enfeebled with Intoxication, and many of them without arms except a Knife which they carry for the most vilanous purposes. The Chiefs of the Kickapoos, Sacks, & Patawatimies, who lately visited me are sensible of the progress of these measures, and their Views amongst themselves—which they are convinced will lead to utter exterpation—and earnestly desire that the introduction of such large quantities of Whiskey amongst them may be prevented.

Whether some thing ought not to be done to prevent the reproach which will attach to the American Character by the exterpation of so many human beings, I beg leave most respectfuly to submit to the Consideration of the President—That this exterpation will happen no one can doubt who knows the astonishing annual decrease of these

unhappy beings. The Delawares are now making an other attempt to become agriculturists—they are forming settlements upon the White river a branch of the Wabash under the conduct of two Missionaries of the Society of "The United Brethren for propogating the gospel amongst the Heathens" otherwise Meravians. To assist them in this plan the Chiefs desire that one half of their next annuity may be laid out in impliments of agriculture, and in the purchase of some domestic animals as Cows and Hogs. The Kaskaskeas & Peankashaws request the same thing and the Patawatimies wish a few corse hoes may be sent with their goods. The sun a great Chief of the last mentioned Nation requests that a Coat and Hat of the Uniform of the United States & to prevent Jealousy a few more may be aded for the other Chiefs, of his nation. Indeed I am convinced that nothing would please the Chiefs of all the Nations so much as a distinction of this kind. It was a method always persued by the British and nothing did more to preserve their Influance. I therefore take the liberty of recommending that about a half dozen Coats made in the uniform of the United States and ordinary Cocked Hats may be sent for each of the nations who have an annuity of one thousand dollars, and Half that number for the Nations who receive 500 dollars—the expence to be taken from the allowance of each nation. The Kickapoos who are a strong and warlike Nation have not a proper proportion of goods allowed them by the United States their annunity is 500 dollars only, which is the sum allowed to the remnant of the Kaskaskias which have only fifteen or twenty warriors. The Kickapoos of the Priaria a large branch of that nation never receive any part of the goods. They frequently steal Horses which are never returned because they do not fear the withholding of their annuity. The Socks a very large nation which Inhabit the Waters of the Illinois River are not bound by any treaty—and will not deliver up horses or prisones in their possession. I have reason to believe that there are several persons

Cholera

still with them which were taken during the late war. They say they are very willing to treat if they are put upon the same footing that the rest of the Indian Nations are.

The contractor to the army had untill lately an agent at this place—from whom I had procured the provisions which were necessary in the Councils I have had with Several nations which have visited me. I have signed an abstract for the quantity furnished. In their issues I have been as economical as possible—perhaps more so than was proper—the whole amount of Issues under my direction until this—amounted only to 13 rations.

Document 38
1810   Indiana
Tecumseh Explains How the United States Got Land from the Indians

Source: Logan Esarey, editor, **Messages and Letters of William Henry Harrison, Collections** (2 vols., Indianapolis: Indiana Historical Commission, 1922), vol. 7 [vol. I, 1800-1811], pp. 463-469. Courtesy of Indiana Historical Bureau.

TECUMSEH'S SPEECH TO GOVERNOR HARRISON 20th AUGUST 1810

Brother. I wish you to listen to me well—I wish to reply to you more explicitly, as I think you do not clearly understand what I before said to you I shall explain it again.

When we were first discover'd it was by the French who told us that they would adopt us as their children and gave us presents without asking anything in return but our considering them as our fathers. Since we have changed our fathers we find it different.

Brother. This is the manner that the treaty was made by us with the French. They gave us many presents and treated us well. They asked us for a small piece of country to live on which they were not to leave and continue to treat us as their children after some time the British and French came to quarrel the British were victorious yet the French promised to think of us as their child and if they ever could serve us to do it. Now my red children I know I was obliged to abandon you in disagreeable circumstances, but we have never ceased to look upon you and if we could now be of service to you we would still be your friends.

The next father we found was the British who told us that they would now be our fathers and treat us in the same manner as our former fathers the French—they would occupy the same land they did and not trouble us on ours; but would look on us as their children.

Brother. We were very glad to hear the British promise to treat us our fathers the French had done they began to treat us in the same way but at last they changed their good treatment by raising the Tomahawk against the Americans and put it into our hands, by which we have suffered the loss of a great many of our young men etc.

Brother. Now we began to discover the treachery of the British they never troubled us for our lands but they have done worse by inducing us to go to war. The Hurons have particularly suffered during the war and have at length become certain of it. They have told us that we must bury the British Tomhawk entirely that if we did not they (the B.) would ere long ask us to take it up.

You ought to know that after we agreed to bury the Tomhawk at Greenvile we then found their new fathers in the Americans who told us they would treat us well, not like the British who gave us but a small piece of pork every day. I want now to remind you of the promises of the white people. You recollect that the time the Delawares lived near the white people (Americans) and satisfied with the promises of friendship and remained in security yet one of their town was surprised and the men women and children murdered.

The same promises were given to the Shawonese flags, were given to them and were told by the Americans that they were now the children of the Americans. Their flags will be as security for you if the white people intend to do you harm hold up your flags and no harm will be done you. This was at length practised and the consequence was that the person bearing the flag was murdered with others in their village. Know my Bro. after this conduct can you blame me for placing little confidence in the promises of our fathers the Americans.

Brother. Since the peace was made you have kill'd some of the Shawanese, Winebagoes Delawares and Miamies and you have taken our lands from us and I do not see how we can remain at peace with you if you continue to do so. You have given goods to the Kickapoos for the sale of their lands to you which has been the cause of many deaths amongst them. You have promised us assistance but I do not see that you have given us any.

You try to force the red people to do some injury. It is you that is pushing them on to do mischief. You endeavour to make destructions, you wish to prevent the Indians to do as we wish them to unite and let them consider their land as the common property of the whole you take tribes aside and advise them not to come into this measure and until our design is accomplished we do not wish to accept of your invitation to go and visit the President.

Measles or Smallpox

The reason I tell you this is—You want by your distinctions of Indian tribes in allotting to each a particular track of land to make them to war with each other. You never see an Indian come and endeavour to make the white people do so. You are continually driving the red people when at last you will drive them into the great lake where they can't either stand or work.

Brother. You ought to know what you are doing with the Indians. Perhaps it is by direction of the President to make those distinctions. It is a very bad thing and we do not like it. Since my residence at Tippecanoe we have endeavoured to level all distinctions to destroy village chiefs by whom all mischief is done; it is they who sell our land to the Americans our object is to let all our affairs be transacted by Warriors.

Brother. This land that was sold and the goods that was given for it was only done by a few. The treaty was afterwards brought here and the Weas were induced to give ther consent because of their small numbers. The treaty at Fort Wayne was made through the threats of Winamac but in future we are prepared to punish those chiefs who may come forward to propose to sell their land. If you continue to purchase of them it will produce war among the different tribes and at last I do not know what will be the consequence to the white people.

Brother. I was glad to hear your speech you said if we could show that the land was sold by persons that had no right to sell you would restore it, that that did sell did not own it was *me*. These tribes set up a claim but the tribes with me will not agree to their claim, if the land is not restored to us you will soon see when we return to our homes how it will be settled. We shall have a great council at which all the tribes shall be present when we will show to those who sold that they had no right to sell the claim they set up and we will know what will be done with those Chiefs that did sell the land to you. I am not alone in this determination it is the determination of all the warriors and red people that listen to me.

I now wish you to listen to me. If you do not it will appear as if you wished me to kill all the chiefs that sold you this land. I tell you so because I am authorised by all the tribes to do so. I am at the head of them all. I am a Warrior and all the Warriors will meet together in two or three moons from this. Then I will call for those chiefs that sold you the land and shall know what to do with them. If you do not restore the land you will have a hand in killing them.

Brother. Do not believe that I came here to get presents from you if you offer us anything we will not take it. By taking goods from you you will hereafter say that with them you purchased another piece of land from us. If we want anything we are able to buy it, from your traders. Since the land was sold to you no traders come among us. I now wish you would clear all the roads and let the traders come among us. Then perhaps some of our young men will occasionally call upon you to get their guns repaired. This is all the assistance we ask of you.

Brother. I should now be very glad to know immediately, what is your determination about the land also of the traders I have mentioned.

Brother. It has been the object of both myself and brother from the beginning to prevent the lands being sold should you not return the land, it will occasion us to call a great council that will meet at the Huron Village where the council fire has already been lighted At which those who sold the land shall be call's and shall suffer for their conduct.

Brother. I wish you would take pity on all the red people and do what I have requested. If you will not give up the land and do cross the boundary of your present settlement it will be very hard and produce great troubles among us. How can we have confidence in the white people when Jesus Christ came upon the earth you kill'd and nail'd him on a cross, you thought he was dead but you were mistaken. You have shaken among you and you laugh and make light of their worship.

Everything I have said to you is the truth the great spirit has inspired me and I speak nothing but the truth to you. In two moons we shall assemble at the Huron Village (addressing himself to the Weas and Pottawatomies) where the great belts of all the tribes are kept and their settle our differences.

Brother. I hope you will confess that you ought not to have listened to those bad birds who bring you bad news. I have declared myself freely to you and if you want any explanation from our Town send a man who can speak to us.

If you think proper to give us any presents and we can be convinced that they are given through friendship alone we will accept them. As we intend to hold our council at the Huron village that is near the British we may probably make them a visit. Should they offer us any presents of goods we will not take them but should they offer us powder and the tomhawk we will take the powder and refuse the Tomhawk.

I wish you *Brother* to consider everything I have said is true and that it is the sentiment of all the red people who listen to me.

By your giving goods to the Kickapoos you kill'd many they were seized with the small pox by which they died.

The Governor began to answer Tecumseh and had proceeded for 15 or 20 minutes. He was explaining the justice used by the U. States towards the Indians and what he said the Interpreter explained to the Shawonese but before it was explained to the Potawatomies and Miamies Tecumseh rose up and a number of his young men with their war clubs tomhawks and spears. He spoke for some time with great vehemence and anger, which when interpreted appeared to be a contradiction of what the Govr. had said and that he had lied. The Governor told him that since he had behaved so illy he would put out the council fire and not set with him again.

August 21.

After some explanation offer'd as an apology by Tecumseh, the council this day met again, when Tecumseh address'd the Governor as follows:

Brother. There are many white people among you who are not true Americans, they are endeavouring to fill the minds of the Indians with evil towards the United States of which I shall now inform you. The person that informed me was a man of sense.

Brother. He said to us. That when you first began to bring about the last treaty you observed the greatest secrecy, after which you went to Fort Wayne and there made the treaty equally secret, declaring that you did not think it necessary to call upon us, but that you were determin'd to confine us to a small piece of land, and that you would bring all the tribes who listen to me, to abandon myself and the Prophet, and then you would know what to do with us.

Brother. This person came to our village shortly after the Treaty at Fort Wayne and said to us—Lallowachika (the Prophet) and you Tecumseh you may believe what I say to you, it is not me alone who speaks to you. I am the agent of a large party of white people who are your friends and will support you, they send me here to inform you everything that, that man the Governor at Vincennes is doing against you; but you must observe great secrecy and by no means inform him of us, or we shall be hung. I was (continues the person) at the Treaty at Fort Wayne and heard the Governor say that the Prophet was a bad man and that he would prevent traders from trading at his village (the Prophet's); or if any did go, they should sell their goods so high that the Indians could not purchase them, and consequently must suffer.

Brother. This man further represented to us that you were yet to remain in office two years and would be succeeded by a good man who was a true friend to the Indians, that you would offer us goods (annuities) but by no means to accept of them, that in order to induce us to take them you would offer us horses with saddles and bridles plated with silver, that all the goods and even the provisions that you give to the Indians is with the intention to cheat them out of their lands. That it was the intention of the United States to oppress the Shawanese before long the white people would push their settlements so near to them and oblige them to use the ax instead of the rifle—therefore recommended to us to take nothing from you.

Brother. Another American told us lately at our village, that you were about to assemble the Indians at Vincennes, for the purpose of making proposals, for more land—that you was placed here by Government to buy land when it was offer'd to you but not to use persuasions and threats to obtain it.

Brother. This man told me that I must go to Vincennes and make my objections to the purchase of land from the Indians, and not be afraid to speak very loud to you—that when you wanted land you was very smooth with the Indians, but at length became very boistrous.

Brother. After my hearing this so often, I could not help thinking otherwise than you wished to sow discord amongst the Indians. I wish you my Bro. to let alone those distractions you have always been endeavouring to establish among the Indians. It is doing them a great injury by exciting jealousies between them. I am alone the acknowledged head of all the Indians.

Here the Governor requested Tecumseh to state explicitly whether surveyors who might be sent to survey the land would be interrupted by the Indians and if the Kickapoos would receive their annuities that were now here—upon which Tecumseh replied.

Brother. When you speak to me of annuities I look at the land, and pity the women and children. I am authorized to say that they will not receive them.

Brother. they want to save that piece of land, we do not wish you to take it. It is small enough for our purposes. If you do take it you must blame yourself as the cause of trouble between us and the Tribes who sold it to you. I want the present boundary line to continue, should you cross it. I assure you it will be productive of bad consequences.

IV
Age of Expansion
1812-1860

Between the War of 1812 and the Civil War, the Industrial Revolution transformed the United States from an agrarian republic resting on the eastern seaboard into a thriving, industrial nation sprawled across a vast continent. The steamboat, cotton gin, reaper, rotary printing press, locomotive, and machines of every kind came into common use and enhanced the lives of America's citizens and aided her growth. Creative activity in literature, art, social theory, and philosophy stamped the generation as remarkable. But at the same time and in stark contradiction, America mistreated the relatively few and mostly impoverished Indian people, inflicting more atrocities and more studied brutalities upon them in this age of material progress and cultural advancement than in any previous time in American history.

The period of industrial expansion began with two major Indian wars. During the War of 1812, United States forces crushed the Northwest Confederacy of Tecumseh and stopped forever any possibility of armed Indian resistance to white development of the Midwest. In 1813-1814, militia forces waged a war against the Creek of Alabama and opened the Southwest to the cotton gin and black slavery.

In the next decade the white population demanded the removal of the Indians who still lived east of the Mississippi River. Church groups and state governments attempted several removals, but a federal law was necessary to define territory in the West and provide clear patents for vacated lands. On May 28, 1830, President Andrew Jackson signed the Indian Removal Bill, authorizing the chief executive to negotiate with the tribes and remove them to a place apart from whites, west of Arkansas, then thought to be a worthless desert.

In the southern states, federal removal officials encountered stiff opposition from the civilized tribes of the Choctaw, Chickasaw, Creek, Cherokee, and Seminole that required the extended use of forgery, fraud, bribery, and intimidation to overcome and achieve their removal. With the Seminole the United States resorted to war to force their removal. The conflict evolved into a struggle lasting from 1835 to 1845, with the United States Army committing numerous atrocities. The number of Indians who died from causes attributable to removal can never be ascertained. Perhaps fifteen thousand perished in the concentration camps where they were held prior to the journey and from disease, cold, mistreatment, and starvation enroute. Speculation in vacated Indian land became a major activity in the South, involving President Jackson, senators, congressmen, and military officers—all plunged avidly into the sordid trade. Some northern businessmen formed companies to speculate in Indian land: one group acquired 1,200,000 acres in west Florida, while others speculated in Indian lands being vacated in the northern states.

Throughout the northern states of New York, Ohio, Indiana, Illinois, and Wisconsin, the federal government continued until 1850 to remove Indians who relinquished their land. White speculators and farmers quickly acquired Indian homes and fields. In New York the Ogden Land Company carried out a particularly vicious campaign of fraud and bribery against the Seneca, who eventually lost most of their 116,000 acres. In 1832, along the Illinois and Wisconsin border the removal of Indians erupted into war when the Sauk under Black Hawk refused to leave and were ruthlessly suppressed and driven west.

In the early 1840s, Americans drifted into the undeveloped West and many moved down into the Mexican border states. These states were under a savage and unrelenting attack by Apache Indians, who were furious about Mexican land speculators, embittered over the traffic in Indian slaves, and intent on retribution for earlier Mexican atrocities against them. Mexican authorities sought to exterminate the Apache by placing a bounty on their scalps and hiring several score of Americans as professional Indian hunters. The scalp hunters killed hundreds of Indians, reducing the number so drastically that profits fell. Then they turned upon Mexican peasants and passed their scalps as Indian. The outraged Mexican government dismissed the Yankees from service.

As a plum of the Mexican War, 1846-1848, the territory of New Mexico passed into American control. Ranchers, merchants, and farmers had long engaged in the enslavement of Navajo, Apache, and other Indian children and killed warriors, old people, and women who were intractable. American conquest did not halt Indian slavery.

In 1849 the territory of California also became an American possession. To the Indians of California, American conquest and occupation meant a continuation of the mistreatment they had experienced for a generation under

Mexican domination. When the American government failed to function for several years in many areas of California, the mining camps, boom towns, and farming communities existed in anarchy. Miners and ranchers often forced Indians into a serfdom comparable to black slavery. Public holidays are recorded that featured Indian hunts as the principal form of celebration. Miners formed "militia" groups to steal and rape Indian women, and individuals commonly committed acts of rape, murder, and perversion against the Indian people, who were considered a subhuman species. On one occasion when local militia companies rode to suppress an Indian "war" incited by white brutalities, they carried a company banner emblazoned with the word "Extermination" embroidered by their wives and daughters. The estimated number of Indian deaths from the beginning of American occupation in 1849 to 1856 is 50,000 out of a population of about 120,000.

Throughout the Great Plains and Rocky Mountains not settled by whites and in the unceded Indian lands of the north woods, fur traders and a class of criminal whites maintained a continual presence among Indians. Through these men, and especially through John Jacob Astor's American Fur Company, whiskey was continually introduced, leading to the deliberate debauching of tribes. The whiskey trade was a principal cause of many tribal clashes and massacres of whites. To the Indians the Christian missionaries' picture of hell closely resembled the white civilization they knew, and they frequently asked, "Why convert the Indians?"

Battle of Bad Axe, August 2, 1832, Black Hawk War.

1813-1814   Southern Alabama
Creek War Atrocities

By 1813 the expanding American nation had pushed up against the Indian boundaries of the Southwest and had begun exerting inordinate pressure upon the tribes for their rich, loam soil. Deep tensions built up among the Creek of Alabama, who were trapped along both the Gulf Coast and further north. White hunger for land was not the only threat; the white men's culture—ranging from cats, shoes, and galluses to plows, coffins, and cattle—began inserting itself into tribal culture. In 1813 the Creek split into warring factions over the issue of how to stop white imperialism. The faction appealing to Creek tradition and culture—Red Sticks, named either for painting their war clubs a deep red or for the color of the ceremonial sticks of their prophets—elected war. On August 30, they attacked the United States stockade, Fort Mims Mobile, defeating the Americans and massacring most of the women and children. A wave of terror swept through the white border states. Immediately, militia armies, with Andrew Jackson of Tennessee as a principal general, were sent to crush the Red Stick faction. Jackson hurriedly pushed his volunteers deep into the Indian forests to "exterminate" them. Then he realized that his brash tactics had removed him from his supplies and left his troops with the possibility of famine. The Cherokee nation furnished his army supplies and, later, a famous regiment that fought with friendly Creek and the American armies against a common foe. Jackson waged a total war against the hated enemy, who possessed few guns and little ammunition, yet stood and desperately fought in some battles almost to the last man. Jackson deliberately leveled Creek towns, burned fine specimens of Indian architecture, and destroyed crops and provisions in order to reduce the tribe to starvation. Many of the women and children survived only by fleeing to the forests, where Cherokee took them captive, presumably as slaves. An example of atrocities is from the autobiography of Davy Crockett, who participated in the Battle of Talleshatchee on November 5, 1813 (document 39).

Document 39
1813   Attack on the Creek   Alabama

Source: **A Narrative of the Life of David Crockett, of the State of Tennessee. Written by Himself** (Philadelphia: E. L. Cary and A. Hart, 1834), pp. 43-44.

And so we passed on each side of the town, keeping near to it, until our lines met on the far side. We then closed up at both ends, so as to surround it completely; and then we sent Captain Hammond's company of rangers to bring on the affray. He had advanced near the town, when the Indians saw him, and they raised the yell, and came running at him like so many red devils. The main army was now formed in a hollow square around the town, and they pursued Hammond till they came in reach of us. We then gave them a fire, and they returned it, and then ran back into their town. We began to close on the town by making our files closer and closer, and the Indians soon saw they were our property. So most of them wanted us to take them prisoners; and their squaws and all would run and take hold of any of us they could, and give themselves up. I saw seven squaws take hold of one man, which made me think of the Scriptures. So I hollered out the Scriptures was fulfilling; that there was seven women holding to one man's coat tail. But I believe it was a hunting shirt all the time. We took them all prisoners that came out to us in this way; but I saw some warriors run into a house, until I counted forty-six of them. We pursued them until we got near the house, when we saw a squaw sitting in the door, and she placed her feet against the bow she had in her hand, and then took an arrow, and raising her feet, she drew with all her might, and let fly at us, and she killed a man, whose name, I believe, was Moore. He was a lieutenant, and his death so enraged us all, that she was fired on, and had at least twenty balls blown through her. This was the first man I ever saw killed with a bow and arrow. We now shot them like dogs; and then set the house on fire, and burned it up with the forty-six warriors in it. I recollect seeing a boy who was shot down near the house. His arm and thigh was broken, and he was so near the burning house that the grease was stewing out of him. In this situation he was still trying to crawl along; but not a murmur escaped him, though he was only about twelve years old. So sullen is the Indian, when his dander is up, that he had sooner die than make a noise, or ask for quarters.

The number that we took prisoner, being added to the number we killed, amounted to one hundred and eighty-six; though I don't remember the exact number of either. We had five of our men killed. We then returned to our camp, at which our fort was erected, and known by the name of Fort Strother. No provisions had yet reached us, and we had now been for several days on half rations. However we went back to our Indian town on the next day, when many of the carcasses of the Indians were still to be seen. They looked very awful, for the burning had not entirely consumed them, but given them a very terrible appearance, at least what remained of them. It was, somehow or other, found out that the house had a potato cellar under it, and an immediate examination was made, for we were all as hungry as wolves. We found a fine chance of potatoes in it, and hunger compelled us to eat them, though I had a little rather not, if I could have helped it, for the oil of the Indians we had burned up on the day before had run down on them, and they looked like they had been stewed with fat meat.

October 5, 1814   Battle of the Thames, Canada
Mutilation of Slain

During the War of 1812, American forces suffered severe reverses in their initial engagements against British and Canadian troops. In the Northwest the Shawnee Tecumseh had united many of the Indian tribes in a confederacy to assist the British, hoping to halt the expansion of the Americans into their homelands. However, at the decisive battle of Put-in-Bay on Lake Erie, the United States Navy under Admiral Oliver Hazard Perry destroyed the British fleet, removed the British dominance of the Great Lakes supply routes, and reversed the fortunes of the American Army. Under General William Henry Harrison, American militia quickly pushed northeast of Detroit into Canada, to engage the demoralized British army. On the River Thames, two miles west of Moraviantown, the British generals decided to stand and fight with their army of regulars and Indians. The Americans crushed them; about two score of Indian warriors, including the valiant Tecumseh, perished. After the battle American militiamen turned to the bodies of the "yellow buggers" and scalped, flayed, and otherwise mutilated them. Many wanted razor straps made from Indian skin, especially from Tecumseh's corpse. The frontiersmen also participated in acts of barbarity, including the murder of an Indian woman and the mutilation of her body. The following excerpt describing the atrocities is taken from the English author, William James, whose history was written mainly for a British audience (document 40). The account is accurate for the time, but historians today agree that the bodies of various slain Indians were mistaken for Tecumseh's, which was never identified. In regard to General Harrison's actions, it is true that whenever he encountered mutilation, he ordered it stopped. Immediately after the battle, though, he burned to the ground the homes and public buildings in the Indian settlement of Moraviantown in accordance with the American scorched-earth policy.

Further reading: Glenn Tucker, *Tecumseh, Vision of Glory* (Indianapolis: The Bobbs-Merrill Co., 1956).

Document 40
1814   Scalping the Slain   Southern Canada

Source: William James, A Full and Correct Account of the Military Occurrences of the Late War between Great Britain and the United States of America . . . (2 vols., London: printed for the author, 1818), vol. I, pp. 293-296.

Full two-thirds of general Harrison's army, at the battle of the Thames, were Kentuckians. As every soldier wore a scalping-knife as part of his accoutrements, and was extremely "dexterous in the use of it;" as the *live* Ken-

tuckians bore to the *dead* Indians (taking Mr. Thomson's estimate) fully as 20 to one; and as one head could conveniently afford but one scalp, we can picture to ourselves what a scramble there must have been for the trophies. For the European reader's edification, we will endeavour at describing the manner in which the operation of scalping is performed. A circular incision, of about three inches or more, in diameter, according to the length of the hair, is made upon the crown of the head. The foot of the operator is then placed on the neck or body of the victim, and the *scalp*, or tuft of skin and hair, torn from the skull by strength of arm. In case the hair is so short as not to admit of being grasped by the hand, the operator, first with his knife turning up one edge of the circle, applies his teeth to the part; and, by that means, quite as effectually disengages the *scalp*. In order to preserve the precious relict, it is then stretched and dried upon a small osier hoop. The western Indians invariably crop their hair, almost as close as if it were shorn; to retaliate upon their enemies, probably, by drawing some of their teeth. As captain M'Culloch's prisoner was a western Indian, we were, therefore, wrong in supposing, that the American officer practised any refinement in the art of *scalping*.

The body of Tecumseh was recognised, not only by the British officers who were prisoners, but by commodor Perry, and several American officers. An American writer (from the spot, it would appear) says:—"There was a kind of ferocious pleasure, if I may be allowed the expression, in contemplating the contour of his features, which was majestic, even in death."—Poor chief! the *majesty* of his features could no longer, now he was dead, awe the Kentuckians; and that majesty was, by their merciless scalping-knives, soon converted into hideousness. Had the "ferocious pleasure" of Americans required no further gratification than Tecumseh's scalp, custom might have been their excuse. The possessor of this valuable trophy would not, it may be supposed, part with a hair of it. Were the other Kentuckians, then, to march home empty-handed?—Ingenuity offered a partial remedy. One, more dexterous than the rest, proceeded to *flay* the chief's body; then, cutting the skin in narrow slips, of 10 to 12 inches long, produced, at once, a supply of *razor-straps* for the more "ferocious" of his brethren. We know that the editor of the United States' government-paper, the "National Intelligencer," not many months ago, flew into a violent rage, because some anonymous writer here had mentioned the circumstance. How will the American government bear to hear the fact thus solemnly repeated, accompanied by the declaration, that some of the British officers witnessed the transaction, and are ready to testify to the truth of it?—But, have we not *American* testimony in support of the charge?—The same writer who was so struck with the *majesty* in Tecumseh's countenance, and who, of course, would, by every means in his power, soften down an account that reflected so high dishonor upon his countrymen, says thus:—"Some of the Kentuckians disgraced themselves by committing indignities on his dead body. He was scalped, and *otherwise disfigured*."

Considering the importance of Tecumseh's death to the American cause, it is difficult to account for general Harrison's omission to notice it; unless we suppose, that the general did transmit the account, but so blended with the "indignities" committed upon the chief's person, that the American secretary at war, finding a difficulty in garbling, suppressed altogether, that paragraph of the letter.

December 24, 1814   Kaskaskia, Illinois Territory
Scalp Bounty—An Act to Promote Retaliation
Upon Hostile Indians

The territorial governments forming along the Mississippi River in the early nineteenth century devised various methods of removing Indians who were considered a menace to white settlement. During the War of 1812, Illinois employed a bounty system. The law passed by the territorial legislature at Kaskaskia is given.

Further reading: Milo M. Quaife, *Chicago and the Old Northwest, 1673-1835* (Chicago: University of Chicago, 1913).

Document 41
1814   Bounty on Indians   Illinois

Source: Francis S. Philbrick, editor, **The Laws of Illinois Territory in Collections of the Illinois State Historical Library,** vol. XXV (Springfield: Illinois State Historical Library, 1950), pp. 177-178.

AN ACT *to promote retaliation upon hostile Indians*

Whereas the hostile incursions of the savages and their indiscriminate slaughters of men women and children, have been often repeated and under circumstances aggravating the honor of such sanguinary scenes, and producing great affliction and distress among the inhabitants of this Territory.

And whereas nothing is so well calculated to check the progress or prevent the repetition of those attacks on the part of those blood thirsty monsters as successful pursuit and retaliation upon them to effect which it becomes expedient to offer sufficient encouragement to the bravery and enterprize of our fellow-citizens, and those other persons now engaged or that hereafter may be engaged in the defence of our frontiers. Therefore

SEC. 1. Be it enacted by the Legislative Council and house of Representatives and it is hereby enacted by the authority of the same. That if any indian or indians shall hereafter make an incursion into our settlements with hostile intentions and shall commit any murder or depreda-

tion, and any citizen or citizens or rangers or other persons engaged in the defence of our frontier shall pursue and overtake and take prisoner or prisoners or kill any indian or indians that may have so offended such person or persons shall if they be citizens merely receive a reward for each Indian so taken or Killed the sum of fifty dollars and if they be rangers or other persons actually at the time engaged in the defence of any frontier such person or persons shall be entitled to a reward of twenty five dollars.

SEC. 2. Be it further enacted that if any party of citizens having first obtained permission of the commanding officer on our frontier to go into the Territory of any hostile indians shall perform any such tour and shall kill any indian warrior, or take prisoners any squaw or child in the country of said hostile Indians such person shall be entitled to a reward of one hundred dollars for each indian warrior Killed and such squaw or child taken prisoner.

Record of treaty

SEC. 3. Be it further enacted that if any party of Rangers or other persons now engaged or that hereafter may be engaged in the defence of our frontier, not exceeding fifteen in number shall with the leave of the officer make a voluntary incursion into the country of any hostile indians and shall Kill any indian warrior or warriors, or take and bring away any squaw or squaws child or children, in and from the country of said Indians such persons as aforesaid shall be entitled to a reward of fifty dollars, for each indian warrior Killed as aforesaid, and each squaw or child so taken prisoner.

SEC. 4. Be it further enacted, that proof of any of the before mentioned facts to entitle any person or persons to the reward given by this law, shall be made before the Judges of any county court, or any two of said Judges who upon full proof being made before them, shall certify the same to the auditor of public accounts who shall audit the amount due to such person or persons and give to him or them a warrant on the Treasurer for the amount thereof which shall be paid out of any money in the public Treasury. This act shall be in force from and after the passage thereof.

RISDON MOORE
Speaker of the House of Representatives
PIERRE MENARD
Approved Dec. 24, 1814   president of The Councel
NINIAN EDWARDS

July 21, 1816   Bribery   Nashville, Tennessee

Indian governments constantly faced the problem of maintaining their principles during the often calamitous meetings with the United States because white politicians frequently destroyed their integrity by the effective use of bribery. This corruption of leadership is demonstrated during the Cherokee negotiations to settle boundary questions arising from the Creek War of 1813-1814. Under the leadership of Andrew Jackson western speculators and frontiersmen forced the Creek into a treaty that signed away much of their central Alabama homeland, including 1,300,000 acres south of the Tennessee River which the Cherokee lived on and claimed as their own. The treaty outraged the Cherokee. They knew Indian boundaries were usually vaguely determined according to ancient custom, but their ownership of most of the disputed land was beyond question. In addition, their vital military contribution to American victory in the recent Creek War should have entitled them to a favorable boundary settlement. Their wounded veterans, numerous widows, and helpless orphans required assistance. Further, the Cherokee suffered severe damage during the war—not from the enemy but from the American frontiersmen, who burned cabins, shot cattle, hogs, and sheep "for mere sport; or prejudice," and left the meat to rot where it fell. By the end of the war the Cherokee people, faced with possible starvation, dispatched a delegation with a list of Indian damage claims compiled by their agent, R. J. Meigs, to Washington to request the Creek cession be staid and their claims be heard. On March 23, 1816, President Madison and Secretary of War William Crawford signed a treaty that satisfied most Cherokee demands. Land speculators considered the treaty an affront to whites and soon inveigled President Madison to appoint a commission chaired by Andrew Jackson to purchase Creek lands that the Cherokee claimed. Forgetting the military valor of the Cherokee and their generous food supplies to the white soldiers, Jackson viewed the Cherokee position as an attempt to plunder the United States of land fairly won in battle. The following is a letter from Andrew Jackson to one of the commissioners who was to negotiate a preliminary boundary line with the Cherokee. Jackson gave him instructions to corrupt the Indian government by bribing its leaders, Brown, Lowry, Path Killer, and The Ridge—to cede their entire claim (document 42). The commissioners were successful in the debauching of many of the leaders. Later with Jackson's personal help, they rammed the treaty ratification through the Cherokee National Council at a poorly attended, forced session in the dead of night.

Further reading: Grace Steele Woodward, *The Cherokees* (Norman: University of Oklahoma, 1963).

Document 42
1816   Bribery   Tennessee

Source: John Spencer Bassett, editor, **Correspondence of Andrew Jackson** (Washington, D.C.: Carnegie Institute, 1927), vol. II, pp. 254-255.

TO BRIGADIER-GENERAL JOHN COFFEE.
                              NASHVILLE July 21, 1816.
(Private)

D'r Genl, I have this moment rec'd by mail the letter to your address here enclosed, having opened it and finding it from Colo McKee and being on the subject of the Choctaw treaty, I enclose it.

From the late date of the meeting of the chiefs it will afford sufficient time for you to attend to the duties on the line. It is really strange that you and Colo Barnett has not rec'd instructions to desist from running the line for the present untill, the event is known, of the treaty ordered with the cherokees, for a recession of those lands lately ceded south of the Tennessee, was it not for so many plunders being lately committed, I would conclude, that there was no reallity in this show of a treaty with the cherokees, or there would have been some others added to the commission. it proves one thing at least, that they have not attached so much importance to this thing, as to the other treaties to be holden, when I view it as the key to all things that can benefit the U. S., and can be obtained by treaty.

I really am not sorry that you are without advice, your orders will compell you to go on and will authorise you to call for the chiefs to attend you, and you can do more with the chiefs, by advice, than will be done by Colo Meigs. I wish you and Colo Barnett would see Colo Brown Lowry the Path Killer and the ridge. should you, you can sound them to the bottom and obtain from them a declaration that they will resign all claim for a very small sum, they know they never had any rights and they will be glad as I believe to swindle the U States out of a few thousand dollars, and bury the claim, if persisted in, which they know, might bury them and there nation. By obtaining a declaration from the chiefs that the[y] will sell, you can tell them I am authorized to buy from them, and expect a full delegation from their nation at the chickasaw treaty to be held on the first of Sept next at the old council house. Colo Meiggs is instructed to have a full delegation there. But as all this may be for the public eye, when really under the Rose advice may be given contrary, we ought to be on our guard, to detect duplicity (if it exist) and expose it, and do all we can justly, to do away that *cursed convention* that may deluge our country in blood. The cherokees are alarmed and justly, and with a little vigilence and good policy, all the evils can be everted only the sum that will have to be paid for the recession.

The hight of my diplomatic ambition is that we may restore to the U states the territory fairly and justly ceded by the creeks, if the convention with the cherokees can be set aside the ballance will follow, as a thing of course, if that cannot be done all that can be obtained from the chickasaws will agrandise the cherokees, whom it delighteth the sec to honor, when I take a view of this whole thing with all its ramifications I cannot determine whether it proceeded from thear weakness or corruption, or from what else it could have proceeded, to say the least, it was a wanton, hasty, useless thing calculated to injure the best interests of the U states, without affording the least hope of benefit to her. we must exert ourselves to get the government honourably clear of this convention that they may be more vigilence and care regain the good opinion of the good citizens of the west, with my best wishes to you and respects to Colo Barnett, adieu

April 8, 1818   St. Marks, Florida
Execution of Prisoners of War

In 1814 the armies of Andrew Jackson crushed the Creek confederacy in lower Alabama, but a thousand recalcitrant members fled into Spanish Florida, where they joined Seminole kinsmen and black refugees from slavery. They continued to be hostile to whites, particularly, northern merchants who attempted to place them in debt to force land cessions in lieu of cash payment. Indians also hated land speculators who, backed by northern merchants, forged title to Spanish land grants totalling millions of acres. American soldiers were sent to expell Creek Indians trespassing on land near the Georgia-Florida border which was ceded to the United States in the Creek Treaty of 1814. The Creek fought and defeated the invading groups and then withdrew into the wilderness of Spanish Florida. Federal authorities had expected Indian resistance; some Indian leaders believed the Creek treaty had been deliberately drawn to create a provocative border incident as an excuse for the United States to invade the feeble Spanish empire and rip from it the territory of Florida. True or not, this is precisely what occurred. When news of the Indian attack reached Washington, Jackson was ordered on December 26, 1817, "to terminate" the conflict. He assembled fifteen hundred militia and regulars, ignored both the law and the token Spanish military presence, and on March 10, invaded western Florida, destroying all homes, crops, and boats belonging to Indians and blacks. Two accounts relating to the capture and execution of two Creek chiefs, Homollimico and Francis, are presented. The first, emphasizing the humanity of the Creek, is by Millee, or *Mahlee*, the beautiful daughter of Francis, given in 1842 to Colonel Ethan A. Hitchcock, who had found her in Indian Territory and recorded her story in his diary (document 43). She describes intervening with her tribesmen to save the life of the American soldier, Duncan McKrimmon, then under sentence of death. In 1844, through the efforts

of Hitchcock, Congress recognized her deed and awarded her its first medal for bravery with an annual stipend of ninety-five dollars. The second document stresses the inhumanity of American military officers and is taken from the nineteenth century historian James Parton's description of the capture and execution of Francis and Homollimico (document 44). Parton quotes from the narrative of a volunteer, J. D. Rodgers, who was present.

Further reading: Marquis James, *Andrew Jackson, The Border Captain* (Indianapolis: The Bobbs-Merrill Co., 1933).

Document 43
1817   Indian Humanity   East Florida

Source: W. A. Croffut, editor, **Fifty Years in Camp and Field. Diary of Major-General Ethan Allen Hitchcock, U. S. A.** (New York: G. P. Putnam's Sons, 1909), pp. 152-153.

In the summer of 1817, a small party of Seminoles surprised and captured while fishing in the river one Captain Duncan McKrimmon, a member of the Georgia militia, and they made arrangements to sacrifice him at the stake near the home of Francis. The following is the story as told by Milly to Colonel Hitchcock—it is the same that Captain McKrimmon told all his life:

"Milly began by saying that an elder sister and herself were playing on the bank of the river, when they heard a war-cry, which they understood to signify that a prisoner had been taken. They immediately went in the direction of the cry and found a white man, entirely naked, tied to a tree, and two young warriors, with their rifles, dancing around him preparatory to putting him to death, as was their right according to custom. She explained to me that in such cases the life of a prisoner is in the hands of the captors—even the chiefs have no authority in the case. She was then but fifteen or sixteen years of age; 'the prisoner was a young man,' said Milly, 'and seemed very much frightened and looked wildly around to see if anybody would help him. I thought it a pity that a young man like him should be put to death and I spoke to my father and told him it was a pity to kill him—for he had no head to go to war with' (meaning that he had been led off by others). 'My father told me,' continued Milly, 'that he could not save him, and advised me to speak to the Indians. I did so. One of them was very much enraged, saying he had lost two sisters in the war and would put the prisoner to death. I told him that it would not bring his sisters back to kill the young man, and so, talking to him for some time, I finally persuaded him, and he said that if the young man would agree to have his head shaved, and dress like an Indian, and live among them, they would save his life.' She then proposed the conditions to the white man, which were joyfully accepted; and the Indians changed the contemplated death scene into a frolic. They shaved the young man's head, excepting the scalp lock, which was ornamented with feathers, and, after painting him and providing him an Indian dress, he was set at liberty and adopted as one of the tribe."

Document 44
April 8, 1818   St. Marks, Florida
American Execution of Prisoners

Source: James Parton, **Life of Andrew Jackson** (New York: Mason Brothers, 1860), vol. 2, pp. 454-456, 457.

A few hours before General Jackson's arrival at St. Marks, Captain McKeever came into the harbor, displaying English colors from the masthead of his vessel. Within the fort was Duncan McKrimmon, whose life Milly Francis had saved. This McKrimmon was destined to be the means of bringing upon his fair deliverer irremediable woe. The circumstances referred to have been obligingly related to me by an American officer who served in General Jackson's army, and was an eye-witness of all the important occurrences of the campaign.

"McKrimmon, upon seeing a vessel coming into port showing English colors, asked leave of the Spanish commandant to go on board of her, alleging that he feared the Indians might reclaim him and put him to death. He had been consigned to the custody of the Spanish commandant by Francis the prophet, whose town was only three miles distant. He went on board with Hambly and Doyle, who were in the same situation as himself—prisoners subject to Indian caprice. To their equal astonishment and delight, they found that the vessel was American, and that their safety was certain.

"They immediately informed Captain McKeever of the return of Francis from England, and of his ardent desire for, and constant expectation of the arrival of supplies to carry on the war against the United States. This prompted the captain to increase his display of English colors, and in the course of the following day—the temptation was too strong to be longer resisted—Francis or Hellis Hajo, with his right-hand chief, Himollemico, obtained a canoe and set off to the fleet at the mouth of the bay, distant ten miles from the fort. Soon they accomplished their journey, and as soon as they got on board Francis asked:

" 'What loaded with?'

"He was informed, 'guns, powder, lead, and blankets for his red friends the Indians.'

"They manifested ecstatic delight; when the captain invited them to his cabin (taking care to deprive them of all their arms), to take a glass with him. They descended the stairs, the captain following in the rear, with a signal to a few Jack tars to accompany him with ropes. No

sooner said than done. Jack made his appearance before the astonished chiefs, who were soon bound and secured beyond the possibility of escape.

"McKrimmon came in to salute the prisoners; when Francis, in fair English, said,

" 'This is what I get for saving your life.' "

. . .

"The next day after the capture by Captain McKeever of Hellis Hajo and Himollemico, he sent them up to the fort, when General Jackson ordered them to be hanged. Francis was a handsome man, six feet high; would weigh say one hundred and fifty pounds; of pleasing manners; conversed well in English and Spanish; humane in his disposition; by no means barbarous—withal, a model chief."

August 23, 1825   Detroit, Michigan Territory
Effects of the Whiskey Trade

John Jacob Astor's American Fur Company systematically debauched the Indians in the Northwest with whiskey, rum, and wine in violation of the laws of the United States. The traffic precipitated border clashes and murder among the Indians (literally thousands of Indians died over the years and at least a hundred and fifty of Astor's men in twenty-five years) and left a trail of misery throughout the north country. The fur trade and whiskey traffic profits made Astor the wealthiest man in the United States and a political power in New York City and Washington. Rarely does one encounter a description of his business methods in a standard account of the fur trade. An eyewitness account of his method of operation is taken from a letter by Colonel J. Snelling of the United States Army to James Balfour, Secretary of War (document 45). The British trade that the colonel refers to was also controlled by Astor.

Further reading: Mari Sandoz, *The Beaver Men; Spearheads of Empire* (New York: Hastings House, 1964).

Document 45
1825   Michigan
Effects of the Whiskey Trade

Source: U.S. Congress. Senate. **The Fur Trade**, S. Doc. 58, 19th Cong., 1st sess., 1826, pp. 11-12.

"In former letters addressed to the Department of War, I have adverted to the mischievous consequences resulting from the introduction of whiskey and other distilled spirits into the Indian country. The pretext is, that our traders cannot enter into successful competition with the British traders without it:"

"If the sale of whiskey could be restricted to the vicinity

of the British line, the mischief would be comparatively trivial, but if permitted at all, no limits can be set to it. A series of petty wars, and murders, and the introduction of every species of vice and debauchery by the traders, and their *engagées*, will be the consequences. It becomes also a fruitful source of complaint with those engaged in the fur trade from the West. The traders who obtain supplies from St. Louis, pass Fort Snelling at the mouth of the river St. Peters, where, in obedience to the orders I have received from the President, their boats are searched and no spiritous liquors are permitted to be taken further. The traders who are licensed for the lakes, spread themselves over the whole country between Lake Superior and the Upper Mississippi; their whiskey attracts a large proportion of the Indians to their trading houses, and the Western traders not only have to complain of the loss of custom, but in many instances, the Indians who have obtained their goods of them are seduced by whiskey to carry the produce of their winter's hunt to others. This has long been one of the tricks of the trade; the traders, who are not generally restrained by any moral rules after they pass the boundary, practise it without scruple whenever opportunities occur, and he who has the most whiskey generally carries off the furs. They are so far from being ashamed of the practice, that it affords them subjects for conversation by their winter fires. I have myself frequently heard them boast of their exploits in that way. The neighborhood of the trading houses where whiskey is sold, presents a disgusting scene of drunkenness, debauchery, and misery; it is the fruitful source of all our difficulties, and of nearly all the murders committed in the Indian country. In my route from St. Peters to this place, I passed Prairie du Chiens, Green Bay, and Mackinac; no language can describe the scenes of vice which there present themselves. Herds of Indians are drawn together by the fascinations of whiskey, and they exhibit the most degraded picture of human nature I ever witnessed. I happened to be at this place in July when the Indians within the territory of the United States visited Malden. The presents they received there were infinitely greater in quantity, and superior in quality, to those received of our agents. These were immediately brought to our store, and exchanged for whiskey. For the accommodation of my family I have taken a house about three miles from town, and in passing to and from it, I had daily opportunities of seeing the road literally strewed with the bodies of men, women, and children, in the last stages of brutal intoxication. It is true, there are laws in this territory to restrain the sale of whiskey, but they are not regarded; too many are interested in what is here considered a profitable trade. I was informed by a person of veracity, that one man, (a Mr. ——— ———) had purchased this season above three hundred blankets for whiskey, they cost him on an average about seventy-five cents each. I passed this man's door daily, it was always surrounded by Indians, and many were passing in, and out, with kegs on their backs.

"If the evil could be confined to the places I have mentioned, it would be of little importance, but the facilities afforded to traders on the upper Lakes, are spreading it through all those extensive regions within the American boundaries."

"The present year there has been delivered to the agent of the North American Fur Company at Mackinac, (by contract) three thousand three hundred gallons of whiskey, and two thousand five hundred of high wines. The practice of using high wines is a favorite one with the traders, as it saves transportation, and the quantity of liquor can be increased at pleasure.

I have been inadvertently led further into this subject than I intended, but I will venture to add that an inquiry into the manner in which the Indian trade is conducted, and especially by the North American Fur Company, is a matter of no small importance to the tranquility of the borders."

1832   Southern Wisconsin
Black Hawk War Atrocities

On April 6, 1832, a thousand Sauk left their Iowa reserve to follow their leader, Black Hawk, across the Mississippi to their former corn fields laying fallow near the mouth of the Rock River. They moved in open defiance of a treaty negotiated a year earlier with a minority faction of the tribe under the leadership of Chief Keokuk; it restricted them to Iowa. The mass movement of so many Indians frightened the frontier settlements in Illinois and Wisconsin, who called for punitive expeditions to search out the intruders and, in the words of President Andrew Jackson, "teach them respect." The Sauk attempted to still the whites' deep fear by withdrawing up the Rock River into its Horicon marsh headwaters in southern Wisconsin, where they hoped to plant crops and solicit allies among the Potawatomi and Winnebago. Withdrawal only incited the whites to more feverish activity, and militia as well as regular army units, including a Menominee company of mercenaries, started to move in on them. By July the Sauk had exhausted their food supply and faced possible starvation. When they sent messengers under a white flag to surrender to the first army to approach their camps, the messengers were shot by militiamen, forcing the Sauk to fight while moving west across southern Wisconsin to Iowa. Pursued by soldiers, they retreated along a path marked by crows and buzzards feasting upon the bodies of ponies, aged men, women, and children who fell by the wayside, dead of starvation (document 47). On August 2, they reached the Mississippi, where the Bad Axe River joins it, and began to cross, when the militia attacked. Black Hawk remarked in his autobiography, "Our braves, but few in number, finding that the enemy paid no regard to age or sex, and seeing that they were murdering helpless women and little children, determined to fight until they were killed." The Sauk fought on the riverbank while their families swam the Mississippi. Then the steamboat *Warrior*, loaded with riflemen and carrying a cannon, blocked the river passage, and the soldiers began shooting the aged, women, and children (documents 48 and 49). Three hundred exhausted Sauk reached the other side, where their hereditary enemies, the Sioux (dispatched by the Americans) viciously

MENOMINEE WAR SONG

Song of Sauk Woman Captured in Black Hawk War

attacked and killed several score. Later, as a token of public appreciation for removal of the Sauk, all militiamen received grants of public lands.

There are numerous atrocities associated with the bludgeoning of the starving, fleeing Sauk. On three occasions the militia refused to allow the Indians to surrender; twice they shot at messengers while they stood under a flag of truce. An account of one incident taken from Black Hawk's autobiography describes his attempt to surrender to Captain Throckmorton of the *Warrior* the day before the Battle of Bad Axe (document 46). We know from other sources that Throckmorton fully understood what was transpiring. At many points across Wisconsin, soldiers bayoneted, scalped, and mutilated unarmed and innocent Sauk. An excerpt from the memoirs of Colonel Charles Whittlesey describes such atrocities. Whittlesey, a citizen of Wisconsin, was then traveling as a civilian. To describe the massacre of Bad Axe, an essay on the Black Hawk War from the noted nineteenth century historian, Reuben Gold Thwaites, is given. Also militiaman John Fonda commented briefly about his activities on board the *Warrior*. Born in New York, Fonda was a highly respected early pioneer of Wisconsin who dictated his memoirs to the editor of the Prairie du Chien *Courier*, where they began appearing with the February 15, 1858, issue. Finally, an account by Perry Armstrong on the desecration of Black Hawk's grave is presented. Armstrong, a noted Illinois attorney, was strongly sympathetic to the Sauk (document 50).

Further reading: Cyrenus Cole, *I Am A Man—The Indian Black Hawk* (Iowa City: Iowa State Historical Society, 1938).

Document 46
1832   Ignoring the White Flag   Wisconsin

Source: **Life of Ma-Ka-Tai-Me-She-Kia-Kiak or Black Hawk . . . , dictated by himself** (Boston: Russell, Odiorne & Metcalf, 1834), pp. 133-134.

Myself and band having no means to descend the Ouisconsin, I started, over a rugged country, to go to the Mississippi, intending to cross it, and return to my nation. Many of our people were compelled to go on foot, for want of horses, which, in consequence of their having had nothing to eat for a long time, caused our march to be very slow. At length we arrived at the Mississippi, having lost some of our old men and little children, who perished on the way with hunger.

We had been here but a little while, before we saw a steam boat (the "Warrior,") coming. I told my braves not to shoot, as I intended going on board, so that we might save our women and children. I knew the captain [THROCKMORTON,] and was determined to give myself up to him. I then sent for my *white flag*. While the messenger was gone, I took a small piece of white cotton, and put it on a pole, and called to the captain of the boat, and told him to send his little canoe ashore, and let me come on board. The people on the boat asked whether we were Sacs or Winnebagoes. I told a Winnebago to tell them that we were Sacs, and wanted to give ourselves up! A Winnebago on the boat called to us *"to run and hide, that the whites were going to shoot!"* About this time one of my braves had jumped into the river; bearing a white flag to the boat—when another sprang in after him, and brought him to shore. The firing then commenced from the boat, which was returned by my braves, and continued for some time. Very few of my people were hurt after the first fire, having succeeded in getting behind old logs and trees, which shielded them from the enemy's fire.

The Winnebago, on the steam boat, must either have misunderstood what was told, or did not tell it to the captain correctly; because I am confident that he would not have fired upon us, if he had known my wishes. I have always considered him a good man, and too great a brave to fire upon an enemy when sueing for quarters.

Document 47
1832   Wisconsin
Atrocities Against Noncombatants

Source: Col. Charles Whittlesey, "Recollection of a Tour Through Wisconsin in 1832," **First Annual Report and Collections of the State Historical Society of Wisconsin, for the year 1854** (Madison: Beriah Brown, 1855), vol. I, pp. 78-79.

It was now early in September, and everything conspired to nerve the system and animate the senses. The sky had not shown a cloud for many days; the air was cooled by an ever moving breeze; countless flowers shone in purple and gold about us, and wherever we chose to move, the ground was firm and smooth as a turnpike. A new and unmingled pleasure diffused itself through the company, of which even the animals seemed to partake.

The path wound around the northern shores of the Four Lakes, from which Gen. Dodge, with a band of mounted militia of the mining district, had lately driven the remnant of Black Hawk's force. The scattering trails of the retreating Indians were still distinct. Sometimes they would all converge into one broad and plain track, then again radiate in different directions, continually branching and spreading over the country, dwindling to a mere trace. This resulted from their method of travel, sometimes in a body, then in classes, these again sub-divided, and so on, for the double purpose of deceiving their pursuers in regard to their true route, and also of dispersion and escape in case of attack. It proved one of the greatest annoyances and hindrances of the expedition. In the present instance, delay on the part of General Dodge became a matter of life and death. From April till the latter part of July, they had evaded the white forces. During this period, they had been driven but little over an hundred miles, that is, from the Sycamore Creek to the Four Lakes. Much of the time their exact position could not be known. They were now suffering by famine, and found it necessary to cross the Wisconsin into the timber country north of that stream, for subsistence. Probably there is not a known instance where attachment to a cause and to a leader has continued under circum-stances of such discouragement. They were encumbered with women and children, and had been so closely watched for two months, that little opportunity occurred to fish or hunt. They had lived upon roots, boiled grass, bark of trees, anything capable of sustaining life, before they would kill the horses upon which the squaws and papooses rode. They were now reduced to a state of utter starvation with thirty miles of country to be traversed, and the whites had discovered their camp-fires the night previous across a small lake. If they could cross the Wisconsin before an attack was made, the fish of the stream would furnish them a meal, and the river itself a protection. The militia were in motion at day-light, and within a few miles of the forlorn band. Along the trail lay the bodies of famished men, women and children; some dead, others helpless and exhausted to the last degree by fatigue and hunger. These wretched and worn-out creatures, if still living, were bayonetted upon the spot. The exasperated frontiersman now finding his victim within reach, imbibed the ferocity of his enemy, dealing instant death to every one that fell in his power. In fact, early in the season, Gen. Atkinson had found it necessary to place a guard over his Indian prisoners, in order to save their lives.

An instance is known of a decrepit old man, to whom a loaf of bread had been given, and he suffered to depart. He had not passed out of hearing, when he was dispatched by the bayonet, and his food distributed among the murderers. At a fight near the Mississippi, just previous to the final action at the Bad Axe, a fine young chief about fourteen years of age, was taken, with silver bracelets on his arm. The militia-man who captured him was only prevented from butchering him on the spot, by a threat from a lieutenant of the regular service, that his own life should instantly answer for that of the prisoner.

Document 48
1832   Massacre   Bad Axe, Wisconsin

Source: Reuben Gold Thwaites, "The Story of the Black Hawk War," **Collections of the State Historical Society of Wisconsin** (Madison: Democrat Printing Company, 1892), vol. XII, pp. 259-261.

Atkinson's men were on the move by two o'clock in the morning of August 2. When within four or five miles of the Sac position, the decoys were encountered. The density of the timber obstructing the view, and the twenty braves being widely separated, it was supposed that Black Hawk's main force had been overtaken. The army ac-cordingly spread itself for the attack, Alexander and Posey forming the right wing, Henry the left, and Dodge and the regulars the center. When the savage decoys retreated up the river, as directed by the chief, the white center and right wing followed quickly, leaving the left wing—with the exception of one of its regiments detailed to cover the rear—without orders. This was clearly an affront to Henry, Atkinson's design doubtless being to crowd him out of what all anticipated would be the closing engagement of the campaign, and what little glory might come of it.

But the fates did not desert the brigadier. Some of Ewing's spies, attached to his command, accidentally discovered that the main trail of the fugitive band was lower down the river than where the decoys were leading the army. Henry, with his entire force, thereupon de-scended a bluff in the immediate neighborhood, and after a gallant charge on foot through the open wooded plateau between the base of the bluff and the shore, found himself in the midst of the main body of three hundred warriors, which was about the number of the attacking party. A desperate conflict ensued, the bucks being driven from tree to tree at the point of the bayonet, while women and children plunged madly into the river, many of them to immediately drown. The air was rent with savage yells and whoops, with the loud cries of the troopers as they cheered each other on, and with the shrill notes of the bugle directing the details of the attack.

It was fully half an hour after Henry made his descent, when Atkinson, hearing the din of battle in his rear, came hastening to the scene with the center and right wing, driving in the decoys and stragglers before him, thus completing the corral. The carnage now proceeded more fiercely than ever. The red men fought with intense desperation, and, though weak from hunger, died like braves. A few escaped through a broad slough to a willow island, which the steamer "Warrior," now re-appearing on the river, raked from end to end with canister. This was followed by a wild dash through the mud and water, by a detachment of regulars, and a few of Henry's and Dodge's volunteers, who ended the business by sweeping the island with a bayonet charge. Some of the fugitives succeeded in swimming to the west bank of the Mississippi, but many were drowned on the way, or coolly picked off by sharpshooters, who exercised no more mercy towards squaws and children than they did towards braves—treating them all as though they were rats instead of human beings.

This "battle," or massacre, lasted three hours. It was a veritable pandemonium, filled with frightful scenes of bloodshed. The Indians lost one hundred and fifty killed outright, while as many more of both sexes and all ages and conditions were drowned—some fifty only being taken prisoners, and they mostly women and children. About three hundred of the band crossed the river successfully, before and during the struggle. The whites lost but seventeen killed and twelve wounded.

Those of the Sacs who safely regained the west bank were soon set upon by a party of one hundred Sioux, under Wabasha, sent out for that purpose by General Atkinson, and one-half of these helpless, half-starved non-combatants were cruelly slaughtered, while many others died of exhaustion and wounds before they reached those of their friends who had been wise enough to abide by Keokuk's peaceful admonitions and stay at home. Thus, out of the band of nearly one thousand persons who crossed the Mississippi at the Yellow Banks, in April, not more than one hundred and fifty, all told, lived to tell the tragic story of the Black Hawk War—a tale fraught with dishonor to the American name.

Document 49
1832   Razor Straps   Wisconsin

Source: John H. Fonda, "Early Wisconsin," **Collections of the State Historical Society of Wisconsin** (Madison: Published by the Society, 1907), p. 263.

One incident occurred during the battle that came under my observation, which I must not omit to relate. An old Indian brave and his five sons, all of whom I had seen on the Prairie and knew, had taken a stand behind a prostrate log, in a little ravine mid-way up the bluff; from whence they fired on the regulars with deadly aim. The old man loaded the guns as fast as his sons discharged them, and at each shot a man fell. They knew they could not expect quarter, and they sold their lives as dear as possible; making the best show of fight, and held their ground the firmest of any of the Indians. But, they could never withstand the men under Dodge, for as the volunteers poured over the bluff, they each shot a man, and in return, each of the braves was shot down and scalped by the wild volunteers, who out with their knives and cutting two parallel gashes down their backs, would strip the skin from the quivering flesh, to make razor straps of. In this manner I saw the old brave and his five sons treated, and afterward had a piece of their hide.

Document 50
1838   Vandalizing of Grave   Iowa

Source: Perry A. Armstrong, **The Sauks and the Black Hawk War** (Springfield: H. W. Rokker, 1887), pp. 539-540.

About the 17th of September, 1838, accompanied by the head men and chiefs of his little band, who, despite all efforts of Keokuk and the United States Government to force them to abandon Black Hawk and recognize Keokuk as their head chief, still adhered to him, he started from his quiet home in Iowa for Rock Island to receive the annuity under the so-called treaty of Fort Armstrong, of September 21, 1832.

He had gone but a short distance, however, ere he was taken quite ill, and an immediate return to his cabin home on the northeast quarter section 2, township 70, range 12, Davis county, Iowa, followed. Here his tired spirit lingered upon the boundary line between the known and the unknown, doubting which path to take, until the 3d of October, when he heard the loved voice of Piasa, his father, from the unknown territory beyond the river, saying: "Black Hawk, your earthly path is ended; come away." Then, with a calm reliance upon, and a fixed faith in the Great Sowana, his wearied spirit fluttered across the line at the age of seventy-one years.

He was buried near his cabin in a full military uniform presented him by the cabinet of President Jackson, in 1833. In his military cap was his totem—a bunch of the tail feathers of the black sparrow-hawk. His body sat upon a board sunk some fifteen inches below the earth's surface, and the earth was then filled in again. His entire bust was therefore left erect above ground. Puncheons were then placed over him so as to form a wooden cone some four feet high, which was sodded over with blue grass. At the head of his grave stood his flag-staff, some thirty feet in height, bearing a silken flag, emblazoned with the stars and stripes. Indian-like, he was always partial to jewelry and ornamentation, and for that purpose his ears were perforated in several places for rings, while he also wore a large silver crescent in his nose, until by some accident the septum was torn, leaving a ragged little piece protruding down about the eighth of an inch.

He had been presented with three medals, one by President Jackson, one by ex-President John Quincy Adams, and the other by the city of Boston, which were suspended around his neck in his conical tomb. Gen. Jackson had given him a sword, and Henry Clay and the English General, Dixon, had each given him an elegant cane. These were buried with him, the canes on his right, the sword on his left side. Here would we fain leave him sweetly slumbering on the north bank of the lovely Des Moines, whose softly rippling waters kept a requiem for the dead; but vandal hands spoiled the scene.... a certain Dr. Turner, of Lexington, Iowa, visited this solitary grave, July 4, 1839, and robbed it of its tenant, sword, canes, medals and jewelry, and sent the body to Alton, Ill., where the skeleton was wired together. From there it was sent to Warsaw, Ill. On discovering that their father's grave had been robbed of its tenant his sons were nearly frantic and demanded the return of the body. Gov. Lucas, of Iowa, took immediate measures for its discovery and return, which were successful, and the body was delivered to his sons in the early part of 1840, who restored it to its conical tomb again. But here it remained but a short time ere vandal hands again carried it away and placed it in the Burlington, Iowa, Geographical and Historical Society, where it was consumed by fire in 1855, with the entire collection of the Society. A slight punishment for so great a crime against humanity.

August 19, 1837 — Cattaraugus Reservation, New York
Contract for Fraud

At the close of the War for Independence, New York settled Massachusett's patent claims to a portion of her territory and obtained cession of the land by agreeing to give the grantees then holding the claims and their heirs and assigns the preemptive right to Indian land in the disputed section. A preemptive right in this instance meant the privilege of the private persons or companies holding it to buy Indian land if the Indians chose to sell. In 1794 and 1802 the United States government stipulated by treaty that the land would be Indian "forever." With the Erie Canal through central New York, steamboats on the Great Lakes, factories along inland waters, and the influx of immigrants, the fertile Indian lands bordering major cities and canals were increasing in value by millions of dollars. By the 1830s the Ogden Land Company possessed the preemptive rights to 116,000 acres of Seneca land and had decided to acquire it by any means possible. In the previous decade the company had successfully removed the Oneida, Stockbridge, and Brotherton groups to Wisconsin and had preempted their land. This complex, earlier scheme had involved federal

authorities and treaties with several tribes, including the Seneca who possessed some minor residual claims to additional Wisconsin land. In 1837 the federal government, at the behest of the Ogden Land Company and its political friends, called a council with the Seneca to purchase their interest in Wisconsin. The council was secretly contrived, however, to remove the Seneca from their New York reservations to the distant Indian territory, and a treaty was drawn up to this effect. To make the treaty binding on the tricked tribe, a majority of the Seneca chiefs had to sign the treaty. The Ogden Land Company proceeded to acquire the necessary signatures by force, fraud, bribery, and intimidation. The following is a contract between Heman Potter, an Ogden Land Company attorney, and Levi Halftown, a Seneca chief, in which Potter promises Halftown money for his aid if the Seneca are removed (document 51). Potter, a member of a New

HYMN 8 / TEYERIHWAHKWATHA

How sad our state by nature is!
  Our sin, how deep it stains!
And Satan binds our captive souls
  Fast in his slavish chains.

Yo ni gonh raks hat ji tyon he
  Yon gwa rib wa ne ren;
Shon gwa ne renks non gwe rya ne,
  Ne o neh shonh ro non.

But there's a voice of sovereign grace,
  Sounds from the sacred word:
"Ho, ye despairing sinners, come
  And trust upon the Lord!"

Eh on de wea na yenh tah kwe,
  Ji non ka kah ya ton:
O se wah rih wa ne ren kats!
  Ren ten ras ne Ni yoh.

My soul obeys the' Almighty's call,
  And runs to this relief:
I would believe thy promise, Lord;
  O help my unbelief!

A gwa don hets on thon da te,
  Eh non ka n'yen hen ge;
T'wa geh tah kon sa rih wis son,
  To genh ske a gen hak.

To the blest fountain of thy blood,
  Incarnate God, I fly:
Here let me wash my spotted soul
  From sins of deepest dye.

Sa ne gwenh sa tyob na we rot,
  Ok sha eh yenk tak he;
Eh non weh en ge no ha re,
  Ji ni wa gen hih ton.

A guilty, weak, and helpless worm,
  Into thy hands I fall;
Be thou my strength and righteousness,
  My Saviour, and my all.

O nya re ji ni gya to denh,
  O to gye na Ni yoh!
I se ta ge shats tenh se ron,
  Sa ya ner a gwe gon.

York State family prominent in land speculation and politics, negotiated many contracts. The 1837 treaty was fought in court by a number of Seneca with the aid of the Society of Friends, but the Supreme Court upheld the validity of the treaty, even though acknowledging it had been gained by fraud and bribery.

Document 51
1837   Contract for Fraud   New York

Source: **The Case of the Seneca Indians in the State of New York. Illustrated by Facts. Printed for the Information of the Society of Friends** . . . (Philadelphia: Merrihew and Thompson, 1840), p. 193.

It is agreed between Heman B. Potter, of Buffalo, of the first part, and Levi Halftown, a Seneca chief of the Cattaraugus reservation, of the second part, as follows:

That if the Seneca Indians shall accept of the offers of the Government of the United States, and remove to the west, and shall sell out their reservations to the preemption owners upon negotiations now pending, and if the said Levi Halftown shall faithfully render his aid, services, and influence in favor of a treaty for the purposes aforesaid, and if such treaty shall be made and ratified by the Senate of the United States, by which the right and title of said Indians shall be effectually abandoned, then, and in that case, the said Heman B. Potter stipulates and agrees, for himself and his associates, that the sum of five hundred dollars shall be paid to the said Levi Halftown in three months after notice of such ratification, and that he shall be entitled to a lease from the said pre-emption owners, or their trustees, for, and during his natural life, of the lot or piece of land where he now lives, on the said Cattaraugus reservation, being about sixty acres, to terminate whenever he shall cease to live on and occupy the same: said lease to be executed as soon as said lands shall have been surveyed into lots, so that said piece of land may or can be described according to the survey.

Witness our hands and seals this 19th day of August, 1837.

H. B. Potter,   [L. S.]
his
LEVI x HALFTOWN, [L. S.]
mark.

Witness—O. ALLEN.

October 27, 1846   Tonawanda Reservation, New York
Result of Fraud

Schemes masterminded in New York affected the lives of Indians in Kansas. Businessmen, who gained enormous wealth from the treaties and whose personal lives were otherwise exemplary, denied as preposterous any responsibility for the deaths of scores of Seneca on the arid Kansas plains. They are not exculpated merely because they utilized third parties to corrupt chiefs and bribe federal officials, or because they left the shattered tribe to the whim of fortune. A letter from the full blood, Levi Parker of New York's Tonawanda band of Seneca, to his brother, Spencer Cone in Kansas, reveals the depth of the tribe's

tragedy (document 52). The brother had collaborated with the land speculators and migrated to Kansas with several score of Seneca. The Parkers (a remarkable family that included Ely S. Parker, who became a Union Army general, and later Commissioner of Indian Affairs under President Grant) had disowned Spencer and required him to change his name to Cone.

Document 52
1846   Result of Fraud   New York

Source: Letter from Levi Parker to Spencer H. Cone, October 27, 1846. Parker Manuscript, American Philosophical Society, Philadelphia. Courtesy of the American Philosophical Society.

Ther is nothing stiring here at presant abot the Law we shall stick to the last minuit, if we can, because we do not want to go to the west. yo say they that have moved their this spring die of fast. and if we should go to we would die it must be mean country i told father he would feel bad after he found out how the country was their. if we look the Law we shall not go their, i should like to go their and see the country but i am so poor i never shall come their, it is an outragious thing for the indians to be driven from their homes and go to the new country if the white will keep driving us from our home we will all die and who will mourn to us their will be not one—

December, 1837   Fort Mellon, Florida
Violation of Truce

The American Indian people reacted in various ways to the removal policies of the United States. The Choctaw actively collaborated, the Seneca sought legal redress, the Potawatomi tried passive resistance, and the Seminole resorted to arms and waged a fierce war. But all were removed and all, regardless of their reaction, suffered high death rates. The Seminole War that began in 1835 and lasted until 1845 required massive deployment of federal and local forces against Indian retreat into the swamps. By 1837 many American citizens, deeply hating the Seminole for the American failure to root out three thousand resisting Indians, encouraged their elected officials to improvise new methods of fighting them. Old methods—bribery, scorched earth and starvation, and open battle—had failed.

The commander of American forces in Florida, General Winfield Scott, suggested that the War Department use a bounty system "for every captured Indian warrior, $500, for every such warrior slain in battle or pursuit, $400." The War Department refused to consider the plan. Some Florida land speculators suggested extermination. The government authorized the use of bloodhounds to track the Indians in the jungles, but the dogs could not be trained properly and were soon discarded. One successful method was to arrange peace councils under a flag of truce and then seize and imprison the Indians. When the Indians grew wary of this tactic, the army resorted to luring chiefs back to the negotiating table. Neutral Indians were solicited to penetrate the swamps, gain Seminole confidence, explain the futility of war, and suggest a meeting at the truce tent, where Americans would betray both Indian groups and seize the Seminole. It was necessary first to deceive by fraud and lies the Indian group employed for making contact with the Seminole. A letter from Cherokee Chief John Ross to Joel Poinsett, Secretary of War, protested this act perpetrated with an unsuspecting Cherokee delegation as the decoy (document 53). Previously the United States, refusing to recognize the main Cherokee nation headed by John Ross, was content in using a small tribal faction, who were bribed to follow American dictates and did not represent tribal opinion. The American request for assistance marked the first recognition of the legitimate Cherokee nation and benefited them in their resistance to removal. The Cherokee also had experienced the power of the United States government and knew how ruthlessly it could be used; they thought a delegation to Florida would assist a distressed brother tribe.

Document 53
1837   Violation of Truce   Florida

Source: U.S. Congress. House. **Indian Prisoners of War.** H. Doc. 327, 25th Cong., 2d sess., pp. 12-14.

WASHINGTON CITY, *January* 2, 1838.

SIR: You have doubtless been informed, through Colonel John H. Sherburne, of the arrival in this city, on the evening of the 30th ultimo, of the Cherokee deputation who were charged with the duty of endeavoring to restore peace between the Seminole Indians and the United States, in the character of mediators. This deputation penetrated the deep swamps and hammocks of Florida, under the escort of Coahachee, one of the captive chiefs; and at Chickasawhatchie, (Chickasaw creek), a distance of sixty miles from Fort Mellon, they met the Seminole and Mickasuky chiefs and warriors in council, and there delivered to them the talk which I, with your approbation, had sent them. After reading and fully explaining its import through the interpreter, the assembled chiefs and warriors at once agreed to receive it in friendship, as coming through their red brethren the Cherokees, with the utmost sincerity and good feelings, from their elder brother the Secretary of War, who represents their father, the President of the United States. When the usual Indian ceremonies on this occasion, in smoking the pipe of peace, &c., were concluded, Micanopy, the principal chief, with twelve

others of his chieftains, and a number of their warriors, agreed to accompany the Cherokee deputation, and accordingly went with them, under a flag of truce, into the headquarters of the United States army, at Fort Mellon. After this successful meeting, further steps were taken for inviting all the people to go in; and whilst some were coming in, the escape of Wild-cat from the fort at St. Augustine, and other events altogether beyond the control of the Cherokee deputation, produced a sudden and unexpected distrust and change of determination in the minds of the chiefs and warriors of the nation who were still out in their fastnesses. Upon being informed of this fact, it is reported that General Jesup immediately ordered his troops to be put in motion for hostile operations, and also caused all the chiefs and warriors who had come in under the Cherokee flag to be forthwith made prisoners of war; they were then placed in the hold of a steamboat, and shipped to the fort at St. Augustine, and there imprisoned. It is further reported that General Jesup told some of these chiefs that, for the first drop of blood which might be spilt by the warriors against whom he had marched his troops in battle array, they (the captive chiefs) shall be hanged. Under this extraordinary state of the affair, it has become my imperious though painful duty, for the defence of my own reputation, as well as that of the deputation who acted under my instructions, for carrying out the humane objects of this mediation; also, in justice to the suffering chiefs and warriors, whose confidence in the purity of our motives, as well as in the sincerity of the Government, by the assurances held out to them under your authority in my talk, had thus placed themselves under the flag of truce before the American army, and I do hereby, most solemnly protest against this unprecedented violation of that sacred rule which has ever been recognised by every nation, civilized and uncivilized, of treating with all due respect those who had ever presented themselves under a flag of truce before their enemy, for the purpose of proposing the termination of a warfare. Moreover, I respectfully appeal to and submit for your decision, whether justice and policy do not require at your hands that these captives should be forthwith liberated, that they may go and confer with their people, and that whatever obstacles may have been thrown in the way of their coming in to make peace may be removed. In a word, under all the circumstances of the case, so far as the particular captives alluded to are concerned, I feel myself called upon, by every sense of justice and honor, to ask that they may be released and placed at liberty, to determine with their people what to do under all the circumstances of their affairs, as freely and untrammelled as they were previous to the council held with them by the Cherokee mediation, as it was through the influence of the Cherokee talk they had consented to go under the flag of truce into General Jesup's headquarters. The detailed report of the deputation of their proceedings on this mission not having as yet been fully made out, I have deemed it important to present the facts herein briefly stated without delay; and should it be deemed necessary, or you shall desire it, I will communicate to you the full report of the deputation as soon as it may be in readiness.

I have the honor to be, sir, your obedient, humble servant,

JOHN ROSS.

HON. JOEL R. POINSETT,
Secretary of War.

1838-1839   Trail of Tears   Tennessee

In the midst of the depression of 1837-1840, the United States Army removed fifteen thousand Cherokee from their ancient homeland in the eastern Tennessee mountains along a "trail of tears" through Kentucky, Illinois, and Missouri to Indian Territory—the most notorious white atrocity against the Indian people (document 54). The grisly tale of suffering and deaths is also remembered for the valiant resistance in the courts by the Cherokee, who ultimately won a victory in the Supreme Court—only to have it reversed by presidential fiat when Andrew Jackson ordered them removed. A dominant school of historians believes that American federal and local governments were incapable of solving the rights of a distinct racial group desiring their own political institutions. They think that the Cherokee who deigned to occupy a beautiful and rich land, administered by Cherokee law and institutions, aroused such intense hatred in the white community that any other decision would have erupted in a race war. Jackson, it is argued, had no choice if the Indians were to survive. This does not mitigate the atrocities levied by federal and local authorities against a small, civilized republic of Cherokee people. The account given below is by the noted white anthropologist, James Mooney, who interviewed many of the participants, white and Indian. Mooney received the account of Tsali's execution by regular army officers from his surviving son, Wasituna (Washington).

Further reading: Dale Van Every, *Disinherited* (New York: William Morrow & Co., 1966).

Document 54
1838-1839   Trail of Tears   Tennessee

Source: James Mooney, **Myths of the Cherokee** in **Nineteenth Annual Report of the Bureau of American Ethnology to the Secretary of the Smithsonian Institution, 1897-1898** (2 parts, Washington: Government Printing Office, 1900), part 1, pp. 130-133.

The history of this Cherokee removal of 1838, as gleaned by the author from the lips of actors in the tragedy, may well exceed in weight of grief and pathos any other passage in American history. Even the much-sung exile of the Acadians falls far behind it in its sum of death and misery. Under Scott's orders the troops were disposed at various points throughout the Cherokee country, where stockade forts were erected for gathering in and holding the Indians preparatory to removal. From these, squads of troops were sent to search out with rifle and bayonet every small cabin hidden away in the coves or by the sides of mountain streams, to seize and bring in as prisoners all the occupants, however or wherever they might be found. Families at dinner were startled by the sudden gleam of bayonets in the doorway and rose up to be driven with blows and oaths along the weary miles of trail that led to the stockade. Men were seized in their fields or going along the road, women were taken from their wheels and children from their play. In many cases, on turning for one last look as they crossed the ridge, they saw their homes in flames, fired by the lawless rabble that followed on the heels of the soldiers to loot and pillage. So keen were these outlaws on the scent that in some instances they were driving off the cattle and other stock of the Indians almost before the soldiers had fairly started their owners in the other direction. Systematic hunts were made by the same men for Indian graves, to rob them of the silver pendants and other valuables deposited with the dead. A Georgia volunteer, afterward a colonel in the Confederate service, said: "I fought through the civil war and have seen men shot to pieces and slaughtered by thousands, but the Cherokee removal was the cruelest work I ever knew."

To present escape the soldiers had been ordered to approach and surround each house, so far as possible, so as to come upon the occupants without warning. One old patriarch, when thus surprised, calmly called his children and grandchildren around him, and, kneeling down, bid them pray with him in their own language, while the astonished soldiers looked on in silence. Then rising he led the way into exile. A woman, on finding the house surrounded, went to the door and called up the chickens to be fed for the last time, after which, taking her infant on her back and her two other children by the hand, she followed her husband with the soldiers.

All were not thus submissive. One old man named Tsali, "Charley," was seized with his wife, his brother, his three sons and their families. Exasperated at the brutality accorded his wife, who, being unable to travel fast, was prodded with bayonets to hasten her steps, he urged the other men to join with him in a dash for liberty. As he spoke in Cherokee the soldiers, although they heard, understood nothing until each warrior suddenly sprang upon the one nearest and endeavored to wrench his gun from him. The attack was so sudden and unexpected that one soldier was killed and the rest fled, while the Indians escaped to the mountains. Hundreds of others, some of

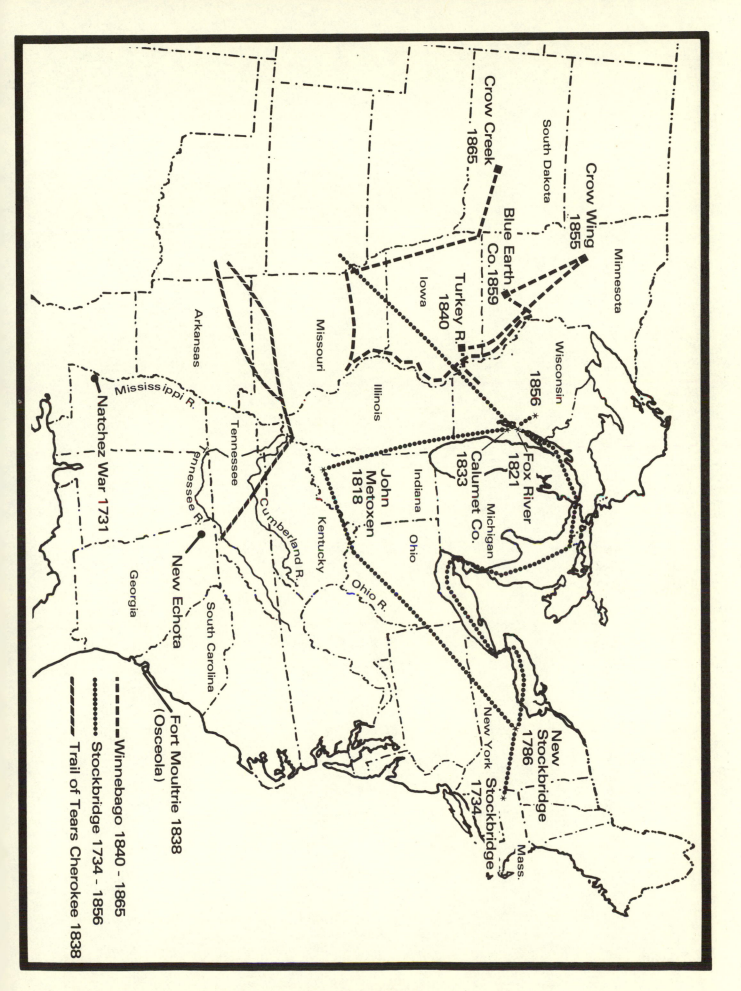

Removals 19th Century

them from the various stockades, managed also to escape to the mountains from time to time, where those who did not die of starvation subsisted on roots and wild berries until the hunt was over. Finding it impracticable to secure these fugitives, General Scott finally tendered them a proposition, through (Colonel) W. H. Thomas, their most trusted friend, that if they would surrender Charley and his party for punishment, the rest would be allowed to remain until their case could be adjusted by the government. On hearing of the proposition, Charley voluntarily came in with his sons, offering himself as a sacrifice for his people. By command of General Scott, Charley, his brother, and two elder sons were shot near the mouth of Tuckasegee, a detachment of Cherokee prisoners being compelled to do the shooting in order to impress upon the Indians the fact of their utter helplessness. From those fugitives thus permitted to remain originated the present eastern band of Cherokee.

When nearly seventeen thousand Cherokee had thus been gathered into the various stockades the work of removal began. Early in June several parties, aggregating about five thousand persons, were brought down by the troops to the old agency, on Hiwassee, at the present Calhoun, Tennessee, and to Ross's landing (now Chattanooga), and Gunter's landing (now Guntersville, Alabama), lower down on the Tennessee, where they were put upon steamers and transported down the Tennessee and Ohio to the farther side of the Mississippi, when the journey was continued by land to Indian Territory. This removal, in the hottest part of the year, was attended with so great sickness and mortality that, by resolution of the Cherokee national council, Ross and the other chiefs submitted to General Scott a proposition that the Cherokee be allowed to remove themselves in the fall, after the sickly season had ended. This was granted on condition that all should have started by the 20th of October, excepting the sick and aged who might not be able to move so rapidly. Accordingly, officers were appointed by the Cherokee council to take charge of the emigration; the Indians being organized into detachments averaging one thousand each, with two leaders in charge of each detachment, and a sufficient number of wagons and horses for the purpose. In this way the remainder, enrolled at about 13,000 (including negro slaves), started on the long march overland late in the fall.

Those who thus emigrated under the management of their own officers assembled at Rattlesnake springs, about two miles south of Hiwassee river, near the present Charleston, Tennessee, where a final council was held, in which it was decided to continue their old constitution and laws in their new home. Then, in October, 1838, the long procession of exiles was set in motion. A very few went by the river route; the rest, nearly all of the 13,000, went overland. Crossing to the north side of the Hiwassee at a ferry above Gunstocker creek, they proceeded down along the river, the sick, the old people, and the smaller children, with the blankets, cooking pots, and other be-longings in wagons, the rest on foot or on horses. The number of wagons was 645.

It was like the march of an army, regiment after regiment, the wagons in the center, the officers along the line and the horsemen on the flanks and at the rear. Tennessee river was crossed at Tuckers(?) ferry, a short distance above Jollys island, at the mouth of Hiwassee. Thence the route lay south of Pikeville, through McMinnville and on to Nashville, where the Cumberland was crossed. Then they went on to Hopkinsville, Kentucky, where the noted chief White-path, in charge of a detachment, sickened and died. His people buried him by the roadside, with a box over the grave and poles with streamers around it, that the others coming on behind might note the spot and remember him. Somewhere also along that march of death—for the exiles died by tens and twenties every day of the journey—the devoted wife of John Ross sank down, leaving him to go on with the bitter pain of bereavement added to heartbreak at the ruin of his nation. The Ohio was crossed at a ferry near the mouth of the Cumberland, and the army passed on through southern Illinois until the great Mississippi was reached opposite Cape Girardeau, Missouri. It was now the middle of winter, with the river running full of ice, so that several detachments were obliged to wait some time on the eastern bank for the channel to become clear. In talking with old men and women at Tahlequah the author found that the lapse of over half a century had not sufficed to wipe out the memory of the miseries of that halt beside the frozen river, with hundreds of sick and dying penned up in wagons or stretched upon the ground, with only a blanket overhead to keep out the January blast. The crossing was made at last in two divisions, at Cape Girardeau and at Green's ferry, a short distance below, whence the march was on through Missouri to Indian Territory, the later detachments making a northerly circuit by Springfield because those who had gone before had killed off all the game along the direct route. At last their destination was reached. They had started in October, 1838, and it was now March, 1839, the journey having occupied nearly six months of the hardest part of the year.

It is difficult to arrive at any accurate statement of the number of Cherokee who died as the result of the Removal. According to the official figures those who removed under the direction of Ross lost over 1,600 on the journey. The proportionate mortality among those previously removed under military supervision was probably greater, as it was their suffering that led to the proposition of the Cherokee national officers to take charge of the emigration. Hundreds died in the stockades and the waiting camps, chiefly by reason of the rations furnished, which were of flour and other provisions to which they were unaccustomed and which they did not know how to prepare properly. Hundreds of others died soon after their arrival in Indian territory, from sickness and exposure on the journey. Altogether it is asserted, probably with reason, that over 4,000 Cherokee died as the direct result of the removal.

January 30, 1838   Fort Moultrie, South Carolina
Osceola's Head

On October 18, 1837, the Seminole war chief Osceola answered General Thomas Jesup's request for a council and, with several leading members of his band, met the Americans under a flag of truce to discuss an end to the hostilities. Jesup surreptitiously encircled the meeting with American soldiers, seized the Seminole, clapped them in prison cells at Fort Moultrie, and began to arrange for their transportation west to Indian Territory. Osceola was suffering from an unknown illness and in captivity continued to grow worse. He died on January 30, 1838. The following account of the preparation of the corpse for burial by the fort physician, Dr. Frederick Weedon, is related by his great-granddaughter and is based on family records (document 55).

Document 55
1838   Osceola's Head   South Carolina

Source: May McNeer Ward, "The Disappearance of the Head of Osceola," **The Florida Historical Quarterly**, vol. XXXIII, nos. 3 and 4 (January-April, 1955); pp. 198-199.

This is the true story of the disappearance of Osceola's head, as given to us by our grandfather. After the death of the Seminole chief, Dr. Weedon was able to be alone with the body. During this time he cut off the head, but left it in the coffin with the scarf that Osceola habitually wore tied as usual around the neck. Not long before the funeral Dr. Weedon removed the head and closed the coffin. Thus, the body was not dug up after burial and the head taken by unknown vandals, as various accounts have stated. Osceola was buried without his head.

Dr. Weedon took the head back to St. Augustine with him, and kept it in his home on Bridge Street, where he also had his office, preserved by an embalming method that he had worked out himself.

Why did he do this? It is hard to know his motives, for we are so far removed by time from the events and the way of thinking of those days. However, doctors then thought nothing of collecting heads of savage tribesmen. Medical museums had collections of heads brought in by sailors from South America, Africa and the South Seas. Phrenology was considered important, for the shape of the skull was thought by scientists to show intelligence as well as talents and aptitudes. Dr. Weedon was an unusual man, and his methods of child training would not find favor today, for he used to hang the head of Osceola on the

bedstead where his three little boys slept, and leave it there all night as punishment for misbehavior.

His daughter Henrietta married a physician, Dr. Daniel Whitehurst, of New York. Dr. Weedon gave the head to his son-in-law five years after the death of Osceola, and Dr. Whitehurst presented it, in 1843, to the most distinguished surgeon of his day, Dr. Valentine Mott. Dr. Mott had been the teacher of Dr. Whitehurst, and was one of the founders of New York University Medical School, as well as of the New York Academy of Medicine.

August 1846   Southwestern Border
Professional Indian Hunters

In the early 1840s, Americans entered the scalp-bounty business of the northern Mexican states, exterminating the Apache and Comanche who plundered Mexico from the mountains of present-day New Mexico and Arizona.

Tzi-kal-tza (referred to himself as "Me Clark"), a Nez Perce, son of one of the members of the Lewis and Clark Expedition.

Organized into companies led by a captain, they hunted for Indians and earned a living from the bounty money paid on scalps from either sex. The profession included a Mexican (Juan N. Armendariz), a Seminole (Coacoochee), a Shawnee (Spybuck), and blacks under the leadership of John Horse. But the top profit makers worked under American leaders with a reputation for ferocity, such as J. J. Glanton, J. Kirker, M. J. Box, and J. Dusenberry. The prices paid on scalps varied with the Mexican state and the particular governor, but a hundred and fifty dollars for warriors' scalps and a hundred dollars for women's and children's scalps were not unusual. There was also a trade in Europe and on the east coast of the United States, where some scalps sold as curios. Thousands of Indians perished under the sustained attack of these killers. When the reduced numbers of the Indians forced the scalp hunters to murder Mexican citizens to maintain profits, the outraged Mexican governments halted the use of foreigners.

The following is an account of an American scalp-hunting team led by James Kirker, told by the English traveler, George Frederick Ruxton, in *Adventures in Mexico and the Rocky Mountains* (1848) (document 56). James Kirker was perhaps the most infamous white man engaged in the scalp business. By his hand he murdered hundreds, and under his command several score of professionals murdered hundreds of men, women, and children for the money their scalps would bring.

Further reading: Ray Brandes, "Don Santiago Kirker, King of the Scalp Hunters," *The Smoke Signal* (Fall, 1962), pp. 2-8.

Document 56
1846   Southwestern Border
Professional Indian Hunters

Source: LeRoy R. Hafen, editor, **Ruxton of the Rockies** (Norman: University of Oklahoma Press, 1950), pp. 146-149. Copyright 1950 by the University of Oklahoma Press.

Chihuahua, the capital city of the state or department of that name, was built towards the close of the seventeenth century, and therefore cannot boast of such antiquity even as the more remote city of Santa Fé. Its population is between eight and ten thousand permanent inhabitants, although it is the resort of many strangers from New Mexico, California, and Sonora. The cathedral, which is considered by the American traders one of the finest structures in the world, is a large building in no style of architecture, but with rather a handsome façade, embellished with statues of the twelve apostles.

Opposite the principal entrance, over the portals which form one side of the square, were dangling the grim scalps of one hundred and seventy Apaches, who had lately been most treacherously and inhumanly butchered by the Indian hunters in the pay of the state. The scalps of men, women, and children, were brought into the town in procession, and hung as trophies, in this conspicuous situation, of Mexican valour and humanity!

. . .

For the purpose of carrying on a war against the daring savages, a species of company was formed by the Chihuahueños, with a capital raised by subscription. This company, under the auspices of the government, offered a bounty of fifty dollars a scalp, as an inducement to people to undertake a war of extermination against the Apaches. One Don Santiago Kirker, an Irishman, long resident in Mexico, and for many years a trapper and Indian trader in the Far West, whose exploits in Indian killing would fill a volume, was placed at the head of a band of some hundred and fifty men, including several Shawnee and Delaware Indians, and sent *en campaña* against the Apaches. The fruits of the campaign were the trophies I saw dangling in front of the cathedral.

In the month of August, the Apaches being then *en paz* with the state, entered, unarmed, the village of Galeana, for the purpose of trading. This band, which consisted of a hundred and seventy, including women and children, was under the command of a celebrated chief, and had no doubt committed many atrocities on the Mexicans; but at this time they had signified their desire for peace to the government of Chihuahua, and were now trading in good faith, and under protection of the faith of treaty. News of their arrival having been sent to Kirker, he immediately forwarded several kegs of spirits, with which they were to be regaled, and detained in the village until he could arrive with his band. On a certain day, about ten in the morning, the Indians being at the time drinking, dancing, and amusing themselves, and *unarmed*, Kirker sent forward a messenger to say that at such an hour he would be there.

The Mexicans, when they saw him approach with his party, suddenly seized their arms and set upon the unfortunate Indians, who, without even their knives, attempted no resistance, but, throwing themselves on the ground when they saw Kirker's men surrounding them, submitted to their fate. The infuriated Mexicans spared neither age nor sex; with fiendish shouts they massacred their unresisting victims, glutting their long pent-up revenge of many years of persecution. One woman, big with child, rushed into the church, clasping the alter and crying for mercy for herself and unborn babe. She was followed, and fell pierced with a dozen lances; and then—it is almost impossible to conceive such an atrocity, but I had it from an eyewitness on the spot not two months after the tragedy—the child was torn alive from the yet palpitating body of its mother, first plunged into the holy water to be baptized, and immediately its brains were dashed out against a wall.

A hundred and sixty men, women, and children were slaughtered, and, with the scalps carried on poles, Kirker's party entered Chihuahua—in procession, headed by the Governor and priests, with bands of music escorting them in triumph to the town.

Nor is this a solitary instance of similar barbarity, for on two previous occasions parties of American traders and trappers perpetrated most treacherous atrocities on tribes of the same nation on the river Gila. The Indians, on their part, equal their more civilised enemies in barbarity; and such is the war of extermination carried on between the Mexicans and Apaches.

1850   Clear Lake Massacre   California

During 1849, Pomo Indians who were held as slaves by two white men named Stone and Kelsey killed their cruel and sadistic rulers and fled to an island in Clear Lake. About a year later white men discovered the location of these essentially pacifistic people and launched a "war" against their village. They first surrounded the island in boats, then landed and methodically killed all the Indians they could.

William Ralganal Benson, a self-educated Pomo chief born in 1862, was known among anthropologists for his honesty and reliability. He related an Indian perspective on the white atrocity that he had received from members of his tribe who survived the attack (document 57). The general accuracy of Benson's account is sustained by several white versions. If anything, he omits many of the savage aspects of the white attack. The term *tuley*, appearing within the text, refers to the thick water grass around the island's edge.

Document 57
1850   Clear Lake Massacre   California

Source: "William Ralganal Benson's Narrative" in Max Radin, "The Stone and Kelsey 'Massacre' on the Shores of Clear Lake in 1849," **California Historical Society Quarterly** (September, 1932), vol. XI, pp. 271-273.

One day the lake watchers saw a boat came around the point.som news coming.they said to each others.two of the men went to the landing.to see what the news were. they were told that the white warriors had come to kill all the indians around the lake.so hide the best you can.the whites are making boats and with that they are coming up the lake.so we are told by the people down there.so they had two men go up on top of uncle sam mountain. the north peak.from there they watch the lower lake.for three days they watch the lake. one morning they saw a long boat came up the lake with pole on the bow with red cloth. and several of them came. every one of the

boats had ten to fifteen men. the smoke signal was given by the two watchmen. every indian around the lake knew the soldiers were coming up the lake. and how many of them. and those who were watching the trail saw the infantrys coming over the hill from lower lake. these two men were watching from ash hill. they went to stones and kelseys house.from there the horsemen went down torge the lake and the soldiers went across the valley torge lakeport. they went on to scotts valley. shoot afew shoots with their big gun and went on to upper lake and camped on Emmerson hill. from there they saw the indian camp on the island. the next morning the white warriors went across in their long dugouts. the indians said they would met them in peace.so when the whites landed the indians went to wellcom them.but the white man was determined to kill them. Ge-Wi-Lih said he threw up his hands and said no harm me good man. but the white man fired and shoot him in the arm and another shoot came and hit a man staning along side of him and was killed.so they had to run and fight back; as they ran back in the tules and hed under the water;four or five of them gave alittle battle and another man was shoot in the shoulder. some of them jumped in the water and hed in the tuleys. many women and children were killed on around this island. one old lady a(indian) told about what she saw while hiding under abank,in under aover hanging tuleys. she said she saw two white man coming with their guns up in the air and on their guns hung a little girl. they brought it to the creek and threw it in the water. and alittle while later, two more men came in the same manner. this time they had alittle boy on the end of their guns and also threw it in the water. alittle ways from her she, said layed awoman shoot through the shoulder. she held her little baby in her arms. two white men came running torge the woman and baby, they stabed the woman and the baby and, and threw both of them over the bank in to the water. she said she heard the woman say, O my baby; she said when they gathered the dead, they found all the little ones were killed by being stabed, and many of the woman were also killed stabing. she said it took them four or five days to gather up the dead. and the dead were all burnt on the east side of the creek. they called it the siland creek. (Ba-Don-Bi-Da-Meh). this old lady also told about the whites hung aman on Emerson siland this indian was met by the soldiers while marching from scotts valley to upper lake. the indian was hung and alarge fire built under the hanging indian. and another indian was caught near Emerson hill. this one was tied to atree and burnt to death.
the next morning the solders started for mendocino county. and there killed many indians. the camp was on the ranch now known as Ed Howell ranch. the solders made camp a little ways below, bout one half mile from the indian camp. the indians wanted to surrender, but the solders did not give them time, the solders went in the camp and shoot them down as tho if they were dogs. som of them escaped by going down a little creek leading to the river. and som

of them hed in the brush. and those who hed in the brush most of them were killed. and those who hed in the water was over looked. they killed mostly woman and children. the solders caught two boys age about 14 or 15. the soldiers took them to lower lake, and then turnd them loose, when the solders started the two boys back, they loded them with meat and hard bread. one said as soon as they got out of site, they threw the meat away and som of the brad also. he said they went on a dog trot for dear life. thinking all the time that the solders would follow them and kill them. he said they would side tract once and awhile and get up on a high peak to see if the solders were coming he said when they got back that night they could nothing but crying. he said all the dead had been taken across to a large dance house had been and was cremated. wetness, Bo-Dom. or Jeo Beatti, and Krao Lah, indian-name. an old lady said her futher dug a large hole in abank of the river and they hed in the hole. one old man said that he was aboy at the time he said the solders shoot his mother, she fell to the ground with her baby in her arms, he said his mother told him to climb high up in the tree, so he did and from there he said he could see the solders runing about the camp and shooting the men and woman and stabing boys and girls. he said mother was not yet dead and was telling him to keep quit. two of the solders heard her talking and ran up to her and stabed her and child. and a little ways from his mother, he said laid a man dieing, holding his boy in his arms the solders also stabed him, but they did not kill the boy, the took the boy to the camp, crying, they gave it evry thing they could find in camp but the little boy did not quit crying. it was aboy about three years of age, when the solders were geting redy to move camp, they raped the boy up in ablanket and lief the little boy seting by the fire raped up in a blanket and was stell crying, and that boy is live today, his name is bill ball, now lives in Boonville; One Old man told me about the solders killing the indiuns in this same camp. he said young man. from the description he gave. he must have been about 18 or 20 years of age. he said he and another boy about the same age was taken by the soldurs and. he said there were two solders in charge of them. one would walk ahead and one behind them. he said the solders took him and the other boy. they both were bearfooted he said when they begin to climb the mountain between mendocino and lake county. he said they were made to keep up with the solders. thir feet were geting sore but they had to keep up with the solders. when they were climbing over the bottlerock mountain. thir feet were cutup by the rocks and thir feet were bleeding and they could not walk up with the solders. the man behind would jab them with the sharp knife fixed on the end of the gun. he said one of the solders came and looked at thir feet and went to abox opened it took acup and diped something out of asack and brought it to them and told them both of them to hold their foots on a log near by. the solder took ahand full of the stuff and rubed it in the cuts on the bottom of their feet. he said he noticed that the stuff the solder put on their feet look like salt. sureenough it was salt. the solder tied clouth over their feet and told them not to take them off. he said the tears were roling down his cheeks. he said all the solders came and stood around them laughing. he said they roled and twested for about two hours. and they also rubed salt in the wounds on their seats and backs wher they jabed them with the solders big knife. as he call it. two or three days later the chife solder told them they could go back. they was then gaven meat and bread, all they could pack. he said they started on thir back journey. he said it was all most difficult for them to walk but raped alot of cloth around thir feet and by doing so made thir way all right. he said the meat and bread got too heavy for fast traveling so they threw the meat and some of the bread away. looking back all the time thiking that the solders would follow them and kill them. now and then they would side tract. and look back to see if the solders were following them. after seen no solders following them they would start out for another run. he said they traveled in such manner untell they got to thir home. he said to himself. hear Iam not to see my mother and sister but to see thir blood scattered over the ground like water and thir bodys for coyotes to devour. he said he sat down under a tree and cryed all day.

V
Civil War
1861-1865

During the Civil War, Indian people endured as much suffering and harsh treatment as they had during other times in their history. Many of their misfortunes stemmed from fighting in the armies of both sides. Small tribes in the older states east of the Mississippi lost as many as a third of their male members to combat and disease. They also faced the unregulated push of whites—who gave little thought to the ultimate fate of the Indians—into the Indian lands of the Great Plains and Far West. Mistreatment of the type inflicted in previous eras accompanied the movement, especially during the frequent wars. Only in Russian Alaska was the picture different. There the government, intent on solving the problem of Indian-white relationships, provided modest institutional access to civilization.

In November, 1861, fighting between rebel and Union forces erupted in Indian Territory, which was the national home of the slave-owning Five Civilized Tribes: Cherokee, Chickasaw, Creek, Choctaw, and Seminole. For many years Indian and white sympathizers with the South had worked to weaken Indian ties with the federal government. In the opening months of the war the United States abruptly transferred the small garrisons of Northern troops from Indian Territory forts to defense positions in Kansas. The act drove the Choctaw, Chickasaw, and many Creek, Cherokee, and Seminole to the Confederacy. Loyal Indians, including black citizens and slaves, attempted to form protective forces against the present and active rebel army, but they were soon attacked and driven northward. During the late autumn of 1861 thousands of loyal Indian people started to withdraw to federal army camps on the barren, frozen Kansas plains, but they were forced to fight pitched battles with white and Indian rebel troops. Intense suffering and hundreds of civilian deaths followed. Throughout the war southern and northern armies fought in the Indian commonwealths and looted and burned the property of the Indians, until nothing but ashes and memories remained over vast areas.

Wars between the Indians and whites did not cease. In August of 1862 the Sioux of Minnesota rose up against the failing Indian management system, then even more callous to human misery because the problems of a distant war absorbed the attention of its leaders. Sweeping down the Minnesota River Valley from their cramped reserve, the Sioux waged war on the farmers. After several battles

with federal forces the defeated Indians negotiated a surrender. A military court hurriedly sentenced 303 to death for the crimes of rape, murder, mutilation of the dead, and participation in the war. After review by President Abraham Lincoln, thirty-eight were hanged, and the remainder were treated as prisoners of war. This repugnant act was not enough to stop the public clamor for severe punishment of the remaining tribesmen; Congress was forced to order all Sioux removed from the state and the fertile reservation land confiscated and sold. The order also included the peaceful Winnebago of southern Minnesota, who had a rapidly maturing settlement based on the agricultural potential of their black-earth homeland. Several hundred of these two tribes were killed by their forced removal to Dakota without sufficient food or clothing.

The year 1863 also saw Navajo Indians of the Southwest removed by military order and marched four hundred miles to a concentration camp in eastern New Mexico called Bosque Redondo. The military commander in New Mexico, Brigadier General James H. Carleton, collaborating with New Mexican land and mineral speculators, sought to remove and civilize the Navajo. The success of the removal depended upon the success of the civilization process. Using the army to destroy Indian crops, herds, and hogans, and issuing "move or die" orders, he gathered the Navajo into groups and marched them to the Bosque. Despite every effort by General Carleton, who sincerely wanted his experiment with humans to work, he failed to impose an alien white civilization upon them. By 1868 the Navajo were released. The attempt at Bosque Redondo to impose a new life-style upon an entire people completely denied democratic principles.

From the California hills to the northern Great Plains bitter warfare between Indians and whites continued. In California attacks upon the fragmented hill bands reached the point of genocide. In the Southwest a war forced the Apache to engage in a bitter resistance. Apache Chief Mangus Colorado's assassination while a prisoner of war and the mutilation of his corpse were but one phase in a bloody episode.

Incessant fighting followed the expanding frontier on the Great Plains, and occasionally a massacre upon Indian villages occurred. The militia attacked the Cheyenne at Sand Creek in eastern Colorado, murdering and mutilating women and children; this event became notorious when the facts were publicized.

December, 1861   Kansas
Plight of Loyal Refugee Indians

The Civil War divided the loyalties of the Five Civilized Tribes of Indian Territory. In late autumn, 1861, a full blood Creek named Opothle Yoholo led about five thousand Creek, Seminole, Cherokee, and fragments of other tribes north to Kansas and the American military camps. As the loyal Indians trudged over the two-hundred mile wilderness route, they were forced to fight several battles with white and Indian Confederate soldiers. On December 26, 1861, at Chustenalah, Confederate forces crushed the rear guard of the beleaguered Indians and overran the train of refugees, capturing all equipment and supplies. The Indians fled the remaining miles to Kansas through a blizzard. Hundreds perished; others suffered severely from the climate and lack of shelter. The following letter from A. B. Campbell, a surgeon in the United States Army, to his superior officer describes the conditions of the Indians (document 58).

Document 58
December, 1861   Kansas
Plight of Loyal Refugee Indians

Source: A. B. Campbell, surgeon, United States Army, to Major J. K. Barnes, Medical Director, Department of Kansas, February 5, 1862, in U.S. Commissioner of Indian Affairs, **Annual Report, 1862** (Washington: Government Printing Office, 1862), pp. 295-296.

It is impossible for me to depict the wretchedness of their condition. Their only protection from the snow upon which they lie is prairie grass, and from the wind and weather scraps and rags stretched upon switches; some of them had some personal clothing; most had but shreds and rags, which did not conceal their nakedness, and I saw seven, ranging in age from three to fifteen years, without one thread upon their bodies. Hogobofohyah, the 2d chief of the Creeks, was sick with a fever. It is time he had received from Mr. Fuller blankets enough to keep him warm, but his tent (to give it that name) was no larger than a small blanket stretched over a switch ridge pole, two feet from the ground, and did not reach it by a foot on either side of him. One or two of the lodges were better, all the rest worse than his. The boxes from the Chicago commission contained thirty-five comfortables or quilts, many of them only two feet and two feet six inches wide, forty pairs of socks, three pairs of pantaloons, seven undershirts, and four pairs of drawers, a few shirts, pillows, and pillowcases. I unpacked the things and piled them up in

the wagon in parcels of the same kind of articles. I had the wagon driven round the margin of the woods. I walked through the woods, and selected the nakedest of the naked, to whom I doled out the few articles I had, and when all was gone, I found myself surrounded by hundreds of anxious faces, disappointed to find that nothing remained for them. The pillow-cases were the most essential articles next to food, for they were the only means that families had to receive their portion of the meal or flour furnished them.

They are extremely destitute of cooking utensils, and axes or hatchets; many can with difficulty get wood to makes fires, either to warm themselves or to cook with, which, together with the want of cooking utensils, compels many of them to eat their provisions raw. They greatly need medical assistance; many have their toes frozen off, others have feet wounded by sharp ice or branches of trees lying on the snow; but few have shoes or moccasins. They suffer with inflammatory diseases of the chest, throat, and eyes. Those who come in last get sick as soon as they eat. Means should be taken at once to have the horses which lie dead in every direction, through the camp and on the side of the river, removed and burned, lest the first few warm days breed a pestilence amongst them. Why the officers of the Indian department are not doing something for them I cannot understand; common humanity demands that more should be done, and done at once, to save them from total destruction.

December, 1862   Mankato, Minnesota
Execution of Thirty-Eight Sioux

After the Sioux uprising in August and September of 1862 had been defeated, the Sioux warriors were tried for war crimes committed against the citizens of Minnesota. The hastily convened army court presented the coffled Indians, heard testimony, and determined guilt or innocence instantly. The court did not permit the Indians to submit evidence against the Indian agents and citizens of Minnesota who for ten years had committed brutal deeds—rapes, beatings, and murders—against them and their families. The army determined that 303 were guilty of rape, murder, and participation in attacks upon unarmed civilians and sentenced them to death. President Abraham Lincoln, repelled by the large number, stayed the execution until he had gone over the list and examined the evidence against them. Preoccupied with the civil rebellion, dependent for information upon a vast patronage system, and faced with a popular demand to kill all the Indians, Mr. Lincoln finally selected thirty-nine to be hung, the rest to be treated as prisoners of war.

The execution order with the list of thirty-nine names (one was later reprieved at the last minute) is given (document 59). The words *by the record* refer to the number each Indian was assigned in the complete list of prisoners submitted to the President. Physical arrangements delayed the simultaneous gibbeting until the twenty-sixth of December. Two innocent men were executed, because in the haphazard process their names were confused with others. An account of the death scene from a contemporary newspaper describes the manner in which the Sioux died (document 60). Although the government permitted Siouan-speaking white preachers to enter the death cell to save the souls of the shackled men, the death ceremonies and customs of the Sioux—not the Christian sentiments the preachers claimed they had instilled—dominated the scene.

Further reading: Kenneth Carley, *The Sioux Uprising of 1862* (St. Paul: The Minnesota Historical Society, 1961).

Document 59
December 6, 1862

White House,
Washington, D.C.

Execution Order

Source: Letter from Abraham Lincoln to H. H. Sibley, December 6, 1862. E. D. Neill, manuscript, Manuscripts Division, Minnesota Historical Society.

Brigadier General H. H. Sibley   Executive Mansion,
St. Paul   Washington,
Minnesota.   December 6th. 1862.

Ordered that of the Indians and Half-breeds sentenced to be hanged by the Military Commission, composed of Colonel Crooks, Lt. Colonel Marshall, Captain Grant, Captain Bailey, and Lieutenant Olin, and lately sitting in Minnesota, you cause to be executed on Friday the nineteenth day of December, instant, the following named, towit

"Te-he-hdo-ne-cha."	No.	2. by the record.
"Tazoo" alias "Plan-doo-ta."	No.	4. by the record.
"Wy-a-tah-to-wah"	No.	5. by the record.
"Hin-han-shoon-ko-yag."	No.	6. by the record.
"Muz-za-bom-a-du."	No.	10. by the record.
"Wah-pay-du-ta."	No.	11. by the record.
"Wa-he-hud."	No.	12. by the record.
"Sna-ma-ni."	No.	14. by the record.
"Ta-te-mi-na."	No.	15. by the record.
"Rda-in-yan-kna."	No.	19. by the record.
"Do-wan-sa."	No.	22. by the record.
"Ha-pan."	No.	24. by the record.
"Shoon-ka-ska." (White Dog).	No.	35. by the record.
"Toon-kan-e-chah-tay-mane."	No.	67. by the record.
"E-tay-hoo-tay."	No.	68. by the record.
"Am-da-cha."	No.	69. by the record.
"Hay-pee-don—or, Wamme-omne-ho-ta."	No.	70. by the record.
"Mahpe-o-ke-na-ji."	No.	96. by the record.
"Henry Milord"—a Half-breed.	No.	115. by the record.

"Chaskay-don"—or Chasyay-etay."	No. 121. by the record.
"Baptiste Campbell" a Half-breed.	No. 138. by the record.
"Tah-ta-kay-gay."	No. 155. by the record.
"Ha-pink-pa."	No. 170. by the record.
"Hypolite Ange" a Half-breed.	No. 175. by the record.
"Na-pay-Shue."	No. 178. by the record.
"Wa-kan-tan-ka."	No. 210. by the record.
"Toon-kan-ka-yag-e-na-jin."	No. 225. by the record.
"Ma-kat-e-na-jin."	No. 254. by the record.
"Pa-zee-koo-tay-ma-ne."	No. 264. by the record.
"Ta-tay-hde-don."	No. 279. by the record.
"Wa-She-choon," or "Toon-kan-shkan-shkan-mene-hay."	No. 318. by the record.
"A-e-cha-ga."	No. 327. by the record.
"Ha-tan-in-koo."	No. 333. by the record.
"Chay-ton-hoon-ka."	No. 342. by the record.
"Chan-ka-hda."	No. 359. by the record.
"Hda-hin-hday."	No. 373. by the record.
"O-ya-tay-a-koo."	No. 377. by the record.
"May-hoo-way-wa."	No. 382. by the record.
"Wa-kin-yan-na."	No. 383. by the record.

The other condemned prisoners you will hold subject to further orders, taking care that they neither escape, nor are subjected to any unlawful violence.

ABRAHAM LINCOLN,
President of the United States.

Document 60
December 26, 1862

Mankato, Minnesota

Execution Scene

Source: The Saint Paul Pioneer, Dec. 28, 1862.

The Reverend Father spoke to them of their condition and fate, and in such terms as the devoted priest only can speak. He tried to infuse them with courage—bade them to hold out bravely and be strong, and to show no sign of fear. While Father Ravoux was speaking to them, old Tazoo broke out in a death-wail, in which one after another joined, until the prison room was filled with a wild, unearthly plaint, which was neither of despair nor grief, but rather a paraoxysm of savage passion, most impressive to witness and startling to hear, even by those who understood the language of music only. During the lulls of their death-song, they would resume their pipes, and with the exception of an occasional mutter, or the rattling of their chains, they sat motionless and impassive; until one among the elder would break out in the wild wail, when all would join again in the solemn preparation for death.

. . .

The influence of the wild music of their death-song upon them was almost magical. Their whole manner changed after they had closed their singing, and an air of cheerful unconcern marked all of them. It seemed as if during their passionate wailing, they had passed in spirit through the valley of the shadow of death, and already had their eyes fixed on the pleasant hunting grounds beyond.

. . .

While Father Ravoux was speaking to the Indians, and repeating, for the hundreth time, his urgent request that they must think to the last of the Great Spirit before whom they were about to appear, Provost Marshall Redfield entered and whispered a word in the ear of the good priest, who immediately said a word or two in French to Henry Milord a halfbreed, who repeated it in the Dacotah to the Indians, who were all lying down around the prison. In a moment, every Indian stood erect, and as the Provost Marshal opened the door, they fell in behind him with the greatest alacrity. Indeed, a notice of release, pardon, or reprieve could not have induced them to leave the cell with more apparent willingness than this call to death. We followed on behind them, and as those at the head of the procession came out of the basement, at the opposite side of the gallows, and directly in front, we heard sort of a

death-wail sounded, which was immediately caught up by all the condemned, and was chaunted in unison until the scaffold was reached. At the foot of the steps there was no delay. Capt. Redfield mounted the drop, at the head, and the Indians crowded after him, as if it were a race to see which would get up first. They actually crowded on each other's heels, and as they got to the top, each took his position, without any assistance from those who were detailed for that purpose. They still kept up a mournful wail, and occasionally there would be a piercing scream. The ropes were soon arranged around their necks, not the least resistance being offered. One or two, feeling the noose uncomfortably tight, attempted to loosen it, and although their hands were tied, they partially succeeded. The movement, however, was noticed by the assistants, and the cords re-arranged. The white caps, which had been placed on the top of their heads, were now drawn down over their faces, shutting out forever the light of day from their eyes. Then ensued a scene that can hardly be described, and which can never be forgotten. All joined in shouting and singing, as it appeared to those who were ignorant of the language. The tones seemed somewhat discordant, and yet there was harmony in it. Save the

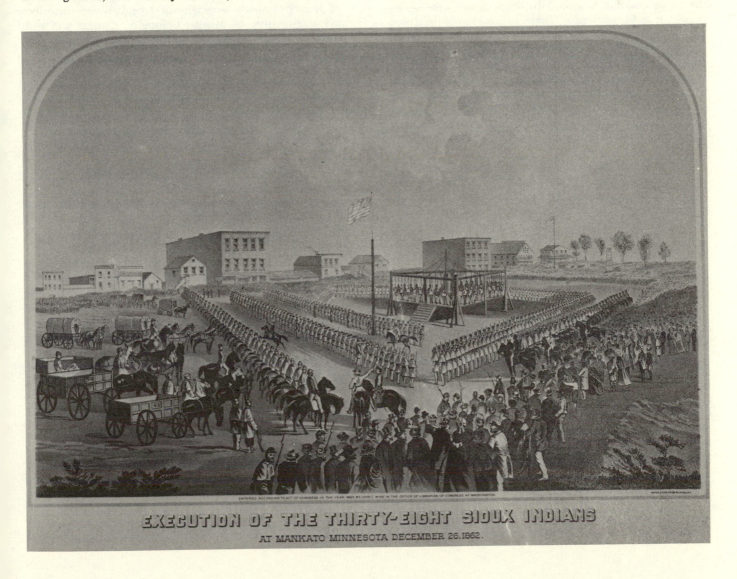

EXECUTION OF THE THIRTY-EIGHT SIOUX INDIANS
AT MANKATO MINNESOTA DECEMBER 26, 1862.

moment of cutting the rope, it was the most thrilling moment of the awful scene. And it was not their voices alone. Their bodies swayed to and fro, and their every limb seemed to be keeping time. The drop trembled and shook as if all were dancing. The most touching scene on the drop was their attempts to grasp each other's hands, fettered as they were. They were very close to each other, and many succeeded. Three or four in a row were hand in hand, and all hands swaying up and down with the rise and fall of their voices. One old man reached out each side, but could not grasp a hand. His struggles were piteous, and affected many beholders.

We were informed by those who understood the language, that their singing and shouting was only to sustain each other—that there was nothing defiant in their last moments, and that no "death song," strictly speaking was chanted on the gallows. Each one shouted his own name, and called on the name of his friend, saying in substance, "I'm here! I'm here!"

THE EXECUTION

Captain Burt hastily scanned all the arrangements for the execution, and motioned to Major Brown, the signed officer, that all was ready. There was one tap of the drum, almost drowned by the voices of the Indians—another, and the stays of the drop were knocked away, the rope cut, and, with a crash, down came the drop. One rope broke, but not until the neck of the victim was dislocated, whose body came down on the drop with a heavy *thud*, and a crash of the boards, there was no struggling by any of the Indians for the space of half a minute—the only movements were the natural vibrations occasioned by the fall.

In the meantime, a new rope was placed around the neck of the one who fell, and, it having been thrown over the beam, he was soon hanging with the others. After the lapse of a minute, several drew up their legs once or twice, and there was some movement of the arms. One Indian, at the expiration of ten minutes, breathed, but the rope was better adjusted, and life was soon extinct. It is unnecessary to speak of the awful sight of thirty-eight human beings suspended in the air. Imagination will readily supply what we refrain from describing.

REMOVING THE BODIES

After the bodies had hung for about half an hour, the physicians of the several regiments present examined the bodies and reported that life was extinct. Soon after, several United States mule teams appeared, when the bodies were taken down and dumped into the wagons without much ceremony, and were carried down to the sand bar in front of the city, and were all buried in the same hold.

. . .

The whole military part of the programme was carried out in the best style. There was no confusion, and every detachment knew its appointed place, and stuck to it. We have never before seen a finer military display in the State.

1863   Arizona
Assassination of Mangus Colorado

In 1863 the Apache chief Mangus Colorado met with the American military at a pre-arranged conference to establish peace terms. He was seized, bound hand and foot, and assassinated. An old man, he had spent his adult life in a bitter war against Mexicans and whites who attempted to conquer his homeland. Two main factors drove his people into war. The first was slavery: slavers actively sought Apache women and children to sell into slavery. The entrance of Americans after 1849 increased the trade. The second was the professional exterminator: he was paid by northern Mexican governments to eliminate the inhabitants of the coveted north lands.

The following excerpt from the first published version of Daniel Conner's biography of Joseph Walker describes the assassination of Mangus Colorado. Conner was with Walker's military group and witnessed the scene (document 61).

Further reading: Dan L. Thrapp, *The Conquest of Apacheria* (Norman: University of Oklahoma Press, 1967).

Document 61
1863   Arizona
Assassination of Mangus Colorado

Source: Daniel Ellis Conner, **Joseph Reddeford Walker and the Arizona Adventure.** edited by Donald J. Berthrong and Odessa Davenport (Norman: University of Oklahoma Press, 1956), pp. 37-41. Copyright 1956 by the University of Oklahoma Press.

He looked careworn and refused to talk and evidently felt that he had made a great mistake in trusting the pale face on this occasion. Our men kept Mangus during that night and on the following day the General concluded that he would take charge of Mangus until the old "brave" accounted for the loss of two plundered government wagons and teams, which were lost on the Rio Grande del Norte some months previously. One of the wagons was loaded with clothing and the other with artillery ammunition, when captured by the Indians, and both were *en route* for Santa Fe, New Mexico, together so these soldiers had been informed. Two soldier sentinels now took charge of Mangus and kept him all day at a fire built of the old cabin logs of the fort, which were lying promiscuously about the camp. Our party had been there long enough to form a regularly beaten path a hundred and fifty paces in length on the west side of the camp by walking sentinel night and day. The soldiery formed their adjoining camp and the sentinel beat at right angles with that of ours, so that the two beats came together, forming a right angle at the fire, where old Mangus was lying on his blanket, a prisoner.

One soldier walked their beat and one citizen walked our beat, and two extra sentinels were placed over the person of Mangus. This was the situation when night came on and it was a bitter cold on that bleak prairie. I was on guard for the forepart of the night, which was exceedingly dark. Being cold and disagreeable, all but the guard retired to their blankets early and soon left the camp wrapped in profound silence. No fire was kept burning except the one at the junction of the two guard beats, where Mangus lay upon his blanket with his trinket under his head for a pillow.

A while before midnight I noticed Mangus moving now and then, drawing up his feet restlessly and tucking the lower end of his blanket with which he was covered, over one foot with the other. I would walk up to the fire and then walk off in the dark of my beat to which I had become so accustomed that I could follow it without difficulty this dark night. When I arrived at the far and lower end and turned to come back to the fire I noticed that the soldiers were annoying Mangus in some way and they would become quiet and silent when I was about approaching the fire, and keep so until I again walked off in the dark on my beat. But my curiosity as to what they were doing to the old Indian became aroused and as soon as I departed into the dark far enough to get beyond the reflection of the firelight I walked rapidly to the lower end of my beat, then turned and walked leisurely back and observed the sentinels' pranks.

I could see them plainly by the firelight as they were engaged in heating their fixed bayonets in the fire and putting them to the feet and naked legs of Mangus, who was from time to time trying to shield his limbs from the hot steel. When I came up to the fire each time they would become innocent and sleepy and remain so until I departed on my beat again, when they would arouse themselves into the decided spirit of indulging this barbarous pastime. I didn't appreciate this conduct one particle, but said nothing to them at the time and really I had some curiosity to see to what extent they would indulge it. I was surprised at their ultimate intentions just before midnight when I was about midway of my beat and approaching the firelight. Just then Mangus raised himself upon his left elbow and began to expostulate in a vigorous way by telling the sentinels in Spanish that he was no child to be playing with. But his expostulations were cut short, for he had hardly begun his exclamation when both sentinels promptly brought down their minnie muskets to bear on him and fired, nearly at the same time through his body. The Chief fell back off of his elbow into the same position in which he had been lying all the forepart of the night. This was quickly followed by two shots through the head by each sentinel's six-shooter, making in all, six shots fired in rapid succession. The old Chief died without a struggle in the precise position that he had occupied continuously since dark. The force of the musket balls marked the frozen ground beyond the body for a distance of five or six feet with an unbroken line of blood plainly indicating the respective directions of the bullets after passing through the body. The four six-shooter balls likewise streamed the old Indian's long hair in strands over his face and straight out upon the ground its full length, indicating the direction of the pistol bullets as they left the victim.

The shooting aroused the whole camp, which soon settled into silence again when the cause was ascertained and the two sentinels retired with the rest of the camp members. Geo. Lount who was to relieve me of guard duty at midnight now promptly took my place, stating that it was not quite midnight but that it was so near it that he would remain up and go on duty immediately.

I retired to my blankets and slept soundly until morning within less than ten paces of the dead body of Mangus, and arose to find the weather extremely cold and found the body of the Indian in the same position and untouched. I raised his head and took from under it quite a number of curious trinkets, one of which was a rectangular wooden block made of oak. It was about four inches in length by about two and a half inches in width and three quarters of an inch thick. It had a hole through one end by which it was fastened to the other trinkets, temporarily. A stout string passed through the hole with its ends permanently tied together forming a loop large enough through which to pass the hand, and I thought that it was to be worn on the wrist, as it was apparently worn smooth by much handling. This block was marked by hieroglyphics which were burned deeply into the wood with some hot instrument and quite neatly executed. The hole had been burned through the block. I gave them to a lieutenant whose name I don't remember, indeed if I ever knew it.

Quite a number of soldiers came to where I was standing near the corpse, and amongst them there was one who called himself John T. Wright of California, who asked the loan of my butcher knife with which to scalp the Chief. I declined upon the ground that my knife was the only cutlery that I possessed with which to prepare my food &c. He then applied to the soldier's cook, Wm. Lallier, who furnished a large bowie knife, with which the soldier took off the scalp of Mangus. He wrapped the long hair around the scalp and put it in his pocket. I thought that I had never seen the skin about the head of a buffalo much thicker than this scalp of Mangus.

It was as before stated very cold and therefore the operation of taking this scalp was a bloodless one, leaving the inner skin as white as the skull from which it was taken. The body was left where it lay till noon, when it was carried on a blanket and dumped into a gully, blanket and all, and covered up.

A few nights after this, some soldiers dug Mangus' body out again and took his head and boiled it during the night, and prepared the skull to send to the museum in New York. I afterward saw the skull frequently before the soldiery departed with it. Thus ended the career of the most notorious chief which the Apaches ever boasted of since the United States has owned Arizona and New Mexico.

August 4, 1863   Wisconsin
Winnebago Discontent

United States Indian agent M. M. Davis investigated allegations of Indian depredations in western Wisconsin and submitted the following report to the Commissioner of Indian Affairs (document 62). The Winnebago had lived in Wisconsin but through a series of treaties various bands had been removed west, principally to Minnesota. Several bands remained in Wisconsin under astute leadership that constantly thwarted white officials' attempts to count them, allot land, and govern them. Chief Dandy was an intrepid defender of his band in Wisconsin; he successfully stymied numerous efforts to remove them or to impose federal regulations on them. The tensions in the white community came not only from those incidents mentioned in the report but also from rumors about the Sioux War of 1862 in neighboring Minnesota and the suspicions of the European immigrants who were unused to the brown-skinned population with an entirely different lifestyle.

Document 62
August 4, 1863   Wisconsin
Winnebago Discontent

Source: U.S. Commissioner of Indian Affairs. **Annual Report, 1863** (Washington: Government Printing Office, 1863), pp. 486-487.

NEW LISBON, *Juneau County, Wisconsin,*
August 4, 1863

SIR: Within the last ten days I have had several urgent applications to visit this section of Wisconsin for the purpose of examining into the alleged Indian depredations, which at present are the cause of much excitement in this part of the State. Although I had no orders to do so, I thought it not inconsistent with duty to comply with requests so urgently made by gentlemen who from long personal acquaintance I entertained the highest respect. Upon inquiring I learned that several Indians had been arrested, and were held in close confinement by order of Brigadier General Smith, commanding in the district of Wisconsin. I therefore at once called upon General Smith at his headquarters in Milwaukie, and from him ascertained

that with one or two exceptions the Indians had been held or kept in close confinement, more for their own protection against the excited white settlers than for any crimes or depredations committed. But General Smith had already issued an order for the release of all Indians, except such as the civil authorities desired to deal with. I reached this place on the morning of the 1st instant. Upon examination I find the Indians complained of to be mostly Winnebagoes, though there are a few lodges of roving Pottawatomies, who have heretofore mostly subsisted in the eastern part of the State, but who, when they get into trouble, will generally claim to be Menomonees. After careful inquiry I am confident that there are but four families who have at any time made it their home on the Menomonee reservation now to be found among any of the Indians west of the Wisconsin river, and these families are a mixture of Winnebago, Pottawatomie, and Menomonee. The Winnebagoes are those who returned from Minnesota after they were removed from this State. Their lodges have been on the headwaters of the Yellow, Lemonwier, and Black rivers. This section of country is good hunting ground; it also affords annually an abundant crop of wild fruit, such as blueberries, whortleberries, blackberries, and cranberries. As soon as the fruit begins to ripen the Indians commence gathering it for sale, and hence make their appearance in considerable numbers in the white settlements. These Indians are exceedingly filthy, uncouth, and generally very impudent. From the most degraded whites they have learned all the vices, and hence they are a terror to most settlers.

The first crime committed by them this season was the murder of a Mrs. Salter, whose husband's business, to a large extent, appears to have been to furnish the Indians with whiskey. This murder was committed about three weeks ago, and while the husband was absent from the house. A drunken Indian was found near the house, and was killed by Salter. The dead Indian's head was cut off with a grub-hoe by a German living near, and stuck upon a stake or pole. Shortly after this an Indian, whom all believe to have been innocent of the murder, came along, and seeing the head of an Indian on a stake became much frightened, when Salter also killed him, beating his brains out with an axe-helve. Since this occurrence Salter and the German believe that the Indians have been hunting them; the German says that the Indians have shot at him. In several instances the Indians have come to the houses of the farmers, in the absence of the farmer himself, and demanded not only food, but the children. Where a demand of this kind was made on the 1st instant, the woman, Mrs. Austin, alleges that she shot the Indian who had entered the window—she used a rifle—the intruder was shot through the breast—fell out of the window he had entered, and was carried off by some of his comrades. Mrs. Austin says that after despatching one Indian she was assailed by another, but with the assistance of a large dog and the rifle she compelled her intruder to retreat.

Whether all the incidents of this encounter are true or not, it has an effect to produce an intense excitement in this section of the State.

Many of the farmers, in the midst of their harvest, leave all, and, with their families, seek the villages for safety. Under this state of things, many of the whites are advocating an indiscriminate slaughter of Indians wherever they may be found.

I called upon the Indians held in custody before they were released. Among them was the Winnebago chief Dandy, noted for his secession proclivities, as well as for his control over the wandering members of his tribe. Dandy expressed his pleasure at seeing me, remarking that he had not seen an Indian agent for many years. He said that all the Indians concerned in the murder of Mrs. Salter should be brought to the white officers to be punished, but that he could not bring them in until he was released. He expressed a decided determination to remain in this country; said that his God first showed him the light here, and that he should not go away and live by some other light. I endeavored to ascertain from this chief the number of Winnebagoes living in this section of the State, but he could give me no idea either as to the number of Indians or Indian lodges. The people here estimate that there are one thousand to fifteen hundred of these roving Indians, but I cannot believe they will exceed five hundred.

While these Indians remain where they are, the further settlement by the whites will cease, but many who have already settled and made substantial improvements will leave and make their homes where Indians cannot molest them.

I have urged the people to act strictly on the defensive, but I apprehend there is considerable danger that a few reckless men have determined to shoot Indians wherever they can find them.

I have the honor to be your obedient servant,
M. M. DAVIS,
United States Indian Agent,
Hon. W. P. DOLE,
Commissioner of Indian Affairs, Washington, D.C.

1860-1865   Indian Slavery   New Mexico

Resistance to slavery and white expansion drove the Apache and Navajo to warfare against the Spanish and American inhabitants of the Southwest. Indian slavery differed little from black slavery with all its horrors and implications. Although a rough estimation, five thousand Navajo were held as slaves in 1860.

A statement on slavery taken from a Congressional investigation of the condition of Indian tribes at the close of the war is given. The testimony is by the Chief Justice of the New Mexican Supreme Court, Kirby Benedict, who practiced law on the Illinois prairies with Abraham Lincoln

and migrated to New Mexico in the late 1850s (document 63).

Further reading: Lynn R. Bailey, *Indian Slave Trade in the Southwest* (Pasadena: Socio-Technical Books, 1966).

Document 63
1860-1865   New Mexico
Indian Slavery in the Southwest

Source: U.S. Congress, Senate. Special Committee Appointed under Joint Resolution of March 3, 1865. **Condition of the Indian Tribes.** S. Rept. 156, 39th Cong., 2d sess., 1867, p. 326.

There are in the Territory a large number of Indians, principally females, (women and children,) who have been taken by force, or stealth, or purchased, who have been among the various wild tribes of New Mexico or those adjoining. Of these a large proportion are Navajoes. It is notorious that natives of this country have sometimes made captives of Navajo women and children when opportunities presented themselves; the custom has long existed here of buying Indian persons, especially women and children; the tribes themselves have carried on this kind of traffic. Destitute orphans are sometimes sold by their remote relations; poor parents also make traffic of their children. The Indian persons obtained in any of the modes mentioned are treated by those who claim to own them as their servants and slaves. They are bought and sold by and between the inhabitants at a price as much as is a horse or an ox. Those who buy, detain and use them seem to confide in the long-established custom and practice which prevails, and did prevail before this country was a portion of the United States. Those who hold them are exceedingly sensitive of their supposed interest in them, and easily alarmed at any movements in the civil courts or otherwise to dispossess them of their imagined property. The rich, and those who have some quantities of property, are those chiefly who possess the persons I have mentioned; those usually have much popular influence in the country, and the exertion of this influence is one of the means by which they hope to retain their grasp upon their Indian slaves. The prices have lately ranged very high. A likely girl of not more than eight years old, healthy and intelligent, would be held at a value of four hundred dollars, or more. When they grow to womanhood they sometimes become mothers from the natives of the land, with or without marriage. Their children, however, by the custom of the country, are not regarded as property which may be bought and sold as has been their mothers. They grow up and are treated as having the rights of citizens. They marry and blend with the general population. From my own observations I am not able to form an opinion satisfactory to my own mind of the number of Indians held as slaves or fixed domestic servants without their being the recipients of wages. Persons of high respectability for intelligence, who have made some calculations on the subject, estimate the number at various figures, from fifteen hundred to three thousand, and even exceeding the last number. The more prevalent opinion seems to be they considerably exceed two thousand. As to federal officers holding this description of persons or trafficking in them, I can only say I see them attending the family of Governor Connelly, but whether claimed by his wife, himself, or both, I know not. I am informed the superintendent of Indian affairs has one in his family, but I cannot state by what claim she is retained. From the social position occupied by the Indian agents, I presume all of them, except one, have the presence and assistance of the kind of persons mentioned; I cannot, however, state positively. In the spring of 1862, when Associate Justice Hubbell and myself conveyed our families to the States, he informed me at Las Vegas that he sold one Indian woman to a resident of that place preparatory to crossing the plains. I know of

MENOMINEE AND UNION ARMY
Song of Enlistment in the Civil War

no law in this Territory by which property in a Navajo or other Indian can be recognized in any person whatever, any more than property can be recognized in the freest white man or black man. In 1855, while holding district court in the county of Valencia, a proceeding in *habeas corpus* was had before me on the part of a wealthy woman as petitioner, who claimed the possession and services of a Navajo girl then twelve years old, and who had been held by the petitioner near seven years. On the trial I held the girl to be a free person, and adjudged accordingly. In 1862 a proceeding in *habeas corpus* was instituted before me by an aged man who had held in service many years an Indian woman who had been, when a small child, bought from the Payweha Indians. The right of the master to the possession and services of the woman on the one side, and the right of the woman to her personal freedom, were put distinctly at issue. Upon the hearing I adjudged the woman to be a free woman; I held the claim of the master to be without foundation in law and against natural rights. In each of the cases the party adjudged against acquiesced in the decision, and no appeal was ever taken.

In the examination of the cases it appeared that before the United States obtained New Mexico, captive and purchased Indians were held here by custom in the same manner as they have been since held. The courts are open to them, but they are so influenced by the circumstances which surround them they do not seem to think of seeking the aid of the law to establish the enjoyment of their right to freedom.

1863   New Mexico Territory
Apologia for Concentration Camps

The Navajo had long waged an intermittent war with land speculators, ranchers, and scalp hunters who believed that the land stretching to the west was rich in precious metals. In the 1850s they faced the U.S. Army and New Mexican citizens who were determined to restrict them to defined areas. The great upheaval caused by the Civil War permitted distant military commanders, such as the regional military commander for New Mexico, Brigadier General James H. Carleton, to carry out Indian policies with little supervision from Washington. Along with New Mexican businessmen he engaged in a project to "open up" the West for exploitation by removing the Indians to a distant area where they could also be taught the fundamentals of white Christian civilization. The project was not a violation of orders, merely the practical exercise of command in carrying out general policy. The Long Walk of the Navajo—four hundred miles to Bosque Redondo in eastern New Mexico—necessitated their roundup first. To implement his scorched earth policy, he destroyed Indian homes and crops to drive them into misery and starvation. Those who then refused to cooperate would be exterminated.

Three letters written by Carleton have been chosen to illustrate the mistreatment. The first letter addressed to Major General Halleck, general in chief of the army in Washington and Carleton's superior officer, clearly states the reasons for extermination (document 64). The second letter was written to Captain William H. Lewis, who was dispatched to collect the Indians for the march to Bosque Redondo (document 65). The third letter, written to the adjutant general, Brigadier General Lorenzo Thomas, in Washington, reveals the intense suffering of Indians subject to the policy (document 66).

Document 64
1863   New Mexico Territory
       Apology for Indian Removal

Source: U.S. Congress. Senate. Special Committee Appointed under Joint Resolution of March 3, 1865. **Condition of the Indian Tribes.** S. Rept. 156, 39th Cong., 2d sess., 1867, p. 110.

Private.]   HEADQUARTERS DEPARTMENT OF
                                    NEW MEXICO,
                        Santa Fé, N. M., May 10, 1863.

MY DEAR GENERAL: I am aware that every moment of your time is of value to the country, and I would not presume to ask you even to read this note did I not believe that what is herewith enclosed would be of interest to you as a general, and, therefore, as a statesman. Among all my endeavors since my arrival here, there has been an effort to brush back the Indians, as you have seen from official correspondence, so that the people could get out of the valley of the Rio Grande, and not only possess themselves of the arable lands in other parts of the Territory, but, if the country contained veins and deposits of the precious metals, that they might be found. So I re-established Fort Stanton, and at least a hundred families have gone to that vicinity to open farms, and they are commencing to find gold there.

I established Fort West, and have driven the Indians away from the head of the Gila, and they are finding gold and silver and cinnabar there. There is no doubt in my mind that one of the richest gold countries in the world is along the affluents to the Gila, which enter it from the north along its whole course. Thus you can see one reason why the rebels want, and why we may not permit them ever to have, a country evidently teeming with millions on millions of wealth.

Last winter I asked for one hundred thousand dollars to make a wagon road from near Fort Craig to the Gila. My request was not listened to, and I endeavored to open the road without help. Strategically, you will see its value. Intrinsically, as I then anticipated, it would be beyond price. My preliminary survey has been unsuccessful, as you observe by Captain Anderson's letter, herewith enclosed. But I do not despair of success. You will also see by the enclosed notes what signs of mineral wealth are already discovered. If I only had one more good regiment of California infantry, composed, as that infantry is, of practical miners, I would place it in the Gila country. While it would exterminate the Indians, who are a scourge to New Mexico, it would protect people who might wish to go there to open up the country, and would virtually be a military colony when the war ended, whose interests would lead the officers and soldiers to remain in the new El Dorado. Pray give all this a thought. It is not a chimera, but a subject that is worthy of the attention of the government *now*. California, you remember, was not considered as valuable an acquisition until its gold startled the whole world. Do not despise New Mexico, as a drain upon the general government. The money will all come back again.

The report of Captain McCleave I allowed to be printed to make others emulous of the self-denial, fixedness of purpose, and hard work of these Californians. This McCleave is the officer I wrote to you about as one who

would not draw his pay while he was a prisoner with the rebels. As a *soldier* you will see he has tolerably fair qualities.

I am, general, very sincerely yours,

JAMES H. CARLETON, *Brigadier General.*

Document 65
1863   **New Mexico Territory**
Order to Kill All Male Indians

Source: U.S. Congress. Senate. Special Committee Appointed under Joint Resolution of March 3, 1865. **Condition of the Indian Tribes.** S. Rept. 156, 39th Cong., 2d sess., 1867, p. 122.

HEADQUARTERS DEPARTMENT OF NEW MEXICO
                        Santa Fé, N. M., August 3, 1863.

Captain: Send a company of infantry from your post to scour the eastern slope of the Sandia mountain country, from Tejerras cañon northwardly towards the Placer mountains, with instructions to kill every male Navajo or Apache Indian who is large enough to bear arms, and who may be living in the fastnesses of the region above described. You are authorized to hire two good guides at a reasonable compensation. The company will keep the field for thirty days. It will start at once.

I am, captain, very respectfully,

JAMES H. CARLETON,
Brigadier General, Commanding.

Document 66
1863   **New Mexico Territory**
Impact of Displacement Policies

Source: U.S. Congress. Senate. Special Committee Appointed under Joint Resolution of March 3, 1865. **Condition of the Indian Tribes.** S. Rept. 156, 39th Cong., 2d sess., 1867, pp. 147-148.

HEADQUARTERS DEPARTMENT OF NEW MEXICO,
                        Santa Fé, N. M., December 12, 1863.

GENERAL: Many of the Navajo women and children which we captured are quite naked, and the children, especially, suffer from the extreme cold. The superintendant of Indian affairs is away in the States, and neither money nor instructions have been left by him, with which or under which blankets or clothing can be procured for them. It is hard to see them perish. Will the War Department authorize the quartermaster department here to buy some cheap blankets for the destitute children, and to issue condemned clothing to these Indians until they can get a start at the Bosque Redondo towards clothing themselves? The Indian department here will do nothing unless under express and urgent instructions from Washington.

I am, general, very respectfully, your obedient servant,

JAMES H. CARLETON,
Brigadier General, Commanding.

1863-1865   Minnesota and Dakota Territory
Removal of the Sioux and Winnebago

In the spring of 1863, Congress capitulated to popular pressure and ordered the removal of the four bands of Minnesota Sioux known as the Santee Sioux to a distant reservation in eastern Dakota. Congress further ordered confiscation of their lands and sale of their lands to the public. In addition, Congress ordered the removal of the Winnebago Indians, even though the shocked Winnebago had not as a tribe participated in the war. Poorly fed, improperly housed, and inadequately clothed, the Indians were placed on a land named Crow Creek. There is no way of knowing accurately how many died, but estimates place the number at several hundred for each tribe. The deaths and suffering were not intended by Congress, but the system of corruption made them unavoidable. Behind the scene were scores of grafters and profiteers who looted the provisions assigned to Indians.

In 1865 a committee of Congress investigating the general condition of Indian tribes solicited information on the removal. The description of the Winnebago is by Chief Little Hill as translated by an interpreter (document 67).

Further reading: Roy W. Meyer, *History of the Santee Sioux. United States Indian Policy on Trial* (Lincoln: University of Nebraska Press, 1967); William E. Lass, "The Removal from Minnesota of the Sioux and Winnebago Indians," *Minnesota History,* XXXVIII (December, 1963), pp. 353-364.

Document 67
1863-1865   Minnesota
Removal of the Winnebago

Source: U.S. Congress. Senate. Special Committee Appointed under Joint Resolution of March 3, 1865. **Condition of the Indian Tribes.** S. Rept. 156, 39th Cong., 2d sess., 1867, pp. 416-417.

DAKOTA CITY, NEBRASKA TERRITORY,
October 3, 1865.

Examination of Little Hill, chief, as to treatment of the Winnebago Indians.

Chief Little Hill spoke as follows:

You are one of our friends, as it appears. We are very glad to meet you here. Here are some of our old chiefs with me, but not all. And we will tell you something about how we have lived for the four years past. Now, you see me here to-day. Formerly I did not live as I do now. We used to live in Minnesota. While we lived in Minnesota we used to live in good houses, and always take our Great Father's advice, and do whatever he told us to do. We used to farm and raise a crop of all we wanted every year. While we lived there we had teams of our own. Each family had a span of horses or oxen to work, and had plenty of ponies; now, we have nothing. While we lived in Minnesota another tribe of Indians committed depredations against the whites, and then we were compelled to leave Minnesota. We did not think we would be removed from Minnesota; never expected to leave; and we were compelled to leave so suddenly that we were not prepared; not many could sell their ponies and things they had. The superintendent of the farm for the Winnebagoes was to take care of the ponies we left there and bring them on to us wherever we went; but he only brought to Crow Creek about fifty, and the rest we do not know what became of them. Most all of us had put in our crops that spring before we left, and we had to go and leave everything but our clothes and household things; we had but four days' notice. Some left their houses just as they were, with their stoves and household things in them. They promised us that they would bring all our ponies, but they only brought fifty, and the hostile Sioux came one night and stole all of them away. In the first place, before we started from Minnesota, they told us that they had got a good country for us, where they were going to put us. The interpreter here with me now (Bradford L. Porter) was appointed interpreter, on the first boat that came round, to see to things for the Indians on the trip round. After we got on the boat we were as though in a prison. We were fed on dry stuff all the time. We started down the Mississippi river, and then up the Missouri to Dakota Territory, and there we found our superintendent, and stopped there, (at Crow Creek.) Before we left Minnesota they told us that the superintendent had started on ahead of us, and would be there before us, and that he had plenty of Indians, and would have thirty houses built for us before we got there. After we got there they sometimes give us rations, but not enough to go round most of the time. Some would have to go without eating two or three days. It was not a good country; it was all dust. Whenever we cooked anything it would be full of dust. We found out after a while we could not live there. Sometimes the women and children were sick, and some of them died; and we think many of them died because they could not get enough to eat while they were sick. We don't know who was to blame for our bad treatment—whether it was our superintendent, Thompson, or whether it was our agent. We don't blame our agent, Balcombe. He used to treat us very well while we were in Minnesota, and we cannot say who was to blame at Crow Creek. For the past three years we supposed our Great Father has sent us enough goods, provisions, and money, but we do not think we have got half of it. Sometimes some of the women and children don't get much of what they ought to have, only a piece of calico, or something like that. After we had remained at Crow Creek awhile we discovered, or found out, that the whole tribe could not stay there. There was not enough to eat. The first winter one party (Minnesheik's gang) started down the Missouri river as far as Fort Randall, where they wintered. Before Clark Thompson, the superintendent, left us, (the first fall after we went there,) he had a cottonwood trough made and put beef in it, and sometimes a whole barrel of flour and a piece of pork, and let it stand a whole night, and the next morning, after cooking it, would give us some of it to eat. We tried to use it, but many of us got sick on it and died. I am telling nothing but the truth now. They also put in the unwashed intestines of the beeves and the liver and lights, and, after dipping out the soup, the bottom would be very nasty and offensive. Some of the old women and children got sick on it and died.

Now, I will speak about our annuity goods. I think some of our goods—I know pretty near where they have gone to. One time Major Balcombe told me to take some goods in the store. Major B. went into our storehouse and got the goods and gave them to me, and told me to take them in the store and leave them, and I did. There were six pieces of calico that I carried into the store. One time I went in the store, and the storekeeper told me they would have goods to-morrow. Next morning I went in again and saw some goods there, and I think the goods belonged to the Winnebagoes, because no teams came there that night from no way. What I have told you, not only I know, but some of these chiefs know also. I know one thing certain, that the pork and flour we left in Minnesota, that belonged to us, was brought over to Crow Creek and sold to us by Hawley & Hubbell, our storekeepers at Crow Creek. I will pass and not say more about the provision, and say of things since we left Crow Creek. For myself, in the first place, I thought I could stay there for a while and see the country. But I found out it wasn't a good country. I lost six of my children, and so I came down the Missouri river. When I got ready to start, some soldiers came there and told me if I started they would fire at me. I had thirty canoes ready to start. No one interceded with the soldiers to permit me to go; but the next night I got away and started down the river, and when I got down as far as the town of Yankton I found a man there and got some provisions; then came on down further and got more provisions of the military authorities, and then went on to the Omahas. After we got to the Omahas, somebody gave me a sack of flour; and some one told us to go to the other side of the Missouri and camp, and we did so. We thought we would keep on down the river, but some one came and told us to stay, and we have been there ever since. Since that time Mr. Graff has been finding rations for us; and I have been chief thirty years, and have never seen such a man. He is a good man. He has been feeding us good beef, flour, and sometimes corn, ever since we have been down there. There is another good man close by us, and that is Colonel Furnas. We the chiefs have no particular complaint to make against our present agent. It is some of our young men that speak against him. We are very glad that Mr. Graff feeds us, and hope he will keep on. We don't know how long he will feed us. You see us here now. We are most all naked; the whole tribe. Some of the tribe are more destitute of clothing than we are. We got some goods here now which the Great Father sent us. They are lying in the Omaha warehouse, and we don't know but that the rats have eat them. There are a good many women and children that are naked and cannot come out of their tents. Some of the young men work out and get something for some of them to wear. The time I went to Washington last winter I asked the commissioner about my goods, and he said the goods had already been sent, and when I got back the agent would give them to us. But when we ask our agent for them he will not give them to us. The reason, I suppose, he will not give us our goods, he is mad with us, because our young men have been talking that the major would be removed and a new agent appointed; and we suppose he was mad about it, and when we went and asked for the goods he told us to go to our new agent. That is the last word I have heard from the agent. Would like you to see about it. We left a good country in Minnesota. We like our present place on the Omaha reservation very well; and, if our treaty is ratified, we shall be well satisfied.

November 29, 1864   Sand Creek,
                                                  Colorado Territory
Sand Creek Massacre

By the late autumn of 1864 deep tensions had come to mark the relations between whites and Indians in Colorado Territory. The frontier population contained a hard core of buffalo-hide hunters, rough miners, draft dodgers, immigrant farmers, and cattlemen who were violently anti-Indian. This was reflected in public officials' demands for the removal of all Indian title to Colorado. A "war" against the Indians would serve several white ends.

Clashes between Indians and whites increased in frequency as the Plains Indians grew restive and militant in the face of white expansion into their homeland. Some, having suffered greatly from regional droughts and the depletion of game resources, had been drawn into the federal annuity system in order to stabilize their life. Cheyenne bands were slowly changing their tribal organization to fit into the white world. Black Kettle's band of

Cheyenne was one who sought federal advice on removing themselves from the impending warfare sought by white volunteer troops in the field. An army officer at Fort Lyons ordered Black Kettle to locate his band of six hundred on Sand Creek, about twenty-five miles from the army camp, and to remain there, assuring Black Kettle that his pacifist position would be honored.

In areas where hostilities existed, United States military policy was "to exterminate the Indians." Colonel James Chivington, who commanded the Third Colorado Volunteer Regiment, a unit enlisted for a hundred days, actively searched for Indians to kill. On one occasion he permitted a massacre of a small band of Indians; another time he murdered five white bank robbers being held as prisoners for civilian authorities. Arriving at Fort Lyons in late November, he learned the location of the Black Kettle band. After receiving additional troops to bring the total under his command to about seven hundred and fifty men, he marched through the night and at dawn attacked and massacred about a hundred and fifty Cheyenne, about a hundred and twenty of whom were probably women and small children. Men and officers mutilated the bodies.

Three federal investigations of the massacre, two Congressional and one military, concluded that political and military leaders of the area, as well as Chivington, were responsible for the mass murder. No punishment was ever meted out. Later many of Chivington's men drew federal pensions for their military service. The examples chosen to document this episode are taken from the investigations. The first one is the sworn testimony of S. A. Browne, a Denver attorney, who relates the speech by Chivington that called for exterminating the Indians, a sentiment Chivington as well as other authorities expressed on numerous occasions (document 68). The second document is the testimony of Robert Bent, a civilian guide, who was the son of a Cheyenne woman and a white man (document 69).

Further reading: C. A. Prentice, "Captain Silas S. Soule, A Pioneer Martyr." *The Colorado Magazine*, Vol. IV (May, 1927); Stan Hoig, *The Sand Creek Massacre* (Norman: University of Oklahoma Press, 1961).

Document 68
1864   Sand Creek, Colorado Territory
Extermination Sentiments

Source: U.S. Congress. Senate. Special Committee Appointed under Joint Resolution of March 3, 1865. **Condition of the Indian Tribes.** S. Rept. 156, 39th Cong., 2d sess., 1867, p. 71.

S. E. Browne sworn:

I have lived in Colorado since May, 1862, during which time have been United States attorney for the Territory;

I have no doubt that if the military and civil management of Indian affairs were in discreet and competent hands Indian difficulties might be avoided; I personally know of no frauds or peculations committed against the government or Indians by any civil or military officers; in February last I was elected colonel of a mounted regiment raised in this Territory to serve for ninety days; late in the month of February I was in General Moonlight's headquarters, who was in command of the district of Colorado at that time, and heard him say that from the first and third Colorado cavalry then mustered out, and the horses and ponies taken at Sand Creek, there were two thousand two hundred head to be accounted for to the government, but of that number only four hundred and twenty-five or four hundred and seventy-five had been accounted for, leaving a deficit of over seventeen hundred that he knew not what had become of; a comparatively small number, I have been informed, have since been recovered; I have seen over a hundred scalps in the city and through the country, said to have been taken at Sand Creek; early in September or late in August last I heard Colonel Chivington in a public speech announce that his policy was to "kill and scalp all, little and big; that nits made lice;" one of the main causes of our difficulties with the Indians comes from the delay in paying the Indians their annuities according to law.

Document 69
1864   Sand Creek, Colorado Territory
Description of Atrocities

Source: U.S. Congress. Senate. Special Committee Appointed under Joint Resolution of March 3, 1865. **Condition of the Indian Tribes.** S. Rept. 156, 39th Cong., 2d sess., 1867. pp. 95-96.

Robert Bent sworn:

I am twenty-four years old; was born on the Arkansas river. I am pretty well acquainted with the Indians of the plains, having spent most of my life among them. I was employed as guide and interpreter at Fort Lyon by Major Anthony. Colonel Chivington ordered me to accompany him on his way to Sand creek. The command consisted of from nine hundred to one thousand men, principally Colorado volunteers. We left Fort Lyon at eight o'clock in the evening, and came on to the Indian camp at daylight the next morning. Colonel Chivington surrounded the village with his troops. When we came in sight of the camp I saw the American flag waving and heard Black Kettle tell the Indians to stand round the flag, and there they were huddled—men, women, and children. This was when we were within fifty yards of the Indians. I also saw a white flag raised. These flags were in so conspicuous a position that they must have been seen. When the troops fired the Indians ran, some of the men into their lodges,

Two Stockbridge being sworn into the Union Army

Struck by the Ree, chief of the Yankton Sioux

14. MAHLU,

1. YOHMI ma okla chito ka pisvt, nvnih chaha yo̱ pit oiya tok ; atuk osh ont binili ma, nan im ai ithvna vhloha hvt im ai ona tok.

2. Mihma itih ha wakvmmi cha, yvmmak ash im abvchi mvt,

3. Chu̱kvsh ilbvsha vhleha yokvto vba apehlichikayak osh immi hokvt nayukpvshke.

4. Nanukha̱klo vhleha yokvto hopohla hi okvt nayukpvshke.

5. Anukhobela iksho vhleha yokvto yakni a̱ isha he vlhpesa hokvt nayukpvshke.

6. Ahopoyuksaka aiahni vhleha hvt hochahafo, itukshihinla aiena hotvto, kaiya hi okv nayukpvshke.

7. Nan i nukhaklo vhleha yokvto ilap ma i nukha̱klo na pisa hi okvt nayukpvshke.

8. Chu̱kvsh kashofa vhleha yokvto Chihowa ya̱ pisa hi okvt nayukpvshke.

9. It i nanaiyvchi vhleha, yvmmak okvto Chihowa ushi hohchifa hi okvt, nayukpvshke.

10. Ahopoyuksaka pulla hatuk mak o̱ isht i palvmmi vhleha yokvto, vba apehlichika yvt immi hokvt nayukpvshke.

11. Vno atuk pulla mak o̱ hatak puta kvt isht hvchi yopulvt, hvchi ilbvshachit, a̱hli keyu kia nana okpulo ilaiyuka puta ka isht hvchi mihahanchikma, na hvchi yukpvshke.

12. Nayukpvt hvchi yukpa fenashke : isht hvchim vlhtoba hi vt chinto hosh vba ya̱ a̱sha hoka ; hopaii vhleha hvchin tikba aiasha ka yakohmichit ilbvshachi tok mak oka.

13. Yakni i hvpi hvchia hoke ; yohmi kia hvpi hvt ho̱mi kvt i kvnia hokmvt, nanta hak o̱ isht a homa hinla cho? yvmmak okvt himmakma nana ho̱ isht ai vlhpiesa he keyu ; amba kocha pit hlaya na hatak puta iyi yosh ahvhlihincha he ak o̱ pulla hoke.

14. Yakni in tohwikeli hvchia hoke. Tvmaha chito yosh nvnih chaha ai on talaia hokvt luma he keyushke.

15. Mikma hatak vt pvla ha̱ pvlalikmvt, tanchi isht vlhpisa nutaka yo̱ talali chatuk keyu ; amba pvla ai-o̱-hikia yo̱ ai o̱

Page from Choctaw Bible, *Matthew V.*

probably to get their arms. They had time to get away if they had wanted to. I remained on the field five hours, and when I left there were shots being fired up the creek. I think there were six hundred Indians in all. I think there were thirty-five braves and some old men, about sixty in all. All fought well. At the time the rest of the men were away from camp, hunting. I visited the battle-ground one month afterwards; saw the remains of a good many; counted sixty-nine, but a number had been eaten by the wolves and dogs. After the firing the warriors put the squaws and children together, and surrounded them to protect them. I saw five squaws under a bank for shelter. When the troops came up to them they ran out and showed their persons to let the soldiers know they were squaws and begged for mercy, but the soldiers shot them all. I saw one squaw lying on the bank whose leg had been broken by a shell; a soldier came up to her with a drawn sabre; she raised her arm to protect herself, when he struck, breaking her arm,; she rolled over and raised her other arm, when he struck, breaking it, and then left her without killing her. There seemed to be an indiscriminate slaughter of men, women, and children. There were some thirty or forty squaws collected in a hole for protection; they sent out a little girl about six years old with a white flag on a stick; she had not proceeded but a few steps when she was shot and killed. All the squaws in that hole were afterwards killed, and four or five bucks outside. The squaws offered no resistance. Every one I saw dead was scalped. I saw one squaw cut open with an unborn child, as I thought, lying by her side. Captain Soulé afterwards told me that such was the fact. I saw the body of White Antelope with the privates cut off, and I heard a soldier say he was going to make a tobacco-pouch out of them. I saw one squaw whose privates had been cut out. I heard Colonel Chivington say to the soldiers as they charged past him, "Remember our wives and children murdered on the Platte and Arkansas." He occupied a position where he could not have failed to have seen the American flag, which I think was a garrison flag, six by twelve. He was within fifty yards when he planted his battery. I saw a little girl about five years of age who had been hid in the sand; two soldiers discovered her, drew their pistols and shot her, and then pulled her out of the sand by the arm. I saw quite a number of infants in arms killed with their mothers. There were trading in the village at the time John Smith, a soldier named Louderback, and a teamster of young Colley's named Clark. They were trading goods said to belong to Dexter Colley and John Smith. The goods traded were similar to those they had been in the habit of trading before. I have heard the Indians charge Major Colley with trading their own goods to them.

1864-1865   Dakota Territory
Barbarity of U.S. Occupation Troops

The-Man-that-was-Struck-in-the-face-by-the-Ree, a principal chief of the Yankton Sioux in Dakota Territory, gave the following statement to a federal commission investigating conditions of the tribes at the end of the Civil War (document 70). A dignified, elderly man noted for his beautiful oratory, he was despondent at the utter failure of the path of peace that he had chosen. Whiskey sellers had wrecked his young men. Agents had robbed the tribe of annuities and stolen their cattle. The army stationed federal regular and volunteer troops among them who raped and prostituted Indian women and spread syphilis, which reduced the number of live born children. Officers and enlisted men freely used derogatory racial epithets. Struck by the Ree's account typifies many military-Indian relations of the Civil War era. The term *grandfather* used by the chief refers to the federal government.

Document 70
1864-1865   Dakota Territory
Barbarity of U.S. Occupation Troops

Source: U.S. Congress. Senate. Special Committee Appointed under Joint Resolution of March 3, 1865. **Condition of the Indian Tribes.** S. Rept. 156, 39th Cong., 2d sess., 1867, pp. 370-371.

My friend, we are now done with the agent, and we will now commence with the soldiers. The first year they came up in this country, I think my grandfather must have told them to commence on me, and that is the reason I commence thus with them. I would like to know if my grandfather told them to commence against me first; I should think so, the way they treated us. The first time they came up our young men had nothing to eat, and had gone over the Missouri river to hunt, and the soldiers killed seven of them. The Two-Kettle band and the Low Yanktonais were friendly, and were then on my reservation at the time, and some of them went out with my young men to hunt, and were among the seven that were killed; they were all friendly to the whites. When General Sully returned from his expedition, and was crossing my reserve, there were some of the Indian women married to half-breeds, and they had houses, and the soldiers went in and drove all the persons in them out, and robbed the houses of all there was in them. I would like to know if my grandfather told them to do so. I do not think he did. (All the chiefs present assent to this.) One of my chiefs, Little Swan, now here, had a house, and the soldiers broke in and destroyed all his goods, furniture, utensils and tools, and all the property of his band, the same being stored there. I would like to know if my grandfather told the soldiers when they returned from the expedition with their horses worn out, lost or stolen, to take horses from the Yanktons, in place of those they had lost or had worn out and broken down; I don't believe he did, but that is the way the soldiers did. I think the way the white men treated us is worse than the wolves do. We have a way in the winter of putting our dead up on scaffolds up from the ground, but the soldiers cut down the scaffolds and cut off the hair of the dead, and if they had good teeth they pulled them out, and some of them cut off the heads of the dead and carried them away. One time one of my young men and two squaws went over the river to Fort Randall, and a soldier wanted one of the squaws to do something with; he wanted to sleep with her, and she refused to sleep with him; one of the Indians asked the other squaw if she would sleep with the soldier, and she said she would; but the soldier would not have her, but wanted the other squaw, and claimed that the Indian was trying to prevent him from sleeping with his (the Indian's) squaw, his wife, and the Indian, fearing trouble, started for the ferry, and the soldier shot the Indian, though the Indian got over it. Another time when General Sully came up he passed through the middle of our field, turned all his cattle and stock into our corn and destroyed the whole of it. The ears of some were then a foot long; the corn was opposite Fort Randall, and they not only destroyed the corn but burnt up the fence. I think no other white man would do so; I do not think my grandfather told them to do so. The soldiers set fire to the prairie and burnt up four of our lodges and all there was in them, and three horses. When my corn is good to eat they cross the river from Fort Randall and eat it, and when it is not good they throw it in the river. I think my reserve is very small; the soldiers cut all my wood and grass, and I think this is bad treatment. The above in regard to the soldiers applies to my three chiefs on the reserve opposite Fort Randall, and I will now speak of things at my agency when the soldiers came down from the expedition last fall. At that time myself and others were out on a hunt, and had put our goods under the floors; but when the expedition came down the soldiers broke open the houses, destroyed our pans and kettles, and fired into the stoves and kettles. The soldiers are very drunken and come to our place—they have arms and guns; they run after our women and fire into our houses and lodges; one soldier came along and wanted one of our young men to drink, but he would not, and turned to go away, and the soldier shot at him. Before the soldiers came along we had good health; but once the soldiers come along they go to my squaws and want to sleep with them, and the squaws being hungry will sleep with them in order to get something to eat, and will get a bad disease, and then the squaws turn to their husbands and give them the bad disease.

I would like to know if my grandfather tells the soldiers to get all my hay. Every year great contracts are made for cutting hay for Fort Randall, and they cut the hay all off our land, and I would like to know if my grandfather gave them permission to cut all the hay and take the money. I never see any of the money myself. They take all of my mowing machines, bought with my money, to cut hay to sell to the soldiers, and I cannot get the mowing machines to cut anything for ourselves, and I have no use

of them. I think the agents are in partnership with these men cutting hay to sell to the soldiers. The reason I think the agent had a hand in cutting hay for the soldiers is, because one year Burleigh gave all of us chiefs fifty dollars each for the hay cut upon the contract. Last spring I asked him for the money for the hay he cut last year, and he told me he could not give it to me, because he had spent it last winter to get us something to eat; but I do not know whether he did or not. I hope you will report these things to my grandfather, and have him stop those men from cutting the hay right off. I think if they would return me my mowing machines I could cut part of the hay on the contract, and I must have some for my ponies; I wish you would attend to it. When I started to come down here they were getting ready to cut hay on another contract for the soldiers at Fort Randall. If they would return our mowing machines we could take the contract ourselves; we have some white men and half-breeds who could assist us, but they want it all themselves. The reason I talk thus is, I think all is wrong. I know the young man who has the contract; I think he has had it two years before. When he breaks any part of the mowing machine he goes to my blacksmith shop and carpenter shop to repair it; it is all paid for out of my annuity fund. It is Hedges who has the contract. Thompson, our blacksmith, has had charge of cutting the hay on the contracts for the past two years, and is getting ready to cut it this year.

Worse than that is the treatment I have received. For the past two winters soldiers have been quartered in my houses, and they go in my blacksmith and carpenter shops and work and repair whatever they have that needs it, and they burn my wood, and I have received no pay for all this. I think, my friend, when you come to see us, you will find a bad smell, and will want to put your coat to your mouth, and will want to get away. I don't know what the soldiers were sent there for, they do us no good. They did their private jobs in and around our houses, and they smell bad. I don't think my grandfather has but very little money; he only sends us about five dollars apiece, and all the white men round come and want to get what we do receive, for horses that some other Indians have stolen, but laid to the Yanktons, because they receive annuities. When the two men were shot the other day at Brulé creek, the governor sent me word to take the Indians away from that place, but none of those Indians belonged to me. Some of the white men come and lay round my place and get out of money, and go and kill their own cattle, and go and lay the killing to the Yanktons, and then go and get pay for them out of our money.

Since I made the treaty I am an American. My new agent told me the other day that the old Commissioner of Indian Affairs had been stealing part of the annuities, and that a better man had been put in his place. At this I felt good, and I put on my hat, I felt so good, my heart so big. My new agent is an entirely different man; he shows me the invoices, and I think he is a good man for us. He hired a blacksmith right off. My friend, what I am going to tell you is the truth. We only get five dollars apiece; we have only had one trader; he often makes us feel bad; he sells us goods so high it makes us cry; I think there ought to be two traders; I want two traders. I think if you come up to our agency you will laugh in the first place, and then be mad to see our storehouse in the same building with the trader's store. I want the store moved away a mile, so that it won't be so handy to our goods; I want you to have this changed. I hope my grandfather will see that the store is moved away from my warehouse, because the trader's store is under the floor where my goods are stored. I sometimes have bad dreams; I feel that there may be cracks that my goods may fall through.

I am done. Again I say, my friend, I am glad you have come to see us, and I hope will report all I have said to the Great Father, and that you will do us good. The Great Spirit knows that I have spoken the truth.

Strike the Ree here ends his speech.

1865   Aftermath of War   Cherokee Nation

At the close of the Civil War, Congress sent peace commissioners to the Indian nations in Indian Territory to settle the problems created by the fighting. While one fourth of the Cherokee had aided the Confederacy, the record of the loyal Cherokee with an exceedingly high enlistment rate and a loss of eight hundred men for the Union was ignored. Instead of helping the Indians eliminate problems caused by the war, the commissioners tried to impose upon the Cherokee a treaty requiring them to relinquish land. Two documents reveal the extent of their suffering. The first document is an excerpt from the annual report of J. Harlan, United States Indian Agent, Cherokee Nation, which accurately describes the impact of war upon them (document 71). The next one, a statement of wrongs done to the Cherokee and a plea for justice, is taken from a memorial to Congress drawn up by the Cherokee leaders, all combat veterans of the war (document 72). The attempt to take Cherokee land was the beginning of massive federal action to destroy the tribal structure and throw the territory open to white settlement. By their protests the Cherokee Nation succeeded in surviving until 1898, when it was abolished by Congress with the Curtis Act.

Document 71
1865   Cherokee Nation
Impact of War on the Cherokees

Source: U.S. Commissioner of Indian Affairs. **Annual Report, 1865.** (Washington: Government Printing Office, 1865), pp. 471-472.

I do not urge their personal suffering with a belief or hope that anything will be allowed for them, but only to strengthen their just claim for property lost to them. Their school-houses and seminaries have suffered in the general destruction which the nation has suffered. Their two fine seminaries would require an outlay of many thousand dollars, before they will be fit for use as seminaries. Their school-houses throughout the nation are many of them burned down, and the bare walls of the balance only left standing.

A very few common schools exist in the nation, and this will be the case while the whole national fund has to be used to supply the destitute with food. They have no means at present to pay teachers, and it must be a long time before they will have, unless the government pays them some part of their losses in this their greatest need. Their churches, heretofore numerous and tolerably well attended, have now gone to decay, and the attendance very much neglected. The Cherokees are—and I am sorry to say it—fast very fast, going backwards in the march of civilization and Christianity. Nothing else ought to be expected from a people only partially civilized, abandoned in their weakness, unprotected by the government for nearly two years after the war commenced, and left a prey to the hate of their rebel brothers, the Cherokees and other tribes who had joined the south in the late rebellion, and worst of all, if possible, to the cupidity of white scoundrels professing loyalty; it is not astonishing that they distrust everybody, white men in particular, and that they are discouraged and disheartened, and on the backward march towards a state of barbarism. Indeed, it would be strange if they were not. The Cherokees were mustered out of the United States service on the thirty-first day of May, and it was nearly three weeks afterwards before they were paid off. The thirty-first day of May is generally too late to plant corn in this country. This year it would have done tolerably well, owing to the late rains. Almost all the corn was planted by the women and children, and partially cultivated before the men were discharged. All that the men could do after their discharge was to assist their women and children in finishing the cultivation of what had been planted. Yet I think they would have enough to make their bread if all that has been raised could be equally divided, but I am sure that cannot be done. The large surplus is in the hands of a few. Many have small surplus, and many have some, but not enough, for their bread, and many poor widows have none and no means of buying any. Some this year will be fed to stock by those who raised it; some will be held over to feed their teams next year, while raising a crop, and much will be wasted. It is apparent that many will have to be fed until another crop shall be raised. I propose to discriminate in favor of those who have none, and those who have some, but not enough to furnish their own bread. They have raised no wheat, and those who have corn should receive a small amount of flour. Occasional changes from corn to flour would promote health, and would enable the many having a small surplus to barter more corn to those who have none.

No one can fully appreciate the wealth, content and comparative happiness the Cherokees enjoyed before the late rebellion, or very shortly after it was begun, unless he had been here and seen it, (which was my case;) and no man can believe more than half of the want, misery and destitution of the Cherokee people now. Blackened chimneys of fine houses are now all that is left, fences burned, and farms laid waste. The air of ruin and desolation envelopes the whole country. None have wholly escaped. No man can pass through the country without seeing all that I have attempted to describe, and no man can fully appreciate it unless he has seen it.

All of which is respectfully submitted.

J. HARLAN,
U. S. Indian Agent, Cherokee Nation.
HON. E. SELLS,
Sup't of Indian Affairs, Southern Superintendency.

Document 72
January 24, 1866   Cherokee Nation
Cherokee Plea for Justice

Source: Cherokee Nation. **Memorial to the President of the United States, and to the Senate and House of Representatives** (Washington, D.C.: January 24, 1866).

To the President of the United States, and to the Senate and House of Representatives.

With hearts full of sorrow, we are constrained to beg your attention to our earnest prayer in behalf of our afflicted and distressed Nation.

We learn that a bill has been introduced into Congress, entitled "A bill to consolidate the Indian tribes, and to establish Civil Government in the Indian Territory."

It is our solemn conviction, and the conviction of our people, that if that bill becomes a law, and is carried into execution, it will crush us as a people, and destroy us as a Nation. In hope of averting such a calamity, we beg your consideration of a few facts, which will show our claim on the United States for justice—our claim on them to observe sacredly, all their treaty obligations to us.

. . .

We cannot adequately depict the scenes which followed in consequence of this failure to obtain help from the Federal army, as seven thousand (7,000) loyal Indians were driven before a foe, infuriated by defeat, and strongly reinforced. With their eyes turned toward the North, ever hoping for succor, the warriors battled in the rear, covering the retreat, while the old men, with women and children, half starved, half clothed, bare footed, waded through the frozen snows, and breasted the keen winds on the

prairies. Never will their sufferings be known. Frozen hands and feet—starved and emaciated frames—swift fevers, and lingering diseases, filling a thousand premature graves, all bear witness to their patriotic sufferings.

The patriotic devotion of these people has rarely been equalled in the annals of history. On the South was Texas—on the East were Arkansas and Missouri—all hostile—to the North it was more than two hundred (200) miles to the nearest aid. A large part of that two hundred miles, was an uninhabited wild, and unprotected from the enemy. Yet that battle was fought by these warriors, and that distance was marched by men, women and children, without aid from the United States Government or people. Had the inhabitants of some county in North Carolina started of their own accord to escape the curse of rebellion, and fought and whipped a rebel brigade, and marched to Washington, even through the cultivated lands of Virginia, they would justly have been lauded as heroes. Had these things been done by the African race, the history of that fight and march would have been sung in paeans of praise all over the land.

After incredible miseries, these Creeks, Seminoles and Cherokees, and individuals of the tribes reached Kansas.

. . .

We boldly claim that we have done our duty, to the full extent of our power, as the friends and allies of the Federal Government. More than three fourths of the able bodied men of the loyal Cherokees, fought in the Federal army, which is a vastly larger proportion of men that any State in the Union has furnished for the war. We fought to the end of the war, and after the last rebel was whipped, we were honorably mustered out of the service. The graves of eight hundred Cherokee warriors, fallen by our side in your service, testify that we have done our duty. Now, having done our whole duty to the Government, all we ask is that the Government do its duty to us—that is fulfill its treaty obligations to us—that it redeem its solemn, reiterated pledges. We ask no gifts, no charities, but simply our rights—the rights for which we have fought and bled in your armies, and for which so many of our noblest men have died.

We make our earnest appeal to the President of the United States and to Congress. We entreat you to regard sacredly your past treaties with us, and to enact no law that shall sweep out of existence those most sacred rights which you have guaranteed to us forever.

. . .

Have we not suffered enough when the torch, both of friend and foe, has consumed our dwellings and desolated our land, and in that the armies of both parties to the war have subsisted on our cattle? While we were fighting the battles of the Union, our land, which you could not protect, though pledged to do so, was infested by "Jayhawkers," and army followers from the North, who drove out and carried from our country, millions of dollars worth of stock and other property, so that we are utterly impoverished. In confirmation of this statement, we quote the words of Hon. Justin Harlan, U.S. Indian Agent, in his report for 1864. Judge Harlan says, "While the rebels, bushwhackers, and guerillas, have taken (from the Cherokees) horses, cattle, hogs, corn, and other crops—all they wanted—white men, loyal, or pretending to be so, have taken five times as much, and all kinds of stock has been driven North and West, and sold." We might quote much more of the same purport.

That which aggravates our sorrow still more, is the fact, that all the robbers and jayhawkers, who have been stealing our stock, and all the faithless officials, who have been plundering both the Government and the Indians, are loud in denouncing the Cherokees as rebels—hoping by their unscrupulous slanders, to divert attention from their own villainy. Thus they have deceived and misled many good and honest men. We are wronged and belied, while war and pestilence and famine have filled our land with mourning and death.

During the progress of the war, white and African refugees have been fed and clothed at public expense. Of this we do not complain. But, when *our people* were driven from their homes, in which the United States was bound to protect them, the Indians' own money was appropriated to feed them, and these appropriations were so used that scarcely a tithe of the money's value ever reached the Indians.

Ye Rulers of America, our cry is unto you as unto God-fearing men. Let justice be done—Let our country, and the sacred right of self-government, guaranteed by treaties, be secured to us—Give us a reasonable indemnity for our losses—Let an equitable settlement be made for our lands in Kansas—Let the interest due and accuring on our investments be paid over, as provided by treaty, that our Government and schools and seminaries may be sustained—that an orphan asylum may be provided for our thousand orphans, many of them the children of heroic soldiers, fallen fighting for the Union.

Now that the unity of your own great Republic has been secured, and the blood and toil and suffering of patriotic Cherokees have helped to cement the Union, we ask that you preserve and protect both the integrity and the peace of our Nation, against the machinations of all those who would rend it to fragments.

Our people are already far advanced in civilization and are all anxious for still further advancement in all that pertains to civilization and Christianity. With the blessing of God, all we want to make us a happy and prosperous people is that the Government secure to us our rights, immovably.

CHEROKEE DELEGATION.
WASHINGTON, D.C. January 24, 1866.

VI
Completion of Expansion
1866-1899

Forty years after the close of the Civil War, America had finished industrializing the West. Railroad and telegraph lines removed forever the old limitations of space and time, bringing settlers into every corner of the vast continent and taking out the treasures of mines, forests, and farms. The unparalleled influx of people and the rapid growth of cities were unplanned and unregulated. The onslaught crushed the Indians and shoved them onto the remnants of their original property base while their basic source of food, the buffalo, died by the uncounted millions under the guns of the hide hunters.

Factors not related to military problems and tactics drove Western Indians to war against the Americans. But, the American military viewed the Indian attacks from the blinkered perspective of a military tactician. A policy resulted based on the premise that only war could ultimately solve the Indian refusal to submit to American civilization; intelligence and planning had no place in army movements. Although a few officers saw the necessity of resolving the Indians' myriad problems, they, like the civilian experts on Indian reform, bungled every practical effort they made. The belief in force as a universal remedy for problems directed military policy in the West. Army strategists were not alone. The majority of public officials and private citizens felt that the West should be settled without regard for orderly procedure or regulations of any kind. War could scarcely be avoided.

By 1877 most of the American wars against the Indian had ceased. A few minor clashes continued until 1919. Initially the military found it difficult to defeat the tribes without long and expensive campaigns. Indian warriors always seemed to escape capture. But under the experienced direction of Civil War generals, the army launched a series of devastating raids against Indian villages, destroying lodges, supplies, ponies, and capturing women and children. Love of family and fear of starvation in the wilderness would sometimes make the Indians capitulate. The scorched earth policy was not fully effective until the extermination of the great buffalo herds. With their elimination the tribes, facing starvation, were forced to become dependent upon federal annuities.

On reservations the Indians did not find refuge from their conquerors, because the white men proceeded to attack the culture of the Indians. By the 1880s the government started to crack the tribal structure through the instrument of allotment—a property expropriation measure which allotted farms to individual tribal members and provided for the sale of the "surplus" to whites. Since the Indians did not have the skills to farm, did not understand taxes, did not wish to destroy their tribal existence, and lacked the skills in English and arithmetic necessary to contend with businessmen, they usually lost their allotment.

In every area where the tribes maintained control of their property, business groups, land speculators, and timber companies made repeated attempts to obtain it. Sometimes these efforts became criminal in nature. Frequently they kept the tribe continually in turmoil, fending off entreaties and complex contractual agreements that would exploit them.

A half-hearted, fumbling attempt was made to provide Indians with the basic elements of Western civilization. In the 1880s the Bureau of Indian Affairs initiated a two-fold process to civilize the Indians. Believing that the Indian life-style was an impediment to economic well-being, the Bureau led an attack against everything Indian. Children would be taught to despise their Indian background and to reject their parents. At the same time an American culture, "superior to any on earth," would be imposed. The program included the use of English as the only language, conversion to Christianity, and the development of mechanical skills. To accomplish this end, total control of the Indians' property as well as their persons had to rest in the Bureau of Indian Affairs.

Further reading: Ralph K. Andrist, *The Long Death, The Last Days of the Plains Indian* (New York: The Macmillan Company, 1964).

April 24, 1866   Smith River, California
Execution of an Indian

The broad power of an Indian agent permitted him to deny Indians under his charge the civil liberties that the rest of America took for granted. The following letter from agent William Bryson to his superintendent, Charles Maltby, requests authority "to execute" an Indian in order to preserve discipline on the reservation (document 73).

Document 73
April 24, 1866   **Smith River, California**
Execution of an Indian

Source: U.S. Commissioner of Indian Affairs. **Annual Report for 1866** (Washington: Government Printing Office, 1866), p. 100.

SMITH RIVER RESERVATION,
April 24, 1866.

SIR: I have the honor to inform you that on Sunday morning, April 22, a fight occurred in the Humboldt Indian ranch, which resulted in the death of one Indian by the unjustifiable interference and act of a third Indian.

The circumstances were these: Some ten weeks ago an Indian and his squaw had a little fuss, and he was correcting her, I suppose a little roughly, when another squaw interfered and used some very unfriendly language to the Indian who whipped his squaw, which caused him to strike her and hurt her severely. I was in Crescent City when this occurred. Some days afterwards they had a

Cherokee Arithmetic

11. ᎠᏬᎠ ᎢᏍᎢ ᏂᏍᏓᏫᎠᎣᏫ 231, 114 ᎠᎦ 324?
           ᏕᏫᎠᏢᏫᎡ 669.

11. What is the sum of 231, 114 and 324?
           Answer 669.

general consultation, and agreed on terms of settlement, and I suppose it was all fixed up without my interference, but the squaw that interfered and got hurt was not willing to settle until her brother drew blood from the Indian that struck and hurt her. When, on Sunday morning last, her brother met this Indian and challenged him to fight, as he was unarmed, he told him he did not want to fight, when the Indian that challenged him made at him and struck him with a knife, inflicting a serious but not dangerous wound on the back. His friend, seeing that he was cut and the blood flowing down his back, took a knife in his hand and ran after this Indian, and came up to him when some others had caught him and were parleying over the matter, stepped up lightly behind him and struck him with a knife and killed him almost instantly; then ran away and made his escape to the woods, and has not yet been caught.

My own opinion, formed from experience, is that this Indian should be hung, and I believe that the peace, safety, and correct discipline on the reservation require it, but in the absence of law and instruction in cases of this nature, I do not feel inclined to take all responsibility upon myself.

I think full instructions should be given me, and some precedent established for my guidance in the future in case similar events should occur.

The military are the proper ones to conduct the execution of an Indian, but General McDowell's order last year forbids any military officer to execute an Indian, and commands him to turn them over to the civil authorities. This order should be modified so as to allow commanders of posts established on Indian reservations to conduct the execution of an Indian, when called upon by the Indian department so to do, if, in their judgment, the punishment is just.

Heretofore I have acted on my own responsibility in cases of this kind, the military concurring, and had in one case an Indian executed, and I know that it had a very soothing influence over the balance of them, and I believe it to be as essential to preserve order and discipline on the reservation to execute an Indian occasionally as it is to furnish them with food and clothing, but I prefer some authority on which to predicate my acts.

I shall not take any decisive action in this case until I hear from you, unless in my opinion our safety require it. The Indian has not yet been caught, (he is lying in the woods,) but I think he will be soon.

The idea of turning over Indians to the civil authorities for trial and punishment I think is wrong. The reservation Indian is under the protection of the general government. The reservation is his home, and there he should receive his rewards and punishments.

I am, very respectfully, your obedient servant,
WILLIAM BRYSON,
Indian Agent, Smith River Reservation.

December 28, 1866   **St. Louis, Missouri**
Extermination Sentiment

The Sioux fought, defeated, and killed an entire company of soldiers under the command of Captain W. J. Fetterman near Fort Philip Kearny. A colonel in the Civil War, Fetterman disobeyed a direct order and marched into the Sioux warriors. The battle was not a massacre. The following telegram was sent by Lieutenant General William T. Sherman, department commander of the region, to General U. S. Grant (document 74).

Document 74
December 28, 1866   **St. Louis, Missouri**
Extermination Sentiment

Source: U.S. Congress. **Letter of the Secretary of War . . .** S. Ex. Doc. No. 15, 39th Cong., 2d sess., 1867, p. 27.

ST. LOUIS, *December* 28, 1866.

GENERAL: Just arrived in time to attend the funeral of my adjutant general, Sawyer. I have given personal instructions to General Cooke about the Sioux. I do not yet understand how the massacre of Colonel Fetterman's party could have been so complete. We must act with vindictive earnestness against the Sioux, even to their extermination, men, women, and children. Nothing less will reach the root of this case.

W. T. SHERMAN,
Lieutenant General,

U. S. GRANT.

Official: E. S. PARKER,
Colonel and A. D. C.

1867   Great Plains
War Against Families and Property

The United States Army faced a difficult task in trying to defeat the warriors of the Plains. The Indians were mobile and very capable fighters. However, the critical need to protect their homes and families and the dependence on wild game, principally the buffalo, made them particularly vulnerable. The army quickly learned to strike hard at the Indian villages and families. On numerous occasions the villages were leveled, and the tribe was reduced to poverty, often in the midst of winter. With countless millions of buffalo available, the loss could be repaired in a year. The following excerpt from the annual report of W. T. Sherman, commanding general in the West, describes implementation of army policy (document 75).

Further reading: Mari Sandoz, *Crazy Horse, the Strange Man of the Oglalas, a Biography* (Lincoln: University of Nebraska Press, 1961).

Document 75
1867   Great Plains
War Against Families and Property

Source: U.S. Congress. **Report of the Secretary of War,** 40th Cong., 2d sess., H. Ex. Doc. No. 1, 1867, p. 34.

Very early in the season Indians of the Cheyenne, Kiowa, and Arapahoe bands had unreservedly notified the commanding officers of posts and the stage drivers and agents that, as soon as the grass grew, they would insist on our withdrawing from these roads. General Hancock also learned that certain Ogalalla and Brulé Sioux had come down from the far north, and were then in treaty with the Cheyennes and Dog-Soldiers, arranging for general hostilities and a concert of action on their part. He accordingly

collected a force, mostly of the new seventh cavalry and thirty-seventh infantry, with light battery B, fourth artillery, and during the month of April he proceeded in person to the threatened country, viz, that embracing Forts Zarah, Larned, and Dodge on the Arkansas, and Forts Harker and Hays on the Smoky Hill. He held full interviews with nearly all the leading men of the tribes I have named, but for reasons fully set forth in his report of May 23, 1867, he, on the 19th of April, burned the village of the Cheyennes and Sioux on Pawnee Fork as a punishment for depredations and murders previously committed. I refer to the general's report on this whole matter, and beg that no indemnification be attempted to these tribes on this account, for it would encourage them to believe themselves warranted to commit any number of murders and thefts, and they would necessarily infer that we feared to strike them in their most vulnerable points, viz., their property and families. It is very difficult to catch their warriors if once on their guard, and the only mode of restraining them is by making them feel that we can reach their families and property.

December, 1869   Wrangel, Alaska
Bombardment of an Alaskan Indian Village

The American acquisition of Alaska required stationing troops at several posts along the shoreline. The Alaskan natives inhabiting villages adjacent to the forts of their new masters had a difficult time adjusting to the change. Unfortunately the army sent too many troops and disrupted a stable political and economic life. Immediately upon disembarking, the troops committed a series of outrages upon the natives, including the looting of a Russian Orthodox Church. In the course of one incident at Wrangel (reported by the post commander), the army shelled the town and hanged an Indian for murdering a white trader (document 77). In his report the chairman of the Board of Indian Commissioners, Vincent Colyer, clearly reveals the racism in the administration of Alaskan justice that led to the fight (document 76).

Document 76
October, 1869   Wrangel, Alaska
Background of Bombardment

Source: U.S. Congress. **Wrangel Alaska, Previous to Bombardment,** 41st Cong., 2d sess., 1870, S. Ex. Doc. 68, p. 7.

On my return trip, while stopping at Wrangel, October 29, Leon Smith, assisted by two half-drunken discharged soldiers, assaulted an Indian who was passing in front of his store. Mr. Smith, ex-confederate officer, said that he was under the impression (mistaken, as he afterward admitted) that the Indian had struck his little boy, and he only shook the Indian. The drunken soldiers standing by then, of their own accord, (unsolicited, Mr. Smith says, by him,) seized the Indian, brutally beat him, and stamped upon him. I had been taking a census of the village that afternoon, and hearing the shouts of the party, met the Indian with his face badly cut and bleeding coming toward his home. I immediately went to the post and suggested to the commandant that he should have the drunken soldiers arrested and retained for trial. He sent a lieutenant, with two or three men, "to quell the disturbance," the Indians meanwhile having become excited, and to "use his own discretion about arresting the men." Lieutenant Loucks returned soon after without the drunken soldiers, and gave as his reason that "the Indian struck Mr. Smith's boy," which, as I have said, was disproved.

The drunken men belonged to a party of over one hundred discharged soldiers who had come down on our steamer from Sitka, and were on their way to San Francisco. Some of them had been drummed out of the service for robbing the Greek [Russian] church at Sitka, and for other crimes. I had informed the commandant of their character the morning after our vessel arrived, and suggested to him the propriety of preventing any of them from landing and going to the Indian village. He replied that he had no authority to prevent any one from landing. I was surprised at this, as I supposed Alaska was an Indian territory, and that the military had supreme control.

Document 77
December, 1869   Wrangel, Alaska
Bombardment of Indian Village

Source: U.S. Congress. **Bombardment of Indian Village at Wrangel, Alaska**, 41st Cong., 2d sess., 1870, S. Ex. Doc. 67, pp. 2-5.

HEADQUARTERS FORT WRANGEL,
Wrangel Island, A. T. December 30, 1869.

CAPTAIN: I have the honor to submit the following report for the information of the major general commanding the department:

About ten minutes after 11 o'clock on the night of December 25, 1869, it was reported to me that one of the laundresses, Mrs. Jacob Muller, had been badly injured by a Stickine Indian, named Lowan, he having, while in her house, just outside of the stockade, and in the act of shaking hands with her, bitten off the third finger of her right hand between the first and second joints, her husband, quartermaster sergeant of this battery, and a citizen, named Campbell, being present at the time. Learning what had taken place, and that the Indian had escaped to the ranch, notwithstanding the efforts of the sergeant to arrest him, I immediately sent Lieutenant Loucks with a detachment of twenty men to take him, with in-

structions to bring him in, if possible, without bloodshed, and only to use their arms in case of resistance or in self-defense. Lieutenant Loucks immediately proceeded to execute the order given him, and returned, bringing with him the dead body of the Indian Lowan and his brother Estone, the latter being badly wounded in the arm, the cause of violent measures having been resorted to. The report of Lieutenant Loucks, herewith appended and marked A, will fully explain. Apprehending trouble, I had turned out the entire force under my command, and as soon as firing was heard at the ranch I immediately sent a detachment of ten men as far as the store of the post trader, some three hundred yards from the garrison, with instructions to act in concert with Lieutenant Louck's party, should they require assistance. A picket guard was stationed around the camp, and everything placed in a condition of defense.

About 10 o'clock a. m. of the morning of December 26, 1869, the sergeant of the guard reported several shots in the direction of the store, and in a few minutes word was brought to me that Mr. Leon Smith, partner of the post trader, W. R. Lear, had been shot near the door of the store. Mr. Smith was soon after brought in to the garrison and taken to the hospital, where his wounds were examined by the surgeon, who pronounced them of a most serious character, fourteen shots having penetrated the body on the left side, just below his heart, and three in the left wrist. Nothing further occurred during the night, and at daylight in the morning I sent Lieutenant Loucks again to the ranch with a detachment under a flag of truce, with instructions to see the chief of the tribe, Shakes, and demand of him the murderer, the Indians to turn the man over to him there, or failing in that, I gave them until 12 o'clock that day to bring him in, notifying them that if at that hour the man Scutd-dor, whom I knew to be in the ranch, was not in my custody, I should open fire upon them from the garrison. I also directed Lieutenant Loucks to inform the principal chiefs of the tribe, Shakes, Torryat, Shonta, Hank, and Quamnanasty, that I wished to see and talk with them at the post as soon as practicable. This message I had sent to each of the chiefs by an Indian woman before Lieutenant Loucks left the post, and I am confident that it was delivered. For the result of Lieutenant Loucks's interview with Shakes and Torryat, I would respectfully call your attention to his report. On the return of Lieutenant Loucks to the post, and reporting to me the refusal of the chiefs to come to the garrison, their indisposition to deliver up the murderer, and the hostile disposition manifested by those present, all of whom were armed, I consulted with the officers present as to the propriety of carrying out my threat of firing on the village, and they were unanimous in the opinion that nothing but the most decided measures would insure the safety of the post. At 12 o'clock no signs were made of any disposition on the part of the Indians to comply with my orders: but their intentions to fight were made evident by the numerous persons engaged in carrying their goods to what they considered places of safety. I waited, however, without avail until nearly 2 o'clock, hoping that they might change their determination; and at 2 o'clock I opened with solid shot on the house in which I knew the murderer, Scutdor, resided; several shots struck the house, but the Indians maintained their position and returned the fire from the ranch, several of their shots striking in close proximity to the men. Later in the day fire was opened on the gun detachments from the hills in rear of and commanding the post, but fortunately without effect. This was replied to from the upper windows of the hospital, and, in connection with a few rounds of canister in that direction, soon drove them away. Firing was kept up on their part all of the afternoon, and a slow fire from the 6-pounder gun on the village was maintained until dark. The next morning, just at day-break, they opened on the garrison from the ranch with musketry, which was immediately replied to, and seeing that they were determined not only to resist, but had become the assailants, I resolved to shell them, but having only solid shot for the 6-pounder, and the distance being too great for canister, I still continued the fire from that gun with shot and from the mountain howitzer with shell. The practice was excellent, considering that I have no breech sights for any of the guns at the post—notwithstanding that three requisitions had been made for the same—and after four shells had been fired, two bursting immediately in front of the houses, and two solid shots just through the house of the principal chief, Shakes, a flag of truce was seen approaching the post, and firing on my part ceased. The flag of truce bore a message from Shakes that he and the other chiefs wished to talk with me, and I replied that I would talk with them in the garrison; but that the murderer must be brought in, for without him "talk was useless."

Soon after the chiefs were seen coming over, and a party behind them with the murderer, who was easily recognized by his dress. Just as they were leaving the ranch a scuffle, evidently prearranged, took place, and the prisoner escaped and was seen making for the bush, no attempt to rearrest him being made. The chiefs on their arrival at the garrison were received by myself and the other officers, and a conference ensued. They were then informed that until "the murderer was brought in no terms would be extended to them; that on that basis alone I would retreat." Finding me determined to have the man at all hazards, they then asked what time would be given and stated that as a proof of their good intentions they would surrender to me the mother of the murderer. I informed them that they must, as they proposed, bring me the hostage at once, and in addition, the sub-chief of the tribe to which the murderer belonged, the head chief being absent up the Stickine River; and that, if the murderer himself was not in my possession by six o'clock the following evening, I would open on them and destroy the entire ranch, together with its occupants.

This closed the conference, and during the afternoon of the same day the woman and the sub-chief were brought in and placed in confinement. That evening, about nine o'clock, the murderer Scutdor was brought in by the chiefs and surrendered to me. The next morning, December 27, a court was organized by general post order No. 76, for the trial of the murderer, who was identified by the five chiefs of the tribe and by his own confession. For the proceedings of the trial I have the honor to call your attention to the accompanying report appended and marked B. In pursuance of the sentence of the court, the man was duly executed by hanging, at twelve o'clock and thirty minutes, on the 29th of December, 1869, in full view of the entire ranch, the five chiefs and the Indian doctor being in immediate attendance at the gallows. The execution passed off without accident, and the body remained hanging until sun-down, when, by my permission, it was taken away by his friends.

Crazy Horse killed

Two much praise cannot be awarded to the officers and men of this command for their coolness and general good behavior, particularly when it is remembered that twenty-two of the men were new recruits, many of whom had never seen any service. I would particularly call the attention of the major general commanding the department to First Lieutenant M. R. Loucks, Second Artillery, whose promptness and decision in carrying out the instructions given him entitle him to the greatest praise, particularly in his interview with the chiefs on his second visit to the ranch.

I would also call your attention to the report of Acting Assistant Surgeon H. M. Rick, United States Army, marked C, of the casualties which occurred during the trouble.

In conclusion, I can only say that, though regretting that extreme measures had to be resorted to, yet under the circumstances I consider nothing else would have accomplished the object in view—that of bringing Mr. Smith's murderer to justice, and reducing the Indians to a state of subjection to the United States authority. Everything is now quiet, and I have no reason to anticipate any future trouble; yet my vigilance is not remitted, nor will it be, as I have no confidence in any promises made by Indians.

They have shown their hostile feelings in this instance, and it is only through fear and the knowledge that any crime committed by them will meet with prompt punishment, that will keep them in proper subjection.

I would also request that the thirty-pound Parrot gun asked for in my last requisition may be sent to me at as early a date as practicable, for, had that gun been in position, I think two percussion shells would have brought the Indians to terms.

Mr. Smith died at eleven o'clock of the night of the 26th of December, 1869. His sufferings were terrible, and death must have been a relief.

Trusting that my action may meet with the approval of the major general commanding the department,

I am, captain, very respectfully, your obedient servant,

W. BORROWE,
First Lieutenant Second Artillery.

April 30, 1871   Camp Grant, Arizona Territory Massacre of Pacifist Apache

In the early months of 1871 five hundred Aravaipa Apache came out of the mountains and voluntarily surrendered to Lieutenant Royal E. Whitman, commander of Camp Grant, an isolated army post seventy-five miles northeast of Tucson, Arizona. Whitman settled them four miles from Camp Grant and wrote to his superiors requesting official orders. In nearby Tucson a group of businessmen, who profited from the Indian wars by trading guns and food to the Apache and then supplying the military regiments with supplies, detested the attempt to settle the Indian question peacefully. Throughout the West and in Washington such groups, or rings, operated to some extent in almost all Indian wars. Usually they were of minor influence. During Geronimo's last campaign, for example, they helped finance and provision the Apache and also sold supplies to the army that chased and fought them. To thwart the military policy the ring decided to intervene in the Apache affair. They hired 142 Mexican and Papago mercenaries who were led by six white men to the camp. At dawn they attacked, killing probably one hundred Apache men, women, and children, and allowing the Papago to carry twenty-seven Apache children away to sell as slaves in Mexico. Dispatched by Lieutenant Whitman to render medical aid to the survivors, Dr. Conant B. Briesly, post surgeon of Camp Grant, describes the massacre scene in the following letter to a military board of inquiry (document 78). His count of the dead is in error.

Further reading: Odie B. Faulk, *The Geronimo Campaign* (New York: Oxford University Press, 1969).

Document 78
April 30, 1871   Camp Grant, Arizona Territory Massacre of Pacifist Apache

Source: U.S. Commissioner of Indian Affairs. **Annual Report for 1871** (Washington: Government Printing Office, 1871), pp. 487-488.

TERRITORY OF ARIZONA, *Camp Grant:*

On this 16th day of September, 1871, personally appeared Conant B. Briesly, who, being duly sworn according to law, deposeth and saith: I am acting assistant surgeon United States Army, at Camp Grant, Arizona, where I arrived April 25, 1871, and reported to the commanding officer for duty as medical officer. Some four hundred Apache Indians were at that time held as prisoners of war by the military stationed at Camp Grant, and during the period intervening between April 25 and 30, I saw the Indians every day. They seemed very well contented, and were busily employed in bringing in hay, which they sold for manta and such little articles as they desired outside the Government ration. April 29, Captain Chiquita and some of the other chiefs were at the post, and asked for seeds and for some hoes, stating that the garden-seeds had been sent for, and would be up from Tucson in a few days. They then left, and I saw nothing more of them until after the killing.

Sunday morning, April 30, I heard a rumor, just before inspection, that the Indians had been attacked, and learned from Lieutenant Whitman that he had sent the two interpreters to the Indian camp to warn the Indians and bring them down where they could be protected, if possible. The interpreters returned and stated that the attack had already been made, and the Indians dispersed, and that the attacking party were returning.

Lieutenant Whitman then ordered me to go to the Indian camp to render medical assistance and bring down any wounded I might find. I took twelve men (mounted) and a wagon and proceeded without delay to the scene of the murder. On my arrival I found that I should have but little use for wagon or medicine; the work had been too thoroughly done. The camp had been fired and the dead bodies of some twenty-one women and children were lying scattered over the ground; those who had been wounded in the first instance, had their brains beaten out with stones. Two of the best-looking of the squaws were lying in such a position, and from the appearance of the genital organs and of their wounds, there can be no doubt that they were first ravished and then shot dead. Nearly all of the dead were mutilated. One infant of some ten months was shot twice and one leg hacked nearly off. While going over the ground we came upon a squaw who was unhurt, but were unable to get her to come in and talk, she not feeling very sure of our good intentions. Finding nothing further could be done, I returned to the post and reported the state of affairs to Lieutenant Whitman, commanding post.

May 1, Lieutenant Whitman, some citizens and myself went out to the Indian camp, and on our way we met two squaws and a buck coming in. They stated that their loss was much heavier than we had supposed, and that some eighty-five had been killed, of whom eight only were men, and that some twenty-five of their number had been taken prisoners. We found six more dead bodies, one of which was an old man, two half-grown boys, and three women. The evening of May 1, Lieutenant Whitman sent two Indians, who had come during the day, into the mountains, mounted on horses furnished by him, to bring in two wounded women. The women were brought in in two days. One of them, a wife of Chipuita Caqitan, was shot through the left arm, and the other had received a gunshot wound through the left lung. The Indians who came expressed themselves as satisfied that we had nothing to do with the murder, and further stated that their only wish was to get back the captives and live at peace.

I know from my own personal observation that during the time the Indians were in after my arrival, they were rationed every three days, and Indians absent had to be accounted for; their faces soon became familiar to me, and I could at once tell when any strange Indians came in. And I furthermore state that I have been among nearly all the various tribes on the Pacific coast, and that I have never seen any Indians who showed the intelligence, honesty, and desire to learn, manifested by these Indians. I came among them greatly prejudiced against them, but, after being with them, I was compelled to admit that they were honest in their intentions, and really desired peace.

C. B. BRIESLY,
Acting Assistant Surgeon United States Army.

Sworn to and subscribed before me this 16th day of September, 1871.

WM. NELSON,
Captain Twenty-first Infantry, Commanding Post.

October, 1871   Texas Panhandle
Camp "Humor"

The Fourth U.S. Cavalry and a company of Tonakaw scouts fought several minor battles with the Comanche. In one battle they killed two Comanche warriors. Captain Robert Carter's memoirs describe the mistreatment of the bodies and the use of the heads for a camp joke (document 79). The heads were eventually deposited with the Smithsonian Institution's large collection of Indian skulls.

Document 79
October, 1871   Texas Panhandle
Camp "Humor"

Source: R. G. Carter, **On the Border with MacKenzie or Winning West Texas from the Comanche** (Washington: Eynon Company, 1935), pp. 199, 201.

As it was getting late, we bivouacked near the spot. The "Tonks" entered the ravine, shot a few bullets into the Comanches' bodies, as was their custom, scalped them, ears and all, and then cut a small piece of skin from each breast, for good luck, or rather "good medicine"—such was the peculiar superstition of the Indian. This, dried in the sun, and placed in a bag, or attached to a string and worn next to the person of the warrier, acts as a safe guard against danger or sickness in any form. It was their "medicine" or "mascot." At night Dr. Rufus Choate, Lieutenant Wentz C. Miller, and two negro boys, field cooks, went up the ravine, decapitated the dead Qua-ha-das, and placing the heads in some gunny sacks, brought them back to be boiled out for future scientific knowledge.

THE BOILING HEADS—AND WOUNDED FARRIER

Shortly after midnight we heard the wolves, which had sniffed the flesh from afar in the keen night air, fighting, snarling, and howling like incarnate fiends over this horrible human feast.

A barbarous and tragical end to a barbarous band, who, while mutilating and heaping red-hot coals upon the nude forms of their writhing victims (as the writer had seen the preceding May at the massacre on Salt Creek prairie) in the peaceful settlements of Texas, during their numerous blood-thirsty raids, had danced for joy at the savage torture inflicted.

Before starting the next morning, a horse litter had to be constructed upon which to carry our wounded man. The poles were lashed to the pack saddles of two mules traveling tandem. Cross-pieces were lashed to them in rear of the croup of one mule and in front of the breast of the other. A head covering was made of a framework of boughs, over which a blanket or shelter tent was thrown. He was thus carried more than two hundred miles, and by the personal nursing and unremitting attention of our faithful and efficient doctor, Rufus Choate, he lived, although his bowels had been perforated.

On this day we had but just gone into camp, and were about to eat our dinner, when Miller shouted to Major Mauck and the writer, from a short distance up the cañon, "Come up, we have something good!" "What is it?" Miller replied, "Soup!" We had observed two camp kettles strung on a pole over the fire. Seizing our cups, never suspecting a joke, we reached the spot. When to our horror we saw the two Comanche scalped heads, with the stripes of paint still on their faces, and with eyes partly opened, bobbing up and down, and rising above the mess kettles, mingled with the bubbling, bloody broth. It was a gruesome spectacle. With hand on our stomachs, we fled, directing "Bob," our valuable, able cook to transfer our dinner and all of our personal belongings further down the cañon, out of sight and reach of our esteemed ethnological head-hunters and skull boilers. A more sickening sight it would be difficult to conceive of. We were no longer hungry that night.

May 18, 1873   Coahuila, Mexico
Massacre of Women, Children and Old Men

During the Civil War era several hundred Kickapoo drifted into northern Mexico and established themselves alongside other tribal bands seeking refuge from American Indian policy. By late 1872 their depredations against Texas ranchers and frontiersmen across the Rio Grande had grown steadily worse, driving the white frontier slowly back as they killed and looted without mercy. They sold the plunder in Mexico to a group of merchants and cattlemen. The Kickapoo raids embroiled the American and Mexican governments in a series of diplomatic disputes on how to stop the raids. Finally, in April of 1873, President U. S. Grant dispatched a delegation of civilian reformers to northern Mexico to open direct negotiations with Mexican officials and Kickapoo leaders with the ultimate goal of returning the Kickapoo to their detested reservation in Indian Territory.

In January, 1873, the United States Army sent Colonel Ranald S. MacKenzie with the Fourth U.S. Cavalry to Fort Concho, Texas, where he was directed to launch a surreptitious and illegal attack on the Kickapoo village in Mexico. Captain R. G. Carter stated that Grant sent the regional commander General P. H. Sheridan, who gave the verbal orders in secret to MacKenzie, promising that Grant and Sheridan would back him if the attack should evoke a public outcry. It is interesting to note that no military or civilian policy maker suggested striking the merchant groups in Mexico that supplied the Kickapoo and manipulated their grievances.

MacKenzie waited until his scouts informed him that the Kickapoo warriors had left their village, then he crossed the Rio Grande to attack. The Fourth marched through rough terrain under exhausting conditions to sneak up at dawn to the sleeping village and make a "glorious" charge against women, children, and old men. They burned and destroyed and took little children and women, many of them wounded, prisoners of war (document 80). The "prisoners of war" were removed to American prison camps to be held as permanent hostages to force the Kickapoo tribe to capitulate to American demands.

The very day the attack was launched against the village, the unsuspecting American civilian reform leaders were in Saltillo, Coahuila, to obtain Mexican assistance in discussions with the Kickapoo. Responding quickly to the changed conditions, they used the captive women and children as a fulcrum to force the Kickapoo warriors to capitulate.

Further reading: Ernest Wallace, *Ranald S. MacKenzie on the Texas Frontier* (Lubbock: West Texas Museum Association, 1964).

Document 80
May 18, 1873   Coahuila, Mexico
Massacre of Women, Children and Old Men

Source: R. G. Carter, **On the Border with MacKenzie or Winning West Texas from the Comanches** (Washington: Eynon Company, 1935), pp. 441-443.

THE FIGHT

The sudden charge proved a complete surprise. The leading company was soon among the grass lodges. Carbines were banging, rifles were cracking. The men were incessantly cheering and scattering in pursuit. The warriors were yelling and flying in every direction, many half naked, from their huts. It was a grand and impressive sight. Sharp and imperative commands alone held the men in ranks, or kept them from dashing individually into the villages. Over mesquite bushes, rocks, pricklypear, and the long, dagger-like points of the Spanish bayonet, dashed the mad, impetuous column of troopers. Here could be seen a horse gone nearly crazy and unmanageable with fright, and running off with its rider, who was almost or wholly powerless to control him. Small, mesquite trees, had to be avoided, and what with controlling the men, dodging obstacles over rough ground, and handling our horses, a more reckless, dare-devil ride we never had.

Soon the rear companies struck the villages, and, dismounting and "fighting on foot" were closely engaged. It was short work. "I" Troop was pursuing the flying warriors across the low, swampy ground, everywhere cut up and intersected by irrigating ditches, and covered with fields of grain, corn, pumpkins, etc. On the left were the pony herds, and stolen stock, the former seemingly as intent upon getting away as their masters.

Mackenzie, remembering Sheridan's injunction to make this a campaign of "annihilation" and "destruction," gave the necessary orders for that work to be done. *Fire the villages!* The dismounted men, already told off for this purpose, making torches of the long pampa plumes and other rank grasses, ran in and quickly fired the tepees or grass lodges, which being made of coarse rushes or grasses, with walls about four feet high and roofs heavily thatched and as dry as tinder, flashed up, roared and burned like powder. The fierce crackling of the flames mingled strangely with loud reports of carbines, sharp crack of rifles, cheers and yells. The destruction was complete.

WAR'S SAD SPECTACLE

Taking a part of "A" Troop, by Mackenzie's order, I struck across to the left for the herds, now stampeding in the distance, and, after much hard riding through the chaparral, which everywhere skirted the villages, expecting momentarily to be ambushed by small parties of Indians who had fled in that direction, I succeeded in rounding up most of the animals, and started back. As I approached the small stream bordering the smouldering lodges, riding at a rapid walk, one of the men shouted "Look out, Lieutenant, there are Indians under the bank!" Turning quickly, I saw, under a large, overhanging bunch of flags and long grass, what appeared to be the form of a large Indian in the act of pointing a weapon. It was about 30 yards and nearly concealed. I was the only officer who had brought a carbine. I had no gun scabbard; it had been strapped to the saddle, but was now loose. Raising it and firing immediately, the Indian fell. The men then opened fire which was replied to from the bushes. Dismounting shortly after and ordering "Cease firing," I approached the bushes and, parting them, witnessed one of those most singular and pitiable spectacles incident to Indian warfare. A small but faithful cur dog was at the entrance of what appeared to be a small cave far under the bank of the stream, savagely menacing our advance. Near him, almost underneath, lay stretched the dead body of a gigantic Indian, and behind him seemed to be more bodies. It was necessary to kill the dog before we could proceed further. The men reaching in, then drew forth two small children, respectively two and four years of age, badly shot through their bodies. One was dead, the other nearly so. Opening the bush still further for more revelations, way in the rear we saw the form of a young squaw, apparently unhurt, but badly frightened. Her black, glittering eyes were fastened upon the group of blue-coated soldiers with a fascinating stare, not unlike that of a snake, expressing half fear, half hatred and defiance. We made signs for her to come out, but, as she refused, she was quitely, and without harm, dragged forth. We thought this was all, but almost covered up under the immense flags, we found still a third child, a girl of about twelve, badly wounded. It was one of those cruel, unforeseen and unavoidable accidents of grim-visaged war. They all had weapons and had fired upon my party. Gathering up our prisoners, we found that we had some forty or fifty, with nearly two hundred ponies and horses, most of the latter being branded stolen stock.

June, 1873   Lava Beds, California
The Plight of the Modoc

The small Modoc tribe originally inhabited northern California. After the settlement of the state, the federal government removed them to a reservation near their hereditary enemies, the Klamath of southern Oregon. They soon exhausted their food resources and faced the possibility of starvation. Captain Jack, their leader, told military authorities and Indian Bureau officials that the tribe preferred death by bullets rather than the slow, painful death of starvation. They fled to California, their old homeland. The army soon cornered them in Lava Beds but failed to drive them out after exhausting attempts. During the prolonged peace negotiations the government refused to give them a new reservation; Captain Jack and several others murdered the peace negotiators. Within a few weeks the army conquered the Modoc and immediately tried the murderers in a military court instead of a civilian court. A small group of reformers launched an immediate protest against the military usurpation of civilian institutions, but they failed to stop the executions.

A letter from Congressman J. K. Luttrell to the Secretary of the Interior accurately depicts the plight of the Modoc before their flight, and he asks that these conditions be investigated (document 81). At the conclusion of the Modoc War the government shipped the Modoc to the hot, dry, malaria-infested plains of northern Indian Territory where many died from the harsh treatment.

Further reading: Keith A. Murray, *The Modocs and Their War* (Norman: University of Oklahoma Press, 1959).

Document 81
June 17, 1873   Lava Beds, California
Plea for Justice

Source: U.S. Congress. **Modoc War**, H. Ex. Doc. 122, 43rd Cong., 1st sess., 1873, pp. 193-194.

HEADQUARTERS, LAVA-BEDS, CAL.,
                                                              June 17, 1873.

DEAR SIR: The Modoc war is over. The Modoc tribe except five or six, are captives. Captain Jack and several of his confederates are soon to be tried by court-martial for the murder of General Canby and the peace commissioners. There can be but one verdict or result, viz, the conviction and execution of all those participating in the murder of settlers and peace commissioners. I have spent several days in the lava-beds and the country adjacent thereto. I have investigated, so far as I could, the cause of the war between the whites and Modoc Indians, and from a careful investigation I can arrive at but one conclusion, viz, that the war was caused by the wrongful acts of bad white men.

In the first place, it is charged by responsible parties here, that the Indians were compelled to slaughter their horses for food on the Klamath reservation to keep from starving, and when they had no more horses to slaughter they were forced by hunger to seek their fishing grounds on Lost River, a tract of land set apart and given to them by the Hon. E. Steele, late superintendent of Indian affairs for California. The land is valuable. Land speculators desired it and sought to have the Indians removed. The Indians say there was but one of two deaths left to them, by starvation on the reservation, or a speedier death by the bullet in the lava-beds. They chose the latter. I am in favor of hanging all those who participated in the murder of the peace commissioners or the settlers, but humanity and justice demand an investigation of the war and its causes, from its first inception. Let us have both sides of the question; let us have the sworn statement of the Indians, which will, I am credibly informed, be corroborated by the testimony of responsible white men. If you have the authority to order it, direct that the testimony of all those who are likely to be convicted and executed be taken. I regret that I have to say it, but I believe that there never was a time since the organization of our Government that there was as much corruption and swindling, not only of the Government and people, but the Indians, as is to-day being practiced on Indian reservations on this coast. Mr. Meacham, and Hon. E. Steele, managed the affairs to the satisfaction of the people and the Indians. I regret that they were not retained as superintendents. I do not know who is to blame, nor do I accuse any particular agent of corruption; but we know that wrongs have been perpetrated, and before launching these Indian chiefs into eternity, let their testimony be taken, that the guilty parties may be found. We have lost many valuable officers and men in this contest; justice demands that if any particular individual or individuals are guilty of inciting the Modocs to war, that he or they should be punished. I am willing, if you can delegate to me the authority, to aid and assist in the investigation of all the causes and charges which may or can be brought out before the court-martial or board, who may be designated to try the prisoners at Fort Klamath. As the Representative of the people immediately concerned, and who have suffered most by reasons of the war, I feel that justice demands a thorough investigation. If I can in any way serve the Government and people in aiding or assisting the investigation, command my services by telegraph at Fort Jones.

Very respectfully yours,

J. K. LUTTRELL,
Member Third Congressional District.

Hon. C. DELANO,
Secretary of Interior, Washington.

1865-1885
Elimination of Indian Food Resources

The settlement of the continent resulted in severely reducing the wild animals and birds that flourished in the forests and on the plains. The senseless process began with the early Pilgrims who helped eliminate the millions of great auk; the trend continued with more species into the nineteenth century to culminate in the slaughter of the passenger pigeon and buffalo. Indian life was organized around natural food resources, and tribes were absolutely dependent upon game. Destroying the game meant that Indians became dependent upon American government policies of food annuities while they learned to cultivate food in the white men's way. Two examples of the destruction of wild game are given, with emphasis on the ferociousness of the approach. The first, taken from a popular journal, is the editor's description of the slaughter of passenger pigeons at the Petoskey, Michigan, roost (document 82). The pigeons numbered in the billions in North America when white men first came. The last wild pigeon was killed near Stevens Point, Wisconsin, at the end of the century; the last member of the species died in 1913 at the Cincinnati zoo. The second document is an excerpt from the Smithsonian Institution's contemporary study of the extermination of the buffalo (document 83). The buffalo numbered somewhere between 50 and 125 million, but by 1885 only a few hundred survived in isolated mountain canyons.

Further reading: Mari Sandoz, *The Buffalo Hunters; the Story of the Hide Men* (New York: Hastings House, 1954); Arlie William Schorger, *The Passenger Pigeon, Its Natural History and Extinction* (Madison: University of Wisconsin, 1955).

Document 82
1878   Petoskey, Michigan
Slaughter of Passenger Pigeons

Source: **Chicago Field** (January 11, 1879), vol. X, pp. 345-346.

On reaching Petoskey we found the condition of affairs had not been magnified; indeed, it exceeded our gravest fears. Here, a few miles north, was a pigeon nesting of irregular dimensions, estimated, by those best qualified to judge, to be *forty* (40) *miles in length, by three to ten miles in width*, probably the largest nesting that has ever existed in the United States, *covering something like* 100,000 *acres of land*, and including not less than 150,000 acres within its limits. At the hotel we met one we were glad to see, in the person of "Uncle Len" Jewell, of Bay City, an old woodsman and "land-looker." Len had for several weeks been looking land in the upper peninsula, and was on his return home. At our solicitation he agreed to remain for two or three days, and co-operate with us. In the village nothing else seemed to be thought of but pigeons. It was the one absorbing topic everywhere. The "pigeoners" hurried hither and thither, comparing market reports, and soliciting the latest quotations on "squabs." A score of hands in the packing-houses were kept busy from day-light until dark. Wagon load after wagon load of dead and live birds hauled up to the station, discharged their freight, and returned to the nesting for more. The freight-house was filled with the paraphernallia of the pigeon hunters' vocation, while every train brought acquisitions to their numbers, and scores of nets, stool-pigeons, etc. The pigeoners were everywhere. They swarmed in the hotels, post-office, and about the streets. They were there, as careful inquiry and the hotel registers showed, from New York, Wisconsin, Pennsylvania, Michigan, Maryland, Iowa, Virginia, Ohio, Texas, Illinois, Maine, Minnesota and Missouri....

Hiring a team, we started on a tour of investigation through the nesting. Long before reaching it our course was directed by the birds over our heads, flying back and forth to their feeding grounds. After riding about fifteen miles, we discovered a wagon-track leading into the woods, in the direction of the bird sounds which came to our ears. Three of the party left the wagon and followed it; the twittering grew louder and louder, the birds more numerous, and in a few minutes we were in the midst of that marvel of the forest and nature's wonderland—the pigeon nesting. We stood and gazed in bewilderment upon the scene around and above us. Was it indeed a fairy land we stood upon, or did our eyes deceive us! On every hand the eye would meet these graceful creatures of the forest, which, in their delicate robes of blue, purple and brown, darted hither and thither with the quickness of thought. Every bough was bending under their weight, so tame one could almost touch them, while in every direction, crossing and recrossing, the flying birds drew a net work before the dizzy eyes of the beholder, until he fain would close his eyes to shut out the bewildering scene. This portion of the nesting was the first formed, and the young birds were just ready to leave the nests. Scarcely a tree could be seen but contained from five to fifty nests, according to its size and branches. Directed by the noise of chopping and falling trees, we followed on, and soon came upon the scene of action. Here was a large force of Indians and boys at work, slashing down the timber and seizing the young birds as they fluttered from the nest. As soon as caught, the heads were jerked off from the tender bodies with the hands, and the dead birds tossed into heaps. Others knocked the young fledglings out of the nests with long poles, their weak and untried wings failing to carry them beyond the clutches of the assistant, who, with hands reeking with blood and feathers, tears the head off the living bird, and throws its quivering body upon the heap. Thousands of young birds lay among

the ferns and leaves dead, having been knocked out of the nests by the promiscuous tree-slashing, and dying for want of nourishment and care, which the parent birds, trapped off by the netter, could not give. The squab-killers stated that "about one-half of the young birds in the nests they found dead," owing to the latter reason. Every available Indian, man and boy in the neighborhood was in the employ of buyers and speculators, killing squabs, for which they received a cent apiece....

We soon struck into an old Indian trail which led us through another portion of the nesting, where the birds for countless numbers surpassed all calculation. The chirping and noise of wings were deafening, and conversation to be audible, had to be carried on at the top of our voices. On the shores of the lake where the birds go to drink, when flushed by an intruder, the rush of wings of the gathered millions was like a roar of thunder and perfectly indescribable. An hour's walk brought us to a ravine, which we cautiously approached. Directed by the commotion in the air, we soon discovered the bough house and net of the trapper. Evidence being what was sought, we stood concealed behind some bushes to await the springing of the trap. The black muck bed soon became blue and purple with pigeons lured by the salt and sulphur, when suddenly the net was sprung over with a "whiz," retaining hundreds of birds beneath it, while those outside its limits flew to adjacent trees. We now descended from the brink of the hill to the net, and there beheld a sickening sight not soon to be forgotten.

On one side of the bed of a little creek was spread the net, a double one, covering an area when thrown, of about ten by twenty feet. Through its meshes were stretched the heads of the fluttering captives, vainly struggling to escape. In the midst of them stood a stalwart pigeoner up to his knees in the mire and bespattered with mud and blood from heat to foot. Passing from bird to bird, with a pair of blacksmith's pincers he gave the neck of each a cruel grip with his remorseless weapon, causing the blood to burst from the eyes and trickle down the beak of the helpless captive, which flowly fluttered its life away, its beautiful plumage besmeared with filth and its bed dyed with its crimson blood. When all were dead, the net was raised, many still clinging to its meshes with beak and claws in their death grip and were shaken off. They were then gathered, counted, deposited behind a log with many others and covered with bushes, and the death trap set for another harvest....

The number of pigeons caught in a day by an expert trapper will seem incredible to one who has not witnessed the operation. A fair average is sixty to ninety dozen birds a day per net, and some trappers will not spring a net upon less than ten dozen birds. Higher figures than these are often reached, as in the case of one trapper who caught and delivered 2,000 dozen pigeons in ten days, being 200 dozen or about 2,500 birds per day. A double net has been known to catch as high as 1,332 birds at a single throw, while at natural salt licks, their favorite resort, 300 and 400 *dozen,* or about 5,000 *birds have been caught in a single day* by one net.

The prices of dead birds range from thirty-five cents to forty cents per dozen at the nesting. In Chicago markets fifty to sixty cents. Squabs twelve cents per dozen in the woods, in metropolitan markets sixty cents to seventy cents. In fashionable restaurants they are served as a delicious tit-bit at fancy prices. Live birds are worth at the trapper's net forty cents to sixty cents per dozen; in cities $1 to $2. It can thus be easily seen that the business, when at all successful, is a very profitable one, for from the above quotations a pencil will quickly figure out an income of $10 to $40 a day for the "poor and hard working pigeon trapper." One "pigeoner" at the Petoskey nesting was reported to be worth $60,000, all made in that business....

There are in the United States about 5,000 men who pursue pigeons year after year as a business. Pigeon hunters with whom we conversed *incognito* stated that of this number there were between 400 and 500 at the Petoskey nesting plying their vocation with as many nets, and more arriving upon every train from all parts of the United States. When it is remembered that the village was alive with pigeoners, that nearly every house in the vast area of territory covered by the nesting sheltered one to six pigeon men, and that many camped out in the woods, the figures will not seem improbable. Every homesteader in the country who owned or could hire an ox team or pair of horses, was engaged in hauling birds to Petoskey for shipment, for which they received $4 per wagon load. To "keep peace in the family" and avoid complaint, the pigeon men fitted up many of the settlers with nets, and instructed them in the art of trapping. Added to these were the buyers, shippers, packers, Indians and boys, making not less than 2,000 *persons,* (some placed it at 2,500) engaged in the traffic at this one nesting. Fully fifty teams were engaged in hauling birds to the railroad station. The road was carpeted with feathers, and the wings and feathers from the packing houses were used by the wagon load to fill up the mud holes in the road for miles out of town. For four men to attempt to effect a work, having for opponents the entire country, residents and nonresidents included, was no slight task.

The majority of the pigeoners were a reckless, hard set of men, but their repeated threats that they would "buck-shot us" if we interfered with them in the woods, failed to inspire the awe that was intended. It was four against 2,000. What was accomplished against such fearful odds may be seen by the following:

The regular shipments by rail before the party commenced operations were sixty barrels per day. On the 16th of April, just after our arrival, they fell to thirty-five barrels, and on the 17th down to twenty barrels per day, while on the 22d the shipments were only eight barrels of pigeons. On the Sunday previous there were shipped by steamer to Chicago, 128 barrels of dead birds and 108 crates of live birds. On the next Sabbath following our arrival the shipments were only forty-three barrels and fifty-two crates. Thus it will be seen that some little good was accomplished, but that little was included in a very few days of the season, for the treasury of the home clubs would not admit of keeping their representatives longer at the nesting, the state clubs, save one, did not respond to the call for assistance, and the men were recalled, after which the Indians went back into the nesting, and the wanton crusade was renewed by pigeoners and all hands with an energy which indicated a determination to make up lost time.

STATISTICS FOR 1878.

The first shipment of birds from Petoskey was upon March 22, and the last upon August 12, making over twenty weeks or five months that the bird war was carried on. For many weeks the railroad shipments averaged fifty barrels of dead birds per day—thirty to forty dozen old birds and about fifty dozen squabs being packed in a barrel. Allowing 500 birds to a barrel, and averaging the entire shipments for the season at twenty-five barrels per day, we find the rail shipments to have been 12,500 dead birds daily, or 1,500,000 for the Summer. Of live birds there were shipped 1,116 crates, six dozen per crate, or 80,352 birds. These were the rail shipments only, and not including the cargoes by steamers from Petoskey, Cheboygan, Cross Village and other lake ports, which were as many more. Added to this were the daily express shipments in bags and boxes, the wagon loads hauled away by the shot-gun brigade, the thousands of dead and wounded ones not secured, and the myriads of squabs dead in the nest by the trapping off of the parent birds soon after hatching, (for a young pigeon will surely die if deprived of its parents during the first week of its life) and we have at the lowest possible estimate a grand total of 1,000,000,000 pigeons sacrificed to Mammon during the nesting of 1878.

Document 83
1865-1885   Great Plains
Slaughter of the Buffalo

Source: William T. Hornaday, "The Extermination of the American Bison," **Report of the United States National Museum under the Direction of the Smithsonian Institution.** 1887 (Washington: Government Printing Office, 1889), pp. 492-496.

The completion of the Union Pacific Railway divided forever the buffaloes of the United States into two great herds, which thereafter became known respectively as the northern and southern herds. Both retired rapidly and permanently from the railway, and left a strip of country over 50 miles wide almost uninhabited by them. Although many thousand buffaloes were killed by hunters who made the Union Pacific Railway their base of operations, the two great bodies retired north and south so far that the greater number were beyond striking distance from that line.

THE DESTRUCTION OF THE SOUTHERN HERD

The geographical center of the great southern herd during the few years of its separate existence previous to its destruction was very near the present site of Garden City, Kansas. On the east, even as late as 1872, thousands of buffaloes ranged within 10 miles of Wichita, which was then the headquarters of a great number of buffalo-hunters, who plied their occupation vigorously during the winter. On the north the herd ranged within 25 miles of the Union Pacific, until the swarm of hunters coming down from the north drove them farther and farther south. On the west, a few small bands ranged as far as Pike's Peak and the South Park, but the main body ranged east of the town of Pueblo, Colorado. In the southwest, buffaloes were abundant as far as the Pecos and the Staked Plains, while the southern limit of the herd was about on a line with the southern boundary of New Mexico. Regarding this herd, Colonel Dodge writes as follows: "Their most prized feeding ground was the section of country between the South Platte and Arkansas rivers, watered by the Republican, Smoky, Walnut, Pawnee, and other parallel or tributary streams, and generally known as the Republican country. Hundreds of thousands went south from here each winter, but hundreds of thousands remained. It was the chosen home of the buffalo."

Although the range of the northern herd covered about twice as much territory as did the southern, the latter contained probably twice as many buffaloes. The number of individuals in the southern herd in the year 1871 must have been at least three millions, and most estimates place the total much higher than that.

During the years from 1866 to 1871, inclusive, the Atchison, Topeka and Santa Fé Railway and what is now known as the Kansas Pacific, or Kansas division of the Union Pacific Railway, were constructed from the Missouri River westward across Kansas, and through the heart of the southern buffalo range. The southern herd was literally cut to pieces by railways, and every portion of its range rendered easily accessible. There had always been a market for buffalo robes at a fair price, and as soon as the railways crossed the buffalo country the slaughter began. The rush to the range was only surpassed by the rush to the gold mines of California in earlier years. The railroad builders, teamsters, fortune-seekers, "professional" hunters, trappers, guides, and every one out of a job turned out to hunt buffalo for hides and meat. The merchants who had already settled in all the little towns along the three great railways saw an opportunity to make money out of the buffalo product, and forthwith began to organize and supply hunting parties with arms, ammunition, and provisions, and send them to the range. An immense business of this kind was done by the merchants of Dodge City (Fort Dodge), Wichita, and Leavenworth, and scores of smaller towns did a corresponding amount of business in the same line. During the years 1871 to 1874 but little else was done in that country except buffalo killing. Central depots were established in the best buffalo country, from whence hunting parties operated in all directions. Buildings were erected for the curing of meat, and corrals were built in which to heap up the immense piles of buffalo skins that accumulated. At Dodge City, as late as 1878, Professor Thompson saw a lot of baled buffalo skins in a corral, the solid cubical contents of which he calculated to equal 120 cords.

At first the utmost wastefulness prevailed. Every one wanted to kill buffalo, and no one was willing to do the skinning and curing. Thousands upon thousands of buffaloes were killed for their tongues alone, and never skinned. Thousands more were wounded by unskilled marksmen and wandered off to die and become a total loss. But the climax of wastefulness and sloth was not reached until the enterprising buffalo-butcher began to skin his dead buffaloes by horse-power. The process is of interest, as showing the depth of degradation to which a man can fall and still call himself a hunter. The skin of the buffalo was ripped open along the belly and throat, the legs cut around at the knees, and ripped up the rest of the way. The skin of the neck was divided all the way around at the back of the head, and skinned back a few inches to afford a start. A stout iron bar, like a hitching-post, was then driven through the skull and about 18 inches into the earth, after which a rope was tied very firmly to the thick skin of the neck, made ready for that purpose. The other end of this rope was then hitched to the whiffletree of a pair of horses, or to the rear axle of a wagon, the horses were whipped up, and the skin was forthwith either torn in two or torn off the buffalo with about 50 pounds of flesh adhering to it. It soon became apparent to even the most enterprising buffalo skinner that this method was not an unqualified success, and it was presently abandoned.

The slaughter which began in 1871 was prosecuted with great vigor and enterprise in 1872, and reached its height in 1873. By that time, the buffalo country fairly swarmed with hunters, each party putting forth its utmost efforts to destroy more buffaloes than its rivals. By that time experience had taught the value of thorough organization, and the butchering was done in a more business-like way. By a coincidence that proved fatal to the bison, it was just at the beginning of the slaughter that breech-loading, long-range rifles attained what was practically perfection. The Sharps 40-90 or 45-120, and the Remington were the favorite weapons of the buffalo-hunter, the former being the one in most general use. Before the leaden hail of thousands of these deadly breech-loaders the buffaloes went down at the rate of several thousand daily during the hunting season.

During the years 1871 and 1872 the most wanton wastefulness prevailed. Colonel Dodge declares that, though hundreds of thousands of skins were sent to market, they scarcely indicated the extent of the slaughter. Through want of skill in shooting and want of knowledge in preserving the hides of those slain by green hunters, *one hide sent to market represented three, four, or even five dead buffalo.* The skinners and curers knew so little of the proper mode of curing hides, that at least half of those actually taken were lost. In the summer and fall of 1872 one hide sent to market represented at least *three* dead buffalo. This condition of affairs rapidly improved; but such was the furor for slaughter, and the ignorance of all concerned, that every hide sent to market in 1871 represented no less than *five* dead buffalo.

By 1873 the condition of affairs had somewhat improved, through better organization of the hunting parties and knowledge gained by experience in curing. For all that, however, buffaloes were still so exceedingly plentiful, and shooting was so much easier than skinning, the latter was looked upon as a necessary evil and still slighted to such an extent that every hide actually sold and delivered represented two dead buffaloes.

In 1874 the slaughterers began to take alarm at the increasing scarcity of buffalo, and the skinners, having a much smaller number of dead animals to take care of than ever before, were able to devote more time to each subject and do their work properly. As a result, Colonel Dodge estimated that during 1874, and from that time on, one hundred skins delivered represented not more than one hundred and twenty-five dead buffaloes; but that "no parties have ever got the proportion lower than this."

The great southern herd was slaughtered by still-hunting, a method which has already been fully described. A typical hunting party is thus described by Colonel Dodge (in Plains of the Great West, p. 134):

"The most approved party consisted of four men—one shooter, two skinners, and one man to cook, stretch hides, and take care of camp. Where buffalo were very plentiful the number of skinners was increased. A light wagon, drawn by two horses or mules, takes the outfit into the wilderness, and brings into camp the skins taken each day. The outfit is most meager: a sack of flour, a side of bacon, 5 pounds of coffee, tea, and sugar, a little salt, and possibly a few beans, is a month's supply. A common or "A" tent furnishes shelter; a couple of blankets for each man is a bed. One or more of Sharps or Remington's heaviest sporting rifles, and an unlimited supply of ammunition, is the armament; while a coffee-pot, Dutch-oven, frying-pan, four tin plates, and four tin cups constitute the kitchen and table furniture.

"The skinning knives do duty at the platter, and 'fingers were made before forks.' Nor must be forgotten one or more 10-gallon kegs for water, as the camp may of necessity be far away from a stream. The supplies are generally furnished by the merchant for whom the party is working, who, in addition, pays each of the party a specified percentage of the value of the skins delivered. The shooter is carefully selected for his skill and knowledge of the habits of the buffalo. He is captain and leader of the party. When all is ready, he plunges into the wilderness, going to the center of the best buffalo region known to him, not already occupied (for there are unwritten regulations recognized as laws, giving to each hunter certain rights of discovery and occupancy). Arrived at the position, he makes his camp in some hidden ravine or thicket, and makes all ready for work."

Of course the slaughter was greatest along the lines of the three great railways—the Kansas Pacific, the Atchison, Topeka and Santa Fé, and the Union Pacific, about in the order named. It reached its height in the season of 1873. During that year the Atchison, Topeka and Santa Fé Railroad carried out of the buffalo country 251,443 robes, 1,617,600 pounds of meat, and 2,743,100 pounds of bones. The end of the southern herd was then near at hand. Could the southern buffalo range have been roofed over at that time it would have made one vast charnel-house. Putrifying carcasses, many of them with the hide still on, lay thickly scattered over thousands of square miles of the level prairie, poisoning the air and water and offending the sight. The remaining herds had become mere scattered bands, harried and driven hither and thither by the hunters, who now swarmed almost as thickly as the buffaloes. A cordon of camps was established along the Arkansas River, the South Platte, the Republican, and the few other streams that contained water, and when the thirsty animals came to drink they were attacked and driven away, and with the most fiendish persistency kept from slaking their thirst, so that they would again be compelled to seek the river and come within range of the deadly breech-loaders. Colonel Dodge declares that in places favorable to such warfare, as the south bank of the Platte, a herd of buffalo has, by shooting at it by day and by lighting fires and firing guns at night, been kept from water until it has been entirely destroyed. In the autumn of 1873, when Mr. William Blackmore traveled for some 30 to 40 miles along the north bank of the Arkansas River to the east of Fort Dodge, "there was a continuous line of putrescent carcasses, so that the air was rendered pestilential and offensive to the last degree. The hunters had formed a line of camps along the banks of the river, and had shot down the buffalo, night and morning, as they came to drink. In order to give an idea of the number of these carcasses, it is only necessary to mention that I counted sixty-seven on one spot not covering 4 acres."

White hunters were not allowed to hunt in the Indian Territory, but the southern boundary of the State of Kansas was picketed by them, and a herd no sooner crossed the line going north than it was destroyed. Every water-hole was guarded by a camp of hunters, and whenever a thirsty herd approached, it was promptly met by rifle-bullets.

1877   **United States**
  Chief Joseph's Complaint

In 1877 several hundred Nez Perce fought and marched over the rugged northern Rocky Mountains in an incredible effort to escape United States Army troops and reach safety in Canada. Defeated in battle, the survivors were shipped to Indian Territory where malaria and other diseases of the strange climate killed many of them. From time to time reformers and military officers visited the leader Chief Joseph who frequently voiced his complaints about the mistreatment the tribe was receiving. The following remarks are excerpted from a long article appearing in *The North American Review* (document 84). Joseph's views and criticisms of the 1877 military campaign against his people and subsequent mistreatment were dictated to a sympathic white minister who actually prepared the article and gave it his own peculiar stamp.

Further reading: Alvin M. Josephy, Jr., *The Nez Perce Indians and the Opening of the Northwest* (New Haven: Yale University Press, 1965).

Document 84
1877   **United States**
  Chief Joseph's Complaint

Source: Young Joseph, Chief of the Nez Perce. With an introduction by the Right Rev. W. H. Hare. "An Indian's Views of Indian Affairs," **The North American Review** (1879), vol. CCLXVI, pp. 426-431.

We understood that there was to be no more war. We intended to go peaceably to the buffalo country, and leave the question of returning to our country to be settled afterward.

With this understanding we traveled on for four days, and, thinking that the trouble was all over, we stopped and prepared tent-poles to take with us. We started again, and at the end of two days we saw three white men passing our camp. Thinking that peace had been made, we did not molest them. We could have killed or taken them prisoners, but we did not suspect them of being spies, which they were.

That night the soldiers surrounded our camp. About daybreak one of my men went out to look after his horses. The soldiers saw him and shot him down like a coyote. I have since learned that these soldiers were not those we had left behind. They had come upon us from another direction. The new white war-chief's name was Gibbon. He charged upon us while some of my people were still asleep. We had a hard fight. Some of my men crept around and attacked the soldiers from the rear. In this battle we lost nearly all our lodges, but we finally drove General Gibbon back.

Finding that he was not able to capture us, he sent to his camp a few miles away for his big guns (cannons), but my men had captured them and all the ammunition. We damaged the big guns all we could, and carried away the powder and lead. In the fight with General Gibbon we lost fifty women and children and thirty fighting men. We remained long enough to bury our dead. The Nez Percés never make war on women and children; we could have killed a great many women and children while the war lasted, but we would feel ashamed to do so cowardly an act.

We never scalp our enemies, but when General Howard came up and joined General Gibbon, their Indian scouts dug up our dead and scalped them. I have been told that General Howard did not order this great shame to be done.

We retreated as rapidly as we could toward the buffalo country. After six days General Howard came close to us, and we went out and attacked him, and captured nearly all his horses and mules (about two hundred and fifty head). We then marched on to the Yellowstone Basin.

On the way we captured one white man and two white women. We released them at the end of three days. They were treated kindly. The women were not insulted. Can the white soldiers tell me of one time when Indian women were taken prisoners, and held three days and then released without being insulted? Were the Nez Percés women who fell into the hands of General Howard's soldiers treated with as much respect? I deny that a Nez Percé was ever guilty of such a crime.

A few days later we captured two more white men. One of them stole a horse and escaped. We gave the other a poor horse and told him he was free.

Nine days' march brought us to the mouth of Clarke's Fork of the Yellowstone. We did not know what had become of General Howard, but we supposed that he had sent for more horses and mules. He did not come up, but another new war-chief (General Sturgis) attacked us. We held him in check while we moved all our women and children and stock out of danger, leaving a few men to cover our retreat.

Several days passed, and we heard nothing of General Howard, or Gibbon, or Sturgis. We had repulsed each in turn, and began to feel secure, when another army, under General Miles, struck us. This was the fourth army, each of which outnumbered our fighting force, that we had encountered within sixty days.

We had no knowledge of General Miles's army until a short time before he made a charge upon us, cutting our camp in two, and capturing nearly all of our horses. About seventy men, myself among them, were cut off. My little daughter, twelve years of age, was with me. I gave her a rope, and told her to catch a horse and join the others who were cut off from the camp. I have not seen her since, but I have learned that she is alive and well.

I thought of my wife and children, who were now surrounded by soldiers, and I resolved to go to them or die. With a prayer in my mouth to the Great Spirit Chief who rules above, I dashed unarmed through the line of soldiers. It seemed to me that there were guns on every side, before and behind me. My clothes were cut to pieces and my horse was wounded, but I was not hurt. As I reached the door of my lodge, my wife handed me my rifle saying: "Here's your gun. Fight!"

The soldiers kept up a continuous fire. Six of my men were killed in one spot near me. Ten or twelve soldiers charged into our camp and got possession of two lodges, killing three Nez Percés and losing three of their men, who fell inside our lines. I called my men to drive them back. We fought at close range, not more than twenty steps apart, and drove the soldiers back upon their main line, leaving their dead in our hands. We secured their arms and ammunition. We lost, the first day and night, eighteen men and three women. General Miles lost twenty-six killed and forty wounded. The following day General Miles sent a messenger into my camp under protection of a white flag. I sent my friend Yellow Bull to meet him.

Yellow Bull understood the messenger to say that General Miles wished me to consider the situation; that he did not want to kill my people unnecessarily. Yellow Bull understood this to be a demand for me to surrender and save blood. Upon reporting this message to me, Yellow Bull said he wondered whether General Miles was in earnest. I sent him back with my answer, that I had not made up my mind, but would think about it and send word soon. A little later he sent some Cheyenne scouts with another message. I went out to meet them. They said they believed that General Miles was sincere and really wanted peace. I walked on to General Miles's tent. He met me and we shook hands. He said, "Come, let us sit down by the fire and talk this matter over." I remained with him all night; next morning Yellow Bull came over to see if I was alive, and why I did not return.

General Miles would not let me leave the tent to see my friend alone.

Yellow Bull said to me: "They have got you in their power, and I am afraid they will never let you go again. I have an officer in our camp, and I will hold him until they let you go free."

I said: "I do not know what they mean to do with me, but if they kill me you must not kill the officer. It will do no good to avenge my death by killing him."

Yellow Bull returned to my camp. I did not make any agreement that day with General Miles. The battle was renewed while I was with him. I was very anxious about my people. I knew that we were near Sitting Bull's camp in King George's land, and I thought maybe the Nez Percés who had escaped would return with assistance. No great damage was done to either party during the night.

On the following morning I returned to my camp by agreement, meeting the officer who had been held a prisoner in my camp at the flag of truce. My people were divided about surrendering. We could have escaped from Bear Paw Mountain if we had left our wounded, old women, and children behind. We were unwilling to do this. We had never heard of a wounded Indian recovering while in the hands of white men.

On the evening of the fourth day General Howard came in with a small escort, together with my friend Chapman. We could now talk understandingly. General Miles said to me in plain words, "If you will come out and give up your arms, I will spare your lives and send you to your reservation." I do not know what passed between General Miles and General Howard.

I could not bear to see my wounded men and women suffer any longer; we had lost enough already. General Miles had promised that we might return to our own country with what stock we had left. I thought we could start again. I believed General Miles, or *I never would have surrendered.* I have heard that he has been censured for making the promise to return us to Lapwai. He could not have made any other terms with me at that time. I would have held him in check until my friends came to my assistance, and then neither of the generals nor their soldiers would have ever left Bear Paw Mountain alive.

On the fifth day I went to General Miles and gave up my gun, and said, "From where the sun now stands I will fight no more." My people needed rest—we wanted peace.

I was told we could go with General Miles to Tongue River and stay there until spring, when we would be sent back to our country. Finally it was decided that we were to be taken to Tongue River. We had nothing to say about it. After our arrival at Tongue River, General Miles received orders to take us to Bismarck. The reason given was, that subsistence would be cheaper there.

General Miles was opposed to this order. He said: "You must not blame me. I have endeavored to keep my word, but the chief who is over me has given the order, and I must obey it or resign. That would do you no good. Some other officer would carry out the order."

I believe General Miles would have kept his word if he could have done so. I do not blame him for what we have suffered since the surrender. I do not know who is to blame. We gave up all our horses—over eleven hundred—and all our saddles—over one hundred—and we have not heard from them since. Somebody has got our horses.

General Miles turned my people over to another soldier, and we were taken to Bismarck. Captain Johnson, who now had charge of us, received an order to take us to Fort Leavenworth. At Leavenworth we were placed on a low river bottom, with no water except river-water to drink and cook with. We had always lived in a healthy country, where the mountains were high and the water was cold and clear. Many of my people sickened and died, and we buried them in this strange land. I can not tell how much my heart suffered for my people while at Leavenworth. The Great Spirit Chief who rules above seemed to be looking some other way, and did not see what was being done to my people.

During the hot days (July, 1878) we received notice that we were to be moved farther away from our own country. We were not asked if we were willing to go. We were ordered to get into the railroad-cars. Three of my people died on the way to Baxter Springs. It was worse to die there than to die fighting in the mountains.

We were moved from Baxter Springs (Kansas) to the Indian Territory, and set down without our lodges. We had but little medicine, and we were nearly all sick. Seventy of my people have died since we moved there.

We have had a great many visitors who have talked many ways. Some of the chiefs (General Fish and Colonel Stickney) from Washington came to see us, and selected land for us to live upon. We have not moved to that land, for it is not a good place to live.

The Commissioner Chief (E. A. Hayt) came to see us. I told him, as I told every one, that I expected General Miles's word would be carried out. He said it "could not be done; that white men now lived in my country and all the land was taken up; that, if I returned to Wallowa, I could not live in peace; that law-papers were out against my young men who began the war, and that the Government could not protect my people." This talk fell like a heavy stone upon my heart. I saw that I could not gain anything by talking to him. Other law chiefs (Congressional Committee) came to see me and said they would help me to get a healthy country. I did not know who to believe. The white people have too many chiefs. They do not understand each other. They do not all talk alike.

1878-1879   Central Plains
Torture and Massacre of Cheyenne

Few episodes in the closing days of the American wars against the Great Plains Indians were more brutal than the crushing of the Northern Cheyenne under Dull Knife. Unable to defeat Indian warriors in open combat, the army levied war against their homes and families and by 1877 reduced them to poverty. The Cheyenne surrendered with the promise they would be allowed to remain in their homeland in the north. However, the government shipped them south to a closely guarded reservation in Indian Territory, where the band deteriorated. Family structure fell apart, the old leadership patterns had no meaning, the women were prostituted by the military, and whiskey was bootlegged. Finally, Dull Knife and other leaders, determined to return home in the north, decided to die fighting rather than to remain and rot. In September 1878, 320 slipped away and fled. Soon the plains became alive with army and militia units hunting down their quarry. The following excerpt from a decision

Mountain West 19th Century

by the United States Court of Claims relates the history of that flight and its bitter end (document 85). The claim arose from a settler seeking payment from the government for the damages alleged to have occurred from Cheyenne during the move north.

Further reading: Mari Sandoz, *Cheyenne Autumn* (New York: Hastings House, 1953).

Document 85
1878-1879   Central Plains
Torture and Massacre of Cheyenne

Source: **Cases decided in the Court of Claims of the United States, at the term of 1897-98** . . . (Washington: Government Printing Office, 1898), pp. 320-323.

On the 25th of November, 1876, Colonel Mackenzie had struck the village of Dull Knife with a column led by Indian scouts, many of whom were Cheyennes. The Indians were surprised, and fled among the rocks with nothing but their arms and ammunition and the clothes they wore. The weather was so intensely cold that on the nights of the 25th and 26th fourteen Indian babies were frozen to death in their mothers' arms. Dull Knife and his band made their way to the camp of Crazy Horse, who received them so coldly that they were deeply incensed, and came in and surrendered and turned against Crazy Horse and the remnant of the Ogalallas who were still hostile. During the ensuing winter friendly relations were cultivated by the officers who had fought them. Captain Bourke writes:

> One day when the Cheyenne chief Dull Knife was at headquarters, I invited him to stay for luncheon.
>
> "I should be glad to do so" he replied, "but my daughters are with me."
>
> "Bring them in, too," was the reply from others of the mess, and Spotted Tail, who was present, seconded our solicitations; so we had the pleasure of the company, not only of old Dull Knife, whose life had been one of such bitterness and sorrow, but of his three daughters as well. They were fairly good-looking—the Cheyennes will compare favorably in appearance with any people I have seen—and were quite young; one of 9 or 10, one of 12, and the oldest not yet 20, a young widow.
>
> Of the other Cheyennes, there was Little Wolf, one of the bravest in fights where all were brave.

This was the condition of Dull Knife's band when the removal to the Indian Territory took place. It had been on the warpath, acting independently of the other members of the tribe, but at the time was merged in the mass of Northern Cheyennes on the reservation, and was with all the others there in amity.

After a year of sickness, misery, and bitterness in the Indian Territory, and repeated prayers to be taken back to the country where their children could live, 320 of them, in September, 1878, broke away from the reservation. Dull Knife and Little Wolf were the leaders of this escaping party, which consisted of their bands.

They were pursued and overtaken. A parley ensued in which Little Wolf, whom Captain Bourke characterizes as "one of the bravest in fights where all were brave," said, "We do not want to fight you, but we will not go back." The troops instantly fired upon the Cheyennes and a new Indian war began.

That volley was one of the many mistakes, military and civil, which have been the fatality of our Indian administration, for the officer who ordered it thereby instituted an Indian war, and at the same instant turned hostile savages loose upon the unprotected homes of the frontier and their unwarned, unsuspecting inmates. The Cheyennes outgeneraled the troops. They fought and fled, scattered and reunited. They fought other military commands and citizens who had organized to oppose them, and in like manner they again and again eluded their opponents, making their way northward over innumerable hindrances. They had not sought war, but from the moment when they were fired upon they were upon the warpath—men were killed, women were ravished, houses were burned, crops destroyed. The country through which they fled and fought was desolated, and they left behind them the usual well-known trail of fire and blood.

At length, on the 3d of October, 1878, in northern Nebraska, the Cheyennes were brought to bay by troops who intercepted and fought them. They surrendered and were carried as prisoners of war to Fort Robinson, numbering then 49 men, 51 women, and 48 children. The war had ended, but the Cheyennes were able to console themselves with the reflection that the officer who began the war had not been able to carry them back to the reservation; that they had killed Lieutenant-Colonel Lewis, 5 soldiers, and 26 settlers, and that the wives and children of their enemies had suffered more bitterly than their own.

But here a new element comes into the case. Shortly before or after the depredations were committed which are the subject of the present action, but before the final capture of the Indians above referred to, Little Wolf and his band separated from the others and turned into the mountains. They disappeared then and as a band have never been seen since. Whether they perished during the ensuing winter or made their way northward and merged with other Indians is conjectural. Only 30 are known to have reached the Cheyenne Reservation on the Rosebud. Dull Knife and his band were carried to Fort Robinson. There they persistently refused to return to the reservation and were kept in close custody. In January, 1879, orders from the Interior Department arrived at Fort Robinson peremptorily directing the commanding officer to remove them to the reservation. On the 3rd of January, 1879, the Indians were told of this, and on the next day gave, through Wild Hog, their spokesman, their unequivocal answer, "We will die, but we will not go back."

The commanding officer apparently shrunk from shooting them down; removing them meant nothing short of that, or of actually carrying each one forcibly to the detested place from which they had escaped. The military authorities therefore resorted to the means of subduing the Cheyennes by which a former generation of animal tamers subdued wild beasts. In the midst of the dreadful winter, with the thermometer 40° below zero, the Indians, including the women and children, were kept for five days and nights without food or fuel, and for three days without water. At the end of that time they broke out of the barracks in which they were confined and rushed forth into the night. The troops pursued, firing upon them as upon enemies in war; those who escaped the sword perished in the storm. Twelve days later the pursuing cavalry came upon the remnant of the band in a ravine 50 miles from Fort Robinson. "The troops encircled the Indians, leaving no possible avenue of escape." The Indians fired on them, killing a lieutenant and two privates. The troops advanced; "the Indians, then without ammunition, rushed in desperation toward the troops with their hunting knives in hand; but before they had advanced many paces a volley was discharged by the troops and all was over." The bodies of 24 Indians were found in the ravine—17 bucks, 5 squaws, and 2 papooses." Nine prisoners were taken—1 wounded man, and 8 women, 5 of whom were wounded. The officer in command unconsciously wrote the epitaph of the slain in his dispatch announcing the result: "The Cheyennes fought with extraordinary courage and firmness, and refused all terms but death." The final result of the last Cheyenne war was, that of the 320 who broke away in September, 7 wounded Cheyennes were sent back to the reservation.

1882   Sitka, Alaska
Native Customs Overthrown by Force

American penetration of Alaska severely disrupted the life of the natives. The conflict between native custom and American law was especially difficult to resolve. In the report which follows from the collector of customs at Sitka to his superior Charles Folger, Secretary of the Treasury, this conflict is revealed (document 86). Many of the Alaskan natives practiced a form of social indemnity or workman's compensation, which required payment or tribute by the employer to the family of a person who was injured or killed while working. To the United States Navy it was an illegal practice, especially when a levy was made against a white man.

Document 86
1882   Sitka, Alaska
Native Customs Overthrown by Force

Source: U.S. Congress, **Shelling of an Indian Village in Alaska,** House Ex. Doc. 9, part 2, 47th Cong., 2d sess., 1883, pp. 1-2.

CUSTOM-HOUSE, SITKA, ALASKA,
COLLECTOR'S OFFICE, *November* 9, 1882.

SIR: On the 28th of last month I had the honor to transmit to the department the following telegram:

"SITKA, *Oct.* 28, 1882.
"SECRETARY TREASURY,
   "*Washington, D. C.:*
"26th inst. Hoochenoo Indians becoming troublesome, capturing property from whites, Commander Merriman repaired thither in Corwin. Became necessary to shell and destroy village, canoes, and make prisoners. Severe lesson taught. Particulars by mail."

It is presumed that all essential information has already been rendered the department by the report of the commander of the Corwin himself, and that as the expedition was a joint one upon behalf of the Navy and Treasury Departments, that the report of the naval commander will also reach the head of this department, hence it will be unnecessary for me to enter into general details, but merely give a synopsis of what I saw myself as an eye witness, and my opinion of the necessity which existed for adopting such stringent measures.

It has been a custom for many years in this territory, when an Indian has been killed or injured by another, or by a white man, for his surviving relatives to demand at the hands of the parties who injured him a certain payment or tribute, consisting generally of blankets. When this levy is made it means potlatch (pay) or die. It has been attempted by the Navy to break up this practice, but without effect.

Shortly previous to the case at bar, whilst an Indian was cutting down a tree for the Northwest Trading Company at Killisnoo, he was warned of the danger, and continued in a position of peril. The tree fell and killed him. Immediately a certain number of blankets were levied as a fine upon the company by his relatives, and payment demanded. The company refused, of course. Matters remained *in statu quo* until the Adams, Commander Merriman, arrived in these waters. He touched at Killisnoo on his way to this port, and complaint was made to him of the exaction, by the superintendent of the company. He informed the Indians that in future no such payments should either be demanded or enforced as far as white men were concerned; that if they persisted in such course he would punish them severely, and that in this instance

Cheyenne Indian Police, Captain Tall Bull at the right hand.

"Trouble," pose for a postcard is an example of the distortion of Indian culture for commercial purposes.

THE INDIAN GHOST DANCE AND WAR

The Red Skins left their Agency, the Soldiers left their Post,
All on the strength of an Indian tale about Messiah's ghost
Got up by savage chieftains to lead their tribes astray;
But Uncle Sam wouldn't have it so, for he ain't built that way.
They swore that this Messiah came to them in visions sleep,
And promised to restore their game and Buffalos a heap,
So they must start a big ghost dance, then all would join their band,
And may be so we lead the way into the great Bad Land.

Chorus:
They claimed the shirt Messiah gave, no bullet could go through,
But when the Soldiers fired at them they saw this was not true.
The Medicine man supplied them with their great Messiah's grace,
And he, too, pulled his freight and swore the 7th hard to face.

About their tents the Soldiers stood, awaiting one and all,
That they might hear the trumpet clear when sounding General call
Or Boots and Saddles in a rush, that each and every man
Might mount in haste, ride soon and fast to stop this devilish band
But Generals great like Miles and Brooke don't do things up that way,
For they know an Indian like a book, and let him have his sway
Until they think him far enough and then to John they'll say,
"You had better stop your fooling or we'll bring our guns to play."

Chorus.—They claimed the shirt, etc.

The 9th marched out with splendid cheer the Bad Lands to explo'e—
With Col. Henry at their head they never fear the foe;
So on they rode from Xmas eve 'till dawn of Xmas day;
The Red Skins heard the 9th was near and fled in great dismay;
The 7th is of courage bold both officers and men,
But bad luck seems to folow them and twice has took them in;
They came in contact with Big Foot's warriors in their fierce might
This chief made sure he had a chance of vantage in the fight.

Chorus.—They claimed the shirt, etc.

A fight took place, 'twas hand to hand, unwarned by trumpet call,
While the Soiux were dropping man by man—the 7th killed them all,
And to that regiment be said "Ye noble braves, well done,
Although you lost some gallant men a glorious fight you've won."
The 8th was there, the sixth rode miles to swell that great command
And waited orders night and day to round up Short Bull's band.
The Infantry marched up in mass the Cavalry's support,
And while the latter rounded up, the former held the fort.

Chorus.—They claimed the shirt, etc.

E battery of the 1st stood by and did their duty well,
For every time the Hotchkiss barked they say a hostile fell.
Some Indian soldiers chipped in too and helped to quell the fray,
And now the campaign's ended and the soldiers marched away.
So all have done their share, you see, whether it was thick or thin,
And all helped break the ghost dance up and drive the hostiles in.
The settlers in that region now can breathe with better grace;
They only ask and pray to God to make John hold his base.

Chorus.—They claimed the shirt, etc.

(W. H. Prather, I, 9th Cavalry).

Popular army ballad sung after the Wounded Knee Massacre, 1890

the company would and should not pay. They submitted with bad grace.

On the night of October 22, whilst this company were whaling in the Kootzenoo Lagoon, a bomb, shot from the whale-boat at a whale, accidentally exploded and killed an Indian *shaman,* who composed one of the crew; whereupon the latter immediately arose, and aided by about one hundred Indians, overpowered the two white men in the boat and took them prisoners; captured the boat, nets, whaling gear, and steam launch of the company, valued at several thousand dollars, and demanded payment of two hundred blankets for the dead man. The white men were kept close prisoners. A plan was formed to murder the engineer of the launch, who fortunately did not take the trail expected.

Capt. J. M. Vanderbilt, the superintendent, at once got up steam on the company's tug-boat Favorite, and started with his family post haste to Sitka for aid from the naval commander. The Indians endeavored to cut off the Favorite, but failed.

As soon as Vanderbilt reported the facts to Commander Merriman, the latter put a howitzer and Gatling gun on the Favorite, sought the co-operation of the revenue-marine steamer Corwin, then in port, and as early as practicable, with a force of about one hundred marines and sailors, started himself for the scene of action, picking up his large steam launch on the way. I accompanied the expedition.

Upon arriving at the lagoon, matters were found exactly as represented by Vanderbilt; the men still prisoners; the Indians increasing in force and very much excited. Commander Merriman lost no time in arresting the ringleaders, and got the two principal chiefs of the tribe on board the Corwin, and informed them that, instead of the Northwest Trading Company paying anything to them, he should inflict upon them a fine of four hundred blankets, payable the next morning, under the penalty of having their canoes destroyed and principal village shelled and burnt.

So temporizing has been the policy pursued within the past two years by the Navy towards the Siwashes that they evidently thought this a game or bluff. They were surly and impertinent, and affected not to think Commander Merriman would put his threat into execution. They, however, took the precaution to make use of the intervening night in taking to a place of security their large canoes and valuables.

On the following day, the Indians having failed to come to time, Commander Merriman made good his threat, destroyed their canoes, shelled and burnt their village.

My object in addressing the department upon this subject is for the purpose of placing my opinion on record as to the propriety of this measure and the absolute necessity which existed for such harsh measures being adopted.

The Hoochenoos are a rich and warlike tribe, very insolent and saucy towards the whites. Not long since they proceeded to Wrangell and attacked the Church Indians there, killing several, amongst them Toyatt, a missionary Indian, a very useful and intelligent man.

As long as the native tribes throughout the archipelago do not feel the force of the government and are not punished for flagrant outrages, so much the more dangerous do they become, and are to be feared by isolated prospecting parties of miners. Once let it be understood by the Siwashes that the life of a white man is sacred, and that they will be severely handled if they harm him, there will be no danger or difficulty in small parties traversing the country in search of minerals and other wealth.

The punishment has been most severe, but eminently salutary, and in my judgment the very thing that was needed, and unhesitatingly, in my opinion, is the prompt and energetic action of Commander Merriman to be applauded, and this occasion is sought to express great confidence in the result of his action and general management of the Indians since he has been on this station.

Owing to the heavy draught of water needed for the Adams, the presence and co-operation of the Corwin were most opportune.

The conduct of Lieutenant Healy in command of said vessel, is especially to be commended, as that of an officer and a gentleman, and a credit to the service. His officers and men conducted themselves well throughout the whole affair, and deserve therefor special mention.

I am, respectfully, your obedient servant,

WM. GOUVERNEUR MORRIS,
Collector

HON. CHAS. J. FOLGER,
Secretary of the Treasury, Washington, D. C.

1890   Wounded Knee, South Dakota   Massacre of the Sioux

The military conquest of Sioux tribes of the Great Plains forced them onto South Dakota reservations where the Secretary of the Interior and the Commissioner of Indian Affairs began to impose civilization upon them. The ancient culture of the Sioux would be crushed forever, the tribes Christianized, and the individual members given small farms, where they would be (like the Secretary and Commissioner) subservient to large railroad, timber, and land corporations. Indian agents attacked Sioux religion, language, hairstyle, food preparation, education, work life, and kinship system. Often incompetent, the agents failed to provide stable guidance to the distressed tribes. Hunger became the Indian's major problem. Disease, illness, and alien moral standards of the encroaching white civilization swept through the camps, instilling a sense of utter helplessness. The Sioux turned to messianic religion and random prophets to salve their misery. At the same time ranchers, land speculators, and land-coveting farmers pressured the federal government to destroy the reservations and "open them up" for civilization.

In the autumn of 1890 the Sioux struggled to meet the conditions of the harsh, uncaring new order and attempted to organize around local leaders. Most frequently the leaders only supplied starving families with food and distressed tribesmen with solace. Instead of releasing food and blankets—which were the property of the Sioux—to the dying, the Bureau of Indian Affairs asked the military to remove the potential leaders of resistance and rebellion. In an attempt to arrest Sitting Bull, the famed war leader of the Sioux was killed. The army began sending large numbers of troops to arrest other alleged recalcitrant leaders. One regiment halted Big Foot's band which was suspected of being armed for war. Big Foot asked the soldiers to discuss the problem. At his camp the soldiers surrounded the several hundred Indians, while a detail searched the lodges for weapons (which they found in small number). From the midst of the gathered warriors, tense and infuriated over the rough search and seizure, a shot was fired. Immediately the army commenced firing upon the warriors until all were killed or wounded. The military then began to slaughter, with small cannon and rifle fire, the fleeing women and children. When the firing stopped after several hours about three hundred Sioux had been killed, most of them women, children, and babies. Sixty soldiers died. The following description of the massacre was provided by Sioux leaders who were called to a conference with military leaders in Washington (document 87).

Further reading: Robert M. Utley, *The Last Days of the Sioux Nation* (New Haven: Yale University, 1963).

Document 87
1890   Wounded Knee, South Dakota
Massacre of Wounded Knee

Source: U.S. Commissioner of Indian Affairs. **Annual Report of 1891** (Washington: Government Printing Office, 1891), pp. 179-181.

[Extracts from verbatim stenographic report of council held by delegations of Sioux with Commissioner of Indian Affairs, at Washington, February 11, 1891.]

Turning Hawk, Pine Ridge (Mr. COOK, interpreter). Mr. Commissioner, my purpose to-day is to tell you what I know of the condition of affairs at the agency where I live. A certain falsehood came to our agency from the west which had the effect of a fire upon the Indians, and when this certain fire came upon our people those who had certain far-sightedness and could see into the matter, made up their minds to stand up against it and fight it. The reason we took this hostile attitude to this fire was

because we believed that you yourself would not be in favor of this particular mischief-making thing; but just as we expected, the people in authority did not like this thing and we were quietly told that we must give up or have nothing to do with this certain movement. Though this is the advice from our good friends in the East, there were, of course, many silly young men who were longing to become identified with the movement, although they knew that there was nothing absolutely bad, nor did they know there was anything absolutely good in connection with the movement.

In the course of time we heard that the soldiers were moving towards the scene of trouble. After a while some of the soldiers finally reached our place and we heard that a number of them also reached our friends at Rosebud. Of course, when a large body of soldiers is moving towards a certain direction they inspire a more or less amount of awe, and it is very natural that the women and children who see this large moving mass are made afraid of it and be put in a condition to make them run away. At first we thought that perhaps Pine Ridge and Rosebud were the only two agencies where soldiers were sent, but finally we heard that the other agencies fared likewise. We heard and saw that about half of our friends at Rosebud Agency, from fear at seeing the soldiers, began the move of running away from their agency towards ours (Pine Ridge), and when they had gotten inside of our reservation they there learned that right ahead of them at our agency was another large crowd of soldiers, and while the soldiers were there there was constantly a great deal of false rumor flying back and forth. The special rumor I have in mind is the threat that the soldiers had come there to disarm the Indians entirely and to take away all their horses from them. That was the oft-repeated story.

So constantly repeated was this story that our friends from Rosebud, instead of going to Pine Ridge, the place of their destination, veered off and went in some other direction, towards the "Bad Lands." We did not know definitely how many, but understood there were 300 lodges of them, about 1,700 people. Eagle Pipe, Turning Bear, High Hawk, Short Bull, Lance, No Flesh, Pine Bird, Crow Dog, Two Strike, and White Horse were the leaders.

Well, the people after veering off in this way, many of them who believe in peace and order at our own agency, were very anxious that some influence should be brought upon these people. In addition to our love of peace we remembered that many of these people were related to us by blood. So we sent out peace commissioners to the people who were running away from their agency. I understood at the time that they were simply going away from fear because of so many soldiers. So constant was the word of these good men from Pine Ridge Agency that finally they succeeded in getting away half of the party from Rosebud, from the place where they took refuge, and finally were brought to the agency at Pine Ridge. Young-man-afraid-of-his-horses, Little Wound, Fast Thunder, Louis

Shangreau, John Grass, Jack Red Cloud, and myself were some of these peacemakers.

The remnant of the party from Rosebud not taken to the agency finally reached the wilds of the Bad Lands. Seeing that we had succeeded so well, once more we went to the same party in the Bad Lands and succeeded in bringing these very Indians out of the depths of the Bad Lands and were being brought towards the agency. When we were about a day's journey from our agency we heard that a certain party of Indians (Big Foot's band) from the Cheyenne River Agency was coming towards Pine Ridge in flight.

CAPT. SWORDS. Those who actually went off of the Cheyenne River Agency probably number 303, and there were a few from the Standing Rock Reserve with them, but as to their number I do not know. There were a number of Ogalallas, old men and several school boys, coming back with that very same party, and one of the very seriously wounded boys was a member of the Ogalalla boarding school at Pine Ridge Agency. He was not on the war-path, but was simply returning home to his agency and to his school after a summer visit to relatives on the Cheyenne River.

TURNING HAWK. When we heard that these people were coming towards our agency we also heard this. These people were coming towards Pine Ridge Agency, and when they were almost on the agency they were met by the soldiers and surrounded and finally taken to the Wounded Knee Creek, and there at a given time their guns were demanded. When they had delivered them up the men were separated from their families, from their tepees, and taken to a certain spot. When the guns were thus taken and the men thus separated there was a crazy man, a young man of very bad influence and in fact a nobody, among that bunch of Indians fired his gun, and of course the firing of a gun must have been the breaking of a military rule of some sort, because immediately the soldiers returned fire and indiscriminate killing followed.

SPOTTED HORSE. This man shot an officer in the Army, the first shot killed this officer. I was a voluntary scout at that encounter and I saw exactly what was done and that was what I noticed; that the first shot killed an officer. As soon as this shot was fired, the Indians immediately began drawing their knives and they were exhorted from all sides to desist, but this was not obeyed. Consequently, the firing began immediately on the part of the soldiers.

TURNING HAWK. All the men who were in a bunch were killed right there, and those who escaped that first fire got into the ravine and as they went along up the ravine for a long distance they were pursued on both sides by the soldiers and shot down, as the dead bodies showed afterwards. The women were standing off at a different place from where the men were stationed, and when the firing began those of the men who escaped the first onslaught went in one direction up the ravine, and then the women who were bunched together at another place went entirely in a different direction through an open field, and the women fared the same fate as the men who went up the deep ravine.

AMERICAN HORSE. The men were separated as has already been said from the women, and they were surrounded by the soldiers. Then came next the village of the Indians and that was entirely surrounded by the soldiers also. When the firing began, of course the people who were standing immediately around the young man who fired the first shot were killed right together; and then they turned their guns, Hotchkiss guns, etc., upon the women who were in the lodges standing there under a flag of truce, and of course as soon as they were fired upon they fled, the men fleeing in one direction and the women running in two different directions. So that there were three general directions in which they took flight.

There was a woman with an infant in her arms who was killed as she almost touched the flag of truce, and the women and children of course were strewn all along the circular village until they were dispatched. Right near the flag of truce a mother was shot down with her infant; the child not knowing that its mother was dead was still nursing, and that was especially a very sad sight. The women as they were fleeing with their babes on their backs were killed together, shot right through, and the women who were very heavy with child were also killed. All the Indians fled in these three directions, and after most all of them had been killed a cry was made that all those who were not killed or wounded should come forth and they would be safe. Little boys who were not wounded came out of their places of refuge, and as soon as they came in sight a number of soldiers surrounded them and butchered them there.

Of course we all feel very sad about this affair. I stood very loyal to the Government all through those troublesome days, and believing so much in the Government and being so loyal to it, my disappointment was very strong, and I have come to Washington with a very great blame on my heart. Of course it would have been all right if only the men were killed; we would feel almost grateful for it. But the fact of the killing of the women, and more especially the killing of the young boys and girls who are to go to make up the future strength of the Indian people, is the saddest part of the whole affair and we feel it very sorely.

I was not there at the time before the burial of the bodies, but I did go there with some of the police and the Indian doctor and a great many of the people, men from the agency, and we went through the battle field and saw where the bodies were from the track of the blood.

May 5, 1894   Antigo, Wisconsin
Difficulties of Indian Leadership

Only an Indian with extraordinary talents and physical
stamina could emerge as a leader against the forces attempting to control Indian lives and property. Typically
when a leader was effective, the fight exhausted his resources and sometimes ruined his health. In 1871, John
Adams became a leader of a Stockbridge faction which
sought to remove the lumber companies' influence over a
minority segment of the tribe. Powerful lumber barons
manipulated the tribe through bribes and carefully contrived arguments while stripping timber from Indian land.
A full-blooded Indian, Adams was a lawyer and a farmer,
a man of good character, and a champion of the oppressed.
His fight against the vested interests took twenty-two
years of effort before he succeeded in 1894. At the last
moment the Senate committee reporting out the bill
(which provided justice for the Stockbridge) denied the
payment of legal fees to Adams on technical grounds.
The following letter from Adams to the Commissioner
of Indian Affairs is a request for the legal fee (document
88).

Document 88
May 5, 1894   Antigo, Wisconsin
Difficulties of Indian Leadership

Source: Letter from John Adams to Daniel M. Browning,
Commissioner of Indian Affairs, May 5, 1894. John Adams
manuscripts, Division of Archives and Manuscripts, The
State Historical Society of Wisconsin.

In connection with the matter of my contract, I desire to
say that I have devoted more than twenty years of my life
in endeavoring to have the wrongs of these people righted.
When I first began this work I was the owner of a good
and well improved farm and had money invested drawing
ten percent interest. My farm and money are both gone,
all being expended in the prosecution of the claims of
these Indians, and today I am entirely destitute of this
world's goods. My whole time has been devoted to this
matter and my services have been persistent, faithful and
successful, but there is much yet remaining to be done.
It does seem to me that the services rendered, hardship
endu[r]ed and losses sustain[ed] entitle me to the most
liberal consideration in the matter. The Indians appreciate
all that I have done for them and the losses sustained by
me in their behalf, and are not only willing but desirous
that I be most liberally compensated. This being so no
technicality in regard to the papers should be considered,
and all formalities waived and the case disposed of upon
the Biblical teaching that "the laborer is worthy of his
hire."

July 9, 1899   Pine Ridge, South Dakota
Demoralizing Effect of Wild West Shows

The Bureau of Indian Affairs frequently loaned reservation Indians to carnivals, circuses, expositions, and Wild
West shows, requiring only the posting of bonds and a
certificate of good character on the part of the white
showmen. Indians traveled throughout Europe and the
United States (except Texas, where federal law forbade
any Indian Bureau or military personnel from sending
Indians "under any pretext whatever"). In the shows and
expositions the Indians displayed their "culture" by stomp-
ing out a scalp or war dance and appearing dressed in
feathers and costume. In 1894 four Winnebago Indians
were abandoned in London. In 1899 thirteen Sioux were
deserted in Duisburg, Germany. William F. Cody, pop-
ularizer of the Wild West show, was one of the great
exploiters of Indians. On one annual tour he took seventy-
two Indians: five died on the road, seven were returned
early in broken health, and the remainder came back worn
and corrupted at the close of the season. Clapp, acting
Indian agent at Pine Ridge Agency in South Dakota,
provides a critique of this practice (document 89).

Document 89
July 9, 1899   Pine Ridge, South Dakota
Demoralizing Effect of Wild West Shows

Source: U.S. Commissioner of Indian Affairs. Annual Report of 1899 (Washington: Government Printing Office,
1899), pp. 41-43.

I have the honor to request that the following may be
brought to the attention of the honorable Secretary of the
Interior, not as in any manner a criticism of action heretofore taken, but as being a statement of fact possibly
useful when the subject again comes before the Secretary
for consideration. I refer to the increasing demand for
Indians for show purposes.
   Having been for some years at this agency, from which
the Wild West show has recruited its Indians annually, I
am in a position to judge of the effects of using them for
exhibition purposes. It is claimed by those desiring to
employ these Indians that the opportunities afforded them
to see what white men have done and are doing, to realize
the resources of the country, both in numbers and in
wealth, would educate the Indian and deter him from
outbreaks, and that seeing the manner in which the whites
lived, would stimulate him to adopt civilized modes of
living. To a limited extent this may have once been true,
but is no longer so. Ten or more years of such going about
in all the cities of this country and many of those in
Europe, together with numerous visits of delegations to
Washington, and constant intercourse with neighboring

towns, leave little either of good or bad connected with the whites for the Indians (at least of this reservation) to learn. The argument has therefore lost any force it may once have had. In point of fact, Indians are not desired by the show people for any purpose but as an attraction, something to stimulate attendance and lure more half dollars into the treasury.

Now, people will not be curious to see civilized Indians— those whom, at great expense, the Government has educated and to some extent civilized. None such are wanted, but only those who are yet distinctively barbarous or who can pose as such. All others are unwelcome and are denied employment. The result is a premium upon barbarism. It is in effect saying to the Indian: "If you retain purely Indian customs—remain a savage, with all the gaud of feathers, naked bodies, hideous dancing, and other evidences of savagery—we want you; and should you have or can procure a dress trimmed with scalps, we want you very much and will pay you accordingly." The Indian is thus taught that savagery has a market value and is worth retaining. The boys in the day schools know it, and speak longingly of the time when they will no longer be required to attend school, but can let their hair grow long, dance Omaha, and go off with shows.

The influence of this sort of thing is far-reaching and seriously retards progress. In the interest of the Indians, whom we are striving to elevate, the Government should not longer permit these exhibitions of that which it is trying at so much expense to suppress.

These shows are not instructive or beneficial to the whites, conveying as they do wrong ideas and impressions regarding the Indians and leading many of them to think that all Indians are such as they see brought out at shows. Such exhibitions have no higher effect than ministering to a morbid curiosity unworthy of civilized human beings. People go to see naked painted Indians from quite the same motives as they do to see freaks—a two-headed girl or a six-legged calf; but I maintain that no good is subserved, whether the exhibition is labeled an "Indian Congress" or a "Wild West Show," but that, on the contrary, the result is harmful to both whites and Indians—to the latter because by such means their civilization is retarded and the efforts made for their advancement become a mockery. The pleadings of missionaries and the zeal of those engaged in teaching are alike futile among all those Indians who under Government sanction are taught that continued barbarism is perhaps after all the best thing for them.

Then also the moral effect upon those Indians who are taken to exhibitions, of whatever sort, is far from good. In the greed for patronage and gain all sorts of things are permitted and encouraged which ordinarily would be suppressed by the police. Not one of these expositions is now complete without its "midway," made

Buffalo Bill with Yellow Hand's scalp.
Nineteenth century popular history illustration.

up of scandalous and suggestively immoral shows for the most part and designedly pandering to the lowest passions. The moral atmosphere about these places is fetid and impure. Indians employed at them have much idle time and, like all others, are free to see all that is to be seen. It is folly to suppose that they do not take advantage of their opportunities. The season over, during which the car lines and the merchants have been enriched and the city boomed, poor Lo comes back to his home with an intimate knowledge of the seamy side of white civilization, his desire for change and excitement intensified, his all too faint aspirations for the benefits of civilization checked, if not destroyed, and with a conviction that the boasted morality of the whites is nothing to be proud of or to copy. The agency physician states that nearly all of the unnamable diseases now occurring on this reservation are traceable to those Indians who have returned from shows and expositions.

VII
The Failure of Institutions
1900-1975

Indian people entered the twentieth century with the promise of admittance to American civilization through the institutions that had emerged over the previous hundred years to aid in that end. In order to join American society they had been required to shed their ancient cultural heritage, which was a bitter experience for Indians. The constant promise by the white conquerors, missionaries, peacemakers, reformers, and, indeed, many of their leaders of a better life in western civilization softened the harshness of conquest. The Indians were deceived. They had their own culture wrenched from them and were not allowed to gain the other. Instead of giving Indians a more meaningful existence, every major institution developed for that purpose by American society failed to function properly and contained such massive structural weaknesses that the Indians continued to suffer from inhumane treatment. The savagery was not reciprocal; from the 1870s onward, the Indians rarely, if ever, inflicted inhumane treatment upon whites.

America's principal failure occurred in politics. For one hundred years America tried to govern Indians by providing them with civil services and directing legal, economic, educational, health, agricultural, and other institutional aids. Congress frequently investigated the problems besetting the Indians, exposed central issues, and proposed and often passed remedial legislation; in the next investigation the problems often reappeared.

In the early years of the century federal control of Indians' property and tribal government was severe. Between 1930 and 1950 a great relaxation occurred, only to be followed in the early 1950s with restrictive federal policy. Among the many controls sometimes imposed upon tribes were restrictions on the right to vote, to free speech, to control one's property, to hire a lawyer, and to inquire about one's tribal status. In 1954, Congress, intent on concluding all federal relations with Indians, sought and devised a way—termination. By the 1960s the Indians had once again undergone severe mistreatment with at least two tribes being crushed by termination, perhaps beyond the point of ever being able to recover. Since 1970 a major reform movement has been in progress.

The legal system has frequently inflicted great suffering upon Indians. This is true throughout the United States but especially in Oklahoma. When Congress killed the thriving nations of Indian Territory, it ordered the legal system to perform the myriad duties of distributing the tribal property among the members; closing schools, orphanages, and asylums; and ending tribal courts. The 101,000 members of the five tribes, including about 20,000 black Indians, possessed 19,500,000 acres of land with vast timber resources, rich mineral deposits, and untapped oil pools. Through the use of Anglo-Saxon legal complexities the courts of Oklahoma removed this property from Indian control and shifted it into the hands of their white protectors. The Indian culture had no concept of probate fees, deeds, mortgages, and other legal devices. The individual Indian, shorn of his nation's protection, stood helpless under the monumental exploitation, some of it financed by banks and conducted as a regular business. For example, county courts were allowed to appoint guardians for Indian children and adults declared incompetent by the court. Many times the legal process consumed the estate of the ward while enriching attorneys, guardians, politicians, and bankers.

The cruelty accompanying this vast legal process of separating Indians from their wealth defies description. The fact that lawyers following the principles of the law became wealthy by drawing guardian fees for several Indian orphans while the orphans suffered from hunger, lacked clothing, and lived without proper shelter or supervision is a testament to the failure of the legal system. The fact that the homes and farms of aged Indians, built by a life time of hard work, were taken by land grafters through the mysteries of legal conveyance, also is a testament to the legal system's failure. By 1925 the task of "adjusting" the Oklahoma Indians to civilization had been largely completed, because little property remained to be taken. The Indians were reduced to common poverty. In 1929 landless Cherokee in eastern Oklahoma starved to death, silent victims of an inhumane legal system.

Throughout their history Indian people have been told that education is the key to a good life. With many exceptions mediocrity has tended to characterize the education provided for them. Although from time to time over the past seventy years federal investigations have publicized the savage treatment sometimes inflicted upon Indian school children, little critical attention has been directed to the low quality of the educational institution. Indian children usually have the poorest teachers; often the school system does not provide instruction on the background and history of the students' tribe or of the Indian people. Indian children suffer discrimination in the white school systems. Current movements to improve the quality of education are marked by a great flurry of federal and state effort. Attempts by state university systems to exploit the money and opportunities for prestige in these programs continue mediocrity as the standard of highest achievement.

The inability of industry to provide a standard of living high enough to sustain a decent life for Indians has been a recurrent theme of the century. Time and again the poverty and bleakness of Indian life has received public notice, only to slip back into obscurity. Since the 1930s efforts have been underway to improve Indian income. These programs take two directions. One type focuses on job training, work opportunities in urban environments, and Indian control and development of tribal property. Another type focuses on reservation tourism and chamber of commerce "culture" shows, complete with live Indians, that will surely cast the Indian in an image that sadly distorts the vitalizing elements of the old culture.

A gradual awakening of reform tendencies in the recent decade and the promise of an emerging Indian nationalism that will attempt to reorder the institutions affecting Indian life are significant for the future. For example, on December 22, 1973 Congress returned the Menominee to federal trust status by repealing the act that terminated the tribe. There is, however, a five-hundred-year-old unrelieved history of American savagery casting its shadow so completely over white-Indian relations that it negates optimism.

August, 1911   Oroville, California
The Last Southern Yana

Ishi, the last living member of the Southern Yana, was "caught" in the California mountains and given a home in the Museum of Anthropology of the University of California. The negative impact of civilization upon American Indians is clearly illustrated in the history of his tribe, which was the victim of concerted effort to exterminate. The curator of the museum, Professor A. L. Kroeber, described the "capture" in the portion of the article given below (document 90). Ishi contracted tuberculosis and died in 1916. Although the material progress of American life seems to preclude a reenactment of the Southern Yana fate using another tribe or ethnic or racial group in the United States, the future is never known.

Further reading: Theodora Kroeber, *Ishi in Two Worlds* (Berkeley: University of California Press, 1961).

Document 90
August, 1911   Oroville, California
The Last Southern Yana

Source: A. L. Kroeber, "Ishi, The Last Aborigine," **World's Work** (July, 1912), pp. 304-305.

At eleven o'clock in the evening on Labor Day, 1911, there stepped off the ferry boat into the glare of electric lights, into the shouting of hotel runners, and the clanging of trolley cars on Market Street, San Francisco, Ishi, the last wild Indian in the United States.

Ishi belongs to the lost Southern Yana tribe that formerly lived in Tehama County, in northern California. This tribe, after years of guerilla warfare, was practically exterminated by the whites by massacre, in 1865. The five survivors took refuge in the utterly wild cañon of Deer Creek in Tehama County, and the last recorded time that any one saw them was in 1870. There were two men, two women, and a child—probably Ishi, for he has told how, when he was a small boy, "so high," the white men came at sunrise and killed his people in their camp.

In November, 1908, a party of water-right surveyors working laboriously down the cañon, came on a hut, from which dashed two or three men or women, leaving one old, decrepit, and sick crone behind. Unable to converse with her, the surveyors left her undisturbed; but all attempts to open negotiations with the other Indians failed, so great was their fear.

Within a year, news of this adventure reached the University of California, where the Indians in question were at once identified, by their condition and location, as the long lost Southern Yana, the relatives of the almost extinct Northern Yana, whose dialect and customs had been investigated by the University ethnologists only a year or two before. After some confirming inquiries in the vicinity, a party was organized in the fall of 1910 to hunt for the Indians. A month in the cañon, in which practically every foot of their territory was gone over, revealed no Indians, but ample evidence of their recent existence—huts, smokehouses, baskets, nets, pestles, flint-chips, and so forth. It was concluded that they had seen the expedition first and had kept consistently out of its way.

Then, at the end of August, 1911, came despatches announcing the capture, near Oroville, some forty miles to the south of Deer Creek, and in a well-settled district, of a lone wild Indian. He had been trying to break into a slaughterhouse, and had been placed in jail, where neither Indians nor whites could converse with him. A member of the staff of the anthropological department of the University of California arrived, armed with a Northern Yana vocabulary and the first communication with the aborigine began, much to the amazement of the local Indians. The next day Sam Batwi, a North Yana interpreter, arrived in response to a telegraphic call, and while finding the dialect different from his own and difficult to manage, was able to make more headway. No formal charge had been placed against the wild man, and in a few days the Sheriff of Butte County obligingly released him to the University authorities—an arrangement sanctioned by the United States Indian Office.

In justice to Ishi, his own version of his "capture" should be given. His people were all dead, he said. A woman and a child had been drowned in crossing a stream. The old woman found by the surveyors was dead. For some time he had been entirely alone—poor, often hungry, with nothing to live for. This, by the way, was no doubt the reason for his drifting, perhaps aimlessly, so far south-ward of his old home. One day he made up his mind to "come in." He expected to be killed, he said, but that no longer mattered. So he walked westward all day, without meeting any one, and at dusk came to a house where meat was hung up. Tired, hungry, and thirsty, he sat down. Soon a boy came out with a lantern, saw him, recoiled, and called a man, who ran up. In response to Ishi's signs, they gave him a pair of overalls—for he was naked except for a rude homemade garment, half shirt, half cape—ordered him into their wagon, and drove him to town, where he was put into a large and fine house—the jail—and very kindly treated and well fed by a big chief—the deputy sheriff.

1915
The Charge Against American Civilization

In 1915 highly educated Indians numbered less than fifty, of whom fewer than a dozen had obtained their training in cultural disciplines. When the Society of American Indians was formed in 1911, these few Indians perforce had to carry the main thrust of the Society's work in developing policies and focusing on issues for the "better-ment of the race." A Seneca, Arthur C. Parker, one of the leading members, became the editor of the *Quarterly Journal,* for which he wrote many editorials and lengthy articles. From one of his major articles an excerpt has been taken that contains a charge against American civilization for crushing the spirit of a people (document 91).

Further reading: Hazel W. Hertzberg, *The Search For an American-Indian Identity: Modern Pan-Indian Move-ments* (Syracuse: Syracuse University Press, 1971).

Document 91
1915   United States
The Charge Against American Civilization

Source: Arthur C. Parker, "Certain Important Elements of the Indian Problem," **The Quarterly Journal of the Society of the American Indian** (January-March, 1915), vol. III, No. 1, pp. 24-28.

There is little understanding of the blight that has fallen upon the red race within the United States. Notwith-standing the immense effort that is put forth by missionary bodies and by the federal government to remedy the un-happy situation of the Indians, neither of these forces acts as if it surely knew the elements with which it was dealing. But between the church and the state, if a com-parison were drawn, the church understands better and responds more intelligently to the vital necessities of the race because its concern is with the man and not his property. Even so, there is no clearly defined philosophy that reveals causes and points out remedies.

The Indian Bureau of the Interior Department is charged by Congressional action with dealing with Indian affairs. Like some vast machine bulky with many ill-fitting, or inferior parts it grinds on, consuming huge sums of money for fuel and lubrication. Its constituted purpose is the protection of Indian property, the transformation of a race by civilization and its education, to the end that the Indians may become good citizens. Yet the Bureau is not achieving as great a measure of success as its Com-missioner and earnest officials might wish.

The church has a similar but broader object, expressed in its own words, "to save the souls of the Indians," in other words, to build manhood and character. But even the church in its various denominations has its trials and its missionaries pray for greater and more permanent influence over the morals of the red man whom they have set out to save.

Neither the church nor the state with all its powers for organization, however, proceeds as if it had discovered why its task was so greatly hampered or why it must apply so much unproductive effort. It appears that the Indians are perverse, are naturally inclined to degradation, are inferior and unmindful as a race, or that they were an accursed people as some of the early colonists thought. Yet both church and state labor on for they feel that Providence has entrusted a benighted people to their keeping. Each factor is an instrument of American civili-zation, the one a civic power, the other a moral force. Each sees the Indian problem through standards of its own race. Each translates its conception of the needs of the Indian in terms of its own liking. Each understands through its own system of thinking, and bases its acts upon the sure assumption of its correctness. No attempt is ever made to outline the plan of its action and to explain why it thinks thus and so, and to submit such a plan to a psychologist, a sociologist or an ethnologist for criticism and suggestion. Each has more or less definitely expressed the idea of "the white man's burden," or the obligation of American civilization and of Anglo-Saxon blood to lead mankind to higher goals. Each body resents any aspersion cast upon the integrity or the inherent moral qualities of the race it represents, for is not the Anglo-American the most charitable, the most conscientious of all races? Even so, there is a fundamental blindness, caused, shall we say, by a moral blind spot; there is a lack of feeling caused shall we say, by local anesthesia; there is a certain cerebral center in the cortices of the brain that seems insensible to certain impressions; there is a coating of the moral nature that is like, shall we say, a callous on the foot, covering an unsuspected nerve. A scratch gives no feeling, but when stepped upon there is a cry, "Keep off!" The development of the human race has not advanced to the point where men are uniformly fair minded. The people of the country who do have the welfare of an unhappy race at heart must come to understand the true nature of the injury the red man has sustained through his violent contact with civilization, and good men must learn to see the injury through the eyes and by the thoughts of the injured man.

For the sake of definiteness and to stimulate constructive argument we wish to lay down seven charges, out of perhaps many more, that the Indian makes at the bar of American justice. Whether the white man believes them just or not, true or not, he cannot discharge his obligation to the red man until he considers them and understands that the Indian makes them because he at least feels them just charges. There will be white Americans who will see the charges as rightfully made and there will no doubt be some Indians, who, trained in the philosophies of the narrow school of the conqueror, will not admit them.

But notwithstanding objections we desire to submit the charges. The Indian's view must be known if his sight is to be directed to broader visions.

The Charge Against American Civilization

The people of the United States through their government agencies, and through the aggression of their citizens have:

1. Robbed a race of men—the American Indian—of their intellectual life;
2. Robbed the American Indian of his social organization;
3. Robbed the American Indian of his native freedom;
4. Robbed the American Indian of his economic independence;
5. Robbed the American Indian of his moral standards and of his racial ideals;
6. Robbed the American Indian of his good name among the peoples of the earth;
7. Robbed the American Indian of a definite civic status.

Each of the factors we have named is an essential to the life of a man or a nation. Picture a citizen of this republic without freedom, intellectual or social life, with no ability to provide his own food and clothing, having no sure belief in an Almighty being, no hero to admire and no ideals to foster, with no legal status and without a reputable name among men. Picture a nation or a people so unhappy. Yet civilization has conspired to produce in varying degrees all these conditions for the American Indians.

So much for the seven great robberies of the race. We have not even cared to mention the minor loss of territory and of resources—these are small things indeed, compared with the other thefts.

But though the robbery has been committed, the Government and great citizens will exclaim, "We have given much to atone for your loss, brother red man."

Let us examine the nature of these gifts. The Federal Government and the kind hearts of friends have—

1. Given reserved tracts of land where the Indians may live unmolested;
2. Given agents and superintendents as guardians and constituted a division of the Interior Department as a special bureau for the protection of the red race;
3. Given schools with splendid mechanical equipment;
4. Given the ignorant and poor, clerks who will think and act for them, and handle their money;
5. Given food, and clothing and peace;
6. Given a new civilization;
7. Given a great religion.

So great and good gifts must have a price, for men cannot have these boons without suffering some disability. Measures are necessary to protect the Government itself from the results of its own charity and leniency to a people but lately regarded as enemies. The Government, therefore, as a price has—

1. Denied the Indians a voice in their own affairs to such an extent that Indian councils may not now meet without the consent of the Commissioner of Indian Affairs;
2. Denied the Indians the stimulus that springs from responsibility;
3. Denied the Indians the right to compete on the same terms as other men;

4. Denied the Indian a definition of his status in the country;

5. Denied the Indian the right to submit his claims against the United States in the Court of Claims, without special consent of Congress;

6. Denied the Indian a true and adequate education;

7. Denied the Indian the right to be a man, as other men of America are.

To be sure, the Indians were not at once denied these fundamental rights of human beings living in an organized civilized community. It was only as the seven great robberies became more or less complete and the reservation system grew, that the seven great denials took effect. The robberies and the denials are of a subtle psychological character and many there are who will ingeniously argue that the Indians still have all the things we have mentioned, or may have them if they will to do it, and that the seven gifts are but the gratuities of a charitable government.

But the men who so argue are devoid of finer spiritual perceptions, or perchance they are unable to see another man's viewpoint when they have one of their own. There are not wanting men and women who are unable to realize that another man can be hungry when their own stomachs are full. There are men having considerable mental endowments and a knowledge of the world who say, "If I were in his place, I would do thus and so. I would seize opportunity and soon all would be well." Men of this character are still mentally blind and spiritually dull, and are the first to deny that any great wrong has been done after all. They are insensible to the fact that the red man has felt his debasement and that his soul and his children's souls are bitter with a grief they cannot express.

The result of such denials of basic human rights to proud men and women is definite and deep. Whether he can express his thoughts in words or not, whether the turmoil in his heart finds voice or not, every American Indian who has suffered this oppression that is worse than death feels that civilization has—

1. Made him a man without a country;
2. Usurped his responsibility and right of acting;
3. Demeaned his manhood;
4. Destroyed his ideals;
5. Broken faith with him;
6. Humiliated his spirit;
7. Refused to listen to his petitions.

The old reservation Indian feels all these things, and they burn into his very soul leaving him unhappy and dispirited.

Only those who have had the comfort of education and the sustaining power of religion have been able to keep up hope, and even these often-times feel the sting the more and thus, a more painful recognition of their humiliation.

If these statements seem to tinge of irony or of invective to the civilized man with the moral blind spot, they are, nevertheless, very real things to the Indian who knows wherein he is wounded. To him this analysis will seem mild indeed for it speaks nothing of a thousand deeds that made the four centuries of contact years of cruel misunderstanding. Yet, to him these earlier years were better years than now, for he was then a free man who could boast a nation, who could speak his thought and who bowed to no being save God, his superior and guardian. Nor will we here mention the awful wars against Indian women and children, the treacherous onslaughts on sleeping villages, the murders of the old and helpless, broken promises, the stolen lands, the robbed orphans and widows, done by men professing civilization and religion—for this is aside from our argument. We mention what is more awful than robbery of lands, more hideous than the scalping and burning of Indian women and babies, more harrowing than tortures at the stake; we mean the crushing of a noble people's spirit and the usurpation of its right to be responsible, self supporting and self governing.

Let it be affirmed as a deep conviction that until the American Indian is given back the right of assuming responsibility for his own acts and until his spirit is roused to action that re-awakened ideals will give him, all effort, all governmental protection, all gifts are of small value to him.

1917   **Union, Mississippi**
                    Peonage

After the era of removal, 1820-1840, several thousand Indians remained in the old South. Some, like the Creek in Alabama, elected not to follow the main tribal body and took land in the state; others, like the Lumbee of South Carolina, were not included in the removal schemes; and still others, like the Cherokee of North Carolina, fled into the forests to avoid the government edict. These scattered Indian groups connected with the economic institutions of the region where they lived, but they kept alive the cultural link with the past. By the twentieth century the basic economic problems facing the Indians were those the South faced. The crop-lien system, a form of peonage, dominated the lives of the lower class of all three races.

The crop-lien system emerged during the tumult of Reconstruction, when Southern businessmen sought to control laborers—white, black, and Indian—to work the land left idle as a result of the Civil War. The freedom of the American economic structure permitted local land owners to provide laborers with a small farm and take the rent in crops instead of in scarce cash. Since the poverty-stricken tenants lacked seed, food supplies, and other essentials, rural merchants advanced these necessities and took a lien on the future crop share of the tenants.

High interest rates were levied. The land owners and merchants were frequently the same person or at least shared the same community of interests. After the harvest the crop-sharing tenants most often found they were still in debt; the third party to the crop-lien system, local sheriffs, entered the relationship. Southern laws did not allow debtors to leave the county. If intimidation, even lynching, did not instill fear and acquiesence in the peons, sheriffs could seize the debtors and place them on the county chain gang. The low quality of food supplied by the merchants lacked essential nutrition. Year in and year out the businessmen required cash crops that depleted the soil and threw the tenants deeper into debt and misery. Illiteracy was essential for control; the white tenants were frequently pitched against the interests of the blacks, and the blacks against the Indians.

A letter from a Choctaw Indian, Tom Stephens, describes the use of force and fear to keep him a peon to a white man (document 92). Illiterate, he dictated the letter to Mrs. Gena Arnold, a school teacher and wife of a white reformer who fought for Indian justice. To work for racial justice in Union, Mississippi, was an act of great courage. The Mississippi Choctaw had always kept their sense of Indian identity, and from 1910-1914 the Indian reform group, the Society of Mississippi Choctaws, sought to advance education, industry, and social justice. Their efforts were deliberately crushed by the federal government.

Document 92
1917
The Crop-Lien System
Union, Mississippi

Source: U.S. Congress, Senate, Committee on Indian Affairs, **Survey of the Conditions of the Indians in the United States, Hearings,** before a Subcommittee of the Committee on Indian Affairs, on S. R. 263, Senate, 71st Cong., 2d sess., 1931, pp. 7827-7828.

UNION, MISS., *September 1, 1917.*
SECRETARY OF THE INTERIOR,

Washington, D.C.

Dear Sir: I, Tom Stephens, am a full-blood Choctaw Indian. I was identified by the Commission to the Five Civilized Tribes, and I gave my name to Hon. John R. T. Reeves, special supervisor, Indian Service, when he was in Mississippi last October.

Since Mr. Reeves was here I have had lots of trouble. A white man has robbed me of everything I had and beaten me nearly to death. I want to tell you all about it and ask you to help me.

It was this way: In December, 1915, I went to visit my sister who lives near Deemer, Miss. A white man, S. Vance Posey, who lives near Deemer, wanted to hire me and my two sons to clear 6 acres of land for him, promising to pay us $5 per acre. We finished this by March, and for this job he paid me alright.

Then he hired me to haul crossties and to plow and do all kinds of work, promising to pay me 75 cents per day. I worked at this from March to June, 1916, but he never would give me a settlement. He would give me a sack of meal some weeks and sometimes a sack of flour and a little bucket of lard, and sometimes I would have to borrow something to eat when he would not give me anything.

In June, 1916, he put me to sawing logs, and my two sons also. We would saw about 10,000 feet per day—sometimes not so much and sometimes a little more; and he had us work about every day at this mill until time to begin farming in February, 1917, but would not make settlement with me, only giving me a little to eat and once in awhile a little money—never more than $1 at a time, and not more than $10 in all; just enough to buy some little thing I had to have.

In February, 1917, he assigned 9 acres of land that I should farm on the halves, and my boys went to work at that while he put me to clearing land and piling and burning brush, which kept me hard at work until about May. And by that time the crop was about layed by, and the 9 acres were all in good corn.

Then when the crop was finished, or at anytime that I and my boys were not working in the field, he had us to saw logs or haul timber. We were working this way June 28, 1917. That morning he put us to hauling post. We got through about 10 o'clock, and when we went up to his house he seemed very angry, like mad man, about something, and he had a knife in his hand and talked very rough and threatening to me, and told me to hurry up and get to work in the timber. He took one of my boys on to the timber with him and sent the other one to plow. I told him I had to go down to my house and get axe and wedge, etc. My old mother lives with me. I told her what he said and that he was angry and had a knife, and she said I must wait until after dinner to go to work with him in the timber. It began to rain hard about noon, so neither I nor my boys went to work that afternoon.

That night after I had been asleep a long time I was awakened by men who came to my house. The leader of them was this man, S. Vance Posey, who had held me in peonage for nearly two years. He had a pistol in one hand, which he held on me, and in the other hand he had a whip or a rope or something awful which he beat and beat me with until it looked like I was dead. One of the other men with him was Arthur Barefield. He had a shot gun and he beat me, too. The other men did not hurt me, they just stood off a little and looked on. It was dark and they did not come near, but I believe two of them were John Tinsley and Linnet Posey.

I was afraid for Vance Posey to see me not dead. So before day the next morning I left home all alone walking on two sticks. It took me all day to go 5 miles to the house of John Robinson. I had to sit down and lie down so much, and was so sick and had had nothing to eat. John Robinson is a white man and lives near McDonald, Miss.

My boys went to work for Vance Posey the next morning after he had almost killed me, and Arthur Barefield told my boy, Felix, that if I did not come to work that afternoon for Vance Posey that 40 men would come get me that night. So my mother and my children were afraid to stay there that night, and they all ran away, of course, leaving everything we have in the world there on Vance Posey's place and now he says he won't let us have anything. So he has, belonging to me and my mother, 26 fruit jars, about 25 chickens, 4 beds, 4 mattresses, violin, 14 quilts, 7 chairs, 1 long table, 1 stove and cooking vessels and dishes, 4 axes, washtubs and pot, shoe last, 2 churns,

1 heater, clock, 2 dish pans, wash pan, water bucket, 3 skillets, and 4 or 5 trunks, which have all our clothes and everything in them, even all my letters from the Government.

In a short time the weather will be cold, and unless you make Vance Posey give up our beds and quilts and clothes my children and my mother and myself may all freeze to death.

Will you have him pay me for the work I did, and give me my half of the corn which is now about ripe in the field?

Please let me know what you will do about it. The white men (some of them) have treated the Choctaws this way all the time since the Dancing Rabbit Creek treaty—everything the Choctaws get the white men take away from them. This is the way they drove our grandfathers

Indian School, Genoa, Nebraska, 1917.

from their homes, and now they take everything from us. I wish the Government would send a man down here to stay all the time to watch out for the Choctaws.

                    Respectfully,   his
                                            TOM X STEPHENS.
                                                    mark

August 7, 1917   Oneida, Wisconsin
Criticism of Trust Patents

On June 13, 1892, the United States allotted the 65,000-acre Oneida reservation to individual Indians. Many spoke only Oneida and did not understand the meaning of private property and taxes. To prohibit the allotted land from being quickly acquired by businessmen speculating in Indian property, trust patents were given for the individual's land. In theory the United States retained legal title. For an Indian to sell his restricted property, the United States had to agree to the alienation or the Indian must have been issued a patent in fee simple, which removed all restrictions against the property. Each allottee had twenty-five years of trust patent protection for his land, after which time a fee patent would be issued. The President could extend the time period. While the time period was extended for ten years, the Secretary of Interior was given new discretionary power in 1906 to remove all restrictions from any Indian property whose owner he adjudged to be competent. The Secretary's power grew to be arbitrary. Under Woodrow Wilson's administration, the removal of restrictions became a major property-expropriation scheme. Typically when property was released from controls, it quickly passed into white ownership. The landless and destitute Indians passed into oblivion. The competency provision acted as a public balm.

The experience of the Wisconsin Oneida is fairly typical of the procedure. In August, 1917, a three-man federal competency board headed by James McLaughlin met the Oneida at Oneida, Wisconsin, to decide the eligibility of those allottees who held land under restriction. After visiting and inspecting the homes of the many restricted allotments, they invited the owners to a meeting where they could express themselves on the question of full citizenship. McLaughlin advised them that the removal of restrictions would give the Oneida "a white man's chance" for a good life. However, many Oneida would become a welfare burden on the township if adjudged competent. Educated Oneida, who were the products of schools such as the Hampton Institute in Virginia, returned home believing that civilization could only be acquired through ownership of private property; they became leading proponents of removing restrictions. In addition, pressure came from Indians and whites who had purchased land on the former reservation.

The suffering endured by the Oneida from the impersonal land system and from the criticism of their educated tribesmen is expressed in the following speech of Civil War veteran John Archiquette, a leader in his tribe (document 93). Literate in Oneida, Archiquette spoke through an interpreter. The Oneida word translated by the secretary of the meeting as G signified deep anguish at the destruction of his beloved people.

Document 93
August 7, 1917   Oneida, Wisconsin
Criticism of Trust Patents

Source: "Typescript of Meeting," James McLaughlin Manuscripts, Division of Archives and Manuscripts, The State Historical Society of Wisconsin.

John Archiquette: (Interpreted by Mr. Webster)

Just a few words in regard to this council. It is not very well understood what this council is here for. I think we all understand it pretty well just what the council is for. Now, it seems to me—for an illustration, there are a few black stars in on this reservation. Call it black stars to represent these trust patent lands and for these black stars to appear here and there it makes the others feel that they ought not to be there. It makes them sore. It makes an eye-sore to see them. Now, the government knows just about exactly what's going on here out here on the Oneida Reservation. They know just about how the people live but there is these few here that don't like to see these black stars. They want to wipe them out and call it clean. It will never be clean until it is wiped out. That is the idea of the people and these few others who are holding the fee simple, they don't care what will become of us when we get our land deeded. We will say what are we going to do. They will say, Do what you can. If you can swim with your head above water, stay above water; if not, go down to the bottom and drown. So there is just one thing I would like to impress upon the representatives of this commission and that is to recommend to the government to extend the time, give us an extension because I really feel that it ought to be given. It ought to be given to us. I am seeing just what is taking place around here. There are those that have changed; they have got their fee simple patents to their lands; they are not getting along the way they ought to. They are suffering and when I see them suffer, I suffer too because I love my people. And many times when I see them suffer, I feel as though I ought to get in and suffer with them too. That is because my heart is with my people and I ask the commission this one thing, to recommend to the department that an extension be given us. Now, these that are in favor, these that are encouraging to get these lands changed into fee simple, they say you going to be elevated, have the same chance as the white man, you are going to be up in G. You will never be up there until your head is bored and your brain is taken out and another one put into it.

1923   Oklahoma
Oklahoma Probate System

In 1898 the United States severed relations with the Cherokee, Choctaw, Chickasaw, and Creek nations and ordered the nations dissolved and the property divided among their citizens. Restrictions were placed upon the property of full bloods to protect them from grafters, a term applied to dealers in Indian lands. Congress then passed the Act of May 27, 1908, removing all restrictions upon sale of inherited lands by full-blood heirs. The exploitation and fraud in progress against orphans and blacks and other classes of former Indian citizens thrust into the rich field of full-blood probate fees. In 1914 the Bureau of Indian Affairs attempted to draw rules of procedure for probate courts in Oklahoma, but the next few years saw the important portions of the procedures negated by Congress and the courts. Finally on July 10, 1923, the Oklahoma Supreme Court struck down the last of these restrictions, leaving each county court a law unto itself. Supported by Congress, the local judges and lawyers joined bankers and merchants in an orgy of fraud and probate manipulation that raised among candid observers the spectre of possible extermination of the full bloods. The grafters—running a highly organized, well-funded public relations campaign to mislead the public—used newspapers, lecture podiums, and chamber of commerce groups to draw a shroud of secrecy over the heinous and lucrative probate procedure. In 1923, Mrs. Gertrude Bonnin, a Sioux Indian, Charles H. Fabens, attorney for the Indian Defense Association, and Matthew K. Sniffen, Secretary of the Indian Rights Association, investigated the condition of the Five Civilized Tribes, including the Seminole. The following is an excerpt from their report (document 94). It was not until the 1933 reform era that serious attempts were made to assist the Indians at a federal level.

Further reading: Angie Debo, *And Still the Waters Run* (Princeton: Princeton University Press, 1940).

Document 94
1923   Oklahoma
Oklahoma Probate System

Source: Gertrude Bonnin, et al., **Oklahoma's Poor Rich Indians. An Orgy of Graft and Exploitation of the Five Civilized Tribes—Legalized Robbery** (Philadelphia: Indian Rights Association, 1924), pp. 26-28, 36-38.

The smothered cries of the Indians for rescue from legalized plunder comes in a chorus from all parts of eastern Okla-

homa. The case cited above is from Tulsa County. And now follows another outrage perpetrated under cover of a County Court in the southern part of eastern Oklahoma.

Little *Ledcie Stechi*, a Choctaw minor, seven years old, owned rich oil property in McCurtain County. She lived with her old grandmother in a small shack back in the hills about two and a half miles from Smithville. They lived in dire poverty, without proper food or clothing and surrounded by filth and dirt. Ledcie Stechi inherited lands from her mother, including twenty acres which became valuable oil property. Other lands she inherited were sold by her uncle, Noel Samuel, for a consideration of $2000 which was deposited in the bank subject to control by the County Judge, who allowed $10 a month for the support of Ledcie Stechi.

After the discovery of oil on the twenty acres above mentioned, her uncle, Noel Samuel, who was her guardian, was induced to resign through a combination of various tactics, force, persuasion and offer of reward which he never got, Mr. Jordan Whiteman, owner of the First National Bank of Idabel, whose attorney was instrumental in Noel Samuel's resignation, was appointed guardian. At the time of Mr. Whiteman's appointment, July, 1921, Ledcie lived with her old grandmother in the hills, and until 1923 they were in a semi-starving condition. Once a week the old grandmother walked to Smithville to buy food on the monthly credit of $15 allowed them by Mr. Whiteman, at Blake's store. They had no conveyance. Sometimes she was too tired to walk back. Then she hired some one to take her home, which cost fifty or sixty cents. During this period from 1921 to 1923, the guardian did nothing to make them more comfortable or to educate the little Indian heiress.

In the fall of 1922 the guardian attempted to sell ten acres of Ledcie's oil land which was producing at the time, and appraised at $90,000, for a consideration of $2000. This attempt was defeated, and with the result that Ledcie Stechi's monthly allowance was increased to $200, from which the guardian allowed the child and grandmother a credit of $15 monthly at a local store. Still, throughout the following year, Ledcie and her old grandmother fared no better than prior to the $200 allowance to the guardian. In April, 1923, they were brought to Idabel, the County seat. The rich little Choctaw girl, with her feeble grandmother, came to town carrying their clothes, a bundle of faded rags, in a flour sack. Ledcie was dirty, filthy, and covered with vermin. She was emaciated and weighed about 47 pounds.

A medical examination showed she was undernourished and poisoned by malaria. After five weeks of medical treatment and nourishment Ledcie gained 11 pounds. Her health improved, she was placed by an employee of the Indian Service in the Wheelock Academy, an Indian school. Mr. Whiteman, evidently fearing to lose his grasp on his ward, demanded the child, and Ledcie Stechi, child of much abuse, was returned to the custody of her legal guardian 24 hours after she was taken to the school where she would have had good care. The last time the aged grandmother had seen Ledcie, and only for a few minutes, was on the 12th of July.

A month later, on the 14th of August, word was brought to the hills that Ledcie was dead. There had been no word of the girl's illness and the sudden news of her death was a terrible blow to the poor old grandmother.

The following day, at dawn, before the corpse had arrived, parties of grafters arrived at the heretofore unknown hovel in the hills and harassed the bereaved old grandmother about the future disposal of Ledcie's valuable properties.

Rival speculators went over with the body of Ledcie Stechie. Some of them sent flowers to be placed on the grave of her, who though but a child, had known only of poisonous thorns. The floral offerings were too late for the child of sorrows, but they were made by hypocrites who hoped thereby to play upon the heart of the aged grandmother, who was now the sole heir to Ledcie Stechi's vast estate.

Greed for the girl's lands and rich oil property actuated the grafters and made them like beasts surrounding their prey, insensible to the grief and anguish of the white-haired grandmother. Feebly, hopelessly, she wailed over the little dead body—its baby mouth turned black, little fingernails turned black, and even the little breast all turned black! In vain she asked for an examination of the body, believing Ledcie had been poisoned. "No use. Bury the body," commanded the legal guardian.

The Court has already appointed a guardian for the grandmother,—against her vehement protest. She, too, will go the way of her grandchild, as sheep for slaughter by ravenous wolves in men's forms, unless the good people of America intervene immediately by remedial Congressional action. Such action is the duty of all loyal Americans for the protection of America's wards.

Incidentally, another heir has been put forward in a contest suit; but, whichever way the case is decided the attorneys expect to come in for fat fees.

. . .

IN BRIEFER FORM

To cite all the cases investigated would be monotonous repetition; suffice it to say, their number is legion, and while there may be variation as to harrowing details, the general result is the same, so far as it concerns the plundering of the Indians, under the "system" as developed in eastern Oklahoma. . . .

The "system" has but one object—GET THE MONEY AND GET IT QUICK!

August 18, 1923   Muskogee, Oklahoma
Creek Protest Against Exploitation

After the abolishment of the national structure of the

Five Civilized Tribes, the individual members were exploited by the Oklahoma legal and political system. The Indians, aware of their predicament, constantly protested against the mistreatment. Their protests, however, seldom reached the public, since Indians lacked institutional access to newspapers and other forms of communication. The following resolution was unanimously adopted by the Creek Indian Baptists' Association held at Montezuma Baptist Church near Muskogee, Oklahoma (document 95).

Further reading: M. K. Sniffen, *"Out of Thine Own Mouth." An analysis of the House Subcommittee Report Denying and Confirming the Looting of Oklahoma's "Poor Rich Indians."* (Philadelphia: Indian Rights Association, 1925).

Document 95
August 18, 1923   Muskogee, Oklahoma
Creek Protest Against Exploitation

Source: U.S., Congress, House, Committee on Indian Affairs, **Five Civilized Tribes in Oklahoma, Hearings,** before the Subcommittee of the Committee on Indian Affairs, House of Representatives, on H. R. 6900, 68th Cong., 1st sess., 1924, pp. 2-3.

RESOLUTION

Whereas by act of Congress the legislative bodies of the Muskogee or Creek Nation have been abolished and its powers supplanted by the State of Oklahoma and the United States of America; and

Whereas since the coming under the jurisdiction of said State, the citizens of the Muskogee or Creek Nation have been humiliated and treated unmercifully in the probate courts by unscrupulous and designing persons who obtain control of their estates through guardianship proceedings for the sole and only purpose of robbing them; that the majority of Creek Indian minors are now landless, due to the fact that guardians have squandered their estates through these same courts on the pretext of obtaining funds for the minors' maintenance and education when it is well known that the Government maintains excellent educational institutions free of all cost to Indians; that the moment an Indian becomes wealthy through the discovery of oil or mineral on his allotment he is brought into court and declared incompetent and one or more guardians appointed, thus placing the Indian in a class with children, insane, and idiotic persons; that the guardianship of wealthy Indian estates are used by candidates of county judiciary offices as a political football and kicked to the person contributing most to his success; and

Whereas it was the sole object and intent of the Creek delegates in inserting article 4, act of Congress approved

March 1, 1901 (31 Stat. 861), as relates to the appointment of guardians, to defeat just such evils as are now being practiced; that by act of Congress the Secretary of the Interior is acting in the capacity of guardian and custodian of the funds of restricted Indians without any cost whatever for such services; and that the dual guardianship as imposed by the State courts is unnecessary, costly, and detrimental to the welfare and best interests of the Indian; and that, owing to the Indians being in the minority and the unscrupulous and grafting element in the majority, no relief or reforms can be expected from the State legislature nor from our Representatives in Congress. Therefore be it

Resolved, That the members of this association strongly protest the further appointment of white or non-Indian guardians over Indians, and that the Secretary of the Interior be urgently requested to take immediate steps to obtain legislation by Congress to correct and stop the aforementioned evils of the probate court system in Oklahoma; that this association strongly favors legislation giving the Secretary of the Interior absolute jurisdiction over the estates of restricted Indians; further

Resolved, That copies of this resolution be sent to the Secretary of the Interior, the Governor of the State of Oklahoma, the Commissioner of Indian Affairs, the chairman of the Committee on Indian Affairs of the United States Senate, the chairman of the Committee on Indian Affairs of the United States House of Representatives, the Superintendent of the Five Civilized Tribes, and the attorney for the Creek Nation.

Approved, August 18, 1923.

1925-1930
Inhumane Treatment of Children

In the 1920s public exposure of the mistreatment of Indian school children in federal schools shocked the national conscience. Two examples have been selected to illustrate the inhumanity of the white schoolmasters. The first is the testimony of Mrs. D. M. Kefauver, Columbus, Ohio, before a Senate committee in Washington. In 1924 Mrs. Kefauver had been appointed head matron of the Ute Indian School at Towaoc, Colorado, with the duty of general supervision of the children. When she first arrived at the school, she discovered a lair of rats in the flour bins and ordered the flour removed. In the excerpt presented, the testimony begins with Louis Glavis (chief investigator for the committee) questioning Mrs. Kefauver about what happened when she informed Mr. McDaniels, superintendent of the school (document 96).

The second document is the testimony of a teacher, Rose Ecoffey, to the same Senate committee conducting hearings at Pine Ridge, South Dakota (document 97). She is questioned by Senator Lynn Frazier and Senator Burton K. Wheeler. Ecoffey's account of the corporal

punishment of the children is sustained by several witnesses, including a school policeman.

Further reading: Lewis Merriam, et al., *The Problem of Indian Administration* (Baltimore: The Johns Hopkins University Press, 1928).

Document 96
1928   Towaoc, Colorado
Malnourishment and Inhumane Treatment of Children

Source: U.S., Congress, Senate, Committee on Indian Affairs, **Survey of the Conditions of the Indians in the United States, Hearings**, before a Subcommittee of the Committee on Indian Affairs, Senate, on S. R. 79, 70th Cong., 2d sess., 1929, pp. 1021-1023.

Mr. GLAVIS. Then what happened when Mr. McDaniels returned? Did you call his attention to the condition of the flour?

Mrs. KEFAUVER. When he came home his wife had reported to him what had been done, and he went over to the kitchen, and he was furious to think that anybody would have the audacity to do a thing like that. He was just furious. His wife whispered to him and told him not to get so furious; he could deal it out as rations. He said, "I will do that."

Mr. GLAVIS. That is, to the older ones?

Mrs. KEFAUVER. To the older ones. He did send it back to the school, because they found mice and rats in the flour afterward, and it was baked, and when they would send it over, every Sunday night they would send the children's food to the dormitories so that they would eat their supper. That was the only time the cook had to get out; and when they would send that over I could not let them put it in the house, it smelled so. It had to be kept outdoors.

Senator PINE. Was that the flour or the bread?

Mrs. KEFAUVER. That was the bread that they baked out of the flour. It was in the most terrible condition that can be imagined.

Mr. GLAVIS. I think one of the witnesses who testified at Yakima, Wash.—Miss Groves—said she found portions of mice in the bread. Did you find any such conditions as that?

Mrs. KEFAUVER. I did not find it myself, but I knew that it had been.

Mr. GLAVIS. You did not, then, get any new flour? You had to use the old flour? Is that so?

Mrs. KEFAUVER. For a few days they brought in a few sacks of other flour, to cover up what they were going to do, I suppose. I took it at that, anyway, because then the other flour commenced to come back in.

Mr. GLAVIS. Did you protest against the other flour coming back?

Mrs. KEFAUVER. I certainly did, but it did not do any good.

Mr. GLAVIS. What about the condition of the meat, if you know?

Mrs. KEFAUVER. The meat was kept over in the basement of the commissary department, which was under the mess hall. I could show you pictures of all those places. There is a large mess hall where the employees eat and where they entertain their guests, and in the basement of that is the commissary that they have for storing the canned goods and such things as that; and the meat was kept there. There was no screen; there was no floor in there, although the cement had been piled up there for a year or more to make the floor, but it never had been done. It was as dirty as it could possibly be; there were no screens, and the meat would be stacked in there in loads. Well, you know, in a hot place like that, how long it would keep fresh. There was no ice to keep it, and it would spoil.

Mr. GLAVIS. Was the condition of the meat called to your attention by the cook at any time?

Mrs. KEFAUVER. The cook came over to the dormitory, and Miss Groves, the teacher, was there; and Mrs. Neher came with her, and in the presence of those two she told me that Mrs. McDaniels had ordered her that day to cook meat that was just alive with maggots for those children.

The CHAIRMAN. Did Mrs. McDaniels have some official position on the reservation?

Mrs. KEFAUVER. Mrs. McDaniels was the wife of the superintendent. She was not under civil service, but she was appointed by Mr. McKean to the position of seamstress. She was the one that censored every new member. In fact, she was the one that was to make out my report, whether I was efficient or not. I was to report to her. You can see her name on the paper.

The CHAIRMAN. Was that a part of her duties as seamstress?

Mrs. KEFAUVER. Her duty? I can only describe what has always been in my mind as to what her duty was. She was the paddle to a mush pot.

Mr. GLAVIS. Did Mrs. McDaniels tell the cook to cook all the meat, or just portions of the meat? What did she say?

Mrs. KEFAUVER. She told her to clean off the maggots and cook the meat, and she said, "I absolutely refuse to cook such meat as that."

The CHAIRMAN. Do you know where they got this meat from?

Mrs. KEFAUVER. I do not know. It was brought in by the wagonload; probably shipped in from Denver.

The CHAIRMAN. How large an attendance did you have in this school?

Mrs. KEFAUVER. There were nearly 200 in all—girls and boys.

Mr. GLAVIS. What about the condition of the milk? Was that all right?

Mrs. KEFAUVER. No. The stables were never cleaned—never. The cows just rolled in the filth. They were milked without being cleaned, and when they put the milk in the separator it was just thick, what was left in the bottom; and that was the milk that they gave those children.

Mr. GLAVIS. You mentioned the separator. Was the separator cleaned?

Mrs. KEFAUVER. The separator was only just rinsed out.

Mr. GLAVIS. With hot, boiling water?

Mrs. KEFAUVER. We never had boiling water. It was very hard to boil the water. In fact, they did not seem to understand that there was a difference between making a fire at an altitude of over a mile and an altitude such as we live in now here, and they did not know. The stove was very poor. It did not have any draft, and consequently things could not be cooked very readily on that stove, and the water could not boil.

The CHAIRMAN. This was a high altitude?

Mrs. KEFAUVER. A very high altitude—between six and seven thousand feet.

Senator PINE. The water would boil before it was hot?

Mrs. KEFAUVER. Yes. They canned a great deal of fruit while I was there, and every bit of it spoiled because they did not seem to understand that they had to have it boiled to make it keep.

Mr. GLAVIS. From what you say, I imagine it gets quite cold at Towaoc in the winter?

Mrs. KEFAUVER. In the winter it gets very cold. There are severe winds that cut through that canyon there, and they are very biting.

Mr. GLAVIS. How were the children dressed? Was the clothing furnished sufficient to keep them warm?

Mrs. KEFAUVER. I will tell you just what those children wore.

Mr. GLAVIS. That is better. Tell just what clothing they wore.

Mrs. KEFAUVER. They had three garments. First was a little thin shirt, a cotton shirt; then they had outing-flannel bloomers, and a thin gingham dress over that. I asked for the coats. There were some little jackets that were there, of serge. I asked for coats for those children. They said they never had any. I said, "Not for winter?" These were all they had all winter long—little thin serge short jackets. The stockings were thin cotton stockings, cheap. The shoes were the cheapest canvas gray shoes that you ever could conceive of.

The CHAIRMAN. Canvas?

Mrs. KEFAUVER. Canvas. They put those shoes on, no matter whether the weather was wet or dry; they kept them on from the time they got up in the morning. They had to walk twelve blocks every day going to and from meals, and if their feet were wet they sat with wet feet until they went to bed at night. That was all they had.

Document 97
1929   Pine Ridge, South Dakota
Physical Abuse of Children

Source: U.S., Congress, Senate, Committee on Indian Affairs, **Survey of Conditions of the Indians in the United States, Hearings,** before a Subcommittee of the Committee on Indian Affairs, Senate, on S. R. 79, 71st Cong., 2d sess., 1930, pp. 2833-2835.

Examination by Senator Frazier:

Q. What is your name?—A. Mrs. Rose Ecoffey.

Q. Were you ever employed in the Indian Service?—A. Yes; I was matron in the school, boys' matron temporarily; I was there in August, September, and part of October. Mr. Jermark asked me to go up there and take the matron's place.

Q. And when they got a regular matron you went home?—A. Yes.

Q. Is that the only time you ever worked at the school?—A. I worked as a nurse in the hospital.

Q. What about the conditions at the school, how were the boys treated?—A. Not good I would call it; runaway boys were whipped and a ball and chain was put on them and they were shaved close to their head; that is the way they punished them for running away.

Q. Why did they do that?—A. Because they run away and played hookey because they did not like the school.

Q. Do you know of any specific instance where they done that?—A. Yes; there was one little one 12 and another one 10, and they put a ball and chain on them and put them to bed and locked the door on them, and when I went in there I wanted to change their bed and the disciplinarian refused to let me; and the second time I went in there, and he sent two boys with me, and it was not fit place for anybody to see. They kept them locked up there three or four weeks or a month. I asked Mr. Wilson, the disciplinarian, about them—he was not here very long—and he said to leave them there.

Q. How long ago was that?—A. In 1925.

By Senator Wheeler:

Q. Were they locked up in that room all the time with a ball and chain on?—A. No; they had to pack them to the boys' building and go up and down the steps with them.

Q. Who was the superintendent of the school?—A. Mr. Guyer.

Q. Is that disciplinarian still here?—A. No; he resigned or was fired or something for being drunk. I went and asked Mr. Guyer what was to be done about the boys having ball and chain, and he would not handle it. Mr. Guyer came to me because I made complaint that the children did not have enough bread to eat and some of the boys said they were hungry, and I spoke to him about it and he said "how many tubs of bread do they get?" and I said "two and a half tubs for 400 children," and I asked him if they can have a little more as you know how these children eat, but I could not get it, and many of these children do not get enough to eat at home, and I have children of my own and I know how they feel. Mr. Jermark asked me to go and fill that position and I appreciate it, but Mr. Guyer told me, "you are not here because I want you," and he was mad at me because I spoke to Mr. Jermark out in the hall, and he told me "you have a hold," and I say "no; I have no pull," and he said "I have no use for you and it is better you and I should not speak."

Q. What is the name of that boy who was whipped?—A. I could not remember his name. The boy went over to the kitchen where his sister was to get some paper and an envelope; he did not know it was against the rules to do that; he was a new boy; and Mielke saw him and hollered at him and he run and caught him and took him to the disciplinarian, Mr. Wilson. He was a boy about 11 years old, and he whipped him in my presence. He laid him across the table and whipped him with a strap; and I said "do you know positively what you whipped the boy for?" and he said "no," only what Mielke told him he was trying to get to his sister; and I turned to the little boy and asked him why he did that, and he said he did not know that he should have permission, and he said they come and chase him around the building and got hold of him. When people have their children in the Government school they want them corrected and punished, but not beat up for nothing; I have seen such things before; this is not the only school I have seen, because if this goes on and we want to put them in Government schools, they will run away.

Q. Did the superintendent of this school know this boy had a ball and chain on?—A. Yes, sir; I told him about it.

Q. Did you tell him about the other conditions existing?—A. I told Mr. Wilson and he says some of the other prisoner boys claim that.

1928   California
Poverty and Disease

The failure of the medical delivery system to administer to Indian need is clearly revealed in the following testimony of Florence Ames, a public health nurse for the California State Department of Public Health. While subjected to squalor and poor medical services, Indians were supposed to acquire the skills of Western civilization (document 98).

Document 98
1928   California
            Poverty and Disease

Source: U.S., Congress, Senate, Committee on Indian Affairs, **Survey of Conditions of the Indians in the United States, Hearings**, before a Subcommittee of the Committee on Indian Affairs, Senate, on S. R. 79, 70th Cong., 2d sess., 1929, pp. 428-429.

Question. Did you see cases where there was a case of tuberculosis actually living with children in a home consisting of simply a 1-room shack?

Answer. Yes, many, and with four and five children; and, so many times, it is the young mother who is the patient.

Question. Speaking of a young mother, I would like to ask you whether you saw, down in the southern reservations, instances of the affliction received by a woman bringing a child into the world?

Answer. Yes; in particular, a maternity case on the Torres-Martinez Reservation.

Question. What did you see there, Miss Ames?

Answer. I found a new maternity case out in a sand pit, beside the hovel, and just in the boiling-hot sun, with nothing—no bedding, nothing for protection.

Question. That was the mother and the child?

Answer. That was the mother and the child. I might say that is one of their customs, to bake them in a hot sun.

Question. There was no physician in attendance, I take it?

Answer. No; none.

Question. And when the mother was moved into the hovel, what conditions did you find there?

Answer. I found they had no bed. They had a sand pit in one corner of the room. They had thrown a few old coats down, and the mother and the babe were on this; and it was the only bed for the whole family, which consisted of the father, and, I think, six other children.

Question. That was at the Torres-Martinez Reservation?

Answer. Yes, sir.

Question. Can you tell us something about trachoma, and whether the Indian Service takes cognizance of its existence?

Answer. Trachoma is recognized by the Indian Bureau as one of the prevalent diseases, but their recognition is primarily when the child enters school. Children are examined by physicians in the boarding school; but very little attention is paid to the preschool cases, or in looking for cases that might exist among adults. The only time I found that they were receiving treatment was when they were entering the boarding schools.

Question. The Indian Service occasionally sends out a specialist. Do you know whether or not the Indians are encouraged to go to him or to his office, or whether he visits them at their homes?

Answer. There are no facilities for visiting the homes. There is a field diagnosis of trachoma; that is, the specialist opens an office in the community, and he expects the Indians to come to him. They don't know whether they have to do it or not. They are supposed to visit him to have treatment and to be diagnosed.

Question. Did you find many cases of Indians who were totally blind from trachoma?

Answer. Yes, sir; a large number of old people, who are blind.

Question. Now, coming to the children, did you find many children with trachoma?

Answer. In the Yuma Boarding School, which has an enrollment of 196 pupils, there were 25 cases of trachoma under treatment. The Sherman Institute has 151 cases of trachoma reported.

By the Chairman:

Question. How large a school is that?

Answer. I don't know just what the enrollment is at the Sherman Institute.

By Mr. Goodrich:

Question. It is close to a thousand pupils, isn't it?

Answer. Yes. This is not my figure, but Miss Mitschke reported it.

Question. She is one of the public health nurses who investigated at Fort Bidwell?

Answer. Yes, sir.

Question. And found how many cases out of 150?

Answer. One hundred and seven.

Question. Did you find infectious skin diseases?

Answer. Yes; they are prevalent in the boarding and day schools, such as scavis and impetego.

Question. Were they receiving any attention to keep it from spreading when you saw them?

Answer. Not what we would call real attention. As to the bathing facilities there is no exclusion, a child with a skin disease is not excluded from bathing with others; and there is very little medical attention given. There are no precautions taken to keep it from spreading among them.

1929   Wisconsin
        Plight of Wisconsin Indians

The 1929 Survey of the Conditions of Indians conducted by the Senate Subcommittee of the Committee on Indian Affairs made public the plight of Wisconsin Indians. It clearly demonstrated that every institution had failed to function properly. The testimony of four witnesses appearing before the Committee accurately depicts the general condition of the seven Indian tribes in Wisconsin.

Poverty is illustrated by the testimony of A. P. Jones, a man with many years acquaintance with the Winnebago (document 99). The failure to provide access to education is accurately depicted by John Callahan, Wisconsin State Superintendent of Public Instruction (document 100). Although he concentrates upon the Winnebago, similar conditions prevailed among the Chippewa and Potawatomi and, to a lesser degree, among the other tribes. S. J. Connolly, a county judge in Forest County, describes the housing, hospital care, and work life of the Forest County Potawatomi and also reveals the misery encountered by Indians because of the county's disdain for citizens termed "federal" (document 101). Finally, a brief statement by Dan Morrison, a citizen living near La Pointe Reservation for Chippewa, suggests the failure of medical institutions (document 102). Senator Lynn Frazier and Senator Robert M. LaFollette, Jr., of Wisconsin, are the questioners.

Document 99
1930   Wisconsin
Poverty

Source: U.S. Congress, Senate, Committee on Indian Affairs, **Survey of Conditions of the Indians in the United States, Hearings,** before a Subcommittee of the Committee on Indian Affairs, Senate, on S. R. 79, 70th Cong., 2d sess., 1930, pp. 1884-1885.

There was still much Federal land owned in Wisconsin and along in the early seventies; they were forceably removed to Nebraska by the United States attorney, and the climate was such down there that a great many of them got sick and died, they all wanted to return to Wisconsin, and in a comparatively few months they all got back and it was necessary to do something for them and they were finally permitted to take up homesteads on the public domain and there was some 200 homesteads taken up in the very poorest part of Wisconsin, practically all were 40-acre homesteads, and I tell you, gentlemen, that not one-fourth of these 100-acre homesteads are worth $100 to-day, and if you could see them you would know that this is a fact, they would not bring that now and they never would have any time since they were taken up. The Wisconsin Winnebagoes have a just cause for complaint for the way they have been treated during the last 100 years by the Government. They were six or eight different treaties entered into and there are many provisions of those treaties that have never been fulfilled, and the matter should, I believe, be determined so that some actual definite liability toward the Indians could be arrived at without them being obliged to pay 20 per cent or whatever might be recovered for attorney fees. The last per capita payment to the Indians, amounting to about $16 or $20, was made about 10 years ago, and since that time they have received no aid from the Government. Now our Indians get along very nicely when they are young, strong, and able-bodied and are able to make a pretty good living for themselves, but when they become old, sick, and diseased it is a different story and many of them are in very hard circumstances. From my experience of nine years among the Wisconsin Winnebagoes, I could tell you lots of instances, and what I want to make clear to you is that there is more destitution, poverty, and want among these Indians than on any reservation I know of or have been through in my lifetime, and I don't think you could see or find anywhere the extreme poverty and the extreme destitution that you find among the Wisconsin Winnebagoes. Something was said about the relief work being done by some of the counties for the Indians; Mr. Hull spoke, I believe, of Jackson County. I know of four at the present time who are receiving aid from the county, they come in and get an order for five or ten dollars' worth of groceries at one of the stores, and there are others I know. The situation is deplorable when you come to consider what the States of Minnesota, Nebraska, and Wisconsin have profited through the transactions of the Government with the Indians, and it is certainly an injustice to the counties and towns within and surrounding the reservations to expect them to bear a burden which rightfully belongs to the Government.

The usual habitation of the Winnebagoes of Wisconsin is simply a teepee, a few birch poles stuck in the ground and a blanket or skins placed over the top, some blankets or robes for a floor, and three or four poles stuck in the ground to cook on, and that is the way they live year in and year out. As many as six or eight live in one teepee, and you can picture the result when one of them contracts tuberculosis, as is the case with many of them. I know of one case in particular where six out of eight died inside of three years due to the insanitary conditions, destitute circumstances, and unhealthful habitation. I know of another instance where the mother had died and the three were left in the Indians' school for three years, and then sent back to the home where the grandmother was tubercular, and you know what the result would be. I don't know that it is necessary to cite any more cases of that kind, I could go on and tell you many of them, but what I am particularly interested in is the old people, those who are no longer able to work and who are living in extreme poverty and destitution; the Government has in a manner provided for the young people by taking them into a Government school and giving them the advantage of an education, but nothing has been done for the old people.

Document 100
1929   Wisconsin
Failure of Education

Source: U.S., Congress, Senate, Committee on Indian Affairs, **Survey of Conditions of the Indians in the United States, Hearings,** before a Subcommittee of the Committee on Indian Affairs, Senate, on S. R. 79, 70th Cong., 2d sess., 1930, p. 1912.

Q. I take it you are more or less familiar with the school situation, particularly with reference to the Winnebago Indians, and we would like to have you tell us about that?—A. My first contact with the Indian problem in school affairs occurred in the Winnebago section in Juneau and Monroe Counties. Several complaints had come in that various school boards were not permitting the Indians living in those districts to attend school. I went to investigate the situation personally and I found that complaints were made by some of the 1-room rural school, that the Indians living in their districts were not paying taxes, and as it was a great expense to keep the schools open and meet expenses, they felt that they were not obliged to take care of Indian children, inasmuch as they considered them wards of the Government and they should be taken care of at the Government-maintained schools for Indians rather than burden the local taxpayers and school districts to which they paid very little if any taxes. After becoming familiarized with the situation, however, I advised them that the Indian children should be accorded school privileges, whether or not their parents paid any taxes. At that time the situation was about this—93 to 95 per cent of the cost of running those schools was derived from local taxation and only about 5 to 7 per cent was contributed by the State. That particular trouble has, I believe, been almost entirely done away with by legislation which the State passed in 1927 whereby they are rendered State and county aid. I believe a great deal of trouble has been caused by the fact that Indian children, as a rule, do not attend school very regularly, particularly is that true of the Winnebagos; the situation with reference to the Oneidas in the vicinity of Green Bay, where their lands were allotted some 30 years ago, is, I believe, a great deal better. The Indians there attend school very regularly.

By Senator Frazier:

Q. Do you find that most of the Indian children attend school?—A. I would say that there are a few hundred children of Indian parents in the State of Wisconsin who are not getting an education, some of them have very little opportunity and others do not have advantage of the opportunity they have.

Q. Do the Government and denominational schools on these reservations compare favorably with the public schools of this State?—A. I have visited the schools at Tomah and Kashena two or three times and I believe they are both good schools so far as Government schools go taking into consideration the fact that school is conducted on a half-day basis. There are only a few private schools on reservations in this State, not over ten or a dozen I would say. There are two at Tomah, one Episcopal and one Catholic, both I believe are good schools; the Indians do not pay to attend those schools and I understand some of them get no aid from the Government. In some cases I believe the Government pays 30 or 40 cents a day for actual attendance of Indian children. We have tried at various times to get aid for some of these schools but are told that they have no money; that situation arose I believe at Radisson and Lac du Flambeau. Some of the schools like the one here at Tomah I feel are doing very good work, particularly in the vocational line, but with the limited amount they have to go on and the facilities they have to work with they can not do very much.

Document 101
1929   Wisconsin
Inadequate Housing and Poor Health

Source: U.S., Congress, Senate, Committee on Indian Affairs, **Survey of Conditions of the Indians in the United States, Hearings,** before a Subcommittee of the Committee on Indian Affairs, Senate, on S. R. 79, 70th Cong., 2d sess., 1930, pp. 1945-1946.

Examination by Senator Frazier:

Q. You may state your name?—A. S. J. Connolly.
Q. Residence?—A. Crandon, Wis.
Q. What official position if any do you hold?—A. I am county judge of Forest County, I have been since January 1, 1926.
Q. I understand you wish to make a statement with reference to conditions among the Indians?—A. Yes, sir.
Q. Go ahead, make it as brief as you can.—A. There are a large number of Potawatamies located within our county and I am more or less familiar with their health and financial condition as I come in contact with them frequently.

By Senator La Follette:

Q. Do you find that there is considerable tuberculosis among the Potawatamies?—A. Yes, there is quite a lot of T. B. Miss Wilson, our field nurse, discovered T. B. among the Indians about the first of the year, and the first two or three cases were handled under the State law the same as any other case, but the number got so great and the expense so large to Forest County that we took the matter up with Washington as there seemed to be no way of handling those cases here. At the present time we are taking care of 16 tubercular Indians and have 3 in the Wisconsin General Hospital with eye trouble. In addition we have two cases of T. B. but have not been so far to get the Indians' consent to removal. Under the State law the

State stands half, and the county the other, making $15 a week in all. We now have 16 cases on which we are paying $7.50 a week. We had an insane man by the name of John Shine, an Indian 85 years old, and we were 30 or 40 days trying to get him into the insane hospital—he had only a pair of trousers and a shirt, no coat or underwear and, of course, no money. Mr. Reedy said he had no funds and was strictly a county charge. I wrote the State board of control and they did not want to send him to Oshkosh, and as the expense would be charged back to Forest County I took the matter up with Mr. Reedy again and he later advised me that there was $160 in his account and to purchase him sufficient clothing, so I made an order committing him. We have two or three applications for vacancies for admission to a sanitarium, and when the necessary authority for their admission was secured they refused to leave home and go away for treatment so we have to treat them out there in their shacks in the woods where they are living.

Q. These shacks are some of the homes built with this so-called improvement fund are they not?—A. Yes; most of them were built with the improvement fund I understand, none of them were built with the thought of sanitation in mind, they are stuck back on the side of a hill or at the bottom of a hill and a lot of these places are not fit for a human being to live in.

Q. What kind of land are these selected forties purchased for the Indians?—A. As a matter of fact it is practically impossible for an Indian or a white man either to make a living on them. The few white men who have tried to make a living on the land adjoining these Indian forties have long since given up and left, practically all of them without exception have pulled out.

Q. What kind of land is it?—A. Mostly cut-over land, very rough and stony, practically no tillable land. Very little of this land has been cleared in the last 14 years. When the Indians came here they tried to do a little farming, cut a little wood and pick berries—wood cutting is about the only income they have. Now, we do not believe that the burden of taking care of these tubercular Indians should be placed upon Forest County. These cases are very hard to handle as the tubercular Indian is not confined, he goes and comes when he pleases, mingles with the whites, go into stores and business places in towns and are a menace to the entire community. We consider that the Indians are wards of the Government and as such the Government should look after them and not expect us to do so with the limited resources we have, of course when they refuse to do so in order to protect the health of the white people in our community we are forced to take care of these Indians. The Indians themselves have no facilities for taking care of one of their number who becomes afflicted with T. B., usually after T. B. is discovered the Indian remains in the home where seven or eight sleep on the floor or in one bed, probably all they have to sleep on is a blanket on the floor. No

sanitary provisions are taken and under such conditions it is only a matter of time until they are all tubercular.

Document 102
1929   **Wisconsin**
Lack of Medical Facilities

Source: U.S., Congress, Senate, Committee on Indian Affairs, **Survey of Conditions of the Indians in the United States, Hearings**, before a Subcommittee of the Committee on Indian Affairs, Senate, on S. R. 79, 70th Cong., 2d sess., 1930, p. 1962.

Examination by Senator La Follette:

Q. Your name is Dan Morrison?—A. Yes, sir.

Q. What do you know about the health conditions among the Indians on the La Pointe Reservation?—A. They are fairly good; not as bad as some other places.

Q. How do these Indians obtain needed medical attention?—A. They call for it through the Government office and they call doctors from Ashland in emergency cases.

Q. Do the doctors always come when the Indians call them?—A. If the Indians have money, they sometimes call the doctors themselves, but if they have funds in the office, they can get doctors.

Q. If they have no funds, what do they do?—A. They would have to get some other method.

Q. In other words, that would mean they would get no medical attention?—A. Yes; that is true sometimes. I know it is hard for them to get medical attention if they have no funds.

Q. How many of these Indians have funds in the office, if you know?—A. Perhaps two-thirds of them have no funds in the agency of their own.

By Senator Frazier:

Q. Many of the Indians there are in poor circumstances, are they not?—A. Yes; many are poor and destitute and have to go without medical attention.

Q. Do you know of your own knowledge of any Indians who could not get medical attention?—A. I just know of one case where a young Indian could not get medical aid and he died.

1930   **Muskogee, Oklahoma**
Starvation

Although federal and local government officials were fully aware of the situation, Indians in the hills of eastern Oklahoma starved to death in 1930. The deaths resulted directly from destruction by the national government of the Five Civilized Tribes and separation of the individual tribal members from their allotted portion of the tribal property. This government act exhibits a fundamental disregard for life itself. At the very least it proves the failure of the political and economic institutions.

The following are excerpts of testimony given in Oklahoma to the Senate committee investigating the conditions of the tribes. The first excerpt is from the testimony of the white field agent for the Bureau of Indian Affairs, Ross Daniel, who was in charge of three counties (document 103). Senator Elmer Thomas is the questioner. The second excerpt is from the testimony of S. W. Peak, a Cherokee, who speaks through an interpreter (document 104).

Further reading: Angie Debo, *And Still the Waters Run* (Princeton: Princeton University Press, 1940).

Document 103
1930   Muskogee, Oklahoma
Starvation

Source: U.S., Congress, Senate, Committee on Indian Affairs, **Survey of Conditions of the Indians in the United States, Hearings,** before a Subcommittee of the Committee on Indian Affairs, on S. R. 263, Senate, 71st Cong., 2d sess., 1931, pp. 6288-6289.

Senator Thomas. How much territory do you have?

Mr. Daniel. Three counties—Cherokee, Adair, and Sequoyah.

Senator Thomas. Where are your headquarters?

Mr. Daniel. At Tahlequah. I noticed some statements by some former witnesses about the condition of the Indians. They are certainly in bad condition. A lot of them do not have bread and grease. They are in the worse sort of condition.

Senator Thomas. Do you actually go into their homes, inside their houses?

Mr. Daniel. Yes, sir.

Senator Thomas. You see what they have to eat?

Mr. Daniel. Yes, sir.

Senator Thomas. Tell the committee what they have to eat.

Mr. Daniel. There are a number of them that do not have any more than I stated a while ago; that bread and grease, and possibly not grease half of the time.

Senator Thomas. What kind of bread?

Mr. Daniel. Some have flour. They have not, as a rule. They all raise a garden. They do the best they can under the conditions existing, but do not get anything for ties. The market is down.

Senator Pine. Are they imposed upon in the sale of their ties?

Mr. Daniel. No; they get the same price. There are any number of them in my district that were allotted in those hills. There is nothing but timber there. There is no tillable land. The timber is practically gone; they have used it up. They have sold the timber and there is very little land over there which has any valuable timber on it any more.

Mr. Hastings. That applies not only to ties but to post timber and other kinds of timber?

Mr. Daniel. Yes.

Senator Frazier. Do you have any other statement you want to make, Mrs. Porter?

Mrs. Porter. No.

Mr. Hastings. Mr. Daniel lives in my home town. He has been in the Indian Service as long as most of them and he is pretty intimately acquainted with conditions around in his district; about the way they live and about the children going to school.

Senator Thomas. Are conditions getting better or worse among the Indians?

Mr. Daniel. I believe they are getting worse.

Senator Thomas. What is the reason for that?

Mr. Daniel. There are several reasons for it. As I said a minute ago, the marketing of timber is worse than it used to be; it is hard to dispose of; and then in connection with the farms, the market has been low on the products they raise. I heard one of the witnesses state the reason why children are not attending school. I agree with that right along, because they do not have proper clothing and proper food. While a good many of them make fair progress in school there are quite a few over the country that do not go to school at all.

Senator Thomas. What do you think is going to happen to the Indian population if things go on like they are now?

Mr. Daniel. If they are not given an education or relieved at this time, I am afraid it will be too late to give them any relief in the next few years.

Senator Thomas. Have you ever heard of any Indians actually starving and dying from want of food?

Mr. Daniel. I do not know that I could name one, but I believe they have died from the effects of improper nourishment. I know of several; yes, sir.

Senator Thomas. You know of Indians that because of lack of food have taken disease or contracted disease?

Mr. Daniel. Yes, sir; I am told by the physician that that is one of the causes of pelagra.

Senator Pine. One of the principal causes?

Mr. Daniel. Yes, sir? I am told that.

Senator Frazier. And a cause of tuberculosis, too?

Mr. Daniel. Yes, sir.

Senator Thomas. Do you think in your jurisdiction many deaths have been caused directly or indirectly because of improper nourishment?

Mr. Daniel. Yes, sir.

Senator Thomas. Failure to have proper food?

Mr. Daniel. Yes, sir.

Senator Thomas. Very many?

Mr. Daniel. Quite a few; yes, sir.

Senator Thomas. In other words, then, the force of your testimony is that these Indians are starving to death?

Mr. Daniel. Well, you might term it that way.

Document 104
1930
Muskogee, Oklahoma
Famine

Source: U.S., Congress, Senate, Committee on Indian Affairs, **Survey of Conditions of the Indians in the United States, Hearings**, before a Subcommittee of the Committee on Indian Affairs, on S. R. 263, Senate, 71st Cong., 2d sess., 1930, pp. 6265-6266.

Senator Thomas. Ask him to tell the committee just what the Indians have to eat for breakfast, noon, and night?

The Interpreter. They do not eat but very little.

Senator Thomas. Tell him not to be backward about it, but to tell us.

The Interpreter. He says he is not backward about telling anything. He says, I am going to tell you the truth. These Indian people are in hard circumstances. Some of these Indian people hardly have two meals a day, and it is very thin at that.

Senator Frazier. What do they eat in those two meals?

The Interpreter. Something like corn bread and gravy, I guess.

Senator Thomas. What is the gravy made of?

The Interpreter. I think it is made out of grease.

Senator Thomas. Where do they get the grease?

The Interpreter. He says whenever they make a pie, they take it down and buy a little can of lard—a small can of lard. That is the way they are getting by.

Senator Thomas. Living on corn bread and gravy?

The Interpreter. Yes, sir; he says he is pretty nearly in the same condition they are in. There is no place to work. You can not sell anything. If you had to sell anything you have just got to give it away.

Senator Thomas. Do the Indians have plenty of corn bread and gravy?

The Interpreter. No, sir. He says this makes the second year that they did not make anything in the way of crops.

Senator Thomas. Ask him if the Indians farm their own land or rent it, as a rule.

The Interpreter. He says they farm it themselves, what little patches they have. Now, he says the Cherokees live up in the hills, back up on the mountains, and that is the reason they have such small patches, and on this good land the negroes and white people are living where the Cherokees had land once, and back there where they are living, why, the jay birds can hardly make a living up there in some places. He says he has been all over the old Cherokee Nation, and I have not found any family that was faring anyways like they ought to.

1948-1950
Arizona
Discrimination Against
Crippled Indian Children

Under the Social Security Act of 1935 federal aid is granted to each state for the care and treatment of crippled children based on the number of children in the state. The Act especially designates that the money be used for children in the lowest income group in the state. Arizona received federal funds for the treatment of crippled children for many years, but it excluded Indian children from its programs. Under pressure to comply with federal regulations, the Arizona Public Welfare Board on December 27, 1949, voted to refuse its annual $100,000 federal grant for all crippled children rather than include Indian children in its program. The state argued that the federal government had facilities on reservations for crippled Indians. The philosophical apology used by Arizona officials was rooted in the states' rights argument and also in their general distaste for the liberal-leaning Social Security program. The officials thought the state should be free from federal money because with it comes control of the citizen. Thus, children with deformities, including about "70 cases of congenital hip dislocation," suffered. On December 25, 1949, the crippled baby girl of the chairman of the San Carlos Apache Tribal Council died because Arizona refused to admit the tiny child to its treatment program.

At the same time Arizona Congressmen were trying to obtain Senate approval for the Bridge Canyon project for central Arizona. This project would have erected a major dam and other works on the Colorado River in northwest Arizona and a dam and other works on New Mexico rivers, primarily to provide supplemental irrigation water for 725,000 acres. The cost would have been more than the costs of the TVA and the Panama Canal construction combined. The actual purpose was to aid the tourist trade and promote the real estate boom for land speculators.

The following remarks by Representative Norris Poulson of California accurately describe the contradiction in philosophy and show the failure of state government (document 105).

Further reading: Felix S. Cohen, "Our Country's Shame," *The Progressive*, May, 1949, pp. 9-10.

Document 105
1948-1950
Arizona
Discrimination Against
Crippled Indian Children

Source: **Appendix to the Congressional Record**, Vol. 96, Part. 14, March 7, 1950, p. A1749.

Mr. POULSON. Mr. Speaker, the State of Arizona, which is now asking the Congress for a $1,500,000,000 reclama-

Angel Decorah, Winnebago, d. 1919, leader in the
Society of American Indians.

Chippewa Indians, Lac du Flambeau reservation, c. 1920

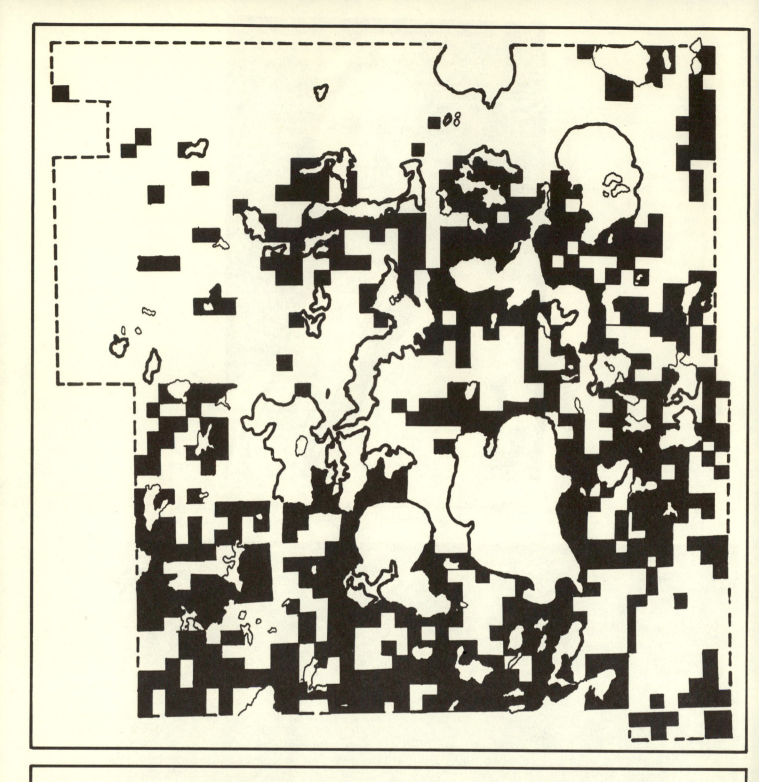

MAP OF
LAC DU FLAMBEAU
INDIAN RESERVATION
WISCONSIN

■ = Unrestricted Land;
    Alienated and Taxed

Other = Restricted; Tribal
        Common and US Trust

½ ¼ 0   1
SCALE OF MILES

tion gift, has just announced a new policy that reveals the great "humanitarian instincts" in the hearts of the Arizona people.

That policy is: No crippled Indian child shall be helped.

The Public Welfare Board of Arizona, which favors the proposed central Arizona project, recently voted to refuse their annual Federal grant of $100,000 for crippled children rather than include Indian crippled children.

All other States provide treatment for crippled Indian children on the same basis as for other crippled children.

Not Arizona.

Arizona is now asking that the Federal Treasury hand out one and a half billion dollars for a project to bring Colorado River water to a few thousand acres of land which is owned by a few large growers and speculators.

This is to be a gift to rich white Arizonians by the American taxpayers.

But what will these rich Arizonians do for the crippled children of their State? Rather than let Indian crippled children be helped, they have refused their annual Federal grant. Thus, they have not only deprived the crippled Indian children, but have deprived the white Arizona crippled children as well.

Regarding this matter, Miss Katharine F. Lenroot, chief of the Children's Bureau, Federal Security Agency, is quoted as follows:

> The Children's Bureau did not voluntarily or arbitrarily withdraw funds for crippled children in Arizona. The decision was that of the Arizona State Board of Public Welfare. Over 2 years ago the Children's Bureau advised the Arizona State Department of Public Welfare that the exclusion of Indian crippled children from the treatment services was contrary to the intent of the Social Security Act.

What has Arizona been doing with the Federal money it received each year for aid of crippled children? The Indian Rights Association states that for years Arizona has been taking this Federal money on the basis of including Indian children, but has refused to help Indian crippled children.

> The victims of this devious and reprehensible practice are physically handicapped Indian children—

Declares the association.

Another indication of how little regard Arizona has for Indians, crippled or not, is the fact that the proposed central Arizona project would flood an Indian reservation, destroying the farms and homes of these Indians, and repay them nothing. The project would, however, make scores of white millionaires at the expense of taxpayers of other States.

In December 1949 the Children's Bureau proposed that Arizona accept Indian crippled children in need of treatment on an equitable basis with non-Indian children, the cost not to exceed 15 percent of the total expenditures

in the State for this program. Indian children make up about 15 percent of the child population in Arizona. The State of Arizona rejected the Bureau's proposal.

Miss Lenroot stated:

> Because of this discriminatory action on the part of the Arizona Welfare Board and its refusal to accept any Indian children for treatment, other crippled children in the State are deprived of the care which could have been purchased with the $100,000 of Federal crippled childrens' funds allocable to Arizona each year.

But even this was not enough for the generous Arizona officials. They had to strike another blow at Indians. The welfare board also decided to discontinue all State funds for children with rheumatic fever who received care from the board of public health. The reason for this action? The public-health program of care included Indian mothers and Indian children.

As stated further by the Indian Association, this unjust action of Arizona fits into a pattern of State discrimination which has for years denied the Indian aged, blind, and dependent children the social-security benefits extended to all other Arizona citizens, including the big landholders who are trying to raid the Treasury for more than a billion dollars.

Under the Social Security Act, Federal aid is granted to all States for the care and treatment of crippled children on the basis of the total number of all children, not just on the basis of non-Indian children.

Apparently this is Arizona's policy:

Free millions for each white landholder, but not one cent for a crippled Indian child.

1946-1952
Racial Expropriation Laws

Starting in 1946 mining and timber interests and land development groups began attacking the property base of the Indian tribes. Working through lobbyists and friends in Congress, they had bills repeatedly introduced to confiscate Indian timber, fishing grounds, and other resources. For example, in 1947 a bill to confiscate Menominee timber was introduced. These bills usually failed to pass Congress, but the increasing strength of the anti-Indian faction forecasted a dismal future for the Indians. To expropriate Indian property would have spelled doom to the efforts to build a modern Indian life. A pious promise in these bills that Indians could later sue for damages belongs in the category of the earlier government promises.

The true meaning of the many expropriation measures (which ultimately crystallized in the termination policy of 1954) is expressed in the following excerpt from a speech by the late Felix S. Cohen, who was the foremost authority on Indian property (document 106). The speech was delivered on February 19, 1948, before the Indian

Rights Association of Philadelphia. Cohen served for many years as associate solicitor and chairman of the Board of Appeals of the Interior Department, as counsel to the Secretary of the Interior, and as general counsel to several Indian tribes. He compiled the *Handbook of Federal Indian Law* (1941) and wrote numerous articles on aspects of Indian law.

Further reading: Felix S. Cohen, *Felix S. Cohen's Handbook of Federal Indian Law* (Albuquerque: University of New Mexico Press, 1971); Angie Debo, *A History of the Indians of the United States* (Norman: University of Oklahoma Press, 1970), pp. 301-318.

Document 106
February 19, 1948
Racial Expropriation Laws

Source: Felix S. Cohen, "Breaking Faith with our First American," **Indian Truth**, March-April, 1948, pp. 7-8.

MASKED PLUNDER

Of course, no assault on Indian lands can succeed if it is formulated as a bare-faced steal. To be successful on a large scale, plunder must always wear the mask of national interest and high moral purpose. The national interest in impoverishing the Indian is generally cast on the assumption that Indians do not know how to develop their own resources, which must therefore be turned over to enterprising corporations in order to ensure full production of commodities needed for war or peace. This line does not always carry much conviction, however, because Indian-owned timber resources and minerals have for years been utilized at a higher rate, and yet with better conservation safeguards, than timber and minerals on the public domain.

The chief justifications for the present raid on Indian resources is therefore the high moral line that reservations and Federal protection of Indian lands are degrading. "Emancipating the Indian" has become the catchword of those who would like to free the modern Red Man from his property. Freeing the Indian from the Indian Bureau has become a high-sounding circumlocution for depriving Indians of promised Federal protection and opening their lands to all forms of encroachment. This appeal to "emancipate" the Indian from his property is highly plausible, because it fits into our national guilt complex about our past treatment of the Indian. The process of separating the Indian from his lands has been accompanied by a corruption and barbarity which give a bad sound to every part of that process. The bad sound attaches even to the one great concession that was made in our earliest land grabs, by which Indians were allowed to "reserve" some part of their original domain for their own use. It was this right to draw a line and keep out the trespassing white prospector or cattleman that made it possible for Indians to regroup their forces and emerge, after a century or more of dealings with white civilization, not as a defeated and suppressed minority but as a vigorous people, increasing in number more rapidly than any other group in our population, contributing in unparalleled proportions to our war efforts, and, with a few dramatic exceptions, making tremendous strides forward in productive enterprises, education, health, and general living standards.

To the unthinking white man, a "reservation" is an undistinguished part of a process that is unpleasant to think about. To the Indian his reservation is home, his "promised land," all that stands between him and the spiritual and physical destruction that most non-reservation tribes have undergone.

The tactic of giving Indian property bad names such as "reservations," "aboriginal rights," or "Indian title," and then "freeing" the Indian from degradation by taking away his property, now has the blessing of Senator Butler, the head of the Senate Public Lands Committee. That tactic will be worked to its limit until the American people realize that a new Century of Dishonor has begun.

I do not want to close on a note of despair. There are several hopeful signs on the horizon today. One is that the American public, according to a recent Gallup poll, is coming to recognize that Indians are human beings entitled to rely on the promises of the United States that they might retain some small fragments of their original domain. When the old slogan "Down with segregation" no longer works to enlist public support of unscrupulous raids on Indian land, we Americans will be able to talk of the sanctity of treaties with straighter faces.

Another hopeful sign is that the American people are coming to realize that the way we treat our oldest minority is a matter of international significance.

When isolationist newspapers and senators, in the midst of a Congressional debate on aid to Europe, discuss starvation among the Navajo, their motives may be less than 99 44/100 percent pure, but the relevance of the facts they present cannot be denied. The same may be said for the cartoon in a Soviet army paper in Berlin, showing a bedraggled Indian observing: "They promised aid to us but they didn't call it the Marshall Plan then." After all, the business of supplying aid to the survivors of wars in which we have engaged has been a serious concern of the United States Government for a century and a half, in the Indian country. We cannot complain if our failures and mistakes in this domain become a fertile source of propaganda in the United States against aid to Europe, and in Europe against aid from the United States. It would be much simpler to set our house in order in our dealings with Indians here at home.

The assurance given us by high Federal officials that we have the resources to help Europe would be more convincing if they were not at the same time advising Congress that we are too poor, as a nation, to pay various Indian tribes in cash for the timber and lands that we are taking, or proposing to take, from them. The good faith of the United States, on which every European nation that enters into an aid agreement must rely, would be clearer in the popular mind if we were living up to our promises to our Indian citizens. And our assurance that we do not intend to interfere with self-government in Europe would carry more conviction if so many senators and congressmen were not at the moment pushing bills which would, in violation of solemn treaty promises, abolish existing Indian municipal councils and land reserves.

WORLD-WIDE SIGNIFICANCE

Attitudes of discrimination and prejudice have a way of transferring from one object to another. That is why prejudice toward any group, however small, however remote, represents so serious a danger to all of us. That is why our treatment of our oldest racial minority in America has an importance that is not to be measured by the number of Indians who are mistreated. Modes of discrimination that were first tried out in California against Indians were effectively transferred to Chinese, then to Japanese and finally to all non-Anglo-Saxon immigrants from the Old World. A single thread of racism runs through the West Coast vigilante wars of the 1850's against Indians and Chinese that led to the first breach in our American policy of welcome to the refugees of Old World oppression. That first breach, the Chinese Exclusion laws of 1884, led in turn to the successive elaborations of legalized xenophobia culminating in our present quota system with its discriminations against all but the non-immigrating immigrants of Anglo-Saxon stock. As the only good Indian was a dead Indian, so today the only good immigrant is one who does not immigrate.

For this reason the racial expropriation laws that are being passed by Congress to remove Indian property from Indian hands have an importance far beyond the dimensions of our Indian population. What is done to Indians or Eskimos of Alaska or Nevada today can be done to Negroes in the South tomorrow and to Jews, Catholics, or descendants of non-Anglo-Saxon strains the day after tomorrow. That is why the efforts of the good people here to break down the stereotypes of racial prejudice in Indian affairs have so large a significance in the world today.

To the extent that our policies as a nation are infected by prejudiced stereotypes of the Navajo, the Eskimo, the French, or the Italian, we are not going to make a success of any national policy of aid to the survivors of big wars or little wars. Favors conferred from pinnacles of racial superiority make enemies, not friends. What we need

most of all today is the sense that made itself manifest in this city in the days of our youth as a nation, that enabled the Founding Fathers of our Republic to promise friendship and equal treatment to all nations and their citizens, to promise "the utmost good faith ... towards the Indians; their land and property shall never be taken from them witout their consent," and to find a basis for both attitudes, and a steady guide to international and domestic policy, in the promise "that all men are created equal."

1950-1953
Restriction of Indian Liberties

In 1950 the federal government began to restrict Indian civil liberties, reversing a twenty-year trend to erase all controls. These restrictions can only be understood in the context of the wider issues of the Cold War, which then dominated the American political scene, drawing public attention away from Indian affairs and stifling criticism. At the same time social tensions gave rise to political leaders with a philosophy of government that saw removing the government from Indian affairs as the only way to resolve their relationship to society. Legal and moral obligations were not considered important. The removal of government, they believed, had to be preceeded by a period of strict regulation or preparation for the promised abandonment. The restrictions were actually the preliminary steps—the bludgeoning of Indian leaders and organizations into submission—before forcing termination upon the cowed tribes. In addition, the Indian property base would be "freed" from federal protection against land, water, timber, and mineral interests.

The following selection, excerpted from an article by Felix S. Cohen, describes the erosion of Indian rights (document 107). He clearly indicates that the restrictions were not the work of one man or one set of men. They were rooted in the decay of institutions.

Further reading: Felix S. Cohen, *Felix S. Cohen's Handbook of Federal Indian Law* (Albuquerque: University of New Mexico Press, 1971).

Document 107
1950-1953
Restriction of Indian Liberties

Source: Felix S. Cohen, "The Erosion of Indian Rights, 1950-1953; A Case Study in Bureaucracy," **Yale Law School Journal**, vol. LXII (February, 1953), pp. 353-355. Reprinted by permission of the Yale Law Journal and Fred B. Rothman & Company.

FREEDOM OF ELECTIONS

In a democracy any interference with the right to vote is, of course, subversive of all other rights, and the general trend throughout the nation has been to diminish such interference. Quite to the contrary, however, is the recent record in the Indian country. During the period 1950-1952 interference with the right to vote increased, chiefly along two lines: the use of federal funds to influence local elections, and direct interference with local election arrangements.

Use of federal funds. A notable instance of the use of federal funds to influence local Indian elections occurred on the Blackfeet Reservation during the June, 1950, tribal election. Thirty-six pages of mimeographed materials attacking certain candidates for local tribal office, charging them with various "criminal" and "illegal" acts (none of which were ever prosecuted and most of which were later shown never to have occurred) were prepared by Government employees at Government expense on Government paper and Government mimeograph machines. Hundreds of copies of this campaign literature were circulated by Government employees on the reservation during the two weeks before the election. The Association on American Indian Affairs wired Secretary Oscar L. Chapman on June 17, 1950, to inquire whether the circulation of such materials was known and approved by the Secretary of the Interior. This question was answered in the affirmative. Such use of federal funds to influence local Indian elections quickly became accepted Departmental practice after June, 1950. In the Blackfeet referendum election of May, 1952, and the Choctaw referendum election of July, 1952, letters from Interior officials on the merits of referendum issues (as seen by the Indian Bureau) were distributed at Government expense with a view to influencing voters.

The Indian Bureau defends its use of federal funds to "enlighten" Indian voters on the ground that it has a trustee's obligation to see that Indians have a proper understanding of the issues on which they vote. But the assumption of superior enlightenment concerning election issues on the part of Government officials runs counter to our American concept of popular government.

Direct interference. Similarly, direct interference with local elections for local offices has increased in frequency during the past three years. When the Blackfeet Tribe held a referendum election on May 9, 1952, on a proposed amendment to the tribal constitution, the Interior Department ran a rival election, managed by Indian Bureau employees; called out its special Bureau police force; closed down one or more tribal polling places; seized tribal funds, without tribal consent, to pay some of the expenses of the Bureau election (notwithstanding Secretary Chapman's assurance that no such action was contemplated); and, in order to validate its own election results, tried to strike more than 1,000 Blackfeet names

from the list of eligible voters. This last move was eventually held by the Solicitor of the Interior Department to be illegal, and so the Bureau's election results were declared invalid. But the Bureau continues to insist that it has the right to run future tribal elections even where, as in the Blackfeet case, the tribal constitution provides that all local elections are to be supervised by the Indians themselves.

At San Ildefonso Pueblo, in New Mexico, the Indian Bureau seized control of valuable lands and proceeded to dispose of the resources of the Pueblo without statutory authority, on the pretext that the Pueblo had failed to elect a Governor. In fact, the elected Governor of the Pueblo is recognized by all the other Pueblos, by the public, and by all of the members of the Pueblo except for a few beneficiaries of the Bureau's illegal acts.

1953-1954
Termination of Federal Responsibility

Beginning in 1946 a movement grew within Congress to sever federal relations with the Indians and "free" them to achieve the good life. By 1948 key committees in Congress were dominated by men who held this view. They lacked sufficient strength, however, to pass legislation until the 1952 election of Dwight Eisenhower to the Presidency. Arthur Watkins of Utah chaired the Senate Indian Affairs Committee and led the attack upon what he falsely termed federal bureaucratic control of the Indian. His problem was how to proceed against the tribes, since each tribe related to the government in a slightly different way and local conditions had to be taken into account. The individual Indian members of the tribes were, on the whole, impoverished, poorly educated, and lacked basic skills. There were very few Indian lawyers, doctors, professors, and technicians. The tribes had property that needed to be more adequately developed by Indians trained in complex skills. The government had failed to train Indians, provide adequate health care, and sustain their cultural sources of history, language, and art—which would have served as a cohesive element in tribal life. Instead of recognizing its failure to govern, Congress resolved to terminate relations. Historically, the removal of governmental protection had meant the massive expropriation of the tribal property by businessmen, farmers, and fishermen.

Two documents illustrate the termination or expropriation era. The first is a senate speech delivered by Senator Watkins on a termination bill for the Menominee of Wisconsin (document 108). Most of the factual references in the speech are inaccurate, especially his reference to the Bureau of Indian Affair's selection in 1947 of ten tribes who were supposedly ready for their "freedom." In 1947 the Public Lands Committee of the Eightieth Congress had compelled the Acting Commissioner of Indian Affairs, William Zimmerman, Jr., to list tribes ready for termination. The Acting Commissioner stated that no criteria existed for making such a selection, but under intense pressure, he gave a "tentative" list. The second document is an excerpt from the testimony of DRUMS, a Menominee Indian movement known as Determination of Rights and Unity of Menominee Stockholders, delivered before the 1971 Senate Committee on Interior and Indian Affairs reviewing termination policy (document 109). The DRUMS statement is accurate and succinct.

Further reading: Gary Orfield, *Report on the Termination of the Menominee Reservation* (Chicago: University of Chicago, 1965); Vine Deloria, Jr., *Custer Died for Your Sins: An Indian Manifesto* (New York: The Macmillan Company, 1969); Alvin M. Josephy, Jr., *Red Power: The American Indians' Fight for Freedom* (New York: American Heritage Press, 1971).

Document 108
July 18, 1953   United States Senate
Speech in Favor of Menominee Termination

Source: **Congressional Record—Senate**, Vol. 99, Part 7, July 18, 1953.

Mr. WATKINS. My reason for bringing the matter to the attention of the Senate today is that it is an actual beginning of something the Government has said for many years it was going to do. To date, there has only been talk about it. In this measure, we actually try to do something.

All available evidence of reports on this tribe, and statistics on its economic and social condition, reinforce the conclusion that this tribe is fully ready for removal from Indian Bureau tutelage. In fact most of the available reports put the Menominees about at the top of advancements among the individual Indian tribes. As long ago as 1930 the Menominees were five-sixths assimilated to modern American ways of life, and evidenced the very least of resistance among the various tribes to adopting the ways of civilization. Yet 23 years have passed without substantial steps being taken toward putting these people on their own.

Moreover, all of the claims of the Menominees in the Court of Claims and in the Indian Claims Commission have been decided, and there remain no outstanding issues between these Indians and the Government regarding property and wardship.

In 1950 the Menominee Tribe of Wisconsin recovered a judgment in the amount of $8,500,000 to compensate them in full for their claims against the Government. The principal claim was, as they alleged, "governmental mismanagement" of the valuable forest lands owned by the tribe. There is now on deposit in the United States Treasury the sum of approximately $9,500,000 which is being administered in trust for the tribe, and costing the Government approximately $200,000 a year in interest alone. The Menominee Indian Reservation of Wisconsin encompasses approximately 233,900 acres of some of the most beautiful forest land in Wisconsin.

Recently I visited that virgin forest, which is a very valuable piece of property. This forest comprises a valuable lumber-producing potential which is being maintained under a sustained yield cutting principle which provides employment for many members of the tribe.

There is also maintained on the reservation a lumber mill which, operated in conjunction with the lumbering enterprise, employs approximately 400 of the 3,150 Indians now on the tribal rolls. This gives approximately one member out of each family on the reservation gainful employment in an Indian owned and Indian operated enterprise. This is based on a family membership of four. They are not poor Indians. It has been estimated that the forest property would approximate $75 million in value. This amount, when added to the $9,500,000 in the Treasury, would indicate that each of the 3,150 members is worth approximately $25,000, or about $100,000 per family.

Yet the Government is appropriating gratuity funds of about $100,000 a year to help this tribe. They are paying most of their own expenses, and have made great advancement, as I could see in a recent visit with them.

To work out the details of the proposed amendment, I visited the tribal reservation in Wisconsin and met many of the members of the tribe, and was very favorably impressed, not only with their potential, but with their past accomplishment and particularly with their competency both as a tribe and as individuals. During that visit I became more convinced than ever before that they are now being hampered by Federal supervision, and that, once placed on their own, as they have long been entitled to be, they will develop their present potentials much more rapidly to their own betterment.

The PRESIDING OFFICER. The Senator's 5 minutes under the rule has expired.

Mr. WATKINS. Mr. President, I ask unanimous consent that I may be permitted to finish my statement. It is not very much longer.

The PRESIDING OFFICER. Is there objection? The Chair hears none, and the Senator from Utah may proceed.

Mr. WATKINS. I visited the tribe for the purpose of working out details of the amendment to the bill now before the Senate. I met many members of the tribe in a big tribal meeting. They had built a gymnasium. I found them to be very intelligent and progressive, and extremely cooperative. The only difference of opinion we seemed to have was that they wanted a longer time in which to terminate the wardship or guardianship of the Government over them.

The amendment which the Interior and Insular Affairs Committee reported, proposes a plan for paying over to these Indians the funds now held in trust for their use. It further provides a plan for ultimate withdrawal of all Federal supervision over the tribe by the 31st day of December 1956. That is a definite date. This plan is unique in that it is the first time, to my knowledge, that a plan of withdrawal has been proposed for termination of all Federal supervision as of a date certain.

This is not an innovation by the Committee on Interior and Insular Affairs. As I have stated, in 1947 Mr. Zimmerman, testifying on Indian affairs, declared that this tribe was one of the tribes of American Indians then ready for complete and immediate withdrawal from Federal supervision. From 1947 until 1953 little, if anything, has been done toward removing this tribe or any tribe from the wardship of the United States. The United States has been sued by this tribe, and the court has awarded a judgment against the Government because of its neglect in managing the Indians' affairs.

Document 109
1954   Menominee County, Wisconsin
History of Menominee Termination

Source: DRUMS, "The Effects of Termination of the Menominee," typescript, pp. 4-8, 10-13; also in U.S., Congress, Senate, **American Indian and Alaska Native Policy, Hearings**, before the Committee on Interior and Insular Affairs, Senate, on S. R. 26, 92nd Cong., 1st sess., 1971, pp. 107-111.

The century of Menominee/federal government relations, 1854-1954, involved both similarities and some important dissimilarities to the experiences of most native Americans in reservations. Like many other Indians bound by the paternalistic rule of the BIA, the Menominees suffered, and resented a lack of meaningful self-government. Unlike many other tribes, the Menominee rejected in the latter part of the nineteenth century BIA attempts to submit them to the government policy of allotment—an "experiment" that imposed private property ownership on Indians, later repudiated by Congress, by which Indians lost nearly 90,000,000 acres of their lands in 50 years. The economic situation of the Menominee was somewhat better than that of many reservation tribes: by virtue of our being situated in the midst of a magnificent forest, our people were able to develop a modest scale lumbering industry which provided the basis for some employment and income. Yet we Menominee had to fight to control our lumbering business, which was run by the BIA. Finally, winning the rights to review the BIA's budget and to sue the Bureau for any mismanagement of the forest, our tribe brought suit in the United States Court of Claims against the BIA for such mismanagement, and in 1951 netted a $7,650,000 judgment for damages. By 1953, we Menominee were anxious to make further gains in

self-government and management of our business and assets; yet we were well satisfied with federal protection of our assets, protection of our treaty rights, and provision of community services. Relative to many other tribes, we Menominee seemed to possess some of the ingredients for future prosperity. We had $10,000,000 in the United States Treasury, a source of employment and income in our lumbering operation, and owned our forest itself, valued at $36,000,000. In addition, we were one of the three Indian tribes in the country who were able to pay for the cost of most of our federal services. But let us stress that these appearances of wealth tend to hide the deeper facts that virtually all *individual* Menominee were poor, that our federal services were not of highest standard, that our housing, health, and education fell far below national norms, and that our stage of self-government was a tender, young one. However, to many Menominee the future seemed to hold the promise of eventual prosperity. But it was at this stage in our history that Congress decided to conduct another social experiment with Indians: termination.

THE ENACTMENT OF TERMINATION
PHASE ONE: 1953-1958

We would like to review in some detail the history relating to the termination of our tribe. We believe this history will help shed a clear light on the reasons why termination is a disasterous policy which should be totally rejected by Congress as it has been by nearly all American Indians.

Early in 1953, we Menominee wanted a portion of our 1951 settlement—about $5,000,000—distributed among ourselves on a $1,500 per capita basis. Since Congressional approval was required for such disbursement of our assets, (then) Representative Melvin Laird and Senator Joseph McCarthy introduced in Congress on behalf of our Tribe a bill to authorize the payment of *our* money to us.

This bill passed the House, but in hearings before the Senate Committee on Interior and Insular Affairs, it ran up against an amendment sponsored by the late Senator Arthur V. Watkins (R. Utah) calling for "termination" of federal supervision and assistance to the Menominee. Watkins and the Committee refused to report the bill favorably, calling upon us Menominee to submit a termination plan *before* we would be given *our* money! "Termination!" What did *that* mean? Certainly at that time, none of us Menominee realized what it meant! Because of the Senate Committee's reaction, a temporary deadlock had resulted. In June, 1953, we Menominee invited Senator Watkins to visit the Reservation and explain "termination" to us.

Senator Watkins badly wanted our termination. He was firmly convinced that factors such as our status as Reservation Indians, our tribal ownership of land, and our tax exemption were blocking our initiative, our freedom, and our development of private enterprise. He wished to see us rapidly assimilated into the mainstream of American society—as tax paying, hard working, "emancipated" citizens. Senator Watkins did *not* believe that *our* consent to termination was necessary for its enactment. Yet he knew that his cause would be helped if he could persuade us to agree to termination.

On June 20, 1953, Senator Watkins spoke for 45 minutes to our General Council. He told us that Congress had already decided on terminating us, and that at most we could have three years before our "affairs would be turned over to us"—and that we would not receive our per capitas until *after* termination.

After he left, our Council had the opportunity to vote on the "principle of termination!" Some opportunity! What little understanding we had of what termination would mean! The vote was 169 to 5 in favor of the "principle of termination." A mere 5 percent of the 3,200 Menominee people participated in this vote. Most of our people chose to be absent from the meeting in order to express their negative reaction to termination. Many who did vote affirmatively that day believed that termination was coming from Congress whether the Menominee liked it or not. Others thought that they were voting *only* in favor of receiving their per capitas. At any rate, it is this farce of "democratic procedure" that is often cited as proof of our own acceptance of termination!

We then set about preparing a termination plan, which the BIA subsequently emasculated, and we received word that Senator Watkins was pressing ahead with his *own* termination bill. *Another* general council meeting was called, one which is seldom mentioned, but at which Menominee voted 197 to 0 to *oppose and reject* termination! But *our* feelings did not matter—and although the Watkins bill met a temporary defeat on technical grounds in the House late in 1953, Senator Watkins reintroduced it in 1954.

We became convinced that there was *no* alternative to accepting termination. Therefore, all we pleaded for was adequate time to plan this sudden and revolutionary change in our lives! On June 17, 1954, the Menominee Termination Act was signed into law by President Eisenhower.

The Act gave us our per capita payments and provided that the Menominee tribal roll would be closed that same day; that the Tribe would submit a plan to provide for future control of tribal assets and that individual Menominee would not be entitled to any of the services provided by the United States for Indians; and that all United States statutes affecting Indians on account of their status as Indians would no longer be applicable to the Menominee. The full burden of providing community services, employment, and protection of our assets was to be transferred to our tribe.

1971   Menominee County, Wisconsin
Impact of Termination

In 1953, Congress expressed through House Concurrent Resolution 108 the principle that Indians ought to be "freed" from all controls and permitted to develop as individuals. Termination policy would provide the "freedom" to work out their problems and slowly grope toward civilization. The rhetoric of "freedom" and "individualism," an appeal to the public mind, obscured the actual sinister function of the policy. In effect, termination policy transferred control and direction of the institutional life of the Indians from the Bureau of Indian Affairs to regional private institutions such as large ranchers and lumber companies and especially banks. These groups then directed the property development. The subsequent poverty, high crime rate, growing illiteracy, and general despair of the Indians are directly attributable to the failure of both Congressional and private design.

Terminated by Act of Congress on June 17, 1954, the Menominee most clearly illustrated the failure of the policy. The following assessment of the impact of termination policy upon the Menominee is taken from a statement by DRUMS, a Menominee Indian group formed to reverse the policy, prepared as part of their testimony before a Senate committee investigating American Indian policy (document 110). State politicians, lawyers, and professors devised the plan whereby the First Wisconsin Trust Company of Milwaukee became the principal controller of Menominee assets. Each Indian was assigned a vote, and the Trust cast the votes of minors and so called "incompetent" adult Indians. It held the majority of votes and elected and controlled the property. It was not organized to combat the growing racism of nearby white school districts, aid in the development of Indian-oriented cultural programs, or confront other social problems. These complex issues have had to be met by the doughty Menominee while they attempt to regain their homeland.

Further reading: Deborah Shames, Co-ordinating editor, Joseph Preloznik, Nancy Lurie, and Jon Ferrara, associate editors, *Freedom with Reservation* (Madison: Impressions, Inc., 1972).

Document 110
1971   Menominee County, Wisconsin
Impact of Termination

Source: DRUMS, "The effects of Termination of the Menominee," typescript, pp. 14-28; also in U.S. Congress, Senate, **American Indian and Alaska Native Policy, Hearings,** before the Committee on Interior and Insular Affairs, Senate, on S. R. 26, 92nd Cong., 1st sess., 1971, pp. 117-131.

The Effects of Termination on the Menominee

THE IMMEDIATE EFFECT

The immediate effect of termination on our tribe was the loss of most of our hundred-year-old treaty rights, protections, and services. No amount of explanation or imagination prior to termination could have prepared us for the shock of what these losses have meant.

Congress withdrew its trusteeship of our lands, transferring to MEI the responsibility for protecting these lands, our greatest assets. As we shall explain, far from being able to preserve our land, MEI has been forced to sell it. And because our land is now being sold to non-Menominee, termination is doing to us what allotment has done to other Indian tribes.

Congress also extinguished our ancient system of tribal "ownership" of land (under which no individual had separate title to his home) and transferred title to MEI. Consequently, we individual Menominee suddenly discovered that we would be forced to buy from MEI the land which had always been considered our own, and to pay for title to our homesites. Thus began the tragic process of our corporation "feeding off" our people.

We Menominee lost our right of tax exemption. Both MEI and individual Menominee found themselves saddled with tax burdens particularly crushing to a small tribe struggling to develop economically.

BIA health, education and utility services ceased. We lost all medical and dental care within the Reservation. Both our reservation school and hospital were closed because they failed to meet state standards. Individual Menominee were forced to pay for electricity and water that they previously received at no cost. Our county found it had to renovate at high cost its substandard sewerage system.

Finally, with termination and the closing of our tribal rolls, our children born since 1954 have been legally deprived of their birthright as Menominee Indians. Like all other Menominee, they have lost their entitlement to United States Government benefits and services to Indians. These children may inherit *only* their parents' portion of Menominee assets—which means that if the parent's share has been lost or dissipated, their children lose forever any chance to share in tribal assets. The only major Menominee treaty right which the government has allowed us to retain has been our hunting and fishing right. Wisconsin had tried to deprive us of this right, but in 1968, after costly litigation, the United States Supreme Court ruled that this treaty right had "survived" termination. This decision raised the question as to whether other rights have also "survived" our termination.

We hope you can appreciate the magnitude of these treaty losses to us. Visualize a situation similar to ours happening in one of your home states. Imagine the outrage of the people in one of your own communities if Congress should attempt to terminate their basic property, inheritance, and civil rights.

LONG-RANGE EFFECTS

We believe that termination has produced three major long-range effects on the Menominee people, each one a disaster in itself.

First, termination has transformed Menominee County into a "pocket of poverty," kept from total ruin only by massive transfusions of special federal and state aid, welfare payments, and OEO spending.

Second, termination has forced our community to sell its assets. Consequently, both tribal and individual assets are being lost at an incredible rate.

Third, the mechanics of the termination plan has denied the Menominee people a democracy.

THE POVERTY OF MENOMINEE COUNTY

First, let us tell you about our people's far-reaching poverty, which extends beyond mere income levels to practically all other areas of our life.

Today Menominee County is the poorest county in Wisconsin. It has the highest birthrate in the state and ranks at or near the bottom of Wisconsin counties in income, housing, property value, education, employment, sanitation and health. The most recent figures available (1967) show that the annual income of nearly 80 percent of our families falls below the federal poverty level of $3,000. The per capita annual income of our wage earners in 1965 was estimated at $881, the lowest in the state.

Our county does not have diversified industry. Over 70 percent of those employed work in our MEI lumber industry. In 1968, 24.4 percent of our people were unemployed, the highest unemployment rate in the state.

This lack of employment opportunities, combined with our high birthrate, forced nearly 50 percent of our county residents to go on welfare in 1968. Welfare costs in the county for 1968 were over $766,000 and our per capita welfare payment was the highest in the state. The majority of Menominee who have left our county to seek work in the cities have become trapped in poverty there also.

With the closing of the BIA hospital, we lost most of our health services, and most Menominee continue to suffer from lack of medical care. There have been no full-time doctors or dentists in Menominee County since termination. Shortly after termination, our people were stricken by a TB epidemic which caused great suffering and hardship because of the lack of medical facilities. Consequently, the state and county had to spend nearly $200,000 in order to bring the epidemic under control. Our people continue to fear the possible recurrence of other such disasters. We feel helpless because resources are not available to provide adequate medical facilities.

Education in Menominee County—which theoretically

should offer our people a hope of future advancement—has also suffered because of termination. The loss of the BIA school required that our youth be sent to Shawano County for their high school training. The Shawano school system has assumed that Menominee children possess the same cultural and historical background as a middle-class white community. Consequently, the school system has shown insensitivity to the cultural background and the special needs of *our* children. In many cases, our children find themselves objects of rejection and discrimination. Since 1961, our high school drop-out rates have increased substantially, absenteeism has soared, and our children apparently are suffering a downward trend in achievement. Comparisons based on educational achievement tests show that Menominee children fall significantly below district and national norms.

How did termination bring our poverty about?

We can answer this question from two viewpoints: economic and cultural.

First, from the economic viewpoint: As we have already mentioned, in 1954 we Menominee seemed prosperous in comparison to other tribes, but deeper examination of our situation would have revealed that our resources were not sufficient for us to finance a county form of government. Our once extensive cash assets were largely eaten up by the expense of termination. The termination act required that MEI lumber our forest by continuous yield. This has meant that year after year only a limited amount of lumber could be taken, and thus, only a limited amount of income could be derived by MEI. Yet after termination became effective, MEI faced the financial burdens of providing employment to the Menominee people and operating a county government. Confronted with inadequate reserves and an inadequate tax base, MEI turned to the first of several drastic measures. To maximize the efficiency of its operation, MEI was forced to reduce its work force, which aggravated an already severe unemployment problem.

The financial strain imposed on individual Menominee was equally devastating. We found ourselves faced with new and heavy expenses, including taxes, utility costs and, worst of all, land payments. These financial burdens, combined with the lack of jobs, resulted in greater poverty than ever before. Thus, termination has weighed down our small, poor community and our single industry with crushing new expenses impossible to meet—all done in the apparent expectation that we then somehow "make it" economically!

The only factor which has prevented us and MEI from complete collapse has been the huge stop-gap financial assistance that the federal and state governments have given us. Since 1961 over $6,000,000 in special federal and state aid has been expended in Menominee County. Over $2,000,000 in state and federal welfare payments has been made to us since 1961, and since 1961 nearly $1,500,000 in OEO money has also been spent within the county.

These payments are only a temporary solution, having been used only to pay for on-going community services and to keep our people from starvation. This special funding does absolutely nothing to attack the basic causes of Menominee poverty: our lack of diversified industry, our dearth of economic opportunities, our negligible investment capital, and our inadequate tax base.

From the cultural viewpoint: Regardless of *how much* money is spent in Menominee County, the essential problem will remain. The government is asking us to make a success of the termination policy which we have bitterly opposed from the start. We are expected to give up our Indianness and adopt a way of life none of us want. Such an experiment as this can never work; it will only continue to impoverish our people.

THE LOSS OF MENOMINEE ASSETS

Termination has trapped Menominee in a vicious circle. Once a community reaches the poverty level of Menominee County, it can exist only by feeding upon itself and its limited assets. This is exactly what is happening to us today, and our assets are being lost at an alarming rate through the actions of both MEI and individual Menominees.

As the 1969 Wisconsin Menominee Indian Study Committee Report states: "The major economic problem of Menominee County has been the need to expand the tax base." Because special federal and state assistance seems to be drying up, MEI must look elsewhere for tax relief. So, with the tragic inevitability that befalls Indians in situations like this, MEI has finally turned to the sale of our most precious asset, our land. In 1968, MEI entered into a joint venture with a private lake developer for the creation in our county of a large artificial lake, Legend Lake, surrounded by homesites to be made available to non-Indians. Through this joint venture MEI has sold 8,760 acres of our most valuable land. If completed, this resort-retirement-vacation Mecca in the heart of our land will offer nearly 2,000 lots for sale to non-Indians.

It is true that this development has temporarily expanded our tax base. On the face of it, MEI has taken a step to attack one of the roots of our poverty. But the negative effects of this policy outweigh the advantages. We have finally been forced to start selling our land to generate cash for payment of community services. This is somewhat like burning down your house to keep warm in a blizzard. The added population of non-Menominee land owners will require additional police and fire protection, road maintenance, and other basic county services; sewerage and water systems will have to be built and maintained. The increased tax income that will result from these property owners will soon be consumed by the cost of these new services. MEI management has indicated that this development is intended only for summer residents and older people who will not require many services.

Nonetheless, the promotional literature for Legend Lake extols the year-round use of Menominee land and suggests the beautiful retirement possibilities. If even one half of the 2,000 lots become permanent homesites, not only will our expanded tax base be eaten up by providing additional services for the new land owners, but this new population of non-Indians, will *outnumber* us Menominee. The probable result is obvious: outnumbered and outvoted, our most valuable land sold, our survival as an Indian community will be doomed.

Menominee assets have also been lost by the individual Menominee. The first asset lost by many of us was our income bond. If a Menominee needed money he could sell his bond to MEI for a fraction of its face value. Although he would gain the advantage of having the cash, he lost forever his claim to the annual 4 percent "stumpage" payment. There was, however, always at least one alternative: welfare. But to qualify for welfare as a Menominee, we must first assign our bond to the State of Wisconsin. By doing so we can meet the State welfare requirement of having not more than $500 in negotiable assets, yet we once again lose our right to a "stumpage" payment. Under this charitable program, Wisconsin has managed to collect over $1,200,000 worth of Menominee bonds. Many of us Menominee have been forced to use our bonds to purchase from MEI the land which used to be considered our own.

In each of the above cases the Menominee loses his only tangible share of the tribal assets. And because of the general misunderstanding and lack of knowledge with regard to the termination agreement, many Menominee falsely believed that because they had lost these bonds, they had also assigned away their rights to vote in MEI affairs, and thus their right to take an active part in the county's operations. Although precise figures are not yet available, it is probably safe to say that most Menominee have by now lost their bonds.

The hardest hit Menominee are those who not only have lost their bonds by using them to buy land from MEI, but who then go on to lose their land on account of their inability to pay taxes. Again, while precise figures are not yet available, it is common knowledge among our people that a great number of us have lost our property through tax delinquency.

Another asset we may lose in the future is our MEI common stock. Although we Menominee recently voted to retain our stock as non-negotiable until 1974, the continuing pressure of poverty might yet force many of us to vote for its negotiability. And once we are compelled to part with our stock, we will then have surrendered the last vestige of our individual share of tribal wealth.

PREVENTION OF MENOMINEE DEMOCRACY

Another frustration which termination brought our people has been our lack of control over our own destiny. As we

previously mentioned, erroneous information, misunderstandings, and our own inability to comprehend the total subject matter prevented us Menominee from taking any meaningful part in the development of our own termination plan.

The corporate-county situation which was established by the termination plan was set up in such a way as to further deny us a voice in our own affairs. The seven member voting trust took upon itself all the voting rights of all the shareholders. We were forced to wait for a full ten years, until 1971, before we could vote to alter or abolish this trust.

As we stated in our introduction, despite the fact that the majority of Menominee who participated in the 1971 election voted to abolish the trust, it was allowed to continue because a majority vote of all *outstanding* shares was required. Thus, any Menominee *not* voting, was, in effect, counted as being in favor of continuance of the Trust. Since many Menominee were scattered all over the country and were unreachable, and since many Menominee do not understand all the legal complications involved in exercising their voting rights, and above all, since the First Wisconsin Assistance Trust "bloc-voted" 48,000 shares to continue the trust, securing such an absolute majority was a next-to-impossible effort. However, a hopeful democratic development has been the enlargement of the voting trust to eleven members, and the election to it of two DRUMS members.

The most blatant denial of democracy which the Menominee have suffered is the imposition of the First Wisconsin Assistance Trust, which manages and votes the Trust Certificates of minor and "incompetent" Menominee. DRUMS is currently challenging the constitutionality of this trust in court. The establishment of the Assistance Trust denied Menominee the right, which is enjoyed by all citizens of Wisconsin, to name or have appointed individual guardians of their own choice. The Trust also denied "incompetents" the right, held by other Wisconsin citizens, to a judicial determination of their alleged incompetency.

As Menominee have been coming of age, the power of this Trust has somewhat declined. But since its inception, the Assistance Trust has wielded an enormous voting power, completely disproportionate to the number of trust certificates it holds. The history of voting for trustees to the Voting Trust at annual meetings of MEI reveals that from 1961 to 1968, while the percentage of trust certificates held by the Assistance Trust has declined from 42 percent to 21 percent, the Trust has in every election voted from 80 percent to 92 percent of the total votes cast. Because the Assistance Trust has dominated the election of the Voting Trustees, in effect, it has indirectly dominated the affairs of MEI. The low percentage of Menominee votes cast in these Trustee elections has resulted from many factors: lack of adequate notice of these meetings by MEI, the increasing dispersal of

Menominee around the country, the continuing lack of understanding by many Menominees of these intricate corporate practices, and the decision of many of our people to boycott elections which they have regarded as essentially undemocratic.

Another way in which self-government has been kept from us concerns the corporate rules regarding sale of our land. Article XII of the MEI Articles of Incorporation requires that in order to "sell, exchange, assign, convey, or otherwise transfer" all or any portion of the real property which it owns, MEI must secure prior approval "by the affirmative vote of the holders of not less than two-thirds of the outstanding shares of stock, entitled to vote thereon." If this Article had been followed by MEI, it would never have received the approval of the Menominee people to sell our land in the Legend Lake project. But the seven members of the Voting Trust interpreted this Article to require only their two-thirds approval. Consequently, the Voting Trust approved this sale of our land, and again, we Menominee people were denied a voice in one of the most crucial decisions ever undertaken in our history.

CONCLUSIONS: THE END OF THE MENOMINEE INDIAN COMMUNITY?

We have told a story which is very tragic, yet it is the true story of the Menominee people since termination. We have told how termination has meant the loss of treaty benefits, has pushed our already poor community further into the depths of poverty, forced our sale of assets; and denied us a democratic community.

Our community is being physically divided by the sale of our heart-land to non Indians. Moreover, the Menominee cannot escape forever the destructive psychological effects of living in destitution. The pride and self-image of the Menominee is threatened by poverty and lack of self-determination.

All of these effects are the result of termination; and they combine to threaten the very existence of our people as an Indian community; an identity which we shall never want to relinquish.

Senate Concurrent Resolution 26

As we stated at the beginning of our testimony, one of our purposes today is to make clear to this committee what termination has meant as a reality in the lives of Indians. By showing you the deadly effects and utter failure of this Congressional policy with regard to us, the Menominee people, we hope that we have helped you realize the imperative need for Congressional repudiation of the policy of termination. When Senator Jackson, introducing Resolution 26, spoke of termination as being "... totally and absolutely unacceptable to the majority of the Indian people ..." he simply spoke the truth. And does not our story today demonstrate why he spoke the truth?

As a *first step* in undoing the disaster of termination we are heartened by, and urge this Committee's acceptance of, Senate Concurrent Resolution 26. We would like to make the following observations concerning Resolution 26:

1. We support the recognition, which Resolution 26 expresses of Federal responsibility "... to protect Indian lands, resources and rights as well as to provide basic community services to Indian and Alaska Native peoples residing on reservations and in other traditional trust areas.

2. We support the Resolution's recognition of Indians' rights "... to share and participate on the same basis as all other citizens in the full range of social and economic development programs authorized by Federal, State, and local units of government."

1975   Gresham, Wisconsin
Disturbance at the Alexian Brothers Novitiate

In the early morning hours of January 1, 1975, 45 armed members of the Menominee Warriors Society broke into the unused Roman Catholic novitiate of the Chicago-based Alexian Brothers, a hospital order. They routed the caretaker and his family and took over the 20-room mansion with its 64-room annex. The Indians demanded that the Brothers deed the 225-acre complex to the Menominee tribe who would use it, they alleged, for a hospital or school. "Deed or death," they vowed.

For the next five weeks in the depths of severe winter weather the novitiate was besieged by armed forces. At first county officers attempted to starve and freeze out the Indians while restraining an increasingly belligerent white citizenry bent upon attacking the Abbey. On January 6 Governor Patrick Lucey ordered the Wisconsin National Guard to assume charge under Colonel Hugh Simonson. A total of 2200 guardsmen would eventually be called. He immediately restored essential services to the novitiate, threw a 22-mile perimeter around the buildings with check points and observation points, and maintained strict control over a tense local situation. The heavily wooded terrain and great distance of the perimeter made a complete seal impossible.

Members of the Warriors Society and their supporters represented one of the factions which appeared within the Indian community during a period of confusion within federal policies. Mostly young people, the members were intensely critical of government philosophy and action, and their interests were often incompatible with the views of tribal leaders. Two spokesmen of the American Indian Movement (AIM) entered the Abbey to serve as communicators for the Warriors. Unlike AIM's takeover of a building at Wounded Knee, South Dakota in 1973, which was accompanied by violence, the disturbance at the Alexian Brothers novitiate was free of casualties. Colonel

The Novitiate Takeover Gresham Wisconsin, Jan./Feb. 1975

N

To Keshena

To SHAWANO

LEGEND

N.G. AREA OF RESPONSIBILITY

NOVITIATE

CHECKPOINT

CHECKPOINT & O.P.

ROADBLOCK

ROVING PATROLS

CP 1 - 2 - 4
CP 16 - 17
CP 16 - 1 - 14
CP 2 - 19
CP 2 - 4
CP 16 Backup

MISSION LAKE

DAM

Red River

BIRCH LANE

BASSWOOD RD

BOXELDER RD

BROADWAY

ELM RD

BEECH RD

BEECH RD

CYPRUS RD

HAZEL DRIVE

OAK AVE

Thornton

HICKORY RD

SOO LINE

CN&W

Highway 29

Highway U

BUTTERNUT RD

CEDAR LANE

JUNIPER RD

CHERRY RD

Abbey

Barn

A

VV

VV

G

1 2 3 4 5 6 9 10 11 11 B 12 13 13 B 14 15 16 17 19 20 21 25 26 27

Simonson's philosophy made the difference: "No building is worth a life."

On February 7 the Brothers agreed to sell; the disturbance was over. The Warriors, having gained national publicity and having aroused public sympathy for the Indian's plight, believed in the seige. Generation of the sums necessary to purchase the property seemed possible. They surrendered to face several felony and misdemeanor charges.

The disturbance highlighted another issue. Tribal leaders had just successfully completed a long and costly struggle to reverse Menominee termination; the tribe had been officially restored to federal status. Now they faced many difficult problems of unemployment, organizing an educational system, implementing a new constitution, and building basic institutions. How would a large complex several miles from the reservation meet Indian needs? How would the novitiate disturbance assist the tribe in meeting its many challenges on the reservation which required

arduous, complicated application of all available resources and would strain the capacities of available trained personnel?

The following map (document 111) depicts the deployment of Wisconsin National Guardsmen during the disturbance.

Further reading: William E. Farrell, "Leader of Guardsmen Credited . . . ," *The New York Times,* February 10, 1975; Sam Martino, "Menominee Militants Jar Indian Efforts," *The Christian Science Monitor,* January 20, 1975.

Document 111
January 7-February 7, 1975   Gresham, Wisconsin
Military Map

Source: Files of the Adjutant General, State of Wisconsin. Madison.

Bibliography

The following books were found useful in our study of North American Indian history. These titles are in addition to those listed under "Further Reading" at the end of the headnotes in the text.

Reference works:

Brandon, William, and Alvin M. Josephy, Jr., *The American Heritage Book of Indians* (New York: American Heritage Publishing Co., Inc., 1961).*

Debo, Angie, *A History of the Indians of the United States* (Norman: University of Oklahoma Press, 1970).

Deloria, Vine, Jr., *Custer Died For Your Sins: An Indian Manifesto* (New York: The Macmillan Company, 1969).*

Gibson, Arrell M., *The American Indian: Prehistory to the Present* (Lexington, MA: D.C. Heath and Company, 1980).

Hagan, William T., *American Indians* (rev'd. ed., Chicago: University of Chicago Press, 1979).*

Hamilton, Charles, ed., *Cry of the Thunderbird: The American Indian's Own Story* (Norman: University of Oklahoma Press, 1972, new edition).*

Jennings, Francis, general editor, The Newberry Center for the History of the American Indian Bibliographical Series (Bloomington: Indiana University Press).* This series includes annotated bibliographies on such diverse topics as:
> Henry F. Dobyns, *Native American Historical Demography* (1976)
> Francis Paul Prucha, *United States Indian Policy* (1977)
> James P. Ronda and James Axtell, *Indian Missions* (1978)
> Helen Hornbeck Tanner, *The Ojibwas* (1976).

Josephy, Alvin M., Jr., *The Indian Heritage of America* (New York: Alfred A. Knopf, 1968).*

McNickle, D'Arcy, *They Came Here First: The Epic of the American Indian* (rev'd. ed., New York: Harper & Row, Publishers, 1975).*

The Navajo Nation: An American Colony. A Report of the United States Commission on Civil Rights (Washington, D.C.: U.S. Commission on Civil Rights, 1975).

Prucha, Francis Paul, ed., *A Bibliographical Guide to the History of Indian-White Relations in the United States* (Chicago: University of Chicago Press, 1977).*

Sturtevant, William C., general editor, *Handbook of American Indians* (Washington, D.C.: Smithsonian Institution). The three well-illustrated volumes published to date include detailed cultural and political histories of the tribal groups in the region.
> Volume 8. Robert F. Heizer, ed., *California* (1978)
> 9. Alfonso Ortiz, ed., *Southwest* (1979)
> 15. Bruce C. Trigger, ed., *Northeast* (1978).

Tyler, S. Lyman, *A History of Indian Policy.* U.S. Department of Interior, Bureau of Indian Affairs. (Washington, D.C.: Government Printing Office, 1973).*

Vanderwerth, W. C., comp., *Indian Oratory: Famous Speeches by Noted Indian Chieftains* (Norman: University of Oklahoma Press, 1971).*

Vogel, Virgil J., *American Indian Medicine* (Norman: University of Oklahoma Press, 1970).*

_____, ed., *This County Was Ours: A Documentary History of the American Indian* (New York: Harper & Row, Publishers, 1972).* Bibliography is excellent.

Washburn, Wilcomb E., *Red Man's Land/White Man's Law: A Study of the Past and Present Status of the American Indian* (New York: Charles Scribner's Sons, 1971).

General Works:

Berkhofer, Robert F., Jr., *The White Man's Indian: Images of the American Indian from Columbus to the Present* (New York: Alfred A. Knopf, 1978).*

Berthrong, Donald J., *The Cheyenne and Arapaho Ordeal: Reservation and Agency Life in the Indian Territory, 1875-1907* (Norman: University of Oklahoma Press, 1976).

Brown, Dee, *Bury My Heart at Wounded Knee: An Indian History of the American West* (New York: Holt, Rinehart & Winston, 1970).*

Danziger, Edmund J., Jr., *The Chippewas of Lake Superior* (Norman: University of Oklahoma Press, 1978).

————, *Indians and Bureaucrats: Administering the Reservation Policy during the Civil War* (Urbana: University of Illinois Press, 1974).

Debo, Angie, *Geronimo: The Man, His Times, His Place* (Norman: University of Oklahoma Press, 1976).

Edmunds, R. David, ed., *American Indian Leaders: Studies in Diversity* (Lincoln: University of Nebraska Press, 1980).*

————, *The Potawatomie: Keepers of the Fire* (Norman: University of Oklahoma Press, 1978).

Foreman, Grant, *Indian Removal: The Emigration of the Five Civilized Tribes of Indians* (Norman: University of Oklahoma Press, 1953, new edition).*

Hudson, Charles M., ed., *Four Centuries of Southern Indians* (Athens: University of Georgia Press, 1975).

Hyde, George E., *Indians of the High Plains: From the Prehistoric Period to the Coming of the Europeans* (Norman: University of Oklahoma Press, 1959).*

————, *Indians of the Woodlands: From Prehistoric Times to 1725* (Norman: University of Oklahoma Press, 1962).*

Jacobs, Wilbur R., *Dispossessing the American Indian: Indians and Whites on the Colonial Frontier* (New York: Charles Scribner's Sons, 1972).*

Jennings, Francis, *The Invasion of America: Indians, Colonialism, and the Cant of Conquest* (Chapel Hill: University of North Carolina Press, 1975).*

John, Elizabeth A. H., *Storms Brewed in Other Men's Worlds: The Confrontation of Indians, Spanish and French in the Southwest, 1540-1795* (College Station: Texas A. & M. University Press, 1975).

Kammer, Jerry, *The Second Long Walk: The Navajo-Hopi Land Dispute* (Albuquerque: University of New Mexico Press, 1980).

Kelly, Lawrence C., *The Navajo Indians and Federal Indian Policy, 1900-1935* (Tucson: University of Arizona Press, 1968).

Martin, Calvin, *Keepers of the Game: Indian-Animal Relationships and the Fur Trade* (Berkeley: University of California Press, 1978).

Miner, H. Craig, *The Corporation and the Indian* (Columbia: University of Missouri Press, 1976).

Otis, D. S., *The Dawes Act and the Allotment of Indian Lands* (Norman: University of Oklahoma Press, 1973) edited with an introduction by Francis Paul Prucha.

Pearce, Roy Harvey, *Savagism and Civilization: A Study of the Indian and the American Mind* (Baltimore: The Johns Hopkins Press, 1953).*

Philp, Kenneth R., *John Collier's Crusade for Indian Reform, 1920-1954* (Tucson: University of Arizona Press, 1977).*

Prucha, Francis Paul, *American Indian Policy in Crisis: Christian Reformers and the Indian, 1865-1900* (Norman: University of Oklahoma Press, 1976).

————, *The Churches and the Indian Schools 1888-1912* (Lincoln: University of Nebraska Press, 1979).

Satz, Ronald N., *American Indian Policy in the Jacksonian Era* (Lincoln: University of Nebraska Press, 1975).*

Savage, William W., Jr., *The Cherokee Strip Live Stock Association: Federal Regulation and the Cattlemen's Last Frontier* (Columbia: University of Missouri Press, 1973).

Spicer, Edward H., *Cycles of Conquest: The Impact of Spain, Mexico, and the United States on the Indians of the Southwest, 1533-1960* (Tucson: University of Arizona Press, 1962).*

Szasz, Margaret C., *Education and the American Indian: The Road to Self-Determination since 1928*, 2nd. ed. (Albuquerque: University of New Mexico Press, 1977).*

Taylor, Graham D., *The New Deal and American Indian Tribalism: The Administration of the Indian Reorganization Act, 1934-45* (Lincoln: University of Nebraska Press, 1980).

Trennert, Robert A., Jr., *Alternatives to Extinction: Federal Indian Policy and the Beginnings of the Reservation System, 1846-1851* (Philadelphia: Temple University Press, 1975).

Vesey, Christopher, and Robert M. Venables, eds., *American Indian Environments: Ecological Issues in Native*

American History (Syracuse: Syracuse University Press, 1980).*

Wallace, Anthony F. C., *The Death and Rebirth of the Seneca* (New York: Alfred A. Knopf, 1970).*

Whitney, Ellen M., comp. & ed., *The Black Hawk War, 1831-1832 Collections of the Illinois Historical Society, volumes XXXV-XXXVIII,* (Springfield: Illinois State Historical Society, 1970-1978).

Periodicals:

Akwesasne Notes, Mohawk Nation, via Rooseveltown, N.Y. 13683 (1969 to the present).

American Indian Culture and Research Journal (Los Angeles: University of California, 1974 to the present).

The Indian Historian (San Francisco: American Indian Historical Society, 1967 to 1979).

Wassaja (San Francisco: American Indian Historical Society, 1973 to 1979).

Wassaja/The Indian Historian (San Francisco: American Indian Historical Society, 1980 to the present).

*available in paperback edition.

INDEX

Indian leaders
  Adams, John, attorney (Stockbridge), 140
  Alémán, Juan, 25
  American Horse (Sioux), 139
  Archiquette, John (Oneida), 149-150
  Big Foot (Sioux), 138-139
  Black Hawk (Sauk), 79, 87-91
    corpse displayed at sideshow, 91
  Black Kettle (Cheyenne), 111-113
  Brant, Joseph (Mohawk), 57
  Chiquita (Apache), 123-124
  Clemente, Don Esteban, 38
  Colorado, Mangus (Apache), 100, 104-106
  Cornstalk (Shawnee), 62
  Crazy Horse (Sioux), 17, 122, 135
  Dandy (Winnebago), 106-107
  Donnaconna (Iroquois), 23-25
  Dragging Canoe (Cherokee), 58
  Dull Knife (Cheyenne), 134-136
  Francis (Creek), 85-86
  Geronimo (Apache), 123
  Great Sun (Natchez), 39-40
  Halftown, Levi (Seneca), 92
  Jack (Modoc), 126-127
  Jacobs (Delaware), 50
  Joseph (Nez Percé), 132-134
  Keokuk (Sauk), 87
  Kiala (Fox), 40-41
  Little Hill (Winnebago), 110-111
  Little Wolf (Cheyenne), 135
  Logan (Mingo), 52, 56
  Massasoit (Wampanoag), 35
  Necotowance (Powhattan), 34
  Old Britain (Miami), 33
  Opechancanough (Powhattan), 28, 34
  Osceola (Seminole), 96
  Parker, Arthur C. (Seneca), 144-146
  Parker, Ely S. (Seneca), 92, 110
  Philip (Wampanoag), 35-37
  Pocahontas (Powhattan), 28
  Popé (Pueblo), 37-38
  Powhattan, 28
  Ridge, The (Cherokee), 84
  Ross, John (Cherokee), 93-94
  Shingas (Delaware), 50
  Sitting Bull (Sioux), 133, 138
  Spotted Horse (Sioux), 139
  Spotted Tail (Cheyenne), 135
  Squanto (Algonquian), 19
  Struck by the Ree (Sioux), 113-115
  Swords (Sioux), 139
  Turk, 25
  Turning Hawk (Sioux), 138-139
  Wabasha (Sioux), 90
  Wild Hog (Cheyenne), 135
  Yellow Bull (Nez Perce), 133

  Yoholo, Opothle (Creek), 101
Indian policy (United States)
  philosophy of, 72, 75, 81, 84-85, 108, 142, 144-146, 162, 163
Indian raid, 16, 33, 125
Indian refugees, 101
Indian Rights Association, 150, 161-162
Indian schools (private)
  subsidized by U.S. government, 157
Indian schools (U.S. government), 151
  conditions at
    Pine Ridge Sioux
      children beaten, shaved, bound with ball and chain, and kept in solitary confinement, 154
    Towaoc Ute
      have inadequate clothing, 153-154
      served filthy food, 152-153
      stored food supplies spoiled but still used, 152-153
Indian Territory
  bill to consolidate proposed in Congress, 116
  references to conditions there, 94-96, 115-117, 126, 132, 134, 134-136
Indian tribes
  Abnaki, 33
  Aleut, 34, 37-50, 58
  Algonquian (Algonkian), 16, 27-28, 29-30, 30-32, 58
  Apache, 38-39, 79, 96-98, 100, 104-106, 107
    pacifist cooperative band massacred, 123-124
    San Carlos, 160-161
  Appalache, 43
  Arapahoe, 120
  Assiniboin, 83
  Blackfeet, 164
  Brotherton, 91
  California tribes, 100
  Cayuga, 47, 57, 64
  Cherokee, 57, 58, 60-62, 79, 84, 93-94, 100, 101, 115-117, 142, 150, 158-160
    exhaustion of timber resources, 159
    ruined by Civil War and Reconstruction, 115-117
  Cheyenne, 100, 111-113, 120, 134
  Chickasaw, 41, 42, 79, 100, 150
  Chippewa, 40, 83, 156, 158
  Choctaw, 41, 43, 79, 100, 150-151, 164
  Choctaw (Mississippi), 147-149
  Comanche, 96, 124
  Conestoga, 44, 52-54
  Creek, 43, 79, 81, 84-85, 100, 101, 116, 146, 150, 150-152
  Delaware, 50-51, 58, 62, 66-68, 73, 76
  Doeg, 33, 34-35
  Eel River, 74
  Ellcombe, 43
  Five Civilized Tribes, 100-101, 150, 151, 159
  Five Nations, see Iroquois